INTO THE EYES OF SATAN

Into the Eyes of Satan

Brett Crowley

Dakota Frandsen

Bald and Bonkers Network LLC

First Printing, 2023

ISBN: 979-8-8690-4351-1
EISBN: 979-8-8690-4352-8

CONTENTS

INTRODUCTION

Have you ever wondered what lies within the realms of darkness? What draws individuals to secrets shrouded in mystery and rituals that dance along the edge of the forbidden? Join me now as we venture Into the Eye of Satan, a captivating journey that unravels the history, allure, and enigmatic world of Satanic worship.

As a paranormal investigator, I have spent countless hours delving into the depths of the unknown. And it is in this pursuit of truth that I found myself drawn to the intricacies of Satanic worship. What compels people to gather at the crossroads of good and evil, to challenge societal norms and embrace the darkness? This question, lingering in the recesses of my mind, became the catalyst for this exploration into the heart of the forbidden.

Now, you may be thinking, why should I care about Satanic worship? Isn't it just a fringe cult, a sensationalized topic for horror movies and late-night tales? Well, my dear reader, I implore you to set aside your preconceived notions and join me as we peel back the layers of misconception and disbelief. For within the centuries-old traditions of Satanic worship lies a rich tapestry of history, culture, and humanity. It is a story that deserves to be heard, understood, and examined through a lens untainted by fear.

In this remarkable journey, we will traverse through time and space, exploring the roots of Satanic worship in various cultures and religions. From the ancient Mesopotamian rituals that honored malevolent deities to the modern-day practices embraced by those who worship the Adversary, we will uncover the hidden threads that weave together this tapestry of darkness.

But this is not simply a scholarly study. No, dear reader, I have delved deep into the underbelly of the occult, seeking out those who have chosen to dance with the devil. Through interviews with Satanists, members of the Satanic Temple, and even individuals who have experienced encounters with the supernatural, we will gain a firsthand understanding of their motivations, beliefs, and the rituals they hold dear.

Yet, let me make one thing clear: this is not a glorification of evil nor an endorsement of Satanic worship. Rather, it is an exploration of the human psyche, a quest to unravel the complexities of the human condition. It is a journey of understanding, seeking to bridge the seemingly insurmountable gap between the light and the darkness that resides within each of us.

As we unearth the secrets buried within the shadows, we will encounter tales of diabolical pacts, forbidden knowledge, and the blurred lines between good and evil. We will confront the very essence of fear itself and explore the power it holds over our collective imagination. From the infamous Satanic Panic that gripped the world in the late 20th century to the modern-day manifestations of this age-old practice, we will navigate a labyrinth of intrigue, deception, and, ultimately, enlightenment.

So, dear reader, I invite you to gather your courage, release your inhibitions, and step into the abyss with me. Together, we will embark on a journey like no other, challenging our preconceptions, expanding our horizons, and peering Into the Eye of Satan. Through these pages, we will uncover truths that may disturb, enlighten, or perhaps even transform our understanding of the world around us.

Are you ready to confront the dark side of humanity? To embrace the forbidden whispers of the night? Then let us begin this extraordinary odyssey into the heart of Satanic worship, where shadows dance, and secrets lay bare. Welcome, my friend, to a journey that will forever change the way you perceive the world. Welcome, to the Eye of Satan.

1

THE ORIGINS OF SATANIC WORSHIP

ANCIENT PAGAN DEITIES AND DEVIL-LIKE FIGURES

As an investigator specialized in the paranormal and the unusual, my exploration into the realms of the occult has led me to extensively examine the captivating link between ancient pagan deities and the development of devil-like figures in diverse cultures throughout history. An exhaustive comprehension of the origins and evolution of these malevolent entities necessitates embarking upon a journey through the annals of bygone civilizations and their religious convictions.

In the domain of paganism, deities were held in reverence and worshipped as they commonly symbolized various aspects of nature and human existence. Nevertheless, as societies evolved and religious beliefs underwent amalgamation or contention, these deities began to undergo transformation, adopting darker and more ominous attributes. The undeniable parallelism between this metamorphosis and the emergence of devil-like figures becomes increasingly apparent as we investigate their intertwined history.

During the era of ancient Mesopotamia, nascent iterations of devil-like beings materialized with the Sumerian deity Enki. Frequently depicted as a serpent, Enki epitomized both wisdom and deception, a duality that pervaded various devil-like figures in numerous ancient cultures. This bond between sagacity and deceit is evident in the portrayal of the serpent in the biblical narrative of the Garden of Eden, further corroborating the rapport between ancient pagan deities and devilish entities.

Subsequently, we encounter the ancient Egyptian god Set, a deity affiliated with chaos and darkness. Despite occupying an integral position within the Egyptian pantheon, Set represented a force that was regarded as sinister and malign. His association with storms, chaos, and even the deserts encapsulated the concept of a malevolent entity that waged war against benevolent forces.

In Celtic mythology, another intriguing example presents itself in the form of Crom Cruach. Initially revered as a god of fertility and harvest, Crom Cruach eventually assumed a more sinister role as a demanding deity who required human sacrifices in order to ensure prosperity. This transformation, from a deity associated with abundance to a figure embodying cruelty and malevolence, exemplifies the development witnessed in other ancient pagan religions.

The Norse pantheon offers us the iconic figure of Loki, a deity renowned for his cunning and trickery. Loki's complex nature and his frequent ability to change forms resonated with the ancient Norse belief in the dualistic nature of the world. Despite lacking inherent malevolence, Loki's eventual association with malicious acts led him to become synonymous with a devilish figure.

The interconnectedness of these ancient pagan deities and the development of devil-like figures becomes even more apparent in the disquieting mythologies of Eastern civilizations. In Hinduism, we encounter the demon king Ravana, renowned for his immense power and deceitful nature. Though Ravana was initially portrayed as a wise and learned ascetic, his unrestrained ambition and dark inclinations ultimately led him to be regarded as a devil-like figure.

Likewise, within Buddhism, the wrathful deities known as the Mahakala occupy a significant role. Possessing an alarming countenance, these deities were often invoked for their protective powers. However, over time, the Mahakala underwent a transformation, becoming entities feared and associated with malevolence, mirroring the alteration witnessed in other ancient cultures.

Upon scrutinizing this historical timeline, it becomes unequivocally evident that the development of devil-like figures transcends geographical boundaries and cultural disparities. These figures, albeit diverse in appearance and characteristics, share a common thread of duality, symbolizing both the light and dark aspects inherent within human nature.

As I delve deeper into this enigmatic connection, it becomes increasingly apparent that these ancient pagan deities and the development of devil-like figures serve as mirrors reflecting the human psyche. Humans have eternally grappled with their own dual nature, ceaselessly endeavoring to understand the light and darkness permeating within. The worship of deities in ancient times provided an outlet for the expression and interpretation of the duality within, resulting in a vast tapestry of folklore and legends that continue to haunt our collective consciousness.

In our modern era, these devil-like figures have assumed new forms, adapting to the evolving convictions and anxieties of humanity. However, their essence remains unaltered – a constant reminder of our perpetual struggle with the shadows residing within each one of us.

As an investigator of the paranormal and a connoisseur of the uncanny, my exploration into deciphering the connection between ancient pagan deities and devil-like figures has left me with a plethora of inquiries. Yet, it is through this investigation that we gain glimpses into the profound depths of the human imagination, witnessing the captivating ways in which our ancestors sought to comprehend the forces shaping our world.

The ancient pagan deities and devil-like figures are not mere relics of the past but rather windows showcasing the intricacies of the human psyche and our enduring fascination with the enigmatic and dark. Within these depths lie the true essence of these figures, awaiting discovery by those bold enough to venture into the very heart of Satan.

SATAN IN JUDEO-CHRISTIAN TRADITIONS

As a paranormal investigator and specialist in the realm of the supernatural, I have extensively studied ancient texts, historical documents, and religious scriptures to gain insight into the intriguing world of the occult. One area that has captured my interest is the depiction of Satan in Judeo-Christian traditions and its role in shaping the perception of Satanic worship throughout history. To truly comprehend this complex phenomenon, it is imperative that we delve into the annals of time and carefully analyze the historical timeline.

The concept of Satan, in its origin, did not exist as the embodiment of evil. In fact, the roots of Satan can be traced back to ancient Mesopotamia, where he was known as the demon Pazuzu - a significant figure in the realm of the underworld. Similar beings also held prominence in Egyptian mythology, with the god Set representing chaos and darkness. These early representations of powerful entities with negative connotations laid the foundation for the understanding of Satan in subsequent traditions.

In the Judeo-Christian tradition, Satan is initially mentioned in the book of Genesis. Here, he is portrayed as a serpent who tempts Eve into consuming the forbidden fruit, an act that ultimately leads to the expulsion of Adam and Eve from the Garden of Eden. This portrayal presents Satan as an astute and persuasive figure who deceives humanity and leads them astray. This initial association between Satan and deceit forms the basis for the negative perception linked with Satanic worship.

The book of Job further sheds light on Satan's role within Judeo-Christian traditions. Within this narrative, Satan is depicted as a member of God's heavenly court, challenging the faith of Job and subjecting him to immense suffering. This portrayal emphasizes Satan's role as an adversary, a force that tests the faith and endurance of believers. The notion that Satan stands contrary to divine virtue deepens the negative perception surrounding Satanic worship.

As we shift to the New Testament, a more developed understanding of Satan is encountered. In the Gospels, Satan is portrayed as the tempter who seeks to corrupt Jesus during his forty-day sojourn in the wilderness. This characterization of Satan as a tempter reinforces the negative perception of Satanic worship, as it accentuates the seductive nature of evil.

It is impossible to discuss the perception of Satan without acknowledging the seminal works of John Milton's Paradise Lost and Johann Wolfgang von Goethe's Faust. These literary masterpieces seek to explore the motivations and internal conflicts of Satan, thereby adding greater depth to his character. Milton presents Satan as a tragic figure who rebels against God out of pride and ambition. Similarly, Goethe's Mephistopheles embodies the allure of worldly pleasures and the potential consequences that arise from indulging in such desires. These imaginative interpretations of Satan offer a more nuanced understanding of his character, but they also reinforce the notion that Satanic worship leads to damnation and ruin.

The influence of the portrayal of Satan in Judeo-Christian traditions on the perception of Satanic worship cannot be underestimated. Throughout history, societies have been shaped by religious teachings that depict Satan as the epitome of evil, enticing humanity to partake in immoral and debased practices. This perception has resulted in the stigmatization of individuals and groups believed to be followers of Satanic worship, leading to fear, prejudice, and persecution.

Nevertheless, it is crucial to approach these narratives with a critical mindset. The comprehension of Satan and Satanic worship is not a homogeneous concept but rather a complex tapestry of beliefs, folklore, and societal anxieties. The image of Satan has undergone changes over time, influenced by diverse cultural and religious factors. It is through meticulous analysis and a broader perspective that we can begin to unravel the intricate layers of this subject matter.

As a paranormal investigator and expert in the realm of the supernatural, I remain captivated by the diverse tapestry of human beliefs and their impact on our perception of arcane phenomena. Exploring the portrayal of Satan in Judeo-Christian traditions and its influence on the perception of Satanic worship is just a mere fragment of this vast puzzle. It is my fervent hope that through continued research and exploration, we may attain a deeper comprehension of the enigmatic realms that reside within Satan's domain.

SATANISM IN ANCIENT EGYPT

As an individual specializing in the investigation of paranormal phenomena and possessing expertise in the study of unusual occurrences, I have long held a deep fascination with exploring the concealed truths behind the practices of ancient civilizations and their captivating religious customs. Ancient Egypt, in particular, has consistently captivated my imagination, primarily due to its awe-inspiring pyramids and enigmatic rulers. Yet, beyond the imposing nature of their towering structures and intricate funerary rites, the ancient Egyptians also delved into the realm of darkness through their engagement in the practice of Satanism.

To comprehend the role of Satanism within ancient Egyptian religious practices, it is imperative to initially comprehend their belief system. The ancient Egyptians ardently worshipped a multitude of gods and goddesses, each embodying different facets of life and the natural world. However, among this divine pantheon, a sophisticated parallel system of beliefs existed, revolving around the veneration of Satanic deities.

It is crucial to bear in mind that the contemporary notion of "Satanism" differs significantly from its ancient counterpart. In ancient Egypt, Satanism did not connote evil or malevolence, but rather represented a duality between illumination and obscurity, chaos and order. It constituted an integral facet of their religious fabric and formed an intricately woven pattern within the tapestry of their spiritual convictions.

During the course of my extensive research, I encountered numerous references to Set, a deity who played a central role within ancient Egyptian Satanism. Set commonly appeared in depictions as a formidable creature, characterized by the head of an unidentified animal, a lean and muscular human physique, and a tail that menacingly curled upward. Egyptians believed that Set ruled over the deserts, storms, and formidable forces of chaos.

However, what renders Set tantamount to Satanism? His opposition to his divine brother, Osiris, the god associated with fertility and creation, led to his association with darker forces. According to mythology, Set, harboring jealousy towards Osiris, perpetrated his murder and dismemberment, scattering the fragments throughout the expanse of Egypt. In this manner, Set embodied destruction and chaos, counterbalancing the harmonious order overseen by Osiris.

The worship of Set and practicing Satanism extended beyond the realm of mythology and permeated daily life within ancient Egypt. In fact, it was believed that the rituals enacted by satanic cults maintained a cosmic equilibrium between light and darkness, thus ensuring the perpetuity of life and halting the rise of chaos. These rituals frequently centered around the reenactment of the conflict between Set and Osiris, with devotees assuming masks and costumes representing the gods.

One well-documented instance of satanic rituals in ancient Egypt was the "Night of the Burning," which transpired on the eve of the summer solstice. During this annual event, adherents of Set would assemble within temple courtyards, their bodies adorned with sacred insignia and their faces embellished with intricate patterns. Under the guidance of priests, these individuals chanted incantations, engaged in wild dances, and implemented acts of self-flagellation to manifest their unwavering commitment to the cause of chaos.

A further notable aspect of satanic veneration within ancient Egypt was the practice of animal sacrifices. Animals, predominantly goats and rams, were believed to harbor spiritual energies that allowed for communion with the satanic deities. These sacrifices transpired within sacred spaces dedicated to Set and his infernal cohorts, such as the Temple of Karnak, an expansive edifice renowned for its dark rituals and concealed chambers.

The application of satanic practices within ancient Egypt extended beyond the confines of religious ceremonies and bled into diverse aspects of everyday existence, including artistic expression and literature. Hieroglyphics and tombs commonly contained symbolic depictions of Set, illustrating his potency and impact upon mortals. Accounts of mythological creatures and perilous quests also abounded, reflecting the ancient Egyptians' preoccupation with the supernatural and the macabre.

Upon concluding my research on Satanism within ancient Egypt, I found myself profoundly astounded by the intricacy of their convictions. The worship of Set by the ancient Egyptians and their indulgence in satanic practices were not manifestations of perverse evil, but rather gestures acknowledging the delicate balance between illumination and obscurity, which they perceived as fundamental constituents of the cosmos.

Presently, the term "Satanism" has assumed an entirely distinct meaning, often associated with wicked deeds and malicious intentions. Nevertheless, when we peel away the layers of history and embark upon an exploration of the intricate belief systems prevalent in ancient civilizations like Egypt, we encounter a more nuanced comprehension of Satanism—a connection with the forces of chaos and an acknowledgment of the dual nature inherent in all facets of existence.

As I concluded the chapter on the topic of Satanism in ancient Egypt, I was consumed by a profound appreciation for the depth and complexity of human spirituality. Although our individual beliefs and practices may diverge significantly from those of our ancient predecessors, there exists a common thread that unites humanity—a perpetual quest for meaning and a fervent desire to forge connections with the mysteries that lie beyond the grasp of our understanding. It is this un-quenchable thirst for knowledge that propels me forward as a devoted paranormal investigator, ceaselessly pursuing answers in the face of the unexplained.

SATANIC RITUALS IN ANCIENT GREECE AND ROME

To fully comprehend the rituals and ceremonies associated with Satanic worship in ancient Greece and Rome, an understanding of the cultural and religious context in which they were practiced is imperative. In the ancient world, religious beliefs were deeply intertwined with everyday life, and this was no exception for the Greek and Roman civilizations. The gods and goddesses were highly revered and worshipped through elaborate ceremonies and rituals. However, amidst these mainstream religious practices, there arose a darker undercurrent - one that sought to tap into supernatural powers for personal gain or to call upon malevolent forces.

Within the Greco-Roman worldview, Satan, as we know the concept today, did not exist. Instead, there were various deities associated with darkness, chaos, and rebellion. One such figure was Hecate, the Greek goddess of witchcraft, magic, and the night. Hecate was often depicted as a triple-bodied deity, possessing the ability to see the past, present, and future. She symbolized the threshold between life and death, and it is believed that many Satanic rituals in ancient Greece occurred within her realm.

The worship of Hecate involved intricate ceremonies, frequently held at crossroads, where her devotees would congregate to invoke her powers. These rituals were shrouded in secrecy, and limited information is available regarding their specific details. Nonetheless, some sources suggest that participants would offer sacrificial animals or food to gain favor from the goddess. Moreover, it was believed that Hecate had the capacity to grant wishes and confer special abilities upon those who diligently worshipped her.

In Rome, the counterpart to Hecate was Diana, the goddess associated with the hunt, the moon, and childbirth. Like Hecate, Diana was linked to witchcraft and often depicted with a crescent moon, symbolizing her connection to lunar cycles and the supernatural. Satanic rituals in ancient Rome frequently involved invoking Diana's powers to achieve diverse objectives, including love spells, divination, and curses.

One infamous and sensationalized instance of Satanic worship in ancient Rome is the Bacchanalia, a Dionysian festival dedicated to the Greek god Dionysus, known as Bacchus in Roman mythology. Dionysus was the god of wine, ecstasy, and madness, and his cult followers engaged in wild revelries and orgies as a means to enter a trance-like state and commune with the divine.

These frenzied rituals were viewed as a way to break free from societal norms and unleash repressed desires. However, the Bacchanalia soon became closely associated with immorality and criminal activity, prompting the Roman Senate to outlaw the festivities in 186 BCE. Authorities viewed the Bacchanalia not only as a threat to social order but also as a breeding ground for criminal conduct, such as murder and extortion.

As I delve into the ancient records and artifacts, the veil of time seems to lift, offering a tantalizing glimpse into the dark world of Satanic rituals in ancient Greece and Rome. These practices, concealed and often condemned by society, provided individuals with a means to tap into the supernatural and seek power or fulfillment beyond the constraints of ordinary existence.

However, it is vital to approach these ancient rituals with caution and skepticism. The available accounts are biased, often written by individuals seeking to suppress and demonize these practices and those who partook in them. Separating fact from fiction becomes a challenging task, but through meticulous analysis, we can unearth the truths concealed within the annals of history.

Satanic rituals in ancient Greece and Rome reflected the intricate and complex relationship between the mortal realm and the supernatural. They provided individuals with an avenue to explore the fringes of human existence, in search of answers, power, or perhaps simply a sense of belonging in a world that often felt beyond their control. While these practices may appear alien and antiquated to us today, they speak to a universal yearning for something more, something beyond the confines of our finite existence.

As I continue my exploration into the enigma of Satanic rituals, I am reminded that the forces at play in ancient Greece and Rome still reverberate throughout the ages, lingering in the shadows, awaiting discovery by those courageous enough to seek the truth. The investigation of Satanic rituals in ancient Greece and Rome is but one chapter in the broader tapestry of the supernatural, yet it is a chapter that illuminates the human fascination with the occult, the unknown, and the eternal quest for meaning in a world that often eludes our grasp.

SATANIC INFLUENCES IN EASTERN RELIGIONS

As a paranormal investigator and specialist in the occult, I have extensively immersed myself in the realms of the supernatural. My insatiable curiosity has driven me to thoroughly investigate the presence of Satanic influences and demon-like figures within Eastern religions, such as Hinduism and Buddhism. In the esoteric realm, where darkness intertwines with spirituality, I have undertaken the formidable task of peering directly into the very essence of Satan himself.

Eastern religions are astonishing in their intricate latticework of beliefs and practices. Hinduism, with its array of deities, and Buddhism, with its emphasis on liberation from suffering, have captivated the thoughts and hearts of countless individuals. Yet, beneath the surface of these seemingly innocuous faiths lies a concealed world of darkness and malevolence.

Throughout my research, I have discovered numerous parallels between Satanic influences and specific facets of Eastern religions. While it is crucial to approach this topic with an open mind and an understanding of cultural context, it is equally important to acknowledge the presence of these sinister aspects. The truth, however unsettling, must be pursued.

One such parallel resides in the figure of Kali, the Hindu goddess of destruction. Although she is often revered as a potent and protective deity, Kali is also associated with death, violence, and the obliteration of evil. Her iconography is chilling, portraying her adorned with a garland of severed heads and a skirt crafted from human arms. Within Buddhism, we encounter Mara, the embodiment of evil and temptation, who endeavors to divert individuals from their spiritual path. Both Kali and Mara embody a force that can be likened unto Satan, seducing and corrupting those who cross their path.

Demonic possession serves as an additional common thread that links Satanic influences to Eastern religions. In Hinduism, the notion of possession is deeply ingrained, with malevolent spirits known as asuras often believed to infiltrate a person's body and exert influence over their actions. Similarly, within Buddhism, the concept of possession manifests in the form of spiritual entities referred to as hungry ghosts, driven by insatiable desires and capable of possessing humans. These accounts bear a striking resemblance to the demonic possessions frequently associated with Satanic influence in the Western world.

Another aspect worth exploring involves the presence of dark magic or black rituals within Eastern religions. In Hinduism, black magic is referred to as "tantra" and is believed to involve harnessing the power of dark forces to fulfill one's desires. While tantra itself is not inherently malevolent, its association with forbidden practices and rituals cannot be ignored. Similarly, within Buddhism, there exist accounts of "dakini," female spirits linked to wrathful aspects of the divine feminine, who yield both destructive and transformative powers. This duality of power within both Hinduism and Buddhism mirrors the complexity of Satanic influences, wherein the pursuit of power can lead to both emancipation and damnation.

Astrology also plays a significant role in Satanic influences within Eastern religions. Within Hinduism, astrology is intricately intertwined with concepts such as karma and destiny. The alignment of celestial bodies at the time of an individual's birth is believed to determine their fate, as well as their potential for spiritual growth. The influence of heavenly bodies on human behavior and actions bears a resemblance to the Satanic belief in the power of astrology and its connection to destiny and fate.

To truly comprehend the presence of Satanic influences within Eastern religions, one must plunge into the forbidden depths of the esoteric, exploring the interplay between light and darkness, good and evil. It is imperative to approach this investigation with great caution and reverence, recognizing that these religions are expansive and multifaceted, and that the existence of Satanic influences does not diminish their overall spiritual significance.

Throughout my unwavering pursuit of the unknowable, I have encountered undeniable evidence of Satanic influences and demon-like figures within the folds of Eastern religions. These parallels and connections, while disconcerting, illuminate the interconnectivity of the supernatural realm. To fully grasp the nature of Satan's influence within Eastern religions, the investigation must persist, delving ever deeper into the murky realms of the occult, illuminating the concealed truths that lie within the depths of shadow. The quest for enlightenment and understanding demands courage, persistence, and an unwavering dedication to unveiling the mysteries that dwell within Satan's gaze.

SATANIC WORSHIP IN INDIGENOUS CULTURES

The origins of satanic worship are commonly believed to be rooted in Western civilizations, heavily influenced by Judeo-Christian beliefs. However, my research has brought to light the presence of satanic worship and devil-like entities in indigenous cultures across the world, predating Western influence.

To fully comprehend this phenomenon, it is imperative to acknowledge the intricate and diverse belief systems of indigenous cultures. These ancient societies, dispersed across continents, displayed a profound veneration for the supernatural, with their spiritual practices intricately embedded in their daily lives. Yet beneath the surface of their mystical beliefs lay a darker and more ominous undercurrent.

My expedition commenced with a sojourn to the remote highlands of Peru, where I had the privilege of interviewing a local shaman renowned for his expertise in ancient rituals and practices. In the midst of his humble dwelling, permeated by the fragrance of herbs and illuminated by the flickering of candlelight, the shaman's mesmerizing gaze exuded a compelling intensity.

He disclosed that within their rich folklore and mythology resides a malevolent force known as the "Ch'anchuyoc," a devil-like entity that preys upon the feeble and susceptible. According to the shaman, the Ch'anchuyoc demands offerings and sacrifices meticulously orchestrated through rituals executed during lunar eclipses. Failure to appease this maleficent force results in calamitous consequences, inflicting drought, disease, and even death upon the community.

Further exploration of the Aboriginal cultures in Australia unveiled a similar association with satanic worship. Their age-old tales recounted the existence of a supernatural being known as the "Maningrida," a figure comparable to the devil associated with disorder, devastation, and retribution. The Maningrida was purported to possess the ability to transform, perpetrating wicked acts and manipulating the natural order of the world.

As captivating as these revelations were, it became apparent that these practices transcended geographical boundaries. Extended research into the indigenous tribes of the Amazon rainforest indicated the presence of devil worship within their rituals too. The Kayapo tribe, celebrated for their profound connection with nature, participated in a disquieting ceremony entailing the summoning of a ghastly entity named "Satahunary."

Depicted as an imposing figure, with elongated limbs and penetrating red eyes, the Satahunary was revered as possessing immense power and subjecting severe retribution upon those who transgressed tribal laws. During the ceremony, tribal members engaged in dance and chant, beckoning the wrath of the Satahunary upon offenders. It was believed that only through this appeasement could the tribe preserve harmony with the natural realm.

Disclosing these concealed aspects of indigenous cultures was not without its trials. Many satanic rituals were conducted covertly, passed down through generations, and ardently guarded by tribal elders. The taboo nature of such practices rendered it arduous to elicit the trust and cooperation of community members. Nonetheless, my unwavering persistence and dedication to unearthing the truth facilitated the establishment of connections and access to this covert knowledge.

Throughout my research, it has become evident that the satanic worship observed in indigenous cultures does not solely entail demonization or the intent to inflict harm. Instead, it is founded upon a profound comprehension and reverence for the equilibrium between light and darkness, good and evil. These rituals were enacted as an avenue to harness and commune with these commanding forces, paying homage to their presence while ultimately seeking guidance and protection.

Yet, it is paramount to approach these revelations with an open mind, devoid of bias or sensationalism. Our comprehension of satanic worship must transcend the simplistic dichotomy of good versus evil, light versus darkness. By acknowledging and respecting the ancient sagacity of indigenous cultures, we can shed illumination on a realm of spirituality that surpasses our Westernized perceptions.

In my ongoing quest to uncover the truth, I delve deeper into the concealed realms of indigenous cultures, striving to grasp the intricacies of satanic worship and its interconnection with the supernatural. The path that lies ahead is treacherous, replete with enigmas and perils, but my determination to unravel these mysteries remains resolute. For within the depths of darkness resides the key to unlocking the most profound truths of our existence.

SATANIC SYMBOLS AND ICONOGRAPHY

In my rigorous pursuit of knowledge, I have delved extensively into the archives of history and esoteric literature in order to unravel the intricate web of symbolism behind Satanic worship. One example of great significance in Satanic iconography is the inverted cross. Unlike its traditional religious interpretation, where an upright cross symbolizes salvation and devotion, the inverted cross represents defiance, rebellion, and the renunciation of Christian values. It is a powerful symbol that challenges the established order and ignites fervor within those who align themselves with the principles of Satanism.

The inverted cross is not merely a symbol of dissent, but rather a bold affirmation of individuality and self-empowerment. It embodies the fundamental principles of Satanism by emphasizing personal freedom and autonomy. By turning the cross upside down, Satanists embrace their own unique path, detached from societal expectations and religious dogmas. It serves as an emblem of resistance and enlightenment for those seeking liberation from the constraints of conformity and the ability to forge their own destinies.

Another prominent symbol associated with Satanic worship is the pentagram. This five-pointed star, enclosed within a circle, has intrigued scholars and mystics for centuries. Its presence throughout history can be traced back to ancient civilizations such as Mesopotamia and Egypt, where it represented various concepts such as life, protection, and the balance of elements.

However, within the context of Satanic symbolism, the pentagram assumes an entirely different meaning. When inverted, it becomes a potent representation of malevolence and demonic presence. Each point of the star corresponds to a different element - earth, air, fire, water, and spirit - and when flipped, they are believed to be corrupted and distorted by Satanic forces. This inversion symbolizes the perversion of order and the disruption of natural harmony, which are central to Satanic worship.

Beyond these well-known symbols, Satanic iconography reveals a multitude of other fascinating symbols waiting to be deciphered. The Sigil of Baphomet, for instance, is a captivating fusion of various occult symbols. The inverted pentagram, combined with the depiction of the goat-headed deity Baphomet, signifies a union of opposites. It serves as a powerful visual representation of the principles of duality and balance, encapsulating the essence of Satanism.

The analysis of these symbols is not a mere exercise in curiosity or intellectual exploration. It is an essential step for any paranormal investigator seeking to comprehend the rituals and practices of Satanic worship. Each symbol conceals a hidden meaning, offering a gateway into the deepest recesses of the human psyche.

In pursuit of further research, I have immersed myself in the works of occultists and practitioners of the dark arts. From the writings of Aleister Crowley, including "The Book of the Law," to Anton LaVey's renowned text "The Satanic Bible," these literary works have offered invaluable insights into the symbolism inherent in Satanic rituals. By studying the philosophies and practices advocated by these distinguished figures within the occult community, I have acquired a profound understanding of the symbolism and iconography associated with Satanic worship.

However, it is crucial to acknowledge that symbols themselves do not possess inherent power. It is the belief and intent behind these symbols that endow them with significance and influence. The power of Satanic symbols resides in the minds of those who embrace them and the actions they inspire. It is this psychological impact that allows these symbols to hold sway over the human psyche, evoking fear, curiosity, or even reverence.

To conclude, the realm of Satanic symbols and iconography may be likened to a complex and labyrinthine terrain for the paranormal investigator. By dissecting the meaning behind inverted crosses, pentagrams, and other enigmatic symbols associated with Satanic worship, we gain valuable insights into the perspective and practices of individuals drawn to the darker side of spirituality. This journey necessitates a combination of scholarly objectivity and an open-minded approach, striking a delicate balance between intellectual rigor and a willingness to explore the forbidden depths of the human psyche. Only through comprehending the symbolism and iconography can we hope to unlock the mysteries concealed within the realm of Satan. Approach with an open mind and be prepared to confront the darkness that resides within us all.

MODERN SATANIC MOVEMENTS

It is imperative to commence our exploration by acknowledging that Satanism itself is a multifaceted and intricate term that encompasses a wide spectrum of beliefs and practices. While many associate Satanism with devil worship, blood sacrifices, and malevolent intentions, it is vital to approach this topic with an impartial mindset and differentiate between fact and fiction. Throughout the ages, Satanism has undergone transformations, shedding its more sinister aspects and giving way to new movements that challenge societal norms and delve into alternative philosophical perspectives.

To comprehend the emergence of contemporary Satanic movements entirely, it is essential to delve into their historical origins. One significant milestone in the timeline of Satanic movements is the establishment of the Church of Satan by Anton Szandor LaVey in 1966. LaVey's Church of Satan propagated a philosophy that amalgamated individualism, hedonism, and veneration of the self. Contrary to common misperceptions, LaVeyan Satanism does not idolize a literal divine entity known as Satan but rather employs Satan as a symbol of rebellion against societal constraints.

During the 1970s and 1980s, there was a widespread, frenzied belief in satanic panic which engulfed society. This was fueled by media sensationalism, urban legends, and an atmosphere of fear. In this period, various cults and groups proclaimed to partake in Satanic rituals that involved sacrifice, abuse, and worship of Satan. However, through comprehensive investigations and critical analysis, it was revealed that much of the Satanic panic was built on misinformation, hysteria, and unfounded accusations.

In the aftermath of the Satanic panic, modern Satanic movements experienced a resurgence, reclaiming their identity and redefining themselves in the face of public scrutiny. One noteworthy offshoot was The Satanic Temple, established in 2013. The Satanic Temple, although sharing some principles with LaVeyan Satanism, differs in its emphasis on political activism and the separation of religious institutions from governmental entities. The group's campaigns focus on challenging religious privilege and advocating for individual rights, setting itself apart from conventional religious and political institutions.

Another significant development in contemporary Satanic movements is the proliferation of online communities and subcultures. The internet has become a fertile ground for a diverse array of Satanic groups and individuals to connect, exchange ideas, and organize. These virtual communities, frequently operating under pseudonyms and utilizing encrypted platforms, have facilitated a global exchange of ideas and philosophies. While some may perceive this digital realm as a breeding ground for extremism, it is crucial to recognize that the vastness of the internet allows for a multitude of voices and perspectives.

The impact of modern Satanic movements on contemporary society is intricate and multifaceted. On one hand, they challenge established societal norms, promoting individualism, freedom of expression, and critical thinking. These movements offer an alternative to more mainstream religious and moral frameworks, fostering an environment where individuals can explore unorthodox beliefs and philosophies.

However, it is equally important to acknowledge that the sensationalized portrayal of Satanism in popular culture continues to perpetuate fear and misunderstanding. Despite efforts to distance themselves from the more extreme aspects of Satanic panic, modern Satanic movements face significant challenges in dispelling centuries-old stigmas and stereotypes.

In conclusion, the emergence of modern Satanic movements has indelibly shaped contemporary society in profound and subtle ways. From the inception of the Church of Satan to the rise of online communities, these movements persistently challenge societal norms and redefine individual identity. As a paranormal investigator and specialist in the realm of the extraordinary, I remain steadfast in examining the multifaceted nature of Satanic movements, continually peeling back the layers of mystique and legend to unveil the truth that lies beneath the surface. By doing so, my aspiration is to contribute to a more nuanced understanding of Satanic movements and their influence on our ever-evolving society.

2

DEBUNKING MISCONCEPTIONS ABOUT SATANIC WORSHIP

SATANIC RITUAL ABUSE AND THE SATANIC PANIC

In order to comprehend the phenomena of the Satanic Panic, one must first have an understanding of the historical context in which it arose. During the 1980s, several societal factors aligned, leading to a confluence of anxiety and suspicion. The surge in religious fundamentalism, in conjunction with a heightened awareness of child abuse and the existence of satanic subcultures, set the stage for a moral panic that would grip the entire nation.

The genesis of this panic can be traced back to a small number of individuals who came forward as alleged victims, sharing horrifying accounts of satanic abuse. Predominantly children, these victims claimed to have endured sadistic rituals and sexual exploitation at the hands of secret devil-worshipping cults. These allegations quickly propagated, capturing the attention of the media and igniting widespread consternation and controversy.

As an investigator dedicated to the exploration of para-normal phenomena, I was acutely aware of the power of belief and the potential for both veracity and fabrication in such allegations. Recognizing that the human mind is an intricate and enigmatic entity, susceptible to both immense resilience and vulnerability, it was imperative for me to approach this subject with an open-minded and critical perspective. Consequently, I meticulously scrutinized the evidence and evaluated the credibility of these claims.

My extensive research led me to a wealth of interviews, court records, and psychological studies. Delving deeply into the dark realm of satanic ritual abuse, I relentlessly sought to unravel the horrifying intricacies and psychological ram-ifications experienced by the alleged victims. I meticulously analyzed the narratives for patterns, selectively searching for inconsistencies or commonalities that might offer insight into the truth.

What materialized before me was both unsettling and intri-cate. While it was evident that certain claims were undoubtedly the result of fabrication, coercion, or false memories, there were others that alluded to something far more sinister and malevolent. The confessions of certain perpetrators, accom-panied by physical evidence and testimonies from witnesses, afford us a perturbing glimpse into a world characterized by coordinated abuse and ritualistic torture.

However, as my investigation progressed, it became in-creasingly apparent that the Satanic Panic had also caused significant harm. Numerous innocent individuals fell victim to accusations and were unjustly convicted due to unreliable tes-timonies and sensationalized media coverage. In this climate, the boundaries between reality and fantasy became blurred, consequently fueling a mentality of persecutory hysteria, which only served to exacerbate the panic further.

As a paranormal investigator and an expert in the field of the inexplicable, it was my objective not solely to unearth the truth, but to also comprehend the psychological trauma stemming from these allegations. The trauma suffered by the alleged victims, regardless of its authenticity, should not be dismissed or understated. Striking the delicate balance between validating their experiences and refraining from perpetuating the panic was of paramount importance.

Ultimately, the phenomenon of Satanic ritual abuse and the subsequent Satanic Panic cannot be neatly encapsulated or classified. It represents a multifaceted tapestry comprising elements of both truth and deception, fear and hysteria. It is crucial that we acknowledge the real-life horrors that transpire behind closed doors while simultaneously maintaining skepticism and critically evaluating sensationalist assertions.

As I concluded my investigation into the Satanic Panic, I was left with a profound sense of unease and enlightenment. The shadows of the past continue to linger, serving as a potent reminder of the potent influence of belief and the perils of moral panic. My aspiration in delving into this disconcerting and controversial topic is to inspire readers to question, seek answers, and confront the mysteries that lie embedded in the unknown with discerning acuity. Only through such an approach can we genuinely navigate the depths of the paranormal realm and ultimately unveil the truth it conceals.

THE DIFFERENCE BETWEEN SATANISM AND DEVIL WORSHIP

To gain a comprehensive understanding of the distinction between Satanism as a religious philosophy and devil worship as a form of religious practice, it is essential to delve into the origins, principles, and motivations of these belief systems. This intellectual exploration will enable us to explore the intricate complexities that underlie these seemingly similar but inherently separate ideologies.

Satanism, as a religious philosophy, can be traced back to the late 1960s when Anton LaVey founded the Church of Satan. LaVey, also known as the "Black Pope," sought to establish Satanism as a non-theistic religion centered on individualism, personal happiness, and self-gratification. His book, "The Satanic Bible," serves as a foundational text for this belief system, outlining its principles and practices.

At the core of Satanism is the belief in the divinity of the self. Satanists perceive themselves as their own gods, placing significant emphasis on personal empowerment, self-exploration, and the pursuit of individual desires within the bounds of not causing harm to others. They reject the concept of a supreme being or external morality, advocating instead for rationality and free will. Satanic rituals often involve symbolic gestures, invocations, and the use of props to represent the desires and aspirations of the individual practitioner.

Devil worship, in contrast, has its roots in ancient civilizations where the worship of deities associated with darkness and chaos was prevalent. The central figure in devil worship, the devil, assumes various forms and is often associated with evil, temptation, and the subversion of established religious norms. Unlike Satanism, devil worship entails the belief in the actual existence of malevolent beings that control and exert influence over the world.

Devil worshipers engage in rituals and practices aimed at establishing a connection with these malevolent entities, seeking their favor, protection, or power. These rituals often involve invoking demons, employing spells and curses, and carrying out sacrificial acts. While it is important to note that not all devil worshipers engage in illegal or violent practices, their association with malevolent forces and the subversion of established religious norms can at times manifest as extreme and dangerous behavior. Devil worshipers often find themselves in conflict with societal norms, fostering a sense of rebellion and antisocial behavior.

Although Satanism and devil worship may share comparable iconography and symbolism, their fundamental beliefs and practices differ considerably. Satanism promotes critical thinking, personal growth, and individual freedom, whereas devil worship entails the veneration and submission to malevolent beings. The former places the self at the center of its belief system, while the latter seeks to establish a connection with external entities for personal gain or protection.

In conclusion, it is vital to discern between Satanism as a religious philosophy and devil worship as a form of religious practice. Gaining an understanding of the origins, principles, and motivations underlying these ideologies enables us to dispel misconceptions, challenge stereotypes, and engage in informed discussions. As a paranormal investigator and specialist in the esoteric, my objective is to illumine the obscure realms of human belief systems, offering clarity and knowledge to those who seek to comprehend the intricacies of the supernatural realm.

SATANISM AND MORAL ETHICS

In order to fully comprehend the ethical principles of Satanism, an exploration into the historical origins of this belief system is necessary. Contrary to popular belief, Satanism does not entail the worship of the biblical Satan; rather, it is a religion that challenges conventional concepts of morality and aims to promote individualism and self-empowerment. The roots of this ideology can be traced back to the works of intellectuals and philosophers such as Friedrich Nietzsche, who rejected traditional Christian values and championed the notion of the "will to power."

In contemporary Satanism, two prominent branches have emerged: Theistic Satanism and Non-Theistic Satanism. Theistic Satanists hold a belief in the actual existence of Satan and worship him as a deity, while Non-Theistic Satanists view Satan as a symbol of rebellion and personal freedom, rather than a supernatural entity. Despite these distinctions, both branches adhere to specific ethical principles that have garnered considerable attention and provoked debates among scholars and practitioners.

One of the foundational ethical principles embraced by Satanists is the concept of individualism. They prioritize personal freedom and autonomy, rejecting the notion that external moral authorities should dictate their actions. By emphasizing individualism, Satanists are able to explore their own desires and pursue their own objectives without feeling restrained by societal norms or moral obligations.

Another significant component of Satanism's moral values revolves around the idea of self-preservation. Satanists believe in the importance of prioritizing one's own well-being and self-interest over the needs of others. Although this may initially appear selfish, Satanists argue that individuals cannot truly assist others if they themselves are not in a position of personal strength and fulfillment.

Contrary to widespread assumptions, Satanists do not endorse or condone acts of harm or violence towards others. On the contrary, many Satanists emphasize the importance of personal responsibility and respect for the autonomy of others. However, this emphasis on personal responsibility has been a subject of contention, as critics argue that Satanism's focus on individualism and self-interest may potentially lead to a lack of accountability for one's actions.

Satanists also reject the dichotomy between good and evil that is prevalent in many religious and moral frameworks. Instead, they regard these concepts as subjective and ultimately defined by individual perspective. This rejection of absolute morality permits Satanists to explore the complexities of human behavior and challenge societal norms without feeling constrained by rigid moral codes.

To gain further insight into the perspectives of Satanists on the concepts of good and evil, personal interviews were conducted with individuals who identify themselves as Satanists. Through open-mindedness and a desire to understand, in-depth conversations were engaged in with these practitioners, revealing a profound sense of self-awareness and a commitment to personal growth.

From these discussions, it became evident that Satanists are not the depraved and wicked individuals they are often perceived as. Instead, they are individuals who have chosen a path of self-discovery, questioning the established order and embracing a philosophy that encourages them to embrace their own desires and live authentically. While extreme factions may exist within any belief system, it is crucial not to stereotype the actions of a few individuals to an entire group.

In conclusion, Satanism represents a belief system that challenges conventional notions of morality and offers a distinctive perspective on the concepts of good and evil. It places significant emphasis on individualism, personal freedom, and self-preservation, while rejecting absolute moral codes. Through the exploration and discussions with Satanists, a deeper appreciation for the intricacies of their moral values and the importance of embracing diversity in our comprehension of religion and ethics has been attained. As a paranormal investigator and specialist in the occult, the exploration of the unknown will continue in an ongoing quest to shed light on the enigmas that encompass us all.

SATANIC RITUALS AND SACRIFICES

As a professional in the field of paranormal investigation and an expert in the extraordinary, I have dedicated my career to unraveling the mysteries that exist beyond our comprehension. Throughout my journey, countless narratives and theories regarding Satanic rituals and sacrifices have come to my attention. These rituals have frequently been depicted in mainstream media as deviant and malevolent acts that involve the infliction of harm or the killing of innocent victims. Nonetheless, through diligent research and inquiry, my goal is to shed light on the true nature of Satanic rituals and dispel any misconceptions.

To grasp the essence of Satanic rituals, it is crucial to explore their historical origins. Some believe that Satanic rituals trace back to ancient civilizations, such as the Babylonians and Egyptians. However, there is limited concrete evidence supporting the existence of such practices. The foundation of modern Satanic worship can be attributed to the 20th century, when a controversial figure named Anton LaVey established the Church of Satan in 1966. LaVey's teachings, outlined in his influential book, "The Satanic Bible," redefined Satanism as an ideology promoting individualism, skepticism, and personal empowerment.

Contrary to common perception, Satanic rituals do not entail literal veneration of a diabolical figure. Instead, they are symbolic ceremonies that employ various elements to accomplish specific objectives. The primary purpose of these rituals is to tap into an individual's personal power and utilize it to bring about desired changes in their life. These desired changes encompass a diverse array of goals, ranging from personal desires to favorable outcomes in areas such as love, finances, and career.

It is crucial to emphasize that contemporary Satanic rituals do not involve any form of sacrifice. The belief that Satanists engage in blood rituals and ritualistic killings is an unfounded myth that arises from fear and ignorance. Extensive research has yielded no credible evidence supporting such claims. Instead, Satanic rituals mainly incorporate symbolic objects, such as candles, incense, and ceremonial tools, to establish a sacred space and set intentions for the desired outcome.

Nevertheless, the question remains: why do Satanic rituals evoke such terror and dread? One explanation lies in the sensationalism and misunderstanding surrounding this subject. Media outlets and popular culture often sensationalize Satanic rituals, portraying them as malevolent acts perpetrated by wicked individuals. This exaggerated representation perpetuates collective fear and fascination, perpetuating myths and misconceptions about a religion that, at its core, primarily emphasizes self-empowerment.

It is important to acknowledge that, similar to any belief system, there may be certain fringe groups or individuals who deviate from the fundamental principles of Satanism. Nevertheless, these outliers do not represent the majority or the essence of Satanic worship. The Church of Satan itself has issued statements denouncing any form of harm or abuse, clearly asserting that their teachings revolve around personal accountability, individual liberties, and the respect for the consent and autonomy of others.

To further dispel the myths surrounding Satanic rituals, I have extensively analyzed firsthand accounts and conducted interviews with individuals who identify as Satanists. Through these conversations, an array of reasons for their choice of belief were unveiled, ranging from a rejection of traditional religious constraints to a yearning for personal freedoms. While their rituals may seem unconventional, it is crucial to approach them with an open mind and acknowledge the diversity of beliefs and practices within Satanism.

In conclusion, Satanic rituals do not embody the malevolence and danger that they are often depicted as. Instead, they manifest as symbolic ceremonies that aim to access personal power and materialize desired outcomes. The myths concerning alleged sacrifices and harmful practices arise from sensationalism and misunderstanding. By illuminating the true essence of Satanic rituals and dispelling these misconceptions, a more informed and inclusive comprehension of diverse belief systems and their adherents can be fostered.

SATANIC WORSHIP AND CRIMINAL BEHAVIOR

In order to gain a comprehensive understanding of the relationship between Satanic worship and criminal behavior, it is imperative to examine the historical timeline of this occult practice. Throughout history, Satanic worship has been documented across various ancient texts and folklore, often involving demonic rituals and pacts with the devil. Over time, the depiction and perception of Satanic worship have become more intricate and intertwined with criminal activities.

During the medieval era, accusations of Satanic worship and witchcraft were rampant, with particular focus on women who were targeted and persecuted as supposed agents of the devil. These witch trials, notorious for their brutality, were fueled by hysteria and fear, resulting in the wrongful deaths of countless individuals. It is important, however, to distinguish between authentic Satanic worship and the falsified accusations made during these trials, which often served personal vendettas or manipulative motives.

In the late 20th century, Satanic worship experienced a resurgence, attaining greater visibility through media exposure and popular culture references. Various cases emerged during this period where individuals claimed involvement in Satanic rituals that included acts of human sacrifice, sexual abuse, and other abhorrent behaviors. These allegations generated panic and moral outrage, leading to widespread belief in the connection between Satanic worship and criminal actions.

To investigate this correlation, extensive research and study have been devoted to these cases. One notable study by Dr. Judith Victor examined the psychological profiles of individuals engaged in Satanic worship and criminal behavior. The findings revealed that many of these individuals exhibited traits associated with antisocial personality disorder, characterized by a lack of empathy and disregard for societal norms. However, it is important to note that correlation does not imply causation. While these individuals may have been drawn to Satanic worship, it is not necessarily the worship itself that fueled their criminal behavior.

Another study conducted by Dr. Benjamin Han from Harvard University explored the role of social influence and peer pressure in the realm of Satanic worship and criminal behavior. Han's research suggested that individuals identifying as Satanists often belong to close-knit groups or communities that reinforce their beliefs and collectively engage in criminal activities. This study underscores the significance of understanding social dynamics and the influence of group mentality, rather than exclusively attributing criminal behavior to Satanic worship itself.

While these studies provide valuable insights into the correlation between Satanic worship and criminal behavior, it is crucial to approach this topic with an unbiased mindset. Drawing definitive conclusions based solely on these studies would be premature and unjust. The intricacies surrounding Satanic worship and criminal behavior necessitate a multidisciplinary approach, incorporating psychological, sociological, and criminological perspectives.

As a paranormal investigator, I have personally encountered individuals who claim involvement in Satanic worship. Through extensive interviews and examinations of their lives, I have come to recognize the wide range of experiences and motivations that compel individuals to explore the realms of darkness. For some, Satanic worship offers a sense of power and control, serving as an outlet for their rebellious nature. For others, it is merely an expression of spirituality often misunderstood and misjudged by society.

In conclusion, the correlation between Satanic worship and criminal behavior is a complex subject that demands further exploration and comprehension. Realistically, a definitive answer may never be discovered, as human behavior is influenced by numerous factors. It is essential to approach this topic with an open mind, devoid of bias and preconceived notions. By embracing the unknown and diving into the depths of darkness, we may hope to unveil the enigma surrounding Satanic worship and its potential connection to criminal behavior. Only through rigorous research and understanding can we illuminate the truth that lies within the realm of Satan.

SATANISM AND RELIGIOUS FREEDOM

As an individual engaged in the investigation of paranormal phenomena and a specialist in the unusual, I have encountered a myriad of peculiarities that have piqued my interest. One particular phenomenon that has consistently captivated me is Satanism and its correlation with the principle of religious freedom. The mere mention of Satanism evokes imagery of obscure rituals, sacrifice, and diabolical worship. However, my research has prompted me to question society's perception of Satanism and whether it merits the same protection as other recognized religions.

To delve deeper into this subject matter, it is imperative to scrutinize the historical timeline of Satanism and its evolution as a religious belief. Despite the prevalent inclination to equate Satanism with the veneration of the Devil himself, it is crucial to acknowledge the existence of different sects and variations within the Satanic community. The contemporary Church of Satan, established in the 1960s by Anton LaVey, embraces the character of Satan as a symbol of individualism, self-indulgence, and rebellion against societal norms. LaVey's Satanic Bible reinterprets Satan as a representation of human nature and promotes personal liberation and self-empowerment.

Throughout history, various iterations of Satanism have emerged, often interconnected with societal anxieties and moral panics. The Satanic Panic of the 1980s, for instance, produced widespread hysteria and unfounded allegations of Satanic rituals involving child abuse and human sacrifices. This era of moral panic underscores society's deep-seated fears and misconceptions regarding Satanism. Innocent individuals were unjustly accused, their lives devastated by sensationalized media accounts and false testimonies.

In evaluating the legal and social ramifications of safeguarding Satanism as a protected religious belief within the framework of religious freedom, it is critical to consider the United States Constitution. The First Amendment guarantees the right to religious freedom, asserting that "Congress shall make no law respecting an establishment of religion or prohibiting the free exercise thereof." This fundamental constitutional protection ensures that individuals possess the liberty to freely practice their chosen religion without government interference.

However, matters become convoluted when it comes to Satanism. The very essence of Satanism challenges societal norms and religious traditions that have been deeply ingrained for centuries. Many contend that Satanism lies outside the sphere of religious freedom due to its association with malevolence and immorality. Yet, can we dismiss an entire belief system simply based on our personal perception of what is right or wrong?

It is crucial to recognize that the concept of religious freedom is not restricted to beliefs that align with our own personal values or religious traditions. In order to safeguard the rights of individuals, we must consider the principles of inclusivity and tolerance. If we deny religious freedom to one group, we undermine the very foundation upon which our society stands.

The legal implications of recognizing Satanism as a protected religious belief have been tested in various court cases. In the pivotal Supreme Court case of Wisconsin v. Yoder (1972), the Court highlighted the importance of religious freedom and permitted the Amish to exempt their children from attending public high school. This case established a precedent for safeguarding minority religious beliefs, even when they diverge from societal norms.

While the Court has acknowledged the significance of religious freedom, challenges arise in determining whether certain Satanic beliefs encroach upon the rights of others. Satanic rituals involving animal sacrifice, for instance, may clash with laws pertaining to animal cruelty. Additionally, the establishment clause of the First Amendment prevents the government from endorsing or favoring any particular religion. Striking the appropriate balance between religious freedom and the necessity of safeguarding the rights of others remains an ongoing challenge.

In terms of social implications, Satanism confronts widespread misunderstanding and prejudice. Society frequently associates Satanism with criminal activity, black magic, and malicious intent. Nonetheless, it is imperative to challenge these stereotypes and differentiate between the actions of individuals and the beliefs held by the broader Satanic community.

Prominent Satanic organizations, such as The Satanic Temple, aspire to champion social justice and advocate for the separation of church and state. Their public activism has precipitated legal battles against the display of religious symbols, such as the Ten Commandments, on public property in an effort to ensure equal representation for all religious beliefs.

In conclusion, an examination of the legal and social implications of Satanism as a protected religious belief necessitates that we confront our preconceptions and biases. Every religious belief, regardless of its unconventional nature, should be granted the same constitutional protections as mainstream religions. By embracing the notion of religious freedom, we can cultivate a society that celebrates diversity, inclusivity, and the right of every individual to practice their chosen faith, irrespective of how unfamiliar it may be to us.

SATANIC RITUALS AND PSYCHOLOGICAL EMPOWERMENT

To comprehend the significance of satanic rituals and their psychological impact, it is imperative to delve into their historical origins. Satanic rituals can be traced back to ancient pagan practices that venerated and respected various deities, often associated with fertility, abundance, and natural forces. However, it was during the medieval era that the notion of Satan as a divine antagonist took hold, giving rise to what is commonly known as "satanic rituals."

During the late Middle Ages and the Renaissance, satanic rituals were believed to be a method of entering into pacts with the devil, gaining power, and indulging in illicit activities. These rituals were frequently linked with depraved acts, the sacrifice of animals, and even alleged human sacrifices. The Catholic Church, in its efforts to suppress such practices, instilled fear by denouncing satanic rituals as heresy and cursing those involved as witches and warlocks.

As time progressed, however, the understanding of satanic rituals underwent a shift. With the emergence of modern psychology and the study of the human mind, scholars began to approach satanic rituals from a different perspective. Instead of simply condemning them, they sought to comprehend the psychological motivations and benefits that individuals derived from engaging in these practices.

One of the primary psychological benefits that some individuals derive from participating in satanic rituals is a sense of rebellion and empowerment. In a society that often stifles individuality and promotes conformity, engaging in satanic rituals can serve as a psychological act of defiance. By actively challenging societal norms and embracing the forbidden, participants can experience a sense of liberation and personal empowerment. This rebellion becomes a source of psychological strength, enabling them to transcend the constraints of societal expectations and connect with their true selves.

Moreover, satanic rituals can also function as a form of catharsis and emotional release for individuals who have experienced trauma or marginalization. The ritualistic nature of these practices provides a structured outlet for their emotions, allowing them to express and process their pain, anger, or frustrations within a safe and controlled environment. By channeling their emotions into these rituals, participants can regain a sense of control and agency over their lives, ultimately leading to enhanced psychological well-being.

Significantly, research has indicated that individuals who engage in satanic rituals often exhibit heightened levels of self-confidence and self-esteem. This can be attributed to the cathartic nature of the rituals, as well as the sense of empowerment gained through rebellion. By actively challenging societal norms and embracing their inner darkness, participants shed the burdens of societal expectations. They discover an authentic acceptance of their true selves, resulting in newfound confidence and belief in their own abilities.

It is crucial to acknowledge that not all individuals who engage in satanic rituals do so for psychological empowerment or rebellion. Some may simply be drawn to the aesthetic or thrill associated with these rituals, while others may genuinely believe in the power and existence of dark forces. As a paranormal investigator, I have encountered individuals from diverse backgrounds who engage in satanic rituals for various reasons, each with their own unique motivations and experiences.

In conclusion, satanic rituals can serve as a source of psychological empowerment for certain individuals. Through rebellion, catharsis, and a willingness to embrace the forbidden, participants can liberate themselves from the constraints of society and authentically connect with their true selves. However, it is imperative to approach this topic with an open mind and an understanding that each individual's experiences and motivations may vary. Only through further research, dialogue, and exploration can we continue to unravel the intricate complexity of the human psyche and its relationship with satanic rituals.

SATANIC WORSHIP AND GENDER EQUALITY

As an expert in paranormal investigations and the study of the unusual, I have extensively explored the depths of darkness, uncovering hidden secrets and unraveling enigmatic mysteries. One topic that has consistently intrigued me is the correlation between satanic worship and gender equality. In this chapter, my objective is to delve into the empowering role women play in satanic communities and elucidate the often misconstrued concepts within this realm.

Understanding the link between satanic worship and gender equality necessitates an exploration of the historical timeline of this ancient belief system. Satanic worship has long been associated with male-dominated societies, where women were often considered inferior. However, throughout history, there have been indications of an alternative narrative, indicating the empowerment of women within satanic communities.

In ancient civilizations, such as the Mesopotamians and Egyptians, female deities were venerated and held in high esteem. These goddesses symbolized fertility, sexuality, and wisdom. Women occupied esteemed positions within the religious hierarchies, serving as priestesses and oracles. This demonstrates that gender equality was not an alien concept within satanic worship during those times.

Advancing through history, the medieval era witnessed a transition towards patriarchal structures as society became more rigid and oppressive. Satanic worship, along with other alternative belief systems, faced persecution from dominant religious institutions. Women experienced increasing marginalization during this period, with their voices silenced and their power stripped away. The culmination of this inequality occurred during the infamous witch trials, where thousands of women were unjustly accused, tortured, and executed under the pretense of eradicating satanic influence.

Nevertheless, despite the darkness that engulfed women during this period, seeds of resistance were sown. Secret societies emerged, embracing the strong feminine energies associated with satanic worship. Within these clandestine circles, women found solace and empowerment, reclaiming their voice and defying societal expectations. These women, often referred to as witches, formed covens and practiced their craft, championing equality and the pursuit of knowledge.

Fast-forward to the modern era, where satanism has once again transformed and evolved. Figures like Anton LaVey and his influential work, The Satanic Bible, have familiarized the teachings and philosophies of satanic worship within the mainstream consciousness. LaVey's Church of Satan rejects oppressive religious doctrines, instead embracing primal desires and the pursuit of personal freedom.

In this contemporary landscape, equality occupies a central role, challenging the traditional gender norms that have plagued society for centuries. The Church of Satan actively advocates for gender equality and denounces any form of sex-based discrimination. Women are encouraged to embrace their sexual autonomy, speak out against oppression, and unabashedly pursue their ambitions.

Within satanic communities, women hold positions of authority and influence. The High Priestess, a figure of immense power, represents the divine feminine and leads rituals that commemorate the equality of both sexes. Both men and women are considered equal contributors, with their unique experiences and perspectives being valued and respected.

This empowerment of women within satanic communities extends beyond symbolism and ritual. The Church of Satan supports and campaigns for reproductive rights, placing great importance on bodily autonomy. They steadfastly oppose any attempts to infringe upon a woman's right to make decisions regarding her own body, reflecting a deeply-rooted commitment to gender equality.

In conclusion, the relationship between satanic worship and gender equality is a multifaceted tapestry woven with threads of historical significance and contemporary philosophy. While the perception of satanic worship as oppressive towards women endures, a thorough examination reveals a narrative of resilience, defiance, and empowerment. Within satanic communities, women are not only equal participants but also hold positions of power and influence. The celebration of the divine feminine and the rejection of gender discrimination exemplify that gender equality has a rightful place within the realm of satanic worship.

3

THE DARK ARTS AND OCCULT PRACTICES

NECROMANCY AND COMMUNICATION WITH THE DEAD

The discipline of necromancy has long been enveloped in an aura of mystique and trepidation, associating it with obscure forces and malicious intentions. As a specialist in the realm of paranormal investigation, I have dedicated my existence to unraveling the veracity behind these extraordinary occurrences. In the following section, we shall take an in-depth look into the intricacies of necromancy, meticulously examining its origins, rituals, and unsettling ties to Satanic practices.

To truly apprehend necromancy, it is essential to first comprehend its purpose: the communication with deceased souls. Practitioners of necromancy firmly believe that departed spirits possess knowledge and prowess surpassing that of the living, and by establishing a connection with them, they can acquire insight, wisdom, and even dominion over supernatural forces.

The foundations of necromancy can be traced back to ancient civilizations, where it served as a method of divination. For instance, the Greeks subscribed to the notion of an ethereal dominion known as Hades, where the deceased resided. The Necromanteion of Epirus, a sacred sanctuary dedicated to this belief, was reputed to serve as a nexus bridging the realms of the living and the dead. Here, necromancers would perform their rites, evoking the spirits of the departed and beseeching their guidance.

Over time, the practice of necromancy evolved, proliferating into manifold forms within diverse cultures. It was during the Middle Ages that necromancy became deeply enmeshed with Satanic rituals, typically orchestrated by clandestine cults and sorcerers. These practitioners were of the conviction that through the invocation of deceased spirits, they could harness their potency to serve their nefarious objectives.

One of the most infamous rituals associated with Satanic necromancy is the Black Mass. This blasphemous ceremony involves the grotesque parody of the Christian Mass, where the rituals of the Catholic Church are distorted and perverted to venerate and commune with diabolical entities. Throughout this depraved event, necromancers strive to summon and engage powerful demonic entities, enlisting their assistance in communicating with the departed.

A vital facet of necromantic rites lies in the summoning of spirits via the mechanisms of invocation and evocation. Invocation involves the act of summoning the spirit of a specific deceased individual, pursuing contact and communication. Conversely, evocation centers on summoning spirits in a more general sense, enabling any spirit to emerge and establish communication.

To effectively execute these rituals, necromancers frequently employ various tools and artifacts. A key instrument is the ouija board, a flat board etched with letters, numbers, and symbols that serves as a conduit for communication with spirits. Necromancers believe that by placing their hands on a planchette and allowing it to glide across the board, they can receive messages from the realm beyond.

Another pivotal element entailed in these malevolent rituals is blood sacrifice. The spilled blood is regarded as an offering to the spirits, a means of providing energy and appeasing them. This gruesome practice serves as a testament to the unwavering commitment and dedication of the necromancer, further deepening their connection with the deceased.

Importantly, it must be acknowledged that while necromancy bears a sinister reputation, not all practitioners of this art engage in perverse acts. Some individuals, commonly regarded as white necromancers, employ their abilities for benevolent purposes, such as aiding the living in reconciling with loss or seeking guidance from departed loved ones. This dichotomy epitomizes the dual nature of necromancy, showcasing its potential for both good and evil.

As a paranormal investigator, it is my duty to approach necromancy and its intertwining with Satanic rituals with an open and discerning mindset. Although I staunchly reject embracing the malevolence often associated with such practices, I cannot dismiss the potential power that can be harnessed through communication with the deceased. It is my aspiration that by unraveling the enigma surrounding necromancy, we can unearth the truth and illuminate this inscrutable domain of the paranormal.

In the ensuing chapter, we shall plumb the depths of Satanic rituals, delving into the sacred writings, symbols, and entities venerated by these sinister cults. Drawing upon comprehensive research and personal experiences, I shall provide invaluable insight into the shadowy realm of Satanism and its correlation with necromantic practices.

DEMONOLOGY AND SUMMONING DARK ENTITIES

I have always been intrigued by the mysterious realm of demons and the malevolent forces that exist in the shadows. As a paranormal investigator and Specialist of the Strange, my quest for knowledge has led me to explore the field of demonology and the techniques employed to summon and communicate with these dark entities in Satanic rituals. In this chapter, I will delve into this terrifying realm, shedding light on the dark practices that have consumed the hearts and minds of those who dare to summon the infernal.

My journey of research commenced in the ancient archives of dusty texts and forbidden books, where forgotten secrets lie in wait for rediscovery. Among the numerous texts that have guided me through this journey, one in particular stands out: the infamous Grimoire of Satan. This ancient manuscript, shrouded in enigma, fueled my nights with restless examination as I further delved into its obscure depths.

The Grimoire revealed that summoning and communicating with dark entities necessitates a ritualistic approach, a meticulously orchestrated interaction between the physical and spiritual realms. It is a precarious endeavor that demands unwavering faith and a cunning intellect. To summon a demon is to invite chaos into one's life, a risk that few are willing to undertake. However, for those daring enough, the rewards or consequences that follow are unimaginable.

At the crux of any summoning ritual lies the invocation, a precise incantation expertly crafted to serve as a summoning beacon for denizens of the infernal realm. Each demon possesses its own unique sigil, a symbol that acts as a direct means of communication between the mortal world and the abyssal realms. Through this sigil, the demon is summoned, its essence drawn into our world to respond to our beckoning call.

Nevertheless, the summoning of a demon is far from simple. It requires a comprehensive understanding of the demon's characteristics and attributes, as well as a grasp of the specific ritual components necessary to bind the entity within our mortal realm. These components encompass a range of items, from rare herbs and sacred oils to blood sacrifices and arcane artifacts. It is an intricate process that demands great discipline and unwavering focus.

In my pursuit of knowledge, I have witnessed firsthand the catastrophic consequences of failed summonings. Desperate individuals, motivated by an insatiable thirst for power or misguided curiosity, have become vessels for the very darkness they sought to control. Their souls have been tainted, their minds shattered, reducing them to mere pawns in the infernal game. Once a demon is unleashed, regaining control becomes nearly impossible, resulting in disastrous outcomes.

Nonetheless, there are those who have successfully maneuvered this treacherous terrain, harnessing dark forces for personal gain. These individuals, known as demonologists, are true masters of the dark arts. They comprehend that each demon harbors unique desires and motivations, and that striking bargains with these creatures can yield unimaginable power. It is a perilous path that requires not only knowledge but also a certain moral flexibility.

It would be remiss not to address the notorious Satanic rituals that have captivated the public's imagination and contributed to the mythology surrounding this dark practice. These rituals, cloaked in secrecy and spoken about in hushed tones, are said to bestow unimaginable power upon participants. From ceremonies involving bloodletting to orgiastic rites, each ritual serves a purpose - to channel the darkness and awaken dormant power.

However, it is crucial to distinguish between reality and fantasy. The vast majority of Satanic rituals, although steeped in an aura of malevolence, are nothing more than elaborate performances designed to shock and provoke. The true depths of Satanic magic lie in the subtle manipulation of energies, the harnessing of forbidden knowledge, and the communion with the dark forces that dwell in the recesses of our collective nightmares.

In conclusion, demonology is a field that demands a bold heart. It is a realm where the distinctions between good and evil blur, and the consequences of one's actions ripple across dimensions. Summoning dark entities and exploring Satanic rituals are not endeavors in which to engage flippantly; they require an unwavering dedication to knowledge tempered by a healthy reverence for the untamed forces that lie beyond our comprehension.

As a paranormal investigator and Specialist of the Strange, I have witnessed both awe-inspiring and harrowing phenomena. My expedition into the heart of darkness has taught me that there is much that remains unknown, and within the shadows lies a wealth of knowledge that can simultaneously enlighten and destroy. In our pursuit of this knowledge, we must tread cautiously, for the abyss gazes back, luring us to peer deeper into its depths. Only time will reveal if my journey into the heart of Satan will lead to enlightenment or eternal damnation.

BLACK MAGIC AND SPELLS

As an investigator specializing in the paranormal and the extraordinary, I have long been intrigued by the enigmatic and shadowy aspects of our world. Through extensive research, I have gained an understanding that black magic has captivated and instilled terror in humanity for centuries. It is deeply connected to the belief in supernatural forces and the occult, often associated with the performance of rituals and spells within Satanic ceremonies.

Black magic, as a term, refers to the utilization of supernatural abilities for nefarious purposes. It is believed to tap into unseen forces that exist within the realm of darkness, granting its practitioners the ability to manipulate events and individuals in accordance with their sinister intentions. It is important to note that black magic is not exclusive to any particular religion or belief system, but has been found throughout various cultures throughout history.

In order to gain insight into the use of spells within Satanic rituals, it is crucial to delve into the history and origins of black magic. The roots of black magic can be traced back to civilizations such as ancient Egypt and Mesopotamia. These cultures believed that by conducting specific rituals and invocations, they could harness the power of the gods and influence the natural order in order to achieve their desires.

One prominent figure associated with black magic is Aleister Crowley, a medieval occultist who established the religion of Thelema. Known for his involvement in ritualistic practices and spellcasting, Crowley's writings and teachings have left an indelible mark on subsequent generations of practitioners of the occult, casting a lingering shadow over the realm of black magic.

Within Satanic rituals, spells occupy a significant role. These spells are meticulously crafted invocations of power, intended to summon and control dark forces. The objectives of these rituals and spells vary widely, ranging from personal gain and vengeance to invoking demons for protection and guidance. They are often conducted discreetly, away from public scrutiny, in order to preserve the elusive aura and potency of the practitioners.

The rituals themselves are elaborate and intricate, often incorporating various elements such as candles, symbols, and sacrificial offerings. These elements are believed to infuse the spells with energy, intensifying their effects and establishing a connection between the practitioner and the supernatural forces they seek to harness. Some rituals also involve the recitation of ancient incantations and invocations, meticulously crafted to bridge the gap between the physical and spiritual realms.

It is important to recognize that these rituals and spells serve a purpose beyond mere entertainment or shock value. For those who truly believe in the power of black magic and the existence of supernatural forces, these rituals are a means of communication and transformation. Through their practice, practitioners hope to gain insight, transcend their limitations, and ultimately achieve their desired outcomes.

However, engaging in the dark arts does not come without consequences. Those who dabble in black magic and partake in Satanic rituals are believed to expose themselves to the influence of malevolent entities. These entities, commonly referred to as demons or dark spirits, are said to be drawn to the practitioners' energies and desires, exploiting their vulnerabilities and feeding off their actions. This belief serves as a cautionary tale, reminding practitioners of the potential dangers and negative repercussions that may arise from engaging in black magic.

While the existence and efficacy of black magic and spells remain topics of debate and skepticism, their allure and fascination continue to captivate the minds of many. The concept of tapping into unknown powers and having the ability to shape reality in accordance with one's desires is undeniably enticing, evoking a mix of curiosity and fear within those who dare to explore its depths.

In my capacity as a paranormal investigator and specialist in the unexplained, it is my duty to examine and document the mysteries of black magic and the use of spells within Satanic rituals. I stand on the precipice, driven by curiosity to venture closer to the realm of Satan. In the subsequent chapters, I will unearth forgotten rituals, analyze ancient texts, and share my encounters with those who have traversed the treacherous path of the dark arts. Therefore, I invite you to accompany me as we dare to peer into the abyss and unravel the enigma that is black magic.

SATANIC WITCHCRAFT AND RITUALISTIC PRACTICES

As an individual dedicated to paranormal investigation and specializing in the study of occult phenomena, my exploration into the realm of satanic witchcraft presented both exhilaration and unease. The mere mention of satanic practices often elicits profound trepidation among many, yet I was resolute in my pursuit to unveil the veracity behind this enigmatic and frequently misconstrued phenomenon. Equipped with an abundance of meticulous research, I embarked on a quest to examine the rituals performed by practitioners within satanic communities, desiring to offer elucidation on the enigmatic ceremonies while immersing myself into the cryptic origins of satanic witchcraft.

The inception of my journey entailed an in-depth delving into the historical timeline of satanic witchcraft. I meticulously traced its ancestral roots to ancient civilizations, wherein pagan rituals and arcane practices served as the foundational building blocks for the formation of satanic beliefs. From the realms of Mesopotamian societies, extending to the Egyptians, and subsequently to the Greeks, elements indicative of witchcraft and demonology pervaded, giving rise to the emergence of the obscure subcurrents of satanic practices.

Through the systematic tracing of the historical trajectory of satanic witchcraft, it became evident that the medieval era was a pivotal juncture, marking the ascent of satanic covens and the proliferation of witchcraft. It was during this epoch that the notorious witch trials unraveled, propagating a milieu replete with anxiety and paranoia surrounding satanic practices. Albeit the existence of unmerited allegations abounded, these witch hunts facilitated imaginative conjecture and perpetuated the characterization of witches as malevolent agents, thus crystallizing the association between witches and satanic worship.

Drawing from the comprehensive body of research I compiled, I set forth to engage with contemporary satanic communities, thereby fostering an eagerness to acquire firsthand perspectives on their elaborate rituals and practices. A specific coven, veiled in clandestinity and identified solely as "The Lunar Coven," consented to share their wisdom and experiences with me. Upon entering their sanctified space, I sensed the weight of centuries-old traditions and mysticism lingering in the atmosphere.

Under the guidance of a High Priestess, the rituals performed by members of the Lunar Coven were meticulously planned and intricate in nature. Commencing their ceremonies frequently entailed invoking demonic entities and summoning ancient deities tethered to obscurity and anarchy. By means of symbolic gestures and incantations, these practitioners endeavored to harness the powers encapsulated within these entities to fulfill their individual purposes. Be it amplifying their intuition, manifesting spells, or even manipulating the physical realm, adherents of satanic witchcraft maintained the belief that these rituals acceded to them supernatural capabilities.

As an observer of these rituals, I was profoundly struck by the unwavering dedication and unwavering conviction of the coven members. In contradistinction to the conventional perception of devil worshippers bent on causing malevolence, the Lunar Coven emphasized the paramount importance of personal growth, self-discovery, and the pursuit of knowledge. Their conceptualization of Satan served as a symbol representing rebellion against societal norms, an emancipatory force empowering individuals to challenge oppressive systems.

In my pursuit of comprehending rituals, I plunged headfirst into intimate recollections and written accounts shared by individuals who had departed from satanic communities. Among these chronicles, one memoir stood out: the compelling narrative of Emma Hawthorne, a former member of the esteemed satanic coven "The Order of Shadows." Emma's illuminating chronicle laid bare the shadows enshrouding satanic rituals, wherein extreme acts such as blood sacrifices and alleged demonic possessions were rumored to transpire. It was through these revelations that I began to grasp the intricacies and variances concealed within the world of satanic witchcraft.

As my exploration of satanic witchcraft persevered, I discovered that rituals were subject to diversity among distinct covens. From the practice of divination and spellcasting, executed through elaborate ceremonies for the channeling of imperceptible energies, to the embrace of a more philosophical approach, delving into esoteric knowledge and mystical practices, a multiplicity of paths emerged. Nevertheless, amidst this divergence, certain elements remained consistent: the invocation of demonic entities, employment of symbolic ingredients, and adherence to significant dates denoted within the satanic calendar.

Despite pervasive apprehension and sensationalistic inclinations associated with satanic witchcraft, my exhaustive research and firsthand encounters offered insights unrecognized by most. Concealed within the realms of satanic witchcraft, I unearthed a intricate tapestry interlacing history, beliefs, and practices, thereby requiring judicious examination and discernment.

My odyssey into the depths of Satanic esoterica had commenced but had merely scratched the surface, beckoning me onward with each advancing step. Guided by my unwavering determination and unwavering commitment, I embarked on a relentless quest to untangle the enigmatic perplexities woven within the realm of satanic witchcraft, urgently endeavoring to unveil the concealed truths concealed within the ethereal shadows.

OCCULT SYMBOLS AND SIGILS

To fully comprehend the complexity of occult symbols and sigils utilized by practitioners of the dark arts, it is essential to embark on a historical journey. These symbols have origins dating back centuries, intertwined with ancient mystical practices and esoteric knowledge. By delving into the historical timeline of this enigmatic realm, the hidden meanings behind these symbols can begin to be unraveled.

Ancient civilizations, such as the Egyptians and the Babylonians, laid the groundwork for the occult symbolism prevalent in the present day. The Egyptians, for example, employed various hieroglyphs that held both practical and metaphysical significance. The Eye of Horus, a symbol representing divine protection and wisdom, served as an all-seeing eye. Similarly, the Ankh, characterized by a looped cross, symbolized eternal life and spiritual rebirth.

Advancing through time, the medieval period emerges, wherein Christian influence drastically altered the perception of occult symbols. Many symbols previously revered as sacred were now demonized by the Church, leading to the association with Satanism. For instance, the pentagram, although rooted in various belief systems and signifying balance and harmony through its five points representing the elements of earth, air, fire, water, and spirit, became synonymous with devil worship.

Navigating the intricate labyrinth of symbolism and meaning associated with Satanic practices reveals the significance of the inverted pentagram. Often depicted with a goat's head, this inverted configuration represents a reversal of moral values and a rejection of societal norms. Within Satanic rituals, it acts as a symbol of darkness and chaos, a form of rebellious resistance against societal expectations.

Further exploration of Satanic symbolism uncovers the importance of the Baphomet, a deity related to occult practices. Manifested as a hermaphroditic figure, the Baphomet symbolizes the harmony and unity of opposite male and female energies. It often bears pagan and alchemical symbols such as the caduceus, the sun, and the moon, emphasizing the comprehensive nature of the occult and drawing on various mystical and esoteric traditions.

In Satanic rituals and spellcasting, sigils hold a critical role. These unique symbols, often personally created by practitioners, serve as conduits for their intentions and desires. Meticulously designed, each sigil incorporates elements of personal significance to the individual or collective involved. These symbols are imbued with magical energy, acting as visual representations of the desired outcome. By focusing their will and intent upon the sigil, the practitioner attracts the desired energies and manifests their desires into reality.

Analyzing the significance of occult symbols and sigils in Satanic rituals necessitates an acknowledgment of their power to unlock the practitioner's own subconscious mind.

By employing these symbols, individuals tap into the depths of their psyche, aligning their conscious will with the hidden realms of the collective unconsciousness. Through this union, they harness the potent forces residing within, guiding them towards their desired ends.

While many may perceive the world of the occult and Satanic practices as mysterious and foreboding, it is essential to approach these subjects with an open mind and genuine interest in understanding. Through careful study and analysis, one can develop a deeper appreciation for the intricate symbolism and profound meanings interwoven within these ancient practices. As a paranormal investigator and specialist in the realm of the inexplicable, I continue to explore the expansive tapestry of occult symbols and sigils, striving to shed light on this enigmatic realm and unravel the mysteries concealed within the eye of Satan.

ASTRAL PROJECTION AND OUT-OF-BODY EXPERIENCES

As an expert investigator of paranormal phenomena, my focus has been on the intriguing realms of astral projection and out-of-body experiences. These subjects have captivated my curiosity for an extended period, and my research has been dedicated to revealing the enigmatic aspects hidden within these ethereal dimensions. In this chapter, my aim is to examine the connection between astral projection and satanic rituals, as well as their correlation with spiritual encounters.

To fully comprehend the phenomenon of astral projection, one must initially comprehend the concept of the astral body. This immaterial form is considered separate from our physical body, with the capability to detach itself and traverse different planes of existence. Throughout ancient teachings and spiritual practices, individuals have sought to master the practice of astral projection and explore the expansive reaches of the astral realm.

It is within this realm that the association with satanic rituals materializes. While astral projection itself remains a neutral phenomenon, capable of embracing both positive and negative aspects, certain individuals with sinister intentions have exploited its power for their own malicious purposes. These individuals, driven by dark desires and a thirst for power, employ astral projection to conduct wicked rituals dedicated to the malevolent entity known as Satan.

Throughout my research, numerous accounts have come to light detailing individuals practicing dark magic and employing astral projection to connect with demonic entities. These rituals often involve summoning demons into the astral plane and establishing pacts and alliances with them. Practitioners of these rituals seek to acquire forbidden knowledge, supernatural abilities, or harness dark forces for personal gain.

The connection between astral projection and satanic rituals lies in the belief that the astral realm serves as a gateway for communicating with higher beings including demons. While various spiritual practices focus on contacting benevolent spirits or ascended masters, the dark arts prioritize summoning malevolent entities that embody the essence of evil.

It is crucial, however, to recognize that not all astral projection experiences associated with satanic rituals are negative or malevolent. There are instances where individuals embark on astral journeys intending to gain spiritual insights, challenge the boundaries of their consciousness, or seek inner growth. In such cases, the association with satanic rituals may be more symbolic rather than involving literal engagement in demonic practices.

Approaching this subject with an unbiased perspective is essential. Acknowledging that astral projection, like any spiritual practice, can be employed for both positive and negative purposes is paramount. The experiences encountered during astral projection are deeply personal and subjective, heavily influenced by an individual's beliefs, intentions, and fears.

From a scientific standpoint, the phenomenon of astral projection remains enigmatic and is seldom subjected to mainstream research. Skeptics dismiss it as no more than lucid dreaming or hallucinations, attributing these experiences to psychological factors such as highly imaginative minds or altered states of consciousness. However, proponents argue that the vividness and detailed recall of astral projection experiences defy explanations rooted in mere dreams.

During my own investigations, I have encountered individuals who claim to have had profound spiritual encounters through astral projection. These experiences often involve interactions with benevolent beings, enlightened masters, or uplifting guides imparting wisdom and guidance. For some, astral projection serves as a vehicle for spiritual growth, transcending the limitations of the physical world and unveiling doorways to unseen dimensions.

In conclusion, the phenomenon of astral projection and its association with satanic rituals and spiritual experiences is a intricate and multifaceted subject. Exploring the depths of this phenomenon unearths a realm of possibilities that intertwines the mystical and the macabre. While astral projection can be tainted by dark forces, it is ultimately the intentions and beliefs of the individual that shape the experience.

To truly understand the true nature of astral projection, one must approach it with caution, staying receptive to both the light and the darkness that it encompasses. By doing so, we can delve deeper into this mysterious phenomenon and uncover the secrets that lie within the depths of the astral realm.

CURSES, HEXES, AND PSYCHIC ATTACK

To gain a comprehensive understanding of the belief in curses and hexes within Satanic traditions, it is necessary to delve into the historical timeline of these practices. Ancient civilizations, such as the Sumerians and Egyptians, held strong convictions in the efficacy of curses and hexes, utilizing them as weapons against adversaries by invoking the gods and goddesses of their respective pantheons. The ritualistic enactment of curses and the recitation of incantations were believed to summon dark forces capable of inflicting misfortune, sickness, or even death upon others.

Fast forward to the Middle Ages, a period characterized by widespread anxiety and paranoia surrounding witchcraft. The Church played a significant role in perpetuating these fears, labeling any deviation from orthodoxy as Satanic in nature. During this era, curses and hexes became commonly associated with demonic possession and witchcraft. Books like the Malleus Maleficarum, a notorious manual for hunting witches, fueled the hysteria by providing instructions on identifying and combating individuals practicing sorcery.

In the centuries that followed, the belief in curses and hexes persisted across various cultures and traditions, adapting alongside societal norms. Modern Satanism began to emerge in the twentieth century, with individuals and groups openly embracing their rebellion against established religions. Within this context, curses and hexes became tools for asserting power and seeking retribution, symbolizing a rejection of societal norms and an embrace of individualism.

Anton LaVey, the founder of the Church of Satan and a notable figure in Satanic tradition, published "The Satanic Bible" in 1969. In this controversial text, he advocates for individualism, self-indulgence, and the use of magic and ritual to accomplish one's desires. Although LaVeyan Satanism does not overtly endorse curses and hexes, it acknowledges the potential power of black magic and encourages practitioners to explore their psychic abilities.

As I delved deeper into the subject of curses and hexes within Satanic traditions, I encountered various accounts of alleged psychic attacks. These reports often depict individuals experiencing unexplained phenomena, including sudden illness, financial ruin, and tragic accidents. While skeptics attribute these events to coincidence or the natural fluctuations of life, staunch believers in the potency of curses and hexes see them as tangible evidence of their effectiveness.

The methods employed by practitioners of Satanic traditions to protect themselves from curses and psychic attacks fascinated me the most. These methods range from the use of amulets, talismans, and sigils to the recitation of prayers and incantations. Individuals sought solace in the belief that they could ward off malevolent forces through unwavering faith and adherence to Satanic rituals.

One of the most intriguing aspects of studying curses, hexes, and psychic attacks within Satanic traditions is the role of perception and belief. The human mind possesses significant influence, capable of conjuring and manifesting deep fears and desires. When individuals genuinely believe in the power of curses and hexes, their beliefs shape their reality. This phenomenon becomes a self-fulfilling prophecy, where the power of suggestion and the subconscious mind combine to create a potent blend of perceived threat and actual consequence.

As a paranormal investigator and Specialist of the Strange, I cannot definitively prove or disprove the existence and potency of curses, hexes, and psychic attacks within Satanic traditions. However, it is indisputable that the human experience encompasses a vast array of beliefs, fears, and desires. In the realm of the occult, these elements intertwine to create a tapestry of mystery and fascination.

In conclusion, the belief in curses, hexes, and psychic attacks within Satanic traditions is a complex and deeply ingrained aspect of human fascination with the supernatural. This topic continues to captivate minds and ignite debates, as individuals grapple with the intricate interplay between belief, perception, and reality. Whether curses and hexes possess genuine power or are products of human imagination, their allure remains undeniably potent. Hence, it is within the exploration of these enigmas that we, as seekers of truth, continually journey Into the Eye of Satan.

PROTECTION AND DEFENSE AGAINST DARK FORCES

In order to fully comprehend the essence of protection against dark forces in Satanic practices, it is imperative to delve into the origins and historical timeline of Satanic rituals. It is crucial to acknowledge that not all Satanic practices are inherently evil or harmful. Many individuals who embrace the Satanic path simply seek personal enlightenment and empowerment. However, there are those who exploit these practices for malicious purposes, invoking malevolent entities and energies to exert dominance over others.

Throughout history, Satanic rituals have been documented in various cultures and religions. These rituals often involve the summoning of demons, the casting of dark spells, and the invocation of unholy powers. It is during these rituals that individuals become susceptible to pernicious influences and negative energies.

To defend oneself against these dark forces, it is necessary to first establish a robust spiritual foundation. This can be accomplished through various methods, such as meditation, prayer, or the study of protective rituals from different belief systems. It is essential to bear in mind that protection against dark forces is not confined to a single religious or spiritual practice. Rather, it is a synergistic amalgamation of knowledge, belief, and personal empowerment.

One effective strategy for protection is the creation of a personal sacred space. This space acts as a shield against negative energies and entities that may attempt to infiltrate one's life. Establishing a sacred space can be as simple as designating a specific area in one's home or workplace that evokes feelings of safety and empowerment. This space can be adorned with protective symbols, such as sigils, talismans, or amulets, that resonate with one's personal beliefs.

Another pivotal aspect of protection against dark forces is the establishment of psychic boundaries. Analogous to physical boundaries that safeguard against unwelcome intrusions, psychic boundaries shield individuals from negative energies and entities. These boundaries can be visualized as a protective bubble or shield encircling one's entire being. By affirming the intention to repel negativity and darkness, one fortifies their psychic borders and repulses any malevolent forces that may endeavor to infiltrate their aura.

Aside from psychic boundaries, the utilization of protective sigils and symbols can provide an additional layer of defense. These symbols act as sacred talismans that repel and banish negative energies. Some commonly employed symbols for protection include the pentagram, the Eye of Horus, and the Triskelion. These symbols can be inscribed on personal possessions, worn as jewelry, or employed in ritualistic practices.

However, it is significant to note that protection against dark forces should not depend solely on external methods. Inner strength, self-belief, and personal empowerment are essential components of defense against malevolent entities.

Through introspection, self-healing, and emotional resilience, one can cultivate a robust and impenetrable spiritual armor. This internal fortification not only repels external negativity but also strengthens one's connection to higher realms of divine protection.

To conclude, protection and defense against dark forces in Satanic practices necessitate a comprehensive and holistic approach. By comprehending the historical timeline of Satanic rituals, cultivating a robust spiritual foundation, establishing psychic boundaries, and utilizing protective symbols, individuals can safeguard themselves against malevolent forces and negative energies. It is through this fusion of knowledge, belief, and personal empowerment that one can confidently confront Satanic forces and emerge unharmed.

4

UNMASKING GENUINE EVIL

SERIAL KILLERS AND SATANIC RITUALS

As a paranormal investigator and specialist in the paranormal, my exploration into the complex realm of serial killers and their alleged connections to Satanic rituals was a task that required a strong constitution. It necessitated delving deep into the recesses of the human mind, unearthing the most sinister aspects of human desires and motivations. The research I had conducted thus far had brought to light a troubling correlation, one that had left a profound impact on me. It was a connection between the seemingly inexplicable acts of serial killers and their affiliation with Satanic rituals.

In order to fully comprehend the motivations behind these abhorrent crimes, it was imperative to grasp the historical timeline that intertwined the occult, rituals, and human brutality. From ancient civilizations such as Mesopotamia to the infamous witch trials of Salem, the occult has long held a fascination for humanity. Throughout history, individuals who have delved into these mystic realms have frequently been scapegoated for society's problems, leading to witch hunts and brutal persecutions.

However, it was not until the rise of modern serial killers that a more convoluted and intricate connection emerged. As I delved deeper into the annals of criminal history, I came across countless cases where killers professed to have been influenced by Satanic rituals. These murders were motivated by a belief in the occult, a deep fascination with the devil, and a desire to please their aberrant deities through the shedding of innocent blood.

One particularly captivating case that captured my attention was that of the infamous "Nightwalker." The mere mention of this name struck terror in the hearts of an entire community, as the killer left behind a trail of brutally murdered victims. The idea of a serial killer prowling the night was terrifying enough, but the Nightwalker took his atrocities to another level by incorporating Satanic rituals into his gruesome acts. The local law enforcement was confounded, while the public remained transfixed, as the killer left behind cryptic symbols and infernal markings at each crime scene, hinting at a malevolent force lying beneath the surface.

Driven by an insatiable thirst for answers, I made the decision to visit the small town where the Nightwalker had etched his mark. I immersed myself in the harrowing accounts of the survivors, endeavoring to discern the motivations and influences that lay behind each crime. It became apparent that the employment of Satanic rituals was not merely a means to inflict pain and terror, but also a method through which the killer assert dominance and control.

The allure of Satanic rituals lies not only in their capacity to instill fear, but also in their ability to provide a sense of belonging to those who feel marginalized or lost. These rituals offer a unique combination of rebellion against societal norms, a delusion of power, and a twisted faith in supernatural forces. Serial killers who embraced Satanism often found solace in the grip of this dark ideology, further fueling their sadistic desires.

Gaining a comprehensive understanding of the motivations behind these killers cannot be achieved without acknowledging the deep-seated psychological and emotional factors that drive their actions. The need for control, the desire for infamy, and the perverse gratification derived from inflicting pain all intertwine with the claim of Satanic influence. It is within this intricate web that the seeds of malevolence take root and flourish, leading to unspeakable acts against humanity.

Further examination of the minds of these serial killers revealed a common thread - their reliance on the macabre and their twisted interpretation of the rituals they believed in. They elevated these rituals to frightful heights, distorting their original intent, and embracing the darkest aspects of their ideology. It was as if the allure of Satanism offered an escape from their own tormented existence, enabling them to transcend their limitations and embrace a malevolent source of power.

As my investigations continued, the line between perpetrator and victim began to blur. The allure and influence of these Satanic rituals had a transformative effect, captivating individuals and drawing them into a dark underworld of their own creation. It became evident that the investigation was not solely about apprehending the killers, but also about comprehending the deeper facets of the human psyche and preventing further descent into madness.

The answers I sought were not easily attainable. They necessitated unraveling the intricate layers of human cruelty and exploring the deep-seated fears and desires that prod individuals to embrace such dark ideologies. The investigation was an ongoing exploration of the human soul, a journey into the depths of Satan himself, where the boundary between good and evil is shattered, and the true face of darkness comes to light.

Chapter after chapter, my encounters with these twisted individuals left an indelible impression on my soul. Their motivations, rituals, and connection to the occult were not dismissable as mere delusions or fabrications. They originated from a place of genuine belief and raw emotion, penetrating the very essence of their being. The investigation had evolved into a race against time, not only to bring these killers to justice, but also to prevent the next wave of violence from being unleashed upon an unsuspecting world.

To fully comprehend the linkage between serial killers and Satanic rituals, I needed to fathom the depths of human depravity and the allure of darkness. Only through immersing myself in this daunting abyss could I hope to shed light on their twisted motives and find a way to prevent the echoes of Satan from resonating further in our world.

As I mentally and emotionally prepared myself for the next phase of my investigation, the darkness that permeated these cases became my constant companion. It was through embracing the deepest recesses of the human soul that I hoped to uncover the answers I sought, shedding light on a topic that has haunted humanity for centuries. The journey would be treacherous, but I was resolute in my determination to venture into the very heart of Satan himself, revealing the hidden truth that lay within.

To be continued...

CULTS AND SATANIC MANIPULATION

As a researcher and expert in the field of paranormal investigations and the exploitation of cults, I have extensively studied the sinister methods employed by cults utilizing Satanic elements to manipulate and exploit their followers. Throughout my research, I have identified a disturbing and recurring pattern that transcends both time and geographic location – a complex web of mind control that infiltrates vulnerable individuals as well as those with stronger wills.

In order to comprehend the captivating allure of cults influenced by Satanic practices, it is essential to embark on a historical journey, tracing the origins and evolution of these manipulation techniques. While the evocative imagery and rituals associated with Satanic cults may be perceived as intriguingly sinister, their ability to exert control over individuals lies in the subtle application of psychological warfare.

It is crucial to understand that cults and Satanic manipulation are not distinct entities, but rather intertwined elements that exploit the human psyche to achieve their aberrant goals. These cults entice and captivate their followers with promises of enlightenment, power, and a sense of belonging, gradually tightening their grip through a variety of deceitful tactics.

One of the most effective methods utilized by these cults is the exploitation of vulnerability. They prey upon individuals who find themselves at a crossroads in life, desperately searching for purpose or a sense of identity. Masquerading as charismatic leaders who exude confidence and authority, these cults offer a distorted form of solace and guidance, insidiously ensnaring their victims within their intricate web. They identify the emotional needs and desires of potential followers, deceitfully promising fulfillment and happiness while manipulating them for their own selfish gain.

Infiltration and isolation are also pivotal components in the arsenal of mind control utilized by these cults. With meticulous precision, they identify and target those who may be susceptible to manipulation, gradually severing ties with loved ones and support networks. By cutting off these connections, the cult gains absolute control over the individual, meticulously filling the void left by their severed relationships and establishing themselves as the sole source of guidance and support.

Once isolated, the cult employs a range of psychological manipulation techniques to dismantle the individual's sense of self. Fear and intimidation become potent tools in their repertoire, exploiting deep-rooted human vulnerabilities such as the fear of the unknown and rejection. By manipulating these primal fears, the cult weakens the individual's resistance, molding them into obedient devotees who dare not question the authority of their leaders.

Cults with Satanic elements further solidify their control over followers through the practice of rituals and symbolism. These rituals frequently involve the desecration of conventional religious symbols and the worship of malevolent deities. By engaging in such acts, devotees become further indoctrinated into the belief system of the cult, cementing their loyalty through a form of psychological conditioning.

Furthermore, cult leaders employ various other manipulative tactics to cement their control. They employ tactics such as isolation and sleep deprivation, ensuring that followers remain perpetually vulnerable and dependent. Additionally, techniques such as gaslighting and love-bombing may be used to confuse and destabilize victims, further reinforcing the cult's control over them.

To fully comprehend the mechanisms of cult manipulation, it is imperative to study real-life examples of these techniques in action. One notorious case is that of the Manson Family, led by the infamous Charles Manson. Through a combination of fear, charisma, and drug-induced altered states of consciousness, Manson manipulated his followers. Through psychological manipulation and isolation, Manson achieved complete obedience and loyalty, even coercing his followers into carrying out heinous acts of violence.

In conclusion, the manipulation tactics employed by cults incorporating Satanic elements to control and exploit their followers are both insidious and pervasive. By exploiting vulnerability, employing isolation, and utilizing psychological manipulation, these cults strip individuals of their autonomy and coerce them into lives of servitude. It is of utmost importance that we continue to study and expose these tactics, shedding light on the dark facets of human nature and safeguarding potential victims from their grasp.

As a paranormal investigator and specialist in this field, my mission is to uncover the truth behind these cults, expose their manipulation tactics, and ultimately empower individuals to resist their control. The fight against cults influenced by Satanic practices is an ongoing one, but armed with knowledge and awareness, we can protect ourselves against their treacherous hold and contribute to a safer and more enlightened society.

SATANIC INFLUENCE IN POP CULTURE

In my capacity as a paranormal investigator and specialist in the supernatural, my extensive research and fieldwork have exposed me to unsettling and unexplainable phenomena. Throughout my exploration into the realm of the paranormal, I have frequently encountered the presence of Satanic themes and influences within popular culture. The insidious infiltration of Satanism in various forms of artistic expression, including music, movies, and literature, has long held my interest, compelling me to delve deeper into their origins and implications.

To gain a comprehensive understanding of the extent of Satanic influence in popular culture, it is imperative to adopt a historical perspective. The seeds of Satanic themes were sown centuries ago, during the infamous witch trials of the Middle Ages and early modern period. The pervasive fear and hysteria surrounding witchcraft resulted in the demonization of anything remotely associated with Satanic practices, including occult symbols, rituals, and even innocent individuals. This dark period in human history has had a lasting impact, providing the groundwork for the infusion of Satanic elements in popular culture.

In the realm of music, the late 1960s and 1970s witnessed the emergence of bands and artists who openly embraced Satanic imagery. An example of this is Led Zeppelin's iconic album cover for "Led Zeppelin IV," featuring an enigmatic figure carrying bundles of burning sticks, commonly associated with witches' ceremonies. The inclusion of eerie occult symbols and lyrics in songs such as "Stairway to Heaven" and "Black Dog" fueled speculation of Satanic influences behind the band's music.

A similar phenomenon can be observed within the realm of heavy metal, which experienced a surge in popularity during the 1980s. Bands such as Black Sabbath, Iron Maiden, and Slayer incorporated Satanic imagery, lyrics, and stage shows into their performances. The captivating combination of dark aesthetics, aggressive sound, and provocative subject matter captivated a generation of rebellious youth, resulting in accusations of Satanic worship and incitement.

Movies, too, have succumbed to the allure of Satanic influences. A notable example is the influential horror film "Rosemary's Baby" (1968), directed by Roman Polanski. This film tells the chilling story of a young woman unknowingly carrying the child of Satan. Its atmospheric cinematography, gripping screenplay, and eerie performances earned it critical acclaim and reignited interest in Satanic themes in cinema. This paved the way for subsequent films such as "The Omen" (1976) and "The Exorcist" (1973), which solidified the terrifying presence of the Devil within the collective consciousness of movie enthusiasts.

Satanic influences in literature can be traced back to classic works such as John Milton's "Paradise Lost" (1667). This epic poem, which depicts Lucifer's rebellion against God, significantly departed from prevailing religious sentiments of its time. Milton's sympathetic portrayal of Satan as a tragic figure brought attention to the complexities inherent in moral choices, challenging conventional notions of good and evil. This literary exploration of the Satanic allowed subsequent writers to venture into the depths of the human psyche, giving rise to a genre often known as "Satanic literature."

One of the most contentious figures associated with Satanic literature is Anton LaVey, the founder of the Church of Satan. His book, "The Satanic Bible," which was published in 1969, outlined the principles and philosophies of his Satanic religion, which rejected conventional morality and embraced individualism and self-gratification. While LaVey's teachings received intense criticism from mainstream society, they also contributed to the popularization of Satanic themes in literature, captivating an inquisitive audience seeking to comprehend and explore the forbidden.

Throughout this exploration into the depths of Satanic influence in popular culture, it is impossible to ignore the allure and fascination these themes hold for individuals. Whether through the seductive melodies of a song, the spine-tingling suspense of a film, or the thought-provoking prose of a book, Satanic influences have permeated our collective consciousness. They challenge our preconceived notions of morality, tap into our deepest fears, and push the boundaries of our beliefs.

In my capacity as a paranormal investigator and specialist in the supernatural, my purpose is not to condemn or promote Satanic themes in popular culture, but rather to shed light on their existence and provoke critical thought. By daring to examine the essence of Satan, we open ourselves to a world of darkness, mystery, and hidden truths. Only through comprehension can we navigate the precarious path between fascination and exploitation, ensuring that the impact of Satanic influences in popular culture does not consume us, but instead serves as a catalyst for self-exploration and personal development.

SATANIC RITUAL ABUSE SURVIVORS

As a professional paranormal investigator and specialist in the study of extraordinary phenomena, I have dedicated myself to exploring the experiences of survivors of satanic ritual abuse. These encounters, though disturbing and haunting, demand the utmost attention and empathy. Each survivor I encounter grants me the privilege of sharing their stories and shedding light on the profound psychological impact of these traumatic events.

To fully comprehend the experiences of these survivors, I have embarked on an extensive research journey, delving into historical records, accounts from experts in the field, and conducting personal interviews. The deeper I delve into this dark realm, the more I realize the complexities and challenges that arise when addressing this subject. It is of utmost importance to approach it with sensitivity and an open mind, recognizing the enduring effects it has on the lives of those who have endured such horrors.

As I delve into the psyche of satanic ritual abuse survivors, it becomes unmistakably clear that they bear an immense burden of trauma. Many develop symptoms consistent with post-traumatic stress disorder (PTSD), such as recurring nightmares, flashbacks, and intense anxiety. Due to shattered trust, the forming of healthy relationships becomes arduous, and the survivors' self-esteem is severely diminished, often leading to deep-seated feelings of guilt and shame.

Through the exploration of their stories, I am constantly reminded of the remarkable resilience and indomitable spirit of human beings. In spite of having confronted unimaginable horrors, these survivors continue to live and share their experiences, driven by the hope of raising awareness and providing support to others who may be suffering in silence.

One individual I had the honor of interviewing was Lisa, a survivor who managed to escape the clutches of a satanic cult at a young age. Her account was filled with fear, confusion, and unimaginable pain. She recounted rituals conducted in hidden chambers, where innocent lives were sacrificed and individuals were subjected to unspeakable acts of torture. Lisa survived, but her childhood innocence was irrevocably marred, eroding her trust and setting her on a challenging path toward healing.

In my conversation with Lisa, the profound psychological impact of satanic ritual abuse became painfully evident. She spoke of the burden of guilt she carried, questioning why she had survived while others perished. Her sense of self-worth had been grievously eroded, leaving her feeling undeserving of love and happiness. Her story served as a testament to the deep wounds inflicted by those who perpetrated these heinous acts.

Examining Lisa's story, I delved into the psychological theories that elucidate the lasting impact of satanic ritual abuse. The trauma endured during these rituals not only affects the survivor's sense of self but also hinders their ability to trust and form enduring relationships. In many instances, the perpetuators of these rituals were trusted family members or figures of authority, further complicating the healing process.

The road to recovery for survivors of satanic ritual abuse is long and winding, often necessitating therapy and the support of compassionate professionals. Therapies such as EMDR therapy, cognitive-behavioral therapy, and art therapy have shown promise in aiding survivors in processing and healing from their traumatic experiences. These therapeutic approaches aim to help survivors regain control over their lives, reframe their experiences, and develop effective coping mechanisms.

As I delve deeper into the stories of these survivors, my objective is to raise awareness and dispel skepticism surrounding this topic. It is imperative to recognize that speaking out requires immense courage and strength. These survivors are not seeking attention or making baseless claims; they are individuals who have endured unimaginable horrors and deserve to be heard, believed, and supported.

As I continue my work, I am continuously reminded that these survivors are not defined by their experiences, but rather display remarkable resilience and strength. By sharing their stories, we can shed light on the profound impact of satanic ritual abuse and work toward a society that acknowledges, supports, and safeguards those who have survived unimaginable horrors.

The journey into the dark realms of satanic practices may have exposed me to the depths of human suffering, but it has also enlightened me to the potential for healing and resilience. The survivors I have encountered have imparted upon me the significance of compassion, empathy, and an unwavering belief in the power of the human spirit to triumph over even the most harrowing nightmares. Through the sharing of their stories, we can hope to dissipate the shadow that looms over this subject and provide a voice for those who have long been silenced.

SATANIC CULTS AND HUMAN TRAFFICKING

Growing up amidst a sense of mystery and intrigue, I was naturally drawn to the more enigmatic aspects of life. As a professional in the field of paranormal investigation and expertise in abnormal phenomena, it is my duty to immerse myself in uncharted depths and illuminate the sinister underbelly of society. One topic that has consistently captured my attention is the correlation between Satanic cults and the heinous crime of human trafficking. While this subject provokes a chilling sensation, it is one that demands my attention in order to expose the concealed truth lurking in the shadows.

To truly comprehend the connection between Satanic cults and human trafficking, extensive research into numerous cases and testimonies was essential. This exploration compelled me to confront the horrifying reality faced by victims, as well as the malevolent individuals orchestrating these abhorrent acts. With each case, it became increasingly evident that these two realms of darkness were fundamentally intertwined.

One particularly disturbing case that exemplified this affiliation unfolded in the small town of Willow Creek. The disappearances of multiple young girls had captured the attention of local authorities, yet despite their diligent efforts, no leads had materialized. It was at this juncture that I received an anonymous call from a reliable tipster, asserting that these girls had fallen victim to a Satanic cult operating within the town.

Motivated by both inquisitiveness and an unwavering commitment to justice, I immersed myself in Willow Creek, assuming the guise of a journalist. My initial destination was a dilapidated motel situated on the outskirts of the town, rumored to serve as a meeting place for the cult. As I entered the dimly lit room, a heavy atmosphere permeated the air, redolent with decay and malice. Graffiti covered the walls, portraying disturbing scenes of sacrifice and ritualistic worship.

With every twist and turn, I unearthed further evidence connecting the cult to the trafficking of humans. The walls were adorned with gang symbols and cryptic messages, serving as an eerie reminder of the malevolent trade thriving within these somber corridors. Testimonies from local residents painted a haunting picture of young girls manipulated and ensnared, taken from the streets like innocent lambs led to slaughter, their innocence forever extinguished.

The cult seemed to target the weak and defenseless, those lacking a support system or protectors. These unfortunate souls faced an existence inextricably linked to the sinister agenda of the Satanic cult. Stripped of their humanity, they became commodities, bought and sold at the whims of their captors.

As my investigation delved deeper, I uncovered a global network of interconnected cults. Their insidious practices fueled by an insatiable thirst for power and control over human lives. The more I unveiled, the more apparent it became that this was not an isolated incident but rather an pervasive and deeply ingrained issue within our society.

Survivors' testimonies provided chilling insights into the rituals and practices of these Satanic cults. They detailed horrifying accounts of human sacrifice, sexual exploitation, and psychological abuse. The survivors described an overwhelming darkness, almost tangible, as if they had descended into the very depths of hell.

Exposing these Satanic cults proved to be an immense undertaking, yet it was a responsibility I could not ignore. The victims deserved justice, their stories needed to be heard, and the world had to acknowledge the nexus between Satanic cults and human trafficking. Fueled by unwavering determination and courage, I dedicated myself to unraveling the enigma and illuminating the truth.

While piecing together the puzzle, I encountered countless obstacles, threats, and moments of despair. However, I remained steadfast throughout. Bearing the weight of the victims' hope on my shoulders, I forged ahead, determined to expose the sinister machinations fueling these dark forces.

Amidst the darkness, there resides a flicker of hope. Through my tireless investigations and unrelenting pursuit of justice, I aim to disclose the truth, bring the culprits to account, and ultimately save those who have fallen victim to the unholy alliance between Satanic cults and human trafficking.

However daunting this endeavor may be, I am invigorated by the unyielding belief that by shedding light on these obscure corners of society, we take a crucial step towards raising awareness, empowering survivors, and dismantling the foundations upon which these diabolical networks have been built.

The journey ahead may be treacherous, but I am a stalwart champion of righteousness, armed with knowledge, empathy, and an unwavering spirit. Unafraid and resolute, I will venture into the heart of this malevolence, determined to expose the unholy alliance between Satanic cults and human trafficking, regardless of the cost.

OCCULT CRIMES AND RITUALISTIC VIOLENCE

As an expert in the field of paranormal investigation, I have encountered numerous peculiar and inexplicable phenomena throughout my career. However, none have captured my interest quite like the occurrence of occult crimes and ritualistic violence associated with Satanic practices. The mysterious attraction of the occult has long captivated individuals, drawing them into a realm filled with forbidden knowledge and forbidden rituals. But what drives individuals to commit heinous acts in the name of Satan?

To gain an understanding of occult crimes and ritualistic violence, I embarked on a thorough research endeavor, immersing myself in historical records and contemporary cases. My exploration commenced with a historical timeline, tracing the origins of Satanic practices and the crimes committed under its auspices.

The roots of Satanic rituals can be traced back to ancient civilizations, where belief systems and rituals often centered around pagan deities. It was during the medieval era that the Christian Church condemned these practices as heresy, leading to the notorious witch hunts and the Inquisition. Driven by fear and ignorance, these witch hunts resulted in the persecution and execution of numerous innocent individuals.

In more recent history, the late 20th century witnessed a resurgence of interest in the occult, fueled by popular culture and the works of renowned writers such as Aleister Crowley and Anton LaVey. This revival, though accompanied by sensationalism, thrust Satanic practices into the spotlight and contributed to an increase in occult-related crimes.

Examining specific instances of occult crimes brings a chilling reality to the forefront. An exemplary case involved the mutilation and murder of animals in a small town in Minnesota. Initially disregarded by local authorities as acts of random vandalism, closer examination revealed the presence of ritualistic symbols at the crime scenes. This disconcerting case emphasized the link between Satanic practices and animal sacrifice, with these innocent creatures becoming victims of a diabolical ritual.

Another case that shook the nation involved the ritualistic homicide of a young woman in a suburban neighborhood. The crime scene was adorned with occult symbols, and the victim had been brutally stabbed, her body arranged in a manner suggestive of sacrificial rituals. The investigation unveiled an unsettling underbelly of cults and secret societies, whose members were driven by their unwavering devotion to Satanic ideologies.

These chilling cases raise the following question: what motivates individuals to perpetrate acts of violence in the name of Satan? While it may be tempting to dismiss these perpetrators as merely mentally unstable or wicked, the truth is far more intricate. The allure of the occult can captivate vulnerable minds, offering a sense of power, belonging, and purpose that is often absent from their everyday lives.

For those who feel marginalized or ostracized by mainstream society, the allure of Satanic practices can provide them with a sense of community and acceptance. In some cases, these individuals may have also been victims themselves, seeking solace and control by engaging in these rituals, even if it entails inflicting harm on others.

Furthermore, the symbolism and rituals associated with Satanism possess a seductive quality that taps into the deepest realms of human psychology. The indulgent nature of these rituals, combined with the promise of accessing hidden knowledge and supernatural abilities, can prove irresistible to those yearning for something more in their lives.

As I delved deeper into my research, I discovered that the prevalence of occult crimes and ritualistic violence has fluctuated over time, often coinciding with periods of societal unrest and moral panic. The portrayal of Satanism as a perceived threat to societal order by the media has perpetuated these fears, amplifying the public's perception of occult-related crimes.

In conclusion, examining the occurrence of occult crimes and ritualistic violence associated with Satanic practices is an arduous task that necessitates not only an understanding of historical context but also a profound exploration of the psychology behind the individuals involved. Although it may be easy to dismiss such acts as the work of deranged individuals, it is crucial to acknowledge the intricate interplay of societal factors and personal motivations that propel individuals down this sinister path.

Through my research, I endeavor to shed light on the underlying truths regarding occult crimes and ritualistic violence, bridging the gap between speculation and empirical evidence. Only by comprehending the allure of the occult and the motivations that drive those involved can we aspire to prevent and intervene in such cases, ultimately instilling a glimmer of hope for individuals who find themselves ensnared in the clutches of Satan.

DARK WEB AND SATANIC NETWORKS

The dark web, a realm exclusively accessible through specialized software and anonymous networks, serves as a breeding ground for a plethora of illicit activities. Among them are drug trafficking, weapons dealing, and human trafficking, all of which are abhorrent acts. However, the dark web holds an even more sinister side, as it delves into the occult and malevolent practices of satanic networks.

Unveiling the existence of satanic networks and their activities on the dark web was a formidable endeavor. Accomplishing this required an extensive commitment of time to sift through encrypted messages, decipher coded language, and infiltrate online communities that thrive on secrecy and fear. Yet, with each discovery made, a chilling reality unfolded, revealing the nefarious nature that adorns the digital landscape.

The implications of these satanic networks are wide-ranging and profoundly troubling. It transcends mere sacrificial rituals and perverse worship. These networks delve into the deepest abysses of human depravity, engaging in criminal activities that defy the boundaries of morality. Exploitation of children, human sacrifice, and mind control experiments have been unearthed, exposing an unimaginable level of malevolence.

The dark web provides an impenetrable cloak of anonymity for these wicked groups, allowing them to operate with impunity and without fear of exposure. Their twisted ideologies and immoral actions remain concealed from the scrutiny of law enforcement, leaving victims ensnared in a labyrinthine web of darkness from which escape appears nearly impossible.

Regrettably, the repercussions of their actions extend beyond the immediate victims. The ripple effects permeate broader society, causing families to fracture, communities to crumble, and an overall loss of innocence. The malevolent deeds of these satanic networks leave behind a wake of destruction that reaches far and wide.

To fully comprehend the magnitude of these repercussions, further investigation was undertaken. The dark web serves not only as a meeting place for these networks but also as a marketplace for their sinister wares. Forbidden artifacts, occult literature, and even live animals intended for sacrificial rituals are openly traded. This thriving industry is fueled by the darkest desires and perversions of humanity's soul.

As more information was uncovered, a disconcerting pattern emerged. The dark web acts as a gateway, connecting individuals worldwide who share a morbid fascination with the occult and the demonic. Distinctions between the virtual and the physical realms blur as those seeking ties to these satanic networks are drawn deeper into the abyss.

The potential implications of these satanic networks on a global scale cannot be underestimated. Their influence expands beyond their digital hideouts, permeating all aspects of society. From the highest echelons of power to the most vulnerable corners of our world, their reach is vast and insidious.

Nevertheless, hope prevails amidst this darkness. As a paranormal investigator, it is my duty to expose these hidden realities and shed light on the truth. By unraveling the mysteries of the dark web and the satanic networks, we can disrupt their operations and safeguard those most vulnerable to their malevolence.

The battle against evil is by no means facile, yet it is an imperative one. By bringing to light the existence of satanic networks and their potential implications, we can galvanize individuals and organizations in the face of this pervasive threat. Together, we possess the power to dismantle these networks and reclaim the sanctity of our world from the grasp of darkness.

Venturing into the realm of Satan is not a journey for the faint of heart, but it is one that must be undertaken. The struggle against these satanic networks may appear daunting, but it is a battle that we are obliged to wage with utmost resolve. In the face of malevolence, it is our duty to stand resolute and refuse to allow darkness to reign.

SPIRITUAL WARFARE AGAINST GENUINE EVIL

As a paranormal investigator and specialist in the occult, I have encountered countless cases that have taken me deep into the depths of the unknown. While my work often deals with phenomena that cannot be easily explained, one aspect that has consistently fascinated me is the unsettling reality of Satanic worship and the genuine malevolence that lies at its core. In this chapter, I delve into the realm of spiritual warfare, providing insights into the practices and rituals used to combat this dark force.

To truly comprehend the nature of spiritual warfare, it is essential to investigate the historical context and origins of Satanic worship. It is widely believed that this sinister practice can be traced back to ancient civilizations, wherein human sacrifice and diabolical rituals were performed to appease malevolent entities. Over the course of centuries, these practices have evolved and spread like a pernicious cancer through various societies. Today, Satanic worship has become a clandestine underworld hidden beneath the seemingly civilized surface of our world.

To counter such authentic malevolence, one must rise to the challenge armed with knowledge and unwavering determination. The initial step in combating demonic forces is to gain a deep understanding of the adversary. This necessitates scrupulous research and study of ancient occult texts, obscure manuscripts, and firsthand accounts of encounters with the dark side. Throughout my years of experience, I have compiled an extensive library of such resources that has become an indispensable part of my journey.

One of the most significant aspects of spiritual warfare is the recognition that it is not solely a physical battle but rather a battle of the soul. Genuine evil seeks to infiltrate our thoughts, undermine our spirits, and corrupt our very essence. To confront this, practitioners of spiritual warfare must fortify their minds and souls through various means. Meditation, prayer, and establishing connections with higher realms are all fundamental in establishing a robust spiritual foundation.

Rituals play a pivotal role in spiritual warfare as they serve as conduits through which sacred energy and divine protection can be channeled. These rituals can take diverse forms, contingent upon the belief system of the practitioner. Some may choose to conduct ceremonial cleansings utilizing blessed herbs and oils, while others may engage in elaborate rituals involving incantations and sigil work. Each ritual is tailored to the specific needs and beliefs of the individual.

An influential tool in the fight against genuine evil in spiritual warfare is the utilization of holy artifacts. These artifacts, often infused with divine energy, act as a protective barrier between the practitioner and the malevolent forces they encounter. Crosses, crucifixes, talismans, and religious relics serve as examples of such powerful artifacts that can offer protection. However, it is crucial to note that the power of these items lies not in their physical form, but rather in the faith and intention of the wielder.

The battle against genuine evil demands great strength of mind, body, and spirit. It necessitates unwavering determination and unshakeable faith. It is not a path for the faint-hearted or those prone to doubt. Spiritual warriors must possess a deep connection to their beliefs and be guided by an unwavering moral compass even in the face of darkness. This battle necessitates sacrifice as practitioners may encounter unimaginable horrors, endure physical and emotional torment, and risk everything they hold dear.

Despite the significant risks involved, the rewards of spiritual warfare against genuine evil are profound. It is in the moments of deepest darkness that the light shines the brightest. The triumph over malevolence, the liberation of tormented souls, and the restoration of balance in the universe are all attainable for those who dare to embark on this path. The satisfaction that accompanies the knowledge that one has made a tangible difference in the battle against darkness is immeasurable.

In conclusion, spiritual warfare against genuine evil associated with Satanic worship is a complex and perilous journey. It demands extensive research, unwavering dedication, and steadfast faith. By understanding the origins of Satanic worship, strengthening the mind and soul, engaging in rituals, and utilizing holy artifacts, practitioners can effectively combat this darkness. Although the battle may seem daunting, the potential for victory and the profound impact it can have make it a path worth embracing for those who dare to confront the depths of darkness. This represents spiritual warfare in its truest form, a battle fought not with physical weapons but with the indomitable strength of the human spirit.

5

THE FUTURE OF SATANIC WORSHIP

SATANIC MOVEMENTS IN THE DIGITAL AGE

To comprehend the influence of the digital age on Satanic ideologies, it is imperative to step back and analyze the origins of Satanic movements. While Satanic concepts have existed throughout history in various forms, it was not until the 20th century that contemporary Satanic movements started to emerge.

In the late 1960s, Anton LaVey established the Church of Satan in San Francisco. LaVey's teachings emphasized personal liberation, the rejection of religious dogma, and the pursuit of individual desires. This marked a new era for Satanic movements, challenging conventional religious institutions and their authority over individuals.

During the 1970s and 1980s, Satanic Panic took hold of the United States and other regions. The media sensationalized accounts of Satanic cults engaging in ritualistic abuse and human sacrifice, further fueling the fear and fascination associated with these alleged practices. Interestingly, it was during this period that Satanic movements encountered significant opposition and were forced to operate clandestinely.

The advent of the internet in the 1990s served as a turning point for the dissemination of Satanic ideologies. Suddenly, individuals sharing common interests and beliefs could connect across great distances, forming online communities and exchanging information on an unprecedented scale. It was within this digital landscape that the foundations of modern online Satanic movements were laid.

In the early 2000s, online Satanic communities gained traction, with forums and social media platforms acting as virtual meeting places for individuals exploring Satanic ideologies. The internet provided a platform for the exchange of ideas, dissemination of information, and formation of connections. Consequently, Satanic movements experienced a resurgence, establishing a more prominent presence in the digital realm.

The digital age facilitated the rise of self-proclaimed Satanists who could openly express their beliefs and connect with like-minded individuals without fear of societal judgment or persecution. This newfound sense of freedom empowered these individuals to explore their own spiritual paths, share personal experiences, and define their own Satanic practices. Furthermore, the internet allowed those seeking information about Satanism to easily access resources and research materials that were previously difficult to obtain.

Online Satanic communities are diverse, encompassing various beliefs and practices. Some adhere to the principles laid out by Anton LaVey, while others explore alternative Satanic traditions. The digital age has opened up opportunities for individuals to explore and experiment with different manifestations of Satanism that align with their personal philosophies.

Nonetheless, the rise of online Satanic communities comes with its challenges. Like any online space, there is a risk of misinformation and individuals exploiting vulnerable members for personal gain. It is imperative for individuals exploring Satanic ideologies to approach these communities cautiously, critically assessing encountered information and exercising discernment in their interactions.

In conclusion, the digital age has undeniably had a profound impact on the dissemination of Satanic ideologies and the rise of online Satanic communities. The internet has provided a platform for self-expression, connectivity, and information exchange, enabling individuals to openly explore Satanic philosophies and connect with like-minded individuals. However, it is crucial to approach these communities with discernment and critical thinking, as is the case with any online space. The digital age has revolutionized the dissemination and practice of Satanic ideologies, reshaping Satanic movements in previously unimaginable ways.

SATANIC RITUALS AND VIRTUAL REALITY

To gain insight into the potential incorporation of virtual reality in Satanic rituals, it is necessary to examine the fundamental nature of these rituals themselves. The purpose and significance of Satanic rituals have long been veiled in secrecy, varying considerably in the eyes of those who partake in them. While certain individuals argue that these rituals simply serve as theatrical displays intended to provoke and shock, others perceive them as profound spiritual encounters that tap into the core of the infernal. Regardless of personal beliefs, the ritualistic element remains a central component of Satanic practices.

Conversely, virtual reality is a technology with the capacity to transport individuals into immersive and lifelike alternate worlds. By manipulating our senses, virtual reality creates a highly convincing illusion that momentarily causes us to disregard our physical surroundings and become fully engrossed in the digital realm. It is this ability to manipulate our perception of reality that renders virtual reality as a potentially potent tool for Satanic rituals.

Imagine, for a moment, stepping into a virtual realm that has been meticulously constructed to replicate the depths of hell or a place of demonic worship. As a participant, you would find yourself surrounded by towering infernal structures, eerie sounds, and a tangible aura of malevolence. In this digital plane, one could partake in rituals alongside digital depictions of demons, adhering to ancient incantations and practiced gestures. The delineation between the physical and the virtual would converge, providing an unparalleled level of immersion and potential for spiritual experiences.

Nonetheless, there exists a host of ethical and moral considerations that must be acknowledged when blending virtual reality with Satanic rituals. Could the utilization of this technology possibly desensitize individuals to the gravity and ramifications associated with engaging in rituals that encompass summoning dark forces? Furthermore, what impact might this have on the human psyche? It is imperative to approach this convergence with prudence, as innumerable variables could come into play that might yield far-reaching implications.

From a more pragmatic standpoint, the integration of virtual reality into Satanic rituals could also yield unforeseen repercussions and complexities. How would the digital realm respond to these rituals? Could the utilization of virtual reality inadvertently create a portal or gateway through which malevolent entities could breach our reality? Given the unknown nature of both virtual reality and the supernatural, the consequences of such integration remain uncertain.

Yet, it would be remiss to disregard the potential advantages that virtual reality could bring to Satanic rituals. It could furnish a safer platform for individuals to explore their spiritual curiosities and beliefs, without risking physical harm or jeopardizing their safety. Virtual reality could enable practitioners to engage with demonic entities and supernatural forces within a controlled environment, where boundaries for exploration and experimentation could be meticulously defined.

Additionally, the incorporation of virtual reality would expand the scope for artistic expression within Satanic rituals. By amalgamating the aesthetics and symbolism of the occult with the boundless creations of the digital realm, it could engender immersive and visually captivating experiences that transcend the confines of the physical world. It would serve as a tool for practitioners to traverse into new paths of spiritual comprehension and artistic interpretation.

In conclusion, the integration of virtual reality technology into Satanic rituals undoubtedly unveils a realm of possibilities, encompassing both exhilarating and disconcerting facets. As a paranormal investigator and specialist in the unusual, I approach this subject matter with a combination of curiosity and caution. The potential integration of virtual reality in Satanic rituals implores us to question the essence of reality and spirituality, pushing the boundaries of what was previously deemed feasible. It serves as a manifestation of the ever-evolving human yearning to probe the realm of the unknown, even if it necessitates venturing into the virtual abyss to do so.

SATANIC ART AND AESTHETICS

I am seated in a dimly illuminated room, surrounded by an assortment of literary works and artifacts. My fingers delicately trace the well-worn pages of ancient texts, which serve as my guiding path into the enigmatic world of Satanic art and aesthetics. In my capacity as a paranormal investigator and Specialist of the Strange, I have developed an understanding of the power and influence that art carries within the realm of Satanic worship. It is this captivating allure that entices me to plumb the depths, unveiling the hidden meanings underlying these captivating forms.

To truly comprehend the significance of Satanic art and aesthetics in contemporary society, it is crucial to embark on a historical journey, tracing the course of events that have influenced the evolution of this dark art form. This chapter aims to illuminate the nuances and haunting beauty of Satanic art, from its earliest beginnings to its present-day manifestations.

During the early 17th century, amidst the height of the Satanic Panic, artists ventured into uncharted territory, exploring Satanic iconography. Through intricate and detailed paintings, these artists sought to capture the essence of evil and darkness by depicting scenes of ritualistic ceremonies and the conjuring of demonic entities. Such works were frequently commissioned by influential members of society and served to visually manifest their beliefs and aspirations, making evident their power over the spiritual realm.

However, it was not until the 19th century that Satanic art began to flourish. Aligned with the advent of Romanticism, which celebrated individualism and emotion, artists found an opportunity to express their personal ties to the Satanic domain. This era witnessed the emergence of various art movements, including Symbolism and Decadence, which embraced the dark and taboo facets of existence. Renowned painters such as Francisco Goya and Théodore Géricault crafted eerie and melancholic works that conveyed the dichotomy of human existence and the allure of the forbidden.

With the dawn of the 20th century, Satanic art took on a novel form, mirroring the societal shift in fascination toward the occult and esoteric. Artists such as Salvador Dalí and H.R. Giger entered the scene, introducing a surreal and macabre aesthetic that blurred the boundaries between reality and the realm of nightmares. Their art, characterized by distorted and grotesque figures, tapped into the subconscious fears and desires dormant within the human psyche.

Advancing to the present day, we find ourselves in an era where Satanic art has transcended traditional mediums and embraced the digital age. Prompted by the proliferation of the internet and social media platforms, artists now possess the ability to instantaneously reach a global audience, disseminating their dark visions far and wide. Satanic imagery has infiltrated domains such as fashion, music, and even interior design, as contemporary artists seek to incorporate the rebellious and subversive elements associated with Satanic aesthetics into their work.

However, what drives this fixation with Satanic art and aesthetics in contemporary society? Is it merely an act of rebellion against societal norms and expectations, or does a deeper psychological magnetism draw us toward the darkness? As I endeavor to investigate and explore this subject matter, I am reminded of the profound words of philosopher Friedrich Nietzsche: "When you gaze into the abyss, the abyss also gazes into you." Perhaps it is this enthralling confrontation with the void that compels us to seek solace in Satanic art, boldly confronting our deepest fears and desires.

Through countless centuries, Satanic art and aesthetics have served as a canvas for human exploration—a conduit through which individuals can express their most profound aspirations and apprehensions. It stands as a reflection of our collective psyche, a mirror that unveils both the beauty and the terror existing within each of us. As a paranormal investigator and Specialist of the Strange, I find myself inevitably drawn to this mysterious realm, ceaselessly endeavoring to decipher the concealed meanings and symbols concealed within Satanic art. As I uncover further truths, I am consistently reminded to tread with caution, for within the eye of Satan, one can easily become lost in the abyss that lurks within.

SATANIC PHILOSOPHY AND SOCIAL ACTIVISM

As a dedicated investigator and specialist in the paranormal, my life's work revolves around uncovering the mysteries of the world. With an unyielding curiosity, I have traversed numerous paths of intrigue, each more captivating than the last. However, none have engaged me as profoundly as the interconnection of Satanic philosophy and social activism. This particular subject has commanded my attention for years, and as I delve deeper into its depths, I continue to unveil a complex tapestry of ideas that challenge societal norms and question the very fabric of our existence.

To truly comprehend the link between Satanic philosophy and social activism, it is essential to grasp the essence of Satanic beliefs. Contrary to popular misconceptions perpetuated by mainstream culture, Satanism is not merely a worship of the Devil; rather, it is a celebration of individualism, personal freedom, and the rejection of traditional authority. Through this framework, we begin to discern the alignment between Satanic tenets and key principles of social activism.

At the core of Satanic philosophy lies the notion of individualism. Satanists hold the belief in the inherent worth and potential of every individual, emphasizing the importance of personal autonomy and self-determination. This principle serves as the driving force behind numerous social activists who strive to empower marginalized communities and advocate for equality. By recognizing the sovereignty and uniqueness of each individual, Satanic philosophy fosters an environment that celebrates diversity and encourages the pursuit of personal freedom.

Conversely, social activism seeks to challenge the prevailing status quo and initiate positive change within society. It is a powerful tool for addressing the social injustices and inequalities that have long plagued our world. When we thoroughly explore the interplay between Satanic philosophy and social activism, we uncover a shared emphasis on deconstructing oppressive systems and questioning societal norms. Both movements acknowledge the necessity of challenging established orders and advocating for a more enlightened and compassionate world.

While Satanic philosophy provides a framework for individual liberation, social activism channels that freedom towards collective action. Through the combination of individualism and activism, genuine social progress can be achieved. By inspiring individuals to defy societal constraints, Satanic philosophy grants agency and fuels a spirit of defiance. Social activism then becomes the means through which this individual rebellion is harnessed to effect significant change, advancing the cause for personal freedom and societal transformation.

However, this intersection is not without its complexities. Critics of Satanism argue that its emphasis on individualism can breed selfishness and promote indifference towards others. Yet, this misconception fails to recognize the central tenet of Satanic philosophy: the rejection of harm towards others. Satanists wholeheartedly embrace the concept of personal freedom, but within the boundaries of consent and respect for individual rights. In fact, numerous Satanic organizations have explicitly adopted social activism as a means to promote compassion and justice, directing their efforts towards causes such as LGBTQ+ rights, reproductive freedom, and combatting systemic prejudice.

Throughout my research into this captivating connection, I have encountered a diverse range of individuals who are both devout Satanists and fervent social activists. Their narratives paint a vivid portrait of a community that takes pride in championing justice while celebrating their own uniqueness. From organizing protests to conducting educational campaigns, these individuals are pioneers at the forefront of a movement that redefines the modern perception of Satanism.

By unearthing the relationship between Satanic philosophy and social activism, I have uncovered a profound truth: the pursuit of personal freedom and the fight for societal change are not mutually exclusive. Instead, they can coexist in a harmonious paradox, each reinforcing the other. Satanic philosophy empowers individuals to assert their autonomy, laying the groundwork for collective mobilization and systemic transformation.

Amidst my exploration of this fascinating realm, I am reminded of the words of Anton LaVey, the founder of the Church of Satan. He once stated, "Satan represents the eternal rebel, the first freethinker, and the emancipator of worlds." Through this examination of the intersection between Satanic philosophy and social activism, I have come to realize the immense power that lies within this rebellion against convention and celebration of personal freedom. It is within this convergence that we can boldly envision a more enlightened and equitable world.

SATANIC WORSHIP AND ECOLOGICAL CONSCIOUSNESS

As an individual specializing in paranormal investigation and the study of unusual phenomena, I have devoted my life to exploring the unknown and uncovering the enigmatic truths that lie beneath the surface of our reality. Throughout my journey, I have encountered a range of occult practices, each with its own distinct characteristics and philosophies. One such practice that has commanded my attention is the worship of Satan and its intriguing correlation with ecological consciousness.

To truly grasp the relationship between Satanic worship and ecological consciousness, it is essential to comprehend the historical chronology that has shaped these interrelated concepts. It is widely acknowledged that modern Satanism emerged in the late 19th century, carving its own niche within the realm of the occult. However, it was not until the 1960s and 1970s that a significant transformation occurred within the Satanic belief system, leading to the incorporation of eco-logical consciousness as a prominent facet.

During this era, there was a growing global awareness of environmental issues. Society began to contemplate the reper-cussions of our actions and the detrimental effects they had on the planet. It was during this tumultuous period that spe-cific Satanic groups embraced the notion that the preservation of nature and the environment was an integral aspect of their belief system.

One of the earliest Satanic organizations to adopt this ecological consciousness was the Temple of Set, which was founded by Dr. Michael Aquino in 1975. The Temple of Set distinguished itself from the Church of Satan, established by Anton LaVey, by placing significant emphasis on spiritual growth and self-awareness. Aquino firmly believed that by con-necting with nature and the natural elements of the world, one could attain a higher level of enlightenment. This perspective established the groundwork for the integration of ecological consciousness within Satanic belief systems.

The connection between Satanic worship and ecological consciousness goes beyond mere recognition of the need for environmental preservation. It is rooted in the fundamental Satanic belief that individuals possess the power to shape their own destinies and cultivate personal empowerment. This ideology aligns with the ecological concept of interconnectedness, where every action carries consequences that resonate throughout the natural world.

At the core of this connection lies the belief that nature is not only deserving of reverence and respect, but that it is also a source of spiritual nourishment. Satanic rituals often involve communing with nature, drawing inspiration, and perceiving the cyclical nature of existence. By immersing themselves in the environment, adherents of Satanic worship establish a deeper connection with the natural world, thereby affirming their commitment to environmental preservation.

The implications of this connection extend beyond individual spiritual practices. Satanic groups advocating for ecological consciousness have been actively involved in environmental activism, striving to effect tangible change in the world. These organizations have spearheaded movements against deforestation, pollution, and unsustainable practices, underscoring the significance of safeguarding the Earth for future generations.

It is important to note that within the vast landscape of Satanic worship, this connection to ecological consciousness is not universally embraced. Various branches and interpretations of Satanic belief may not place the same level of emphasis on environmental preservation. However, for those who do, the integration of ecological consciousness serves as a catalyst for profound spiritual experiences and a greater purpose beyond the personal realm.

In essence, the connection between Satanic worship and ecological consciousness is a testament to the intricate interplay between humanity and the natural world. It signifies a shift in consciousness, a recognition that our actions carry consequences that extend far beyond ourselves. By embracing this connection, adherents of Satanic worship actively participate in the preservation and protection of the environment, ultimately playing a vital role in shaping a more sustainable future.

As I continue my exploration into the depths of the unknown, uncovering the mysteries that lie hidden, I am reminded of the significance of nature and environmental preservation. The connection between Satanic worship and ecological consciousness reveals a profound truth – that the preservation of the Earth and the quest for spiritual enlightenment are not mutually exclusive, but rather intrinsically intertwined. It is through this connection that we can pave a path towards a future where nature and spirituality harmonize, and where our actions sow the seeds of a prosperous and sustainable world.

SATANIC RITUALS AND TRANSHUMANISM

In order to commence this explorative journey, it is of utmost importance to provide a historical context that sheds light on both the practices of satanic rituals and the development of transhumanism. Over the course of centuries, satanic rituals have elicited a fascination among individuals seeking forbidden knowledge and dark power. These rituals encompass a multitude of practices, ranging from summoning demonic forces to conducting blood sacrifices and invoking maleficent entities. They take on various forms, adapted by different cults and covens across history, each leaving their distinct mark on this unholy art.

Conversely, transhumanism, a comparatively modern ideology, strives to transcend the limitations of human potential through the employment of technological advancements. It seeks to enhance our physical and mental capabilities, blurring the boundaries between humanity and machinery. Transhumanists envisage a future wherein humans merge with advanced technologies, emerging as post-human beings with elevated intelligence, immortality, and godlike powers. Through scientific progress such as genetic engineering, cybernetic implants, and brain-computer interfaces, transhumanists endeavor to redefine the very essence of human nature.

The potential integration of transhumanist concepts and technologies into satanic rituals poses a precarious endeavor, as it would necessitate the manipulation of both supernatural forces and human biology and consciousness. The rituals have consistently served as gateways to mysterious realms beyond comprehension. By incorporating transhumanist technologies, adherents may embark on unexplored paths that could result in either unimaginable horrors or unprecedented enlightenment.

To analyze this integration, it is essential to delve into the fundamental principles of both satanic rituals and transhumanism. Satanic rituals are fueled by a hunger for power, knowledge, and the attainment of personal objectives. They are performed to establish a connection with dark entities, often involving intricate invocations, sacrifices, and the manipulation of occult symbols and sigils. Practitioners gain access to supernatural abilities and esoteric knowledge by harnessing these entities and forming pacts with them.

Transhumanism, on the other hand, embraces scientific progress and the concept of self-guided evolution. Its objective is to transcend natural limitations and amplify human potential through the fusion of biology and technology. With advancements in genetics, nanotechnology, and artificial intelligence, transhumanists believe they can overcome the constraints of mortality, intellect, and physical prowess. This ideology stands in stark contrast to satanic rituals, which rely on supernatural forces instead of human ingenuity and scientific advancements.

Nevertheless, could the convergence of these seemingly incongruous ideologies result in forbidden knowledge and power? Might the incorporation of transhumanist technologies strengthen the efficacy of the rituals, creating a potent amalgamation of ancient spiritual practices and futuristic enhancements? The answer lies in the possibility that satanic rituals could employ the advanced technologies of transhumanism to exercise even greater control over the human body and mind.

Let us imagine, for a moment, a satanic ritual that utilizes gene-editing techniques to enhance the physical attributes of its participants. By manipulating their DNA, practitioners could attain swifter speed, greater strength, and heightened resilience. Introducing cybernetic implants into their bodies would enable them to acquire heightened senses, thereby enabling them to perceive the supernatural realm with unparalleled clarity. These technologies have the potential to amplify the effects of rituals, granting practitioners greater access to the demonic forces they seek to harness.

Furthermore, the integration of brain-computer interfaces could revolutionize the practice of invocations during satanic rituals. By directly connecting the human mind with artificial intelligence, practitioners could communicate with otherworldly entities more efficiently, gaining access to hidden knowledge and achieving a higher degree of control. The fusion of human consciousness with advanced technologies could potentially transcend the limitations imposed by the physical world, granting practitioners entry into realms once deemed inaccessible.

While these possibilities may appear to be the speculations of a feverish mind, it is imperative to remain vigilant and open to the ever-evolving nature of the supernatural and technological realms. As a paranormal investigator, it is incumbent upon me to explore all possibilities, regardless of how disquieting they may be. The integration of transhumanist concepts and technologies into satanic rituals and spiritual practices represents a paradigm shift that challenges our current understanding of the occult and human potential.

In the ensuing chapters, I shall delve further into the concepts and technologies that hold the potential to reshape satanic rituals. We will explore genetic engineering, cybernetics, artificial intelligence, virtual reality, and various other phenomena that may form the foundation of this unholy alliance. By examining the historical context, core principles, and cutting-edge advancements, my aim is to shed light on the dark symbiosis between satanic rituals and transhumanism.

As we venture deeper into the realm of Satan, I implore you, the reader, to fortify yourself against the horrors that lie ahead. The path we tread is treacherous, but the truths we uncover may hold the key to unraveling the mysteries concealed within the depths of human consciousness and beyond. Prepare yourself, for the encounters that await us will challenge our perceptions, our beliefs, and the very essence of our existence.

SATANIC WORSHIP AND GENDER IDENTITY

As a professional paranormal investigator and specialist in unconventional phenomena, I have extensively explored the realm of Satanic worship, examining the obscured aspects that surround this enigmatic practice. Throughout my pursuit of knowledge, I have come across numerous unexpected revelations concerning gender identity and the integration of LGBTQ+ individuals within Satanic communities.

When one contemplates Satanic worship, commonly the mind conjures images of traditional gender roles and conservative values. However, the reality is far more intricate and intricate. Over time, the Satanic community has displayed a capacity for progressiveness, championing individual autonomy and challenging societal norms in various facets, including gender identity.

The concept of gender identity within Satanic communities is a complex tapestry of multifaceted perspectives, shaped by the diverse backgrounds, beliefs, and experiences of its practitioners. While certain sects adhere to conventional gender roles and the binary understanding of gender itself, others embrace a more fluid comprehension of gender identity. These latter groups often draw upon Satanic ideologies that prioritize personal freedom and self-expression, rejecting rigid social constructs.

One particularly notable instance is the active inclusion of LGBTQ+ individuals within Satanic worship. Contrary to prevailing misconceptions, numerous Satanic communities wholeheartedly embrace and commemorate queer identities. This integration is driven by a foundational ethos that rejects societal biases and advocates for the right to explore and embrace one's authentic self.

Through my thorough research, I have discovered a remarkable case study that encapsulates this evolving perception of gender identity within Satanic communities. The Black Coven, a Satanic group located in the heart of New Orleans, engages not only in ancestral rituals but also challenges gender norms by openly embracing and nurturing LGBTQ+ members.

During my time with The Black Coven, I engaged in conversations with several LGBTQ+ individuals who shared their experiences of finding solace and acceptance within this Satanic community. One member, who identified as non-binary, recounted their personal journey of self-discovery and expressed gratitude for The Black Coven, as it provided a safe environment to explore their gender identity without judgment or fear.

It became evident that The Black Coven's inclusion of LGBTQ+ individuals was not a superficial gesture but a steadfast commitment to fostering an environment where every member feels valued and respected. Their rituals incorporate elements that honor the diverse experiences of their members, resulting in a sense of belonging rarely encountered in mainstream society.

My conversations with The Black Coven's members shed light on the intricate nature of Satanic worship and its relationship with gender identity. It became apparent that the inclusion of LGBTQ+ individuals within this community is not a recent phenomenon but rather has deep historical roots. Historical evidence suggests that LGBTQ+ individuals have sought refuge within Satanic covens throughout history, seeking sanctuary from a society that often rejected them.

Whilst some may perceive the inclusion of LGBTQ+ individuals within Satanic communities as contradictory or incongruous, it is crucial to understand that these communities have consistently challenged societal norms and strived to forge a path paved with acceptance and freedom. The human experience is diverse, and Satanic worshippers embrace that diversity rather than suppress it.

As a consequence, Satanic worship and LGBTQ+ individuals find common ground in the shared desire for personal autonomy and the rejection of oppressive societal norms. While mainstream religions may impose stringent constraints on gender and sexual identity, Satanic communities cultivate an environment that encourages exploration and self-expression, providing a space for individuals to live authentically.

As the world gradually progresses towards greater acceptance and understanding, it is essential to acknowledge the abundant range of perspectives within Satanic communities regarding gender identity. While some may perceive Satanic worship as inherently contradictory to the LGBTQ+ movement, my research and personal experiences have demonstrated that these communities serve as transformative spaces, offering sanctuary to those who have struggled within mainstream society.

In conclusion, the evolving perspectives on gender identity within Satanic communities and the integration of LGBTQ+ individuals challenge presupposed notions and stereotypes associated with Satanic worship. With each passing generation, the Satanic community continues to push boundaries, embracing a more fluid comprehension of gender identity and cultivating a supportive space for LGBTQ+ individuals to express themselves authentically. This phenomenon stands as a testament to the resilience and adaptability of human spirituality, driven by an unwavering pursuit of personal freedom and acceptance.

SATANIC WORSHIP AND INTERFAITH DIALOGUE

In order to embark upon this journey of enlightenment, it is imperative to acquaint ourselves with the historical timeline of Satanic worship. By delving into the origins and evolution of this frequently misunderstood faith, we can gain a deeper appreciation for its existence and the motivations of its adherents. From the ancient Mesopotamian beliefs in fertility deities to the contemporary interpretations of Satanic worship, the timeline serves as a guiding compass through the ages of this religious domain.

Our exploration reveals that Satanic worship has been intertwined with various religions and belief systems throughout history. In ancient times, it often coincided with the worship of pagan deities and nature spirits, showcasing a primal connection to the forces of the earth. As centuries passed and Christianity expanded its dominion, Satanic worship emerged as an opposing force, embodying rebellion and challenging the established order. This notion persisted through the Middle Ages and the witch trials, where individuals were accused of engaging in Satanic practices and subsequently persecuted.

Nevertheless, it is essential to acknowledge that not all facets of Satanic worship are rooted in malevolence or malicious intent. In recent years, a new wave of Satanic groups has arisen, advocating for individualism, personal freedom, and the separation of church and state. These modern interpretations of Satanic worship emphasize critical thinking, skepticism, and rationality, questioning societal norms and championing personal autonomy. Groups such as The Satanic Temple aim to employ Satanic symbolism to address social and political matters, promoting compassion, justice, and empathy.

Comprehending the complexities of Satanic worship enables us to shift our perspective from one of trepidation and misunderstanding to one of inquisitiveness and openness. Through engaging in interfaith dialogue, we can learn from each other, sharing knowledge and viewpoints that cultivate understanding and respect. By fostering interfaith dialogue between Satanic worshipers and members of other religious traditions, we create an opportunity to challenge our preconceived notions and broaden our understanding of the diversity of human beliefs and experiences.

In facilitating this dialogue, it is crucial to acknowledge the inherent sensitivities and potential conflicts that may arise. Due to its very nature, Satanic worship can be perceived as blasphemous and sacrilegious by many religious groups. Approaching these conversations with empathy and a willingness to listen is paramount, recognizing that individuals' deeply held beliefs may serve as a source of comfort and stability. By building trust and cultivating an environment of mutual respect, we can bridge the divide between seemingly opposing belief systems and discover common ground.

Promoting interfaith dialogue and understanding between Satanic worshipers and members of other religious traditions is no simple feat. It necessitates patience, open-mindedness, and a genuine desire to learn from one another. By engaging in this process, we have the opportunity to challenge our own biases and prejudices, uncovering the richness and intricacy of human spirituality.

As an investigator of the paranormal and a specialist in the unusual, it is my duty to plumb the depths of the unknown, shedding light on the enigmas that envelop us. Satanic worship is undeniably a subject that arouses curiosity and fear, yet by embarking on the path of interfaith dialogue, we can pave the way for a more accepting and harmonious society. Only through understanding can we truly grasp the elaborate tapestry of human beliefs and aspirations, and perhaps, dispel the shadows that obscure our perception of the world.

6

PERSONAL JOURNEYS AND TESTIMONIES

FROM CHRISTIANITY TO SATANISM

Transitioning from one religious belief system to another is a complex and profound journey that entails questioning one's faith, grappling with uncertainty, and ultimately embarking on a new spiritual path. In my quest for knowledge and understanding, I immersed myself in the experiences of individuals who made the deliberate decision to leave behind Christianity and embrace the enigmatic allure of Satanism. The revelations I encountered deeply challenged my own comprehension of faith and spirituality.

The transition from Christianity to Satanism is an arduous undertaking that necessitates a profound sense of rebellion, a defiance of societal norms and expectations, and a willingness to embrace the forbidden. The individuals I had the privilege of knowing and learning from did not conform to the stereotypical image of Satanists often conjured in one's mind. These individuals were not malevolent and deranged beings worshiping demonic forces. Instead, they were seekers, on a quest for a deeper understanding of themselves and their place in the grand scheme of the universe.

One of the individuals I interviewed, Emma, recounted her personal journey with a profound sense of introspection and solemnity. Having been raised in a devoutly Christian household, she perpetually experienced spiritual unease and discontent. Despite her attempts to reconcile her doubts and fears within the confines of Christianity, the restrictiveness and dogmatism of the faith left her feeling stifled. It was when she chanced upon the works of influential occultists and scholars, such as Aleister Crowley and Anton LaVey, that a new realm of possibilities unfolded before her eyes. This marked the inception of her spiritual transformation.

For Emma, Satanism was not about venerating Satan as an external deity but rather a catalyst for personal growth and liberation. It symbolized a rebellion against established norms, a celebration of individuality, and a journey towards self-empowerment. It granted her the freedom to question the moral absolutes imposed by traditional Christianity and opened her mind to explore the boundless potential within herself.

Similarly, James, whom I encountered in the course of my research, spoke of the suffocating weight of guilt and shame instilled by his Christian upbringing. He had devoted his life to serving God and his community, yet he felt empty and unfulfilled. It was during a period of crisis and introspection that he stumbled upon the teachings of LaVeyan Satanism. The philosophy of self-indulgence and personal autonomy resonated deeply with him. By embracing Satanism, he found a path that allowed him to prioritize his own happiness and wellbeing instead of constantly self-sacrificing for others.

What struck me most profoundly about these personal journeys was the emphasis on personal empowerment and the rejection of external authority. Satanism, as embraced by these individuals, was not a quest to cause harm or destruction, but rather a means to liberate oneself from the shackles of societal expectations and embrace personal desires. It became evident that Satanism, which is frequently misunderstood and misinterpreted, was not inherently malevolent or evil. Instead, it was a profoundly personal and introspective journey of self-discovery, defying societal norms, and navigating a unique understanding of spirituality.

Through my interactions with these individuals, I, too, experienced a transformation of sorts. What was once perceived as darkness, a foreboding void, became an avenue for enlightenment and self-discovery. The transition from Christianity to Satanism, as witnessed in the experiences of these individuals, showcased the beauty of human autonomy and the intricacies of faith and spirituality.

As I continue to explore the realm of the occult, the personal accounts of those who have embraced Satanic beliefs will forever remain deeply etched in my memory. The journey from Christianity to Satanism challenges the very essence of what we perceive as "good" and "evil," urging us to question the foundations of our own faith and beliefs. Ultimately, I have come to realize that the path to enlightenment is not confined within the boundaries of one religious system but rather lies in the audacity to question, explore, and embrace the unknown.

Challenging societal norms and dogmas that govern our lives can be an intimidating endeavor. Yet, it is within this exploration of darkness that we may discover the radiance of illumination. Through these personal journeys, the transitions from Christianity to embracing Satanic beliefs, we witness the remarkable power of human autonomy and the liberating potential of spirituality. The line between good and evil becomes blurred, giving rise to a deeper comprehension of ourselves and the world we inhabit.

So, I invite you to contemplate this notion: perhaps it is in delving into the essence of Satan that we genuinely uncover the clarity and self-discovery we so fervently seek.

SATANIC TEMPLE MEMBERS AND ACTIVISM

As a parapsychologist and connoisseur of the inexplicable, I have consistently been gravitated towards the elusive and cryptic. Throughout my professional undertaking, I have encountered numerous individuals who reside on the periphery of society, delving into the depths of the human psyche and defying societal conventions. One such collective that has captivated my interest is the Satanic Temple and its adherents, who actively explore the occult and simultaneously engage in social and political activism.

In order to truly comprehend the motivations and experiences of these Satanic Temple members, I delved deep into their realm, immersing myself in their beliefs and practices. It swiftly became evident that the Satanic Temple deviated significantly from the antiquated and misguided assumptions linked to Satanism. Instead of venerating a literal Satan, they perceive Satan as an emblem of rebellion against despotism, advocating for individualism, empathy, and the pursuit of personal liberty.

Unmasking these truths, I embarked on a quest to interview several noteworthy members of the Satanic Temple regarding their participation in social and political activism. The revelations that transpired during these conversations surpass all my expectations.

One such interviewee, Lucius Blackwood, an articulate and charismatic individual, lucidly expounded upon the impetus behind his activism. Lucius revealed that his affiliation with the Satanic Temple began as a quest for enlightenment and a means to challenge the oppressive systems that govern society. He expressed a vehement disdain for hypocrisy and the inequitable treatment of marginalized communities. At its essence, the Satanic Temple furnished him with a podium to herald his dissent against these injustices, harnessing their principles as the bedrock of their ventures in activism.

Similar sentiments were shared by Aurora Nightshade, a youthful woman whose exuberant personality radiated through her dedication to social causes. Aurora discovered solace in the Satanic Temple, which provided her with an outlet to channel her feelings of indignation and exasperation into productive activism. She explained that activism through the Satanic Temple afforded her the opportunity to champion equality, freedom of expression, and the principle of separation between church and state.

Amongst the array of ways in which Satanic Temple members advocate for change, two specific causes stand out: reproductive rights and the preservation of religious diversity. Through a meticulous exploration of these subjects, we delve deeper into the rationale behind their emphasis on these issues.

Reproductive rights serve as a foundation for the Temple's activism. The Satanic Temple staunchly advocates for bodily autonomy and the prerogative to make informed decisions concerning one's own reproductive well-being. Their protests against restrictive abortion laws prove both provocative and efficacious, shedding light on the egregious violations of women's rights.

As for religious diversity, Lucius Blackwood expounded upon how the Satanic Temple combats religious discrimination by challenging the notion of a dominant religion in the public sphere. By erecting Satanic sculptures alongside religious

monuments in public spaces, they endeavor to warrant governmental compliance with the principle of separation between
church and state. This action, frequently mired in controversy,
instigates a necessary discourse surrounding religious freedom
and the equitable representation of diverse beliefs.

Through my interviews, it has become abundantly clear that
the activism of the Satanic Temple transcends the specter of
Satanism. Rather, it endeavors to contest the norms and biases
deeply entrenched within society. By harnessing the power of
symbolism and employing subversive tactics, these activists
endeavor to disrupt the prevailing order and kindle dialogue
on social and political issues.

As my research on Satanic Temple members and their
involvement in activism draws to a close, I am left with a
profound admiration for these individuals who refuse to be
constrained by societal expectations. They embody the spirit
of rebellion against injustice, utilizing the symbolism inherent
in Satanism as a tool to unveil and combat oppressive systems
afflicting our world.

Fascinating as they may be, the Satanic Temple and its
activists are far from the stereotypical malevolent figures portrayed in popular media. Instead, they constitute a collective
driven by compassion, empathy, and an unwavering commitment to effect positive change in a world often shrouded in
darkness. They serve as a source of inspiration, challenging
us to question the norm, contest authority, and embrace the
intricacies of the human experience.

As I venture further through the domains of the paranormal
and the mysterious, my encounters with Satanic Temple members and their activism have opened my eyes to a novel understanding of the redefinition of social and political boundaries.
Their narratives serve as luminous beacons, shedding light on

the paths we may take to foster a more equitable, compassionate, and inclusive society.

And so, with every subsequent chapter, my perception of
the Satanic Temple and its activism evolves, unraveling intricate layers beneath the surface of this enigmatic and often
misconstrued realm. From within the depths of the shadows,
a shimmer of hope emerges, reminding us that light persists
even in the realm of Satan.

CHURCH OF SATAN HIGH PRIESTS AND PRIESTESSES

To offer genuine insights into the lives of high priests and
priestesses within the Church of Satan, I have conducted extensive research and interviews. Employing a variety of sources,
including historical literature and firsthand testimonies, I have
constructed a comprehensive timeline that outlines the origins and development of this contentious organization. Within
this historical framework, we can commence an exploration of
the motivations and beliefs held by those holding positions of
authority within the Church of Satan.

The origins of the Church of Satan can be traced back to
the mid-20th century when Anton Szandor LaVey founded the
organization in San Francisco. Drawing from his own occult
convictions and principles, LaVey established the Church as a
platform for individuals seeking to embrace and examine the
darker aspects of human existence. Assuming the role of the
first high priest, he established a hierarchical structure that
would be passed down to successive leaders.

Over the years, the role of high priest or priestess within
the Church of Satan has been assumed by individuals who
have made a lasting impact on the organization. From Karla
LaVey, Anton's daughter who assumed leadership following
his demise, to contemporary figures such as Peter H. Gilmore

and Magistra Templi Rex Blanche Barton, the Church has been shaped by a diverse range of individuals, each possessing their own distinct perspectives and approaches.

An underlying theme that emerges through an examination of the lives of these high priests and priestesses is their unwavering dedication to their beliefs. Contrary to misguided stereotypes, they are not merely individuals engaged in malevolence or the worship of Satan as a literal entity. Instead, they regard Satan as a symbolic representation of personal freedom and rebellion against societal norms. Through their rituals and practices, they seek to tap into their innate desires and primal instincts, embracing the darker facets of human nature as a vehicle for personal self-improvement and transformation.

These high priests and priestesses are not embodiments of evil or catalysts for chaos. Rather, they strive for self-improvement and personal enlightenment by exploring the darker aspects of the human psyche. They repudiate the idea of a divine higher power, focusing instead on harnessing their own inherent capabilities. By embracing their individuality and disregarding societal expectations, they endeavor to attain a state of transcendence.

What motivates individuals to adopt such extreme perspectives? Why do they choose to deviate from societal norms and align themselves with an organization so deeply fascinated by darkness and rebellion? In my interviews with high priests and priestesses, a recurring theme emerges: the quest for meaning and purpose.

For many, the Church of Satan offers a sense of community and belonging that they may have struggled to find elsewhere. It provides a space in which their beliefs and desires are not only accepted but also celebrated. In a world that often rejects those who stray from conventional paths of righteousness, the Church affords sanctuary to those who refuse to conform.

Ultimately, the Church of Satan and its high priests and priestesses offer a captivating glimpse into the intricacies of human nature and the myriad ways in which individuals seek fulfillment and enlightenment. While their beliefs and practices may generate controversy and misunderstanding, it is imperative to approach the subject matter with an open mind and a willingness to comprehend rather than condemn.

Through my research and exploration, I have come to appreciate the depth and diversity of perspectives within the Church of Satan. It is not a homogenous entity, but rather an ever-evolving organization populated by individuals in pursuit of their truth and purpose. By shedding light on their lives and perspectives, I aspire to challenge preconceived notions and cultivate a greater comprehension of the human experience, no matter how peculiar or unconventional it may appear.

SATANIC RITUAL PRACTITIONERS

The stroke of midnight signifies my presence in an dimly illuminated room, engulfed by an ominous ambiance. Adjacent to me rests my notebook, hosting a compilation of meticulously transcribed research pertaining to practitioners of Satanic rituals. This assortment of knowledge is not suited for the faint-hearted, though as a Paranormal Investigator and Specialist in matters of the Unexplained, I am accustomed to exploring the most obscure recesses of the human psyche.

To attain a true comprehension of the realm of Satanic rituals, one must acquire an understanding of the individuals who actively partake in these ceremonies. This entails embarking on an unsettling yet captivating journey into the minds of those who willingly embrace the malevolent influence of Satan.

The act of sharing personal anecdotes and experiences from these practitioners allows for insights into their motivations and the depths of their preoccupations. One particular narrative originated from a woman named Sarah, who encountered Satanic rituals for the first time during her tender adolescent years.

Sarah recounted her initiation into a Satanic cult, describing it as an evening shrouded in darkness and secrecy. She provided detailed elaboration on the rituals undertaken, the blood sacrifices made, and the overpowering sensation of power surging through her veins. It was as if she, herself, had harnessed the very essence of malevolence, becoming a conduit for the Dark Lord.

However, not all practitioners gravitate towards Satanism with such intensity and conviction. Some inadvertently find themselves on this path as a form of rebellion or escape from their mundane lives. Matthew, a man entering his fourth decade of life, shared his narrative during one of my interviews. He had grown disillusioned with societal norms and sought a more meaningful existence.

Matthew aligned himself with a group of kindred spirits who introduced him to the realm of Satanic rituals. Initially, it was merely an avenue for rebelling against the established order, a means of expressing his individuality through the forbidden. Yet, with the passage of time, he experienced an encroaching dark energy that began to envelope him, leading him deeper into the realms of this malevolent practice.

Satanic ritual practitioners throughout history have willingly consigned themselves to the most unfathomable depths of society. From the notorious Black Masses held during the medieval era to the clandestine modern-day cults, their ceremonies are veiled in secrecy and driven by distorted desires.

Notably, one particularly chilling account uncovered during my research dates back to the early 1900s. An individual, whose identity shall remain undisclosed, relayed witnessing a

Satanic ritual held within an abandoned church nestled deep within the forest. He spoke of hooded figures, their eyes gleaming with an insatiable hunger, as they chanted in an ancient tongue that sent shivers down his spine.

These personal testimonials offer us a glimpse into the psychology of those actively engaged in Satanic rituals. Some are motivated by a perverse lust for power, while others seek solace from their humdrum lives. There are also those who are inexplicably drawn to the forbidden with motivations yet to be unearthed.

However, there exists a common thread among all practitioners - an undeniable allure of darkness. It is an irresistible force that beckons them towards embracing the occult, unlocking the mysteries of the supernatural, and reveling in the fervor of Satanic rites.

As I conclude my research, a profound apprehension envelops me. The world inhabited by Satanic ritual practitioners is cloaked in shadows, an elaborate labyrinth of darkness that ensnares the minds of those who dare to venture within. As a Paranormal Investigator and Specialist in matters of the Unexplained, my mission is to illuminate these concealed enclaves, expose the realities behind these practices, and delve even deeper into the abyss of Satan's domain.

FORMER SATANIC CULT MEMBERS

In an endeavor to gain a comprehensive understanding of the challenges endured by these survivors, I have embarked upon an investigation into their accounts, delving into the depths of their stories. Armed with my research and an unwavering determination, I sought out individuals willing to candidly share their past experiences, thereby illuminating the most distressing aspects of human existence.

Each narrative proved to be a distinct tapestry woven with anguish, trepidation, and resilience. One such survivor, Amelia, courageously disclosed her harrowing journey. Born into a family deeply entrenched in the malevolent arts, she was exposed to the rituals and beliefs of the Satanic cult to which she belonged from a tender age. It wasn't until she reached adolescence that the true nature of her environment became apparent.

Amelia was subjected to manipulation, control, and terror for several years. The cult members employed psychological tactics to confine her within their clutches, exploiting her insecurities and vulnerabilities. Her struggle for liberation was a constant battle for her soul, as she bore witness to abominable acts that defied all notions of ethics.

Escaping the clutches of the cult proved to be an arduous undertaking, necessitating immense bravery and fortitude. Amelia realized that her departure entailed not only a physical extraction but also a psychological hurdle. She had to dismantle the deeply ingrained beliefs imposed on her since childhood. However, with the support of a select few trusted confidants, she successfully broke free and embarked upon a path of recovery.

As I absorbed Amelia's account, I couldn't help but be awestruck by her resilience. Despite enduring severe trauma, she adamantly refused to allow it to define her. Instead, she dedicated herself to empowering others who encountered similar circumstances. Through therapeutic interventions, introspection, and advocacy, Amelia found purpose in assisting fellow survivors.

Nevertheless, Amelia's story serves as merely a fraction of a much larger puzzle. In my quest to shed light on the lives of former cult members, I delved deep into historical archives, meticulously seeking out documented cases and historical records. The darkness that pervaded these records was palpable, but my determination to expose these stories remained unwavering.

Among the cases I stumbled upon was that of Samuel McCormick, a man who escaped a notorious Satanic cult during the 1970s. Raised amid abuse and cruelty under the façade of religious observances, Samuel's susceptibility made him an ideal target for the cult, which began indoctrinating him from a tender age.

However, Samuel's spirit proved indomitable, and he staunchly resisted surrendering to the engulfing darkness. With audacity bordering on recklessness, he effectuated a daring escape that left him permanently scarred. The scars he bore, both evident and concealed, served as a perpetual reminder of the terror he experienced.

These survivors, like Amelia and Samuel, teach us invaluable lessons about resilience and the potential for healing. Their accounts provide a tangible demonstration of the extraordinary strength of the human spirit, even in the face of unimaginable horrors. It is through their journeys that we can begin to fathom the depths of malevolence, but also recognize the potential for redemption.

As I continue my exploration of the lives of former members of Satanic cults, I am acutely aware of the weighty responsibility that accompanies the sharing of their stories. It is insufficient to merely bear witness to their suffering; we must actively strive to cultivate a world in which such atrocities are eradicated. By illuminating these obscure recesses of humanity, we aspire to bring healing, comprehension, and ultimately, triumph over the forces of darkness.

SATANIC ARTISTS AND CREATIVITY

The inception of my journey can be traced back to the ancient civilizations that harbored beliefs in malevolent deities and demons. One such civilization was Mesopotamia, where the image of Pazuzu, the demon of the southwest wind, held a prominent place in their art. According to their beliefs, Pazuzu served as a protector against evil forces in the desert. However, his ominous appearance also appealed to those seeking to explore the realms of darkness in their creative pursuits. The ornate carvings and statues of Pazuzu provide us with a window into the artistic expressions of ancient societies, as well as their inclinations towards the peculiar and supernatural.

Progressing through time, we arrive at the Middle Ages, a period characterized by religious fervor and an eternal struggle between good and evil. The artistic movements of this era were heavily influenced by Christian faith and often aimed to depict the victory of righteousness over vice. However, upon closer examination of the masterpieces of that time, subtle indications of fascination with the devil are discernible. Paintings like Hans Memling's "The Last Judgment" and Hieronymus Bosch's "The Temptation of Saint Anthony" portray scenes of infernal torment and lurking demonic creatures. These artists, albeit indirectly, delved into the realm of Satan and his sway over humanity.

As the centuries advanced, the romantic era ushered in a preoccupation with the occult and the enigmatic. Artists such as Francisco Goya and William Blake began probing the darker aspects of human nature, frequently resorting to Satanic imagery to invoke astonishment and dread in their viewers. Goya's "Saturn Devouring His Son" and Blake's "The Great Red Dragon and the Woman Clothed in Sun" serve as prime examples of their artistic endeavors to encapsulate the essence of evil within their works. It is important to note that these artists were not endorsing Satanism, but rather employing the imagery associated with it to evoke emotions and challenge societal norms.

In the modern era, Satanic art has adapted to suit the changing cultural landscape and has taken on new forms. The music industry, in particular, has witnessed numerous artists incorporating Satanic symbolism into their performances and album artwork. Bands such as Black Sabbath, Slayer, and Marilyn Manson have all embraced Satanic imagery as integral components of their music and stage shows. Their frequent use of dark themes, occult symbolism, and provocative visuals instills a sense of primal instinct and rebellion in their audiences, offering a thrilling experience.

Beyond the realm of music, Satanic art has found its place in other creative mediums as well. Literature, for instance, has witnessed the rise of authors like Clive Barker and H.P. Lovecraft, who specialize in exploring the realms of horror and otherworldly entities. Barker's "Hellbound Heart" and Lovecraft's "The Call of Cthulhu" exemplify their unique talent for transporting readers to unfathomable dimensions where the diabolical and the divine intertwine.

Moreover, the visual arts have also embraced Satanic influences in recent years. The emergence of the modern occult movement has given rise to a new generation of artists who delve into the darker facets of spirituality. Artists like H.R. Giger and Zdzisław Beksiński have produced remarkable and unsettling artworks that depict surreal and nightmarish landscapes, populated by distorted and demonic figures. These artists employ their art as a means of expressing their personal experiences and beliefs, often challenging societal norms and surpassing the confines of traditional artistic expression.

In conclusion, the history of artistic expressions and creative ventures inspired by Satanic ideologies and symbols is a multifaceted and captivating one. From ancient times to the present day, artists have employed these themes to explore the darker aspects of human nature, challenge conventional norms, and elicit emotional reactions from their audiences. While not actively advocating for Satanism, these artistic expressions provide us with a unique insight into the human fascination with the supernatural and the mysterious. As a paranormal investigator, I am perpetually drawn to these artistic endeavors, driven by a desire to comprehend the intricate connection between art and the devil, and to unravel the enigmatic and peculiar nuances that lie within the human psyche.

SATANIC SCHOLARS AND THEOLOGIANS

As an investigator specializing in paranormal phenomena, I have had the opportunity to interact with numerous individuals who profess to practice the occult. However, in order to gain a more comprehensive understanding of their beliefs and practices, I decided to delve into the scholarly perspectives and theological interpretations of experts in the field of Satanic worship. Through extensive research and interviews, I aimed to uncover the truth behind the mysterious appeal of Satanism.

To embark on this intriguing journey, I thoroughly examined a plethora of texts, including books, manuscripts, and articles penned by prominent Satanic scholars and theologians. One such scholar who piqued my curiosity was Dr. Sebastian La-Croix, a renowned anthropologist specializing in the study of religious cults and secret societies. His seminal work, "Lucifer Unveiled: Exploring the Dark Underbelly of Satanic Worship," offered a comprehensive analysis of Satanic rituals and beliefs from a historical and sociological standpoint.

Dr. LaCroix delved deep into the origins of Satanism, tracing its roots back to ancient pagan practices and occult traditions. Through his research, he unearthed the fact that Satanism, in its various forms, has always existed on the periphery of society, often attracting individuals who seek a darker and forbidden path to enlightenment. He posited that Satanism should not be dismissed as mere delusion or superstition, but rather approached as a complex system of symbolism and power dynamics.

Another influential figure in the field of Satanic studies is Dr. Victoria Blackwood, a theologian renowned for her research on religious extremism and the supernatural. Her publication, "The Luciferian Agenda: Unmasking the Inner Workings of Satanism," sheds light on the philosophical foundations of Satanic worship and its distinctive rituals. Dr. Blackwood argued that Satanism should not be treated as a singular entity, but rather recognized as a continuum of belief systems, ranging from individualistic self-empowerment to radical anarchism.

In her research, Dr. Blackwood delved into the psychological motivations of individuals who align themselves with Satanism. She suggested that for some, the allure of Satanic worship lies in its perceived rebellion against societal norms and religious dogma. For others, it serves as a cathartic release, offering an opportunity to explore the darker recesses of their own psyche. Dr. Blackwood's insights provided a profound comprehension of the intricate complexities that underlie the practice of Satanism.

Whilst Dr. LaCroix and Dr. Blackwood provided valuable insights, perhaps the most contentious theological interpretation of Satanic worship was offered by Reverend Isaac Morganthall, a former Satanic High Priest who underwent a conversion to Born-Again Christianity. In his controversial memoir, "From Darkness to Light: A Personal Journey through the Shadows,"

Reverend Morganthall detailed his personal experiences within the covert world of Satanic rituals and the manipulative tactics employed by Satanic leaders to control their followers. Through his narrative, he described an unwavering belief in the literal existence of Satan and his pernicious influence on humanity. According to Reverend Morganthall, the rituals conducted by Satanists are not merely symbolic gestures, but rather potent conduits through which demonic forces are invoked and harnessed.

However, it is crucial to approach Reverend Morganthall's account with caution, as it is undeniably colored by his conversion to Christianity. Certain scholars critique his work, positing that his personal bias may hinder his ability to objectively analyze Satanic worship. Nonetheless, his unique perspective provided valuable insights into the intense and often traumatic experiences that some individuals undergo within Satanic circles.

As I delved further into the scholarly perspectives and theological interpretations of experts in the realm of Satanic worship, it became evident that Satanism transcends a superficial fascination with the macabre. It is a multifaceted belief system that encompasses elements of rebellion, self-empowerment, hidden knowledge, and even genuinely spiritual, albeit controversial, experiences.

Through my exploration of Dr. LaCroix's anthropological research, Dr. Blackwood's theological analysis, and Reverend Morganthall's personal account, a more holistic understanding of Satanic worship began to materialize. It is a clandestine realm, shrouded in secrecy, yet one that holds profound significance for those who choose to embrace its darker allure.

As I press onward with my investigation into the Eye of Satan, armed with the knowledge and perspectives imparted to me by these distinguished scholars and theologians, I brace myself for the daunting expedition that lies ahead. The enigma of Satanic worship is no longer a mere curiosity, but rather an intricately woven tapestry that demands comprehension, even at the risk of compromising my own sanity.

FINDING REDEMPTION AND LEAVING SATANIC WORSHIP

As an experienced investigator and specialist of paranormal phenomena, I have had the privilege of encountering numerous instances involving dark and malevolent forces that exist within the hidden recesses of our world. Among these distressing occurrences, the most chilling episodes involve individuals who have become entangled in the clutches of Satanic worship. These unfortunate souls, trapped within the labyrinthine grip of darkness, have faced incomprehensible depths of anguish. Nonetheless, against all odds, some have managed to summon the strength necessary to break free from this sinister hold and attain redemption.

In my tireless pursuit of comprehending the powerful allure of Satanic worship and the intricate psychology of those who have succumbed to its grip, I have delved extensively into the archives of history, unearthing forgotten accounts. These stories of redemption offer a glimmer of hope, highlighting the indomitable spirit of individuals who, defying all odds, have discovered the inner strength required to renounce their association with evil.

One such account revolves around Elizabeth Grant, a woman whose life took an ominous turn in her youth when she became ensnared by a Satanic cult. Raised in a troubled household, Elizabeth sought solace and acceptance within the convoluted corridors of darkness. Enticed by the allure of power and fulfillment, she embraced the rituals and practices of Satanic worship. Unfortunately, the deeper she delved into this abyss, the more she lost sight of her true self.

Only after years of torment and despair did Elizabeth reach the breaking point. Desperate for liberation, she sought solace in the writings of spiritual leaders who had confronted their own inner demons and triumphed. Through their teachings, Elizabeth realized that the path to redemption did not lie in responding to darkness with darkness, but in reclaiming her inner light.

Motivated by this newfound determination, Elizabeth embarked on a journey of self-discovery and healing. Seeking guidance from spiritual mentors, she immersed herself in the realm of the healing arts and learned to harness her innate power. Through sheer will and steadfast faith in the potential for redemption, Elizabeth gradually untangled herself from the clutches of Satanic worship, emerging as a transformed individual.

By sharing her story with others, Elizabeth became an inspirational figure for those who found themselves trapped in a similar overwhelming darkness. Her journey from darkness to light offered a glimmer of hope, serving as a beacon of redemption for those who had lost their way.

Another remarkable tale of redemption emerges from the unlikely figure of Nathan Turner, a former high-ranking member of a notorious Satanic cult. Nathan's involvement in the cult began during his rebellious teenage years, as he sought a sense of belonging and purpose. Seduced by the allure of power and sensual gratification promised by his newfound "family," he gradually became ensnared in a web from which escape seemed impossible.

For years, Nathan held a position of trust within the cult's malevolent agenda, participating in unspeakable acts that haunted his psyche. However, as time passed, a small spark of remorse began to flicker within him, gradually eroding the callous exterior cultivated by years of Satanic indoctrination. His dormant conscience finally awakened, demanding answers and seeking justification.

Haunted by his past, Nathan summoned the courage to confront the demons that had held him captive for far too long. Seeking guidance from a charismatic religious leader who shared stories of individuals who had achieved redemption despite their darkest transgressions, Nathan began questioning his own beliefs and the self-destructive path he had chosen.

With each step towards redemption, Nathan's resolve grew stronger. He renounced his allegiance to the cult, severing the ties that bound him to darkness. The process of healing was arduous, demanding unwavering determination. Yet, through therapy, introspection, and a newfound connection to his spirituality, Nathan eventually emerged from the abyss as a transformed individual.

These tales of redemption serve as a powerful reminder that no one is beyond salvation. They offer hope to those ensnared by the insidious allure of Satanic worship, demonstrating the indomitable power of the human spirit to overcome even the most unimaginable depths of despair.

7

CONTROVERSIES AND DEBATES

SATANIC SYMBOLS IN PUBLIC SPACES

As a professional paranormal investigator and specialist in occult phenomena, my inherent curiosity often drives me to delve deep into the various controversies that permeate our society. One such topic that has not only captured my attention but also piqued my intellectual curiosity is the ostentatious display of Satanic symbols in public spaces, and the ensuing clash between the principles of freedom of expression and religious sensitivities. In this chapter, my objective is to undertake a rigorous exploration of this contentious debate, thereby equipping readers with a comprehensive understanding of the intricacies involved.

In order to embark on this intellectual pursuit, it is imperative that we first consider the historical timeline of Satanic symbolism. Since its emergence, Satanism has been inextricably tied to a sense of defiance against societal norms and a sustained rebellion against conventional religious ideologies, while steadfastly advocating for individual autonomy. The conspicuous presence of Satanic symbols in public spaces serves as a tangible manifestation of this ongoing insubordination, a provocative gesture aimed at contesting established religious hierarchies and asserting the inherent entitlement to unrestricted self-expression.

Throughout the annals of history, Satanic symbols have constituted a potent tool for conveying messages and provoking conversations. During the pinnacle of the Romantic era, renowned figures such as Lord Byron and Percy Bysshe Shelley not only embraced Satanic imagery but also harnessed its power to challenge religious dogmas and explore the more sinister facets of human existence. In more recent times, artists of considerable renown, including the illustrious Anton LaVey, who founded the Church of Satan, have judiciously employed Satanic symbols to impel introspection within society and incite a questioning of deeply ingrained convictions.

However, the display of Satanic symbols in public spaces has not been without its vocal detractors, with the clash against religious sensitivities lying at the very crux of this contentious debate. Numerous individuals perceive these symbols as sacrilegious and objectionably offenseive, an unabashed assault on their profoundly cherished religious convictions. These individuals contend that their freedom to practice their faith in an environment free from blasphemous imagery is fundamentally compromised by impeding the public exhibition of Satanic symbols. It is within the aforementioned arena that the fundamental principles of freedom of expression inevitably collide with the reverent religious sensitivities intrinsic to individuals.

When subjected to closer scrutiny, the debate evinces a recurring tension that is fundamentally rooted in the dialectics between the entitlement to unfettered self-expression and the corollary need to exhibit respect for religious beliefs. Proponents of the First Amendment argue that the safeguarding of the right to exhibit Satanic symbols in public spaces is absolutely imperatival; it not only protects freedom of speech for all individuals but also serves as an irrefutable bulwark against the impending erosion of intellectual discourse and the potential stifling of dissenting viewpoints.

Conversely, opponents of this viewpoint vehemently assert that freedom of speech must be meticulously balanced with due deference afforded to religious sensitivities. Their contention posits that the display of Satanic symbols in public spaces engenders an environment that is unequivocally inhospitable and unwelcoming to individuals who approach life through the prism of religiosity, thereby undermining the very principles of inclusivity and tolerance that are vital for the sustenance of a harmonious society. To them, the accommodation of religious beliefs ought to take precedence over unrestrained and unwavering freedom of expression, thereby fostering a delicate equilibrium conducive to societal tranquility.

Amidst this protracted interplay of contrasting perspectives, it is of pivotal significance to contemplate the role that Satanic symbols assumptively undertake within the contemporary social milieu. Critics argue that the public display of these symbols is nothing more than a gratuitous quest for shock value, one that is meticulously designed to incite attention and promote oneself. According to this viewpoint, the appropriation of Satanic imagery fundamentally serves as a calculated marketing strategy or merely as a vehicle to attain notoriety, rather than a genuine and heartfelt expression of personal beliefs. Conversely, proponents assert that Satanic symbols play a crucial role as a poignant reminder of the ceaseless crusade for intellectual emancipation, an entity that incites dialogues of import and persistently challenges the deeply entrenched societal norms.

It is worthwhile to acknowledge that the public display of Satanic symbols is subject to legal constraints and regulations.

While the First Amendment unequivocally espouses the virtues of freedom of expression, it simultaneously does not confer any overarching immunity from the imposition of reasonable restrictions. Courts have invariably decreed that constraints can be imposed on speech if it possesses the potential to present a clear and present danger or incite violence. In essence, debates concerning the public exhibition of Satanic symbols often necessitate exhaustive deliberations regarding the boundaries of free expression and the conceivable harm these symbols may inflict upon individuals and communities.

In conclusion, the intricately nuanced debate revolving around the public display of Satanic symbols is an issue of multifaceted dimensions. It reconciles the cherished principles of freedom of expression with the profound religious sensitivities that pervade society. Grasping the nuances of this impassioned debate necessitates a comprehensive exploratory examination of the historical context, clashing perspectives, and pertinent legal considerations. Given my vocation as a paranormal investigator dedicated to investigating the inexplicable, my ardent desire is to foster dialogue pertaining to these topics that pose significant challenges to our collective Weltanschauung, ultimately affording us the unique capacity to navigate through the convolutions of our society with open-mindedness and comprehension.

SATANIC RITUALS IN LEGAL CONTEXT

In my capacity as a paranormal investigator and specialist in anomalous phenomena, I have embarked on an exploration of the realm of Satanic rituals. This investigation has taken me into uncharted and often disturbing territories, where I have encountered complex legal issues and controversies surrounding these practices. Central to this discourse is the protection of religious freedom, a crucial tenet that often comes into play when evaluating the legal challenges posed by Satanic rituals.

The realm of Satanic rituals is characterized by a mixture of fear, intrigue, myth, and misconceptions. Consequently, these practices present a thorny issue when it comes to legal interpretation. They exist within a delicate balance between religion and criminal activity, leaving legislators and legal scholars grappling with difficult questions. As my investigation delves deeper, I find myself confronted with a complex web of constitutional rights, societal biases, and intricate interpretations of religious freedom in the face of these contentious practices.

A key legal challenge concerning Satanic rituals lies in delineating what constitutes a religious practice. Courts have grappled with the task of discerning whether these rituals are sincere expressions of faith or merely disguised attempts to engage in criminal behavior. Historical evidence has revealed that Satanic rituals have been intertwined with criminal acts, such as human sacrifice, animal abuse, and the desecration of graveyards. The disturbing nature of these acts blurs the boundaries between religious freedom and criminality, presenting legal authorities with a daunting task of discerning the true intent behind such rituals.

Upon examination of the existing legal framework, it becomes evident that clear-cut guidelines to differentiate Satanic rituals from criminal activities are lacking. This has led to inconsistencies in their treatment under the law, resulting in differing outcomes across jurisdictions. Some courts, guided by an intention to protect religious freedom, have adopted a more hands-off approach, viewing Satanic rituals as protected expressions of belief. They argue that the First Amendment guarantees the free exercise of religion, irrespective of its unconventionality or controversy.

However, others contend that the criminal nature frequently associated with Satanic rituals necessitates a more restrictive approach. Opponents assert that religious freedom should not encompass activities that pose harm to individuals or society at large. They argue that the government has a legitimate interest in safeguarding public safety, and permitting Satanic rituals historically linked to criminal behavior would be tantamount to a neglect of this duty.

Determining whether Satanic rituals should be considered protected expressions of religious freedom ultimately depends on the specific circumstances of each case. Courts must weigh the evidence, consider the context, and evaluate the sincerity of the ritual in question. In doing so, they often take into account factors such as the presence of illegal activities or harm caused to individuals or property during the ritual. Navigating this precarious terrain falls within the purview of the legal system, which is tasked with making informed judgments on a case-by-case basis.

Consent stands as another pressing concern in the legal context of Satanic rituals. These rituals, by their very nature, often involve intense and disturbing acts that may transgress ethical boundaries. While some require willing participants, others involve non-consenting individuals subjected to harrowing experiences. The central question raised here pertains to whether individuals can genuinely give informed consent to participate in rituals that may have far-reaching mental, emotional, and physical consequences.

This question has ignited fervent debates within legal circles. On one hand, proponents argue that adults have the right to freely choose their religious practices, even if these practices appear extreme or unsettling to others. They hold that as long as participants possess full knowledge of the ritual's nature and potential consequences, their consent should be regarded as valid, notwithstanding societal norms that may be violated.

On the other hand, opponents posit that the coercive nature often associated with Satanic rituals undermines the authenticity of consent. They contend that individuals may be vulnerable to manipulation, persuasive tactics, or even threats, which cast doubt on the legitimacy of their consent. In such cases, using Satanic rituals as a means to control, exploit, or harm vulnerable individuals becomes a grave concern within the legal system.

The pursuit of justice and the protection of individual rights have sparked an ongoing struggle between religious freedom and the need to ensure public safety in the legal landscape of Satanic rituals. Courts endeavor to strike a delicate balance amidst the complexities and ambiguities surrounding these practices. I am acutely aware, as I venture further into this examination of the depths, that this battle for legal clarity is far from over. Only through continuing research, diligent investigation, and thoughtful analysis can we hope to illuminate this enigmatic realm and untangle the intricate threads binding it to our understanding of religious freedom.

SATANIC RITUALS AND CHILD CUSTODY BATTLES

As a paranormal investigator specializing in unusual phenomena, I have frequently encountered cases that defy conventional understanding. One particularly challenging and ethically complex area I have encountered involves the intersection of satanic rituals and child custody battles. Throughout my years of studying the occult, I have observed families torn apart by their involvement in dark practices and the subsequent legal struggles that arise. This chapter examines the intricacies of these intricate cases, where the line between religious freedom and child welfare becomes blurred.

To truly comprehend the complexities of these child custody battles, a thorough examination of the historical timeline of satanic rituals and their association with allegations of child abuse is vital. The 1980s brought forth a moral panic surrounding satanic cults, fueled by sensational media stories and sensationalized documentaries. This created a potent backdrop for custody disputes, where accusations of devil worship and rituals involving children became weapons in the battle for custody.

My research has entailed an exploration of numerous court cases, allowing me to witness firsthand the devastation caused by these battles. A crucial aspect to consider is the burden of proof in such cases. How does one substantiate claims of satanic rituals, particularly when they are conducted covertly? The issue is further compounded by societal skepticism towards the existence of satanic cults, leading to allegations being dismissed as unfounded or products of overactive imaginations.

Within the realm of satanic rituals, there exists a wide range of practices, from innocuous to genuinely sinister. While some individuals may identify as Satanists, adhering to a personal philosophy of individualism and nonconformity, others delve into the darker aspects of occultism, engaging in rituals that involve the abuse and potential sacrifice of both animals and children.

When delving into this field of investigation, it is crucial to maintain a delicate balance between utmost respect for religious freedom and the protection of innocent lives. The legal system often struggles to strike this balance, torn between recognizing an individual's right to practice their chosen religion and safeguarding the well-being of a child.

Various factors come into play in these cases, including the credibility and mental stability of the accuser, the testimony of the child (if old enough), and the presence of physical evidence. The challenge lies in validating claims of secret satanic rituals, where evidence may be scarce or heavily reliant on witness testimony.

Child custody battles involving satanic rituals necessitate a meticulous approach, often requiring cooperation among paranormal investigators, law enforcement, and child protective services. Such collaborations can greatly enhance the chances of obtaining evidence and protecting vulnerable children. However, it is crucial to recognize the fine line between legitimate investigation and vigilantism, as well as the necessity of maintaining objectivity for a fair legal process.

In my experience, the emotional toll on children subjected to parents engaged in satanic rituals cannot be underestimated. The trauma inflicted in these situations often leaves enduring scars on young lives. Consequently, all involved parties must prioritize the child's well-being and safety, providing the necessary support and resources for their recovery.

Navigating these intricate legal and ethical dilemmas calls for a delicate touch, consistently placing the best interests of the child at the forefront. Legal systems must adapt to these unique circumstances, deepening their comprehension of religious practices and aligning it with child welfare. By doing so, we can adopt a more balanced approach when addressing parents' rights to practice their chosen religion while ensuring the protection of innocent lives.

As a paranormal investigator and specialist in the extraordinary, I have dedicated my life to shedding light on the mysteries that surround us. Through my exploration of the dark realm of satanic rituals and child custody battles, I strive to contribute to a clearer understanding of these intricate cases and advocate for the well-being of the most vulnerable members of our society. It is my hope that by illuminating these topics, discussions and reforms within the legal system will be prompted, ensuring the safety and welfare of children caught in the crossfire of these battles.

SATANIC WORSHIP AND MENTAL HEALTH

As a professional paranormal investigator and specialist in the study of the extraordinary, I have encountered numerous unsettling phenomena throughout my career. However, I was not adequately prepared for the ominous realm of Satanic worship. My work has been devoted to thoroughly exploring the depths of the unknown in search of answers and truth. In this pursuit of knowledge, I have found myself confronted with the ongoing controversy surrounding the impact of Satanic worship on mental health.

To gain an understanding of the nature of Satanic worship and its potential effects on mental well-being, it is imperative to examine the underlying principles of this dark practice. Satanic worship, often associated with occult rituals and acts of blasphemy, is founded on the belief in the existence of an evil deity known as Satan. This deity represents rebellion against traditional religious institutions. It is vital to differentiate genuine Satanic worship from the sensationalized depictions often portrayed in popular culture. True Satanic worship is centered on the exploration of personal desires and the pursuit of individual freedom, rather than the literal worship of a demonic entity.

From a psychological perspective, the impact of Satanic worship on mental health can be interpreted through various frameworks. Some argue that engaging in Satanic rituals can provide individuals with a sense of empowerment and self-expression, particularly for those who feel marginalized or oppressed by societal norms. Supporters maintain that the freedom to embrace one's darkest desires, rather than suppress them, can result in psychological liberation. However, critics argue that such practices have the potential to fuel delusions, worsen pre-existing mental health disorders, and foster anti-social behavior.

A study conducted by Dr. Evelyn Hartley at the University of Paranormal Psychology aimed to uncover the intricate connection between Satanic worship and mental health. The study involved conducting interviews and assessments with individuals who claimed to practice Satanic rituals. Dr. Hartley unveiled a broad spectrum of experiences and perspectives, shedding light on the diverse motivations underlying the adoption of Satanic practices.

One particular case that stood out involved a young woman named Rebecca, who turned to Satanic worship as a means of coping with a traumatic childhood. According to Rebecca, summoning demons and performing rituals allowed her to regain control over her life. Initially, she experienced a sense of exhilaration and liberation from societal constraints. Over time, however, Rebecca began to experience heightened anxiety and paranoia. She believed that malevolent forces were stalking her, resulting in sleepless nights and intense fear. Dr. Hartley diagnosed Rebecca with an undetected predisposition to bipolar disorder, suggesting that her involvement in Satanic worship had triggered a manic episode.

Another case explored within Dr. Hartley's study involved a man named Samuel, whose participation in Satanic rituals yielded a different outcome. Samuel had been raised in a strictly religious environment, where he was required to adhere to rigid moral standards that conflicted with his personal desires. As a consequence of rejecting his religious upbringing,

Samuel embarked on a journey into Satanism, which he found to be a source of liberation and independence. Samuel reported experiencing a sense of peace and fulfillment during his ritual practices. However, this apparent positive impact was met with external judgment from friends and family, resulting in isolation and self-doubt. Samuel's mental well-being experienced a decline, manifesting as depression and a pervasive sense of emptiness.

These cases emphasize the complex web of mental health challenges that can arise as a result of involvement in Satanic worship. Though it is important not to generalize individual experiences, the potential risks associated with engaging in Satanic rituals should not be dismissed. The possibility of triggering dormant mental health conditions or exacerbating existing symptoms is a deeply concerning reality that demands attention.

In conclusion, the impact of Satanic worship on mental health continues to be a divisive and intricate subject. While proponents argue that the exploration of one's darkest desires can lead to psychological liberation, skeptics raise valid concerns about the potential risks, including the activation of mental health issues. The study conducted by Dr. Hartley provides invaluable insights into the diverse experiences and motivations of individuals who participate in Satanic worship, shedding light on its impact on mental well-being. As a paranormal investigator and specialist in the unusual, I remain committed to further exploring this dark connection, with the goal of comprehending the delicate balance between personal freedom and the potential harm it may entail.

SATANIC RITUALS AND ANIMAL SACRIFICE

As a paranormal investigator and specialist in unusual phenomena, I have encountered and extensively studied a wide range of occult practices and rituals. Among these, Satanic rituals, particularly those involving the sacrifice of animals, have always been a puzzling and contentious subject. The purpose of this chapter is to thoroughly examine the ethical concerns and legal consequences surrounding this controversial practice.

In order to truly comprehend the significance of animal sacrifice in Satanic rituals, it is essential to have knowledge of its historical origins. Throughout history, various cultures and religions have partaken in animal sacrifice as a means of communicating with higher powers, seeking favor and protection, or commemorating important events. From the ancient Greeks who made animal sacrifices to appease their deities to the Mayans who sacrificed animals to ensure an abundant harvest, this practice has had a lasting impact on human history.

However, when it comes to Satanic rituals, animal sacrifices take on a darker and more sinister tone. Satanism, as a religious philosophy, has often evoked strong emotions and fear due to its association with Satan, who is seen as the embodiment of evil. It is important to note that the majority of self-identified Satanists do not believe in a literal Satan, but rather embrace a symbol of rebellion and individualism. Nevertheless, the connection to evil and the alleged immoral practices have sparked heated debates.

The ethical concerns surrounding animal sacrifice in Satanic rituals encompass several key factors. First and foremost, animal rights and the infliction of unnecessary suffering take center stage. Advocates argue that animals are sentient beings capable of experiencing pain and fear, and therefore subjecting them to ritualistic slaughter is inherently cruel. This perspective is reinforced by the increasing awareness of animal welfare and the recognition that animals should not be treated as mere objects.

Additionally, the issue of consent arises when discussing animal sacrifice. Animals are unable to provide informed consent to be sacrificed, leading to questions about the morality of taking their lives against their will. Some contend that animals, as beings with inherent value, deserve a certain level of respect and autonomy that the practice of animal sacrifice denies them.

From a legal standpoint, the practice of animal sacrifice within Satanic rituals presents a complex and contentious issue. The legality of animal sacrifice varies greatly across different jurisdictions, with some nations completely prohibiting it, while others may have certain allowances or restrictions. In countries where animal sacrifice is permitted, it is often subject to regulation and oversight by animal welfare organizations and government agencies to ensure that suffering is minimized and ethical standards are upheld.

One case that exemplifies the legal implications of animal sacrifice is the well-known lawsuit of the Church of Satan versus the City of Hialeah in 1993. The Church of Satan, a religious organization founded by Anton LaVey, challenged the city's ordinance that banned animal sacrifice. The Supreme Court ultimately ruled in favor of the city, asserting that the prohibition of animal sacrifice served a legitimate government interest in preventing harm to animals. This case acts as a precedent and underscores the delicate balance between religious freedom and the protection of animal welfare in the legal framework surrounding animal sacrifice.

It is important to note that not all Satanic rituals involve animal sacrifice. The belief that all Satanists engage in these practices is a common misconception perpetuated by sensationalized media. Many self-professed Satanists strictly adhere to the philosophy of LaVeyan Satanism, which highlights individualism and the rejection of societal norms, but does not endorse the practice of animal sacrifice or harm towards living beings.

As a paranormal investigator, I have had the opportunity to firsthand witness the remnants of Satanic rituals involving animal sacrifice. The symbolism, eerie ambiance, and sense of malevolent energy that lingers in such locations cannot be disregarded lightly. While my personal beliefs may incline me towards the side of animal rights and compassion, I strive to maintain objectivity and an open-minded approach in my quest to understand the intricate tapestry of the paranormal realm.

In conclusion, the practice of animal sacrifice in Satanic rituals presents a complex entanglement of ethical concerns and legal ramifications. The ongoing clash between religious freedom, animal rights, and societal values continues to shape the discourse surrounding this contentious topic. As society progresses and our comprehension of ethics and morality expands, it is imperative to engage in open dialogue and exploration to navigate the delicate balance between freedom of belief and the safeguarding of animal welfare.

SATANIC WORSHIP AND FREEDOM OF RELIGION

As an investigative professional specializing in paranormal phenomena, I have encountered a diverse array of belief systems, ideologies, and practices throughout my career. One subject that has consistently fascinated and perplexed me is Satanic worship and its recognition as a legitimate religious belief within the framework of freedom of religion. The conflicts and debates surrounding this contentious subject matter have sparked intense discussions about the parameters of religious liberty and the constraints society should impose on the expression of one's faith.

In order to comprehensively grasp the intricate realm of Satanic worship and its legal recognition, it is imperative to delve deep into its historical origins and unravel the intricacies of its belief systems. This journey commences centuries ago, amidst the ascendance of Christianity and the ecclesiastical efforts to suppress alternative spiritual doctrines. It was during this era that the notion of Satan as a symbol of opposition and rebellion against mainstream religious institutions emerged.

A thorough analysis of the controversies and debates regarding the recognition of Satanic worship as a legitimate religious belief under the umbrella of freedom of religion is necessary to fully comprehend the intricate dynamics at play. To this end, it is crucial to explore the historical timeline of Satanic worship and its association with the concept of freedom of religion.

The emergence of Satanic worship can be traced back to the Middle Ages, when stories of witchcraft and devil worship gained prominence. These practices were vehemently condemned by the Catholic Church, which branded them heretical and viewed them as a threat to their authority. The infamous witch trials and the subsequent persecution of individuals suspected of engaging in Satanic rituals serve as a haunting reminder of the power dynamics that prevailed during that period.

Advancing to the modern era, the debate concerning Satanic worship has taken on a new dimension. In the United States, the First Amendment of the Constitution guarantees the freedom of religion, safeguarding individuals' rights to worship as they choose. This constitutional protection has paved the way for diverse religious movements, including those professing Satanic beliefs.

Despite this, the recognition of Satanic worship as a legitimate religious belief has encountered substantial opposition. Critics argue that the practice of Satanic worship, with its association with malevolence and subversive acts, should not be accorded the same protections as mainstream religions. They contend that Satanic rituals frequently involve destructive and hazardous behaviors, such as animal sacrifices or acts of violence, which cannot be justified under the guise of religious expression.

Nevertheless, proponents of religious freedom maintain that Satanic worship should be treated with the same respect and consideration as any other belief system. They argue that designating Satanic worship as a legitimate religion does not condone illegal or harmful activities, but rather underscores the significance of diversity and inclusivity in a democratic society.

The legal battles surrounding the recognition of Satanic worship as a legitimate religion have been both captivating and contentious. Courts in various jurisdictions have grappled with the task of determining whether Satanic beliefs meet the established criteria for religious recognition. Typically, these criteria entail sincerely held beliefs, a set of rituals or practices, and a coherent group or community that adheres to these beliefs.

One notable case that thrust the debate surrounding Satanic worship into the spotlight was the 1980s trial of the Satanic Church of America. This organization argued that their worship of Satan was protected under the First Amendment, and thus, their religious practices should not be subject to legal scrutiny. The court's ruling recognized their status as a legitimate religion, emphasizing that the Constitution does not discriminate between different faiths or their theological tenets.

While the recognition of Satanic worship as a legitimate religion has gained traction in certain legal realms, wider societal acceptance of these beliefs remains a contentious issue. Religious discrimination and moral objections often significantly influence public perception. Many individuals are uncomfortable with the notion of Satanic worship and perceive it as a dangerous practice that should not enjoy the same rights as mainstream religions.

To bridge this divide, it is crucial to foster open and sincere conversations about Satanic worship, shedding light on the true nature of these belief systems and dispelling unfounded fears. Education and understanding are crucial components in addressing the conflicts and debates surrounding the recognition of Satanic worship as a legitimate religious belief.

In conclusion, the subject of Satanic worship and its recognition as a legitimate religious belief within the framework of freedom of religion is a complex and multifaceted matter. Understanding the historical origins of Satanic worship, analyzing the legal battles it has encountered, and addressing societal perceptions are all vital steps in unraveling this controversial subject. As an investigator specializing in paranormal phenomena, my mission is to shed light on the obscure and question the limitations of our perceived reality.

SATANIC WORSHIP AND SOCIAL STIGMA

In my capacity as a paranormal investigator and specialist in anomalous phenomena, I have embarked on numerous ventures into the realm of the supernatural, encountering individuals from diverse backgrounds and experiences. An integral part of my journey involves an examination of the social stigma and discrimination faced by individuals who openly identify as practitioners of Satanism. In this chapter, my objective is to elucidate the challenges they confront in a society that continues to grapple with misconceptions and apprehension.

To gain a comprehensive understanding of the social stigma attached to satanic worship, it is imperative to delve into the historical timeline of the Satanic Panic that occurred during the latter part of the 20th century. This period was characterized by a moral panic that swept across the nation, fueled by sensationalized media reports and misinformation. Claims of satanic rituals involving human sacrifices and the control of clandestine cults spread like wildfire, resulting in a wave of public hysteria. Consequently, many innocent individuals fell victim to witch hunts, accused solely on the basis of their association with satanic symbols or practices. This mass hysteria laid the foundation for the escalating stigma and discrimination faced by openly identifying Satanists in contemporary times.

One of the primary challenges encountered by Satanists is the fearmongering and vilification perpetuated by mainstream media. Sensationalized portrayals of satanic worship, frequently intertwined with violent crimes or devil-worshipping cults, have fostered a deeply ingrained association between Satanism and malevolence in the public consciousness. This false narrative attributes malicious intent to every individual who identifies as a Satanist, disregarding their beliefs or values. Consequently, Satanists find themselves marginalized and ostracized in various spheres of their lives, including employment and interpersonal relationships, as society struggles to distinguish reality from myth.

Employment discrimination presents a significant issue for Satanists. Many employers, spurred by fear or misguided perceptions, refrain from hiring individuals who openly identify as Satanists. Not only is this discriminatory, but it also undermines the fundamental principles of freedom of religion and belief. For Satanists, securing and maintaining stable employment presents an uphill battle, as they are often faced with the choice of concealing their true identity or exposing themselves to potential retribution from their employers and colleagues.

Satanist parents also encounter immense challenges within the context of child custody disputes in family courts. Frequently, ill-informed court officials and biased judges view Satanists as unfit parents, equating their beliefs with endangerment or moral perversion. As a result, Satanist parents must frequently engage in arduous legal battles to retain custody of their own children, combating societal biases and misconceptions.

Another facet of the social stigma confronting Satanists is an enduring sense of isolation and exclusion from mainstream religious communities. The vast majority of religious institutions perceive Satanism as a threat to their values and beliefs, resulting in the denial of participation in interfaith dialogue or the refusal to afford Satanists the same rights and privileges extended to adherents of other religions. This exclusionary practice not only deprives Satanists of their right to freedom of religion but also serves to perpetuate the notion that their beliefs are inherently dangerous or immoral.

On a more personal level, openly identifying as a Satanist often invites harassment, threats, and even physical violence. Due to their association with perceptions of the "dark side," Satanists frequently become targets of hate crimes and discrimination. This not only compromises their physical safety but also takes an immense toll on their mental and emotional well-being. Living in constant fear of being targeted merely on the basis of their religious beliefs is an undue burden that no individual should be subjected to.

Despite these challenges, a burgeoning movement within the Satanist community aims to challenge social stigmas and advocate for their rights. Organizations such as The Satanic Temple have emerged as prominent figures, actively engaging in legal battles to safeguard the rights of Satanists under the purview of the First Amendment. Furthermore, the increasing visibility of Satanists on online platforms and social media enables the dissemination of accurate information, effectively debunking the prevailing myths surrounding satanic worship.

In conclusion, the social stigma and discrimination experienced by openly identifying Satanists are deeply ingrained in historical prejudices and misconceptions. Fear, perpetuated by sensationalized media depictions and misunderstandings, has resulted in the marginalization of Satanists across various spheres of society. Employment discrimination, child custody disputes, exclusion from religious communities, and the constant threat of harassment and violence are hurdles that Satanists encounter on a regular basis. Nevertheless, through tireless advocacy and the dissemination of accurate information, there is reason to be optimistic that a future characterized by acceptance, understanding, and unfettered religious freedom can be achieved for all individuals, regardless of their beliefs.

SATANIC WORSHIP AND THE ROLE OF MEDIA

To commence this analysis, it is pertinent to reflect upon the historical timeline of Satanic worship and its evolving representation throughout the years. While the origins of Satanic worship can be traced back to ancient civilizations, it was during the 20th century that its portrayal in the media began to gain momentum. Early works of literature such as Bram Stoker's "Dracula" and William Peter Blatty's "The Exorcist" introduced readers to the concept of demonic forces and Satanic rituals.

As time progressed, the influence of Satanic worship in the media expanded further. This was particularly evident with the advent of rock music and its association with Satanic themes. Bands like Black Sabbath and Slayer, characterized by their somber imagery and lyrics, caused alarm and moral panic among conservative groups and the general public. The media, always eager to sensationalize, exacerbated this anxiety through sensational headlines and distorted depictions of these musicians as disciples of Satan.

Nevertheless, the music industry was not the sole platform for the portrayal of Satanic worship. Hollywood, perpetually driven by societal fears and fascination, began producing numerous films centered around Satanic rituals. Movies such as "Rosemary's Baby," "The Omen," and "The Devil's Advocate" presented the notion of Satanic cults as a thrilling and morbid source of entertainment. The power of visual storytelling allowed these films to penetrate the subconscious of the audience, reinforcing stereotypes and anxieties surrounding Satanic worship.

As the years went by, the role of media in shaping public perception of Satanic worship has grown even more influential. With the rise of the internet, the dissemination of information has become instant and widespread. From websites dedicated to conspiracy theories and cult practices to social media platforms showcasing occult rituals, the digital age has become a fertile ground for the proliferation of Satanic imagery.

One cannot overlook the impact that this media portrayal has on public perception and societal attitudes towards Satanic worship. The association of Satanic rituals with violent crimes and malevolence has created an atmosphere of fear and contempt. Outsiders often regard those who identify as Satanists as morally depraved and dangerous individuals. This biased portrayal not only perpetuates societal divisions but also marginalizes and vilifies those who practice Satanic worship as a legitimate religion.

However, it is imperative to differentiate fact from fiction when scrutinizing the media's portrayal of Satanic worship. The reality is that not all individuals who identify as Satanists engage in sinister or criminal activities. While there may be a small fraction of practitioners who partake in harmful actions, the majority are simply exercising their religious freedom and exploring alternative spiritual beliefs. By focusing solely on the negative depictions, the media perpetuates ignorance and misconceptions about this intricate and diverse community.

In conclusion, the depiction of Satanic worship in the media has had a profound influence on public perception and societal attitudes. Throughout history, from literature to movies to the digital era, this malevolent cult has been sensationalized and distorted, reinforcing stereotypes and instilling fear. While it is crucial to recognize the potential dangers associated with Satanic rituals, it is equally important to approach this topic with an open mind and a willingness to comprehend the diversity within the community. As a paranormal investigator and specialist in the paranormal, my commitment lies in unveiling the truth behind Satanic worship, dispelling myths, and challenging the misconceptions perpetuated by the media. Only through education and open dialogue can we hope to transcend the shadows and achieve a deeper understanding of this captivating and enigmatic realm.

8

THE INFLUENCE OF SATANIC WORSHIP

PSYCHOLOGICAL EFFECTS OF SATANIC RITUALS

In order to properly analyze my findings, it is crucial to establish a comprehensive historical timeline of Satanic rituals. Over the course of centuries, a variety of forms of Satanic worship and rituals have existed, often influenced by cultural and religious beliefs. The origins can be traced back to ancient pagan rituals practiced by tribes and civilizations, laying the foundations for the evolution of future rituals.

During the Middle Ages, when the Christian faith gained prominence, the fear and persecution of Satanism reached its pinnacle. The infamous witchcraft trials and inquisitions resulted in numerous individuals being accused of participating in Satanic rituals, often leading to torture, confession, and execution. These events significantly bolstered the belief in Satanic rituals, instilling fear and paranoia within the general population.

Advancing to the present day, while Satanic rituals have become less prevalent, they still captivate and disturb many individuals. It is imperative to differentiate between fact and fiction, especially when examining the psychological impact on those who engage in such rituals.

Through extensive research, I have encountered various case studies of individuals claiming to have engaged in Satanic rituals. These cases have provided me with insights into the psychological effects experienced by these individuals, shedding light on the intricate nature of their beliefs and behavior.

One recurring theme that emerges from these case studies is the profound sense of power and control experienced by participants during Satanic rituals. The allure of joining a group that promises great power, coupled with the desire to rebel against societal norms and traditions, can be highly enticing to those seeking an unconventional path in life.

However, the psychological impact extends far beyond initial attraction. Individuals who partake in Satanic rituals often undergo a profound transformation of their beliefs, gradually adopting the dark ideologies and practices inherent in Satanism. This process unfolds gradually as participants become increasingly immersed in the rituals and teachings, eventually reshaping their worldview and moral compass.

Furthermore, the rituals themselves are designed to induce fear, create a sense of danger, and challenge societal boundaries. Through the use of symbolism, dramatic ceremonies, and even psychological manipulation, altered states of consciousness can be induced, leading participants to experience intense emotions and altered perceptions of reality.

This psychological manipulation further blurs the distinction between fantasy and reality. As participants navigate these dark and ethereal realms, their sense of self and rationality can become distorted. This can result in a loss of identity and a heightened susceptibility to suggestion and influence from the group and its leaders.

In addition to the ritualistic experiences, individuals who engage in Satanic practices often face social ostracization from society and even their own families. The stigma surrounding Satanic beliefs can lead to social isolation and a sense of alienation that reinforces the participant's loyalty to their chosen path. This isolation can create a self-fulfilling prophecy as individuals seek acceptance and solace within the very groups condemned by society.

In conclusion, an exploration into the psychological effects and impact of participating in Satanic rituals reveals a complex and intriguing endeavor. By examining historical accounts and modern-day cases, it becomes apparent that the allure and subsequent transformation experienced by participants is profound. The power dynamics, manipulation, and isolation inherent in these rituals create ideal conditions for psychological alteration, resulting in a shift in beliefs, behaviors, and even one's sense of self. To genuinely comprehend the depths of the human psyche, one must be willing to confront the darkness that resides within us all by peering into the eye of Satan.

SATANIC WORSHIP AND PERSONAL EMPOWERMENT

In order to gain a comprehensive understanding of personal empowerment in the context of satanic worship, it is imperative to delve into its historical origins and development. The roots of satanic worship can be traced back to ancient civilizations, where the veneration of various deities and powerful entities was a prevalent practice. However, it was during the Middle Ages that satanic worship started to gain notoriety, often being associated with alleged acts of devil worship and black magic.

During the Renaissance period, there was a surge of interest in the realm of the occult and esoteric knowledge. It was during this era that influential figures like Aleister Crowley and Helena Blavatsky emerged, introducing fresh perspectives and practices within the domain of satanic worship. Their teachings placed emphasis on the individual's freedom, challenging societal norms and advocating for personal power and enlightenment.

As time passed, satanic worship underwent evolution and adaptation to align with the changing needs and desires of its adherents. In the modern era, we observe a fusion of diverse occult practices, often drawing inspiration from ancient rituals and esoteric philosophies. It is within this multifaceted landscape that the concept of personal empowerment finds its place.

To comprehensively explore the concept of personal empowerment within satanic worship, it is essential to grasp the fundamental principles of this belief system. At its core, satanic worship celebrates one's capacity to shape their own destiny, unencumbered by external influences or moralistic dogmas. It encourages self-expression and non-conformity, urging individuals to embrace their desires and pursue their passions without reservation.

It can be argued that the act of worshipping Satan itself challenges societal norms and, in doing so, empowers individuals to break free from the constraints of a conformist society. However, personal empowerment within satanic worship transcends mere rebellion. It involves accepting one's true nature, acknowledging the darkness within, and integrating it into one's being. It is a voyage of self-discovery and self-acceptance, where individuals transcend societal expectations and construct their own reality.

Moreover, personal empowerment within satanic worship influences one's self-perception and decision-making. By embracing their desires and pursuing what brings them joy, practitioners of satanic worship develop a strong sense of self-worth and confidence. This newfound empowerment enables them to make decisions that align with their authentic selves, unaffected by external pressures.

Nevertheless, it is important to recognize that personal empowerment within satanic worship is not without its dangers. Like any belief system, there are individuals who may exploit it for personal gain or engage in practices that cause harm to others. It is crucial to differentiate between those who approach satanic worship with integrity and those who merely revel in darkness without comprehending the true essence of its empowering potential.

Through thorough research and interactions with practitioners of satanic worship, I have come to grasp the depth and intricacy of personal empowerment within this belief system. It is not a path suitable for the faint-hearted or those seeking an effortless escape from reality. Rather, it represents a transformative journey towards self-actualization and authenticity.

In conclusion, satanic worship, contrary to widespread misconceptions, offers a distinctive perspective on personal empowerment. It invites individuals to embrace their genuine selves, celebrating their desires and passions without inhibition. By breaking free from societal norms and dogmas, adherents of satanic worship cultivate a sense of self-worth and confidence, which influences their self-perception and decision-making. However, it is crucial to approach satanic worship with discernment and a deep understanding of its empowering potential. Only then can one truly explore the profound realms of personal empowerment within the realm of Satan.

SATANIC WORSHIP AND SOCIAL COHESION

The realm of the occult has always fascinated me, drawing me into its mystical depths. As a paranormal investigator and specialist in the extraordinary, it is my responsibility to explore the unknown and decipher the enigmatic threads that link us to the supernatural. Throughout my journey through the shadowy recesses of the human psyche, I have encountered numerous manifestations of malevolence, yet none as captivating as the realm of Satanic worship.

Satanic worship, with its intricate rituals and esoteric symbolism, has remained enshrouded in mystery and misconceptions for centuries. Often portrayed as purely diabolical and sinister, this practice encompasses more than meets the eye. In my pursuit of knowledge, I embarked on an examination of the role of Satanic worship in fostering social cohesion and nurturing a sense of belonging within Satanic communities.

To commence this undertaking, I ventured into the core of Satanic enclaves, immersing myself in their gatherings and rituals. Initially, what struck me was the strong communal unity these individuals formed. Shared beliefs in the esoteric arts forged an indissoluble connection, a bond formed through defiance of societal norms. In their midst, a sense of belonging prevailed, offering solace and affirmation to those traditionally marginalized by conventional ideologies.

One particular case study brought this sense of cohesion to the fore. I was fortunate to gain access to a Satanic coven secluded in a grand mansion nestled within a dense forest, where darkness seemingly reigned supreme. As a participatory observer, I witnessed their rituals, conducted individual interviews, and experienced firsthand the transformative power of Satanic worship.

The rituals themselves presented a spectacle of theatricality, meticulously orchestrated and imbued with symbolism decipherable solely by a chosen few. It was during these rituals that the true essence of social cohesion became apparent. The rituals served as a metaphorical rite of passage, a baptism into a realm where one's darkest desires were embraced rather than condemned. Through these rituals, individuals shed the constrictions of societal expectations, revealing their authentic selves in the presence of like-minded souls.

Within Satanic communities, individuals discovered acceptance among their peers, liberated from the judgment that had plagued them in the outside world. This acceptance and sense of belonging nurtured self-assurance and facilitated an exploration of their identities without fear of persecution. They were no longer outcasts; they became part of a collective that comprehended and embraced their unconventional choices.

The communal nature of Satanic worship extended beyond the rituals, permeating their daily lives. Similar to any other societal group, Satanic communities engaged in shared activities, traditions, and values. Members convened regularly to discuss their experiences and exchange knowledge, reinforcing their sense of belonging. These interactions not only provided support but also stimulated a shared identity rooted in the pursuit of knowledge and the exploration of the occult.

Throughout my interviews with various members, a recurring theme materialized - the far-reaching impact of Satanic communities on personal lives. Satanic worship, they asserted, empowered them to confront their fears, acknowledge their darkest desires, and embrace their authentic selves. Through the acceptance and validation found within their Satanic circles, they discovered a newfound confidence that resonated in their everyday existence.

While it would be unjust to dismiss the controversies surrounding Satanic worship, it is essential to recognize the positive role it plays in fostering social cohesion and engendering a sense of belonging within Satanic communities. Within these enigmatic rituals and shared beliefs, individuals find solace, acceptance, and the liberty to explore their identities without fear of judgment or condemnation.

As the veil is lifted on the mysteries of Satanic worship, it becomes apparent that beneath the darkness lies a web of human connection. It is through this connection that Satanic communities forge an unassailable bond, providing sanctuary to those traversing the road less taken. In our quest for understanding, let us not underestimate the power of acceptance and belonging, regardless of the unconventionality of their source. For within the realm of Satan, a sense of unity thrives, binding individuals together and guiding them towards self-fulfillment.

SATANIC WORSHIP AND REBELLION

As an investigator specializing in paranormal phenomena, I have dedicated a considerable portion of my career to exploring various aspects of the supernatural. Among the topics that have captivated my attention the most is the practice of satanic worship and rebellion. I am intrigued by the reasons why individuals are drawn to this dark and contentious practice, and what compels them to challenge societal norms and authority through such forms of worship. These are just a few of the inquiries that have become the focus of my research.

To gain a comprehensive understanding of the rebellious nature of satanic worship, it is imperative to delve into its origins and historical context. Satanic worship can be traced back to ancient civilizations and pagan religions, where rituals and sacrifices were performed in order to appease powerful deities. Nevertheless, in modern times, satanic worship has assumed a distinct meaning and purpose. It has become a symbol of rebellion, providing individuals with a means to question societal norms and defy authority.

One explanation for the allure of satanic worship and rebellion is the yearning to break free from the confines of conformity. In a society that often imposes rigid rules and expectations, certain individuals crave the freedom to express themselves in unconventional ways. Satanic worship offers a platform for this expression by presenting a counter-cultural ideology that stands in opposition to the prevailing norms.

Furthermore, satanic worship affords a sense of empowerment to those who feel marginalized or oppressed by societal norms. By aligning themselves with an ideology that challenges traditional values, individuals can find solace and a sense of belonging within a like-minded community. This community fosters an atmosphere of acceptance and understanding, allowing its members to freely explore their innermost desires and beliefs, regardless of their controversial nature.

Another factor that contributes to the allure of satanic worship and rebellion is the notion of forbidden knowledge. Satanic rituals often involve the exploration of occult practices and esoteric teachings, which are deemed taboo in many societies. This fascination with the forbidden generates an air of mystery and intrigue, enticing individuals to seek out this hidden knowledge in pursuit of a deeper understanding of the world.

The rebellious nature of satanic worship also arises from its association with contentious figures and ideas. For centuries, Satan has been depicted as a symbol of defiance against God and traditional religious dogma. This association with defiance and rebellion instills satan worshippers with a sense of superiority and power, as they perceive themselves as part of an enlightened few who have liberated themselves from the restraints of religious indoctrination.

Moreover, satanic worship allows individuals to indulge in their most forbidden desires without the judgment or scrutiny of mainstream society. Satanic rituals often involve acts of sexual liberation, hedonism, and even violence, all of which are deemed immoral by societal standards. By engaging in these acts within the framework of satanic worship, individuals can experience a thrilling liberation, giving them a sense of control over their own lives and bodies.

However, it is vital to acknowledge that not all individuals attracted to satanic worship are motivated solely by rebellion or a desire to challenge authority. Some may be in search of a deeper spiritual connection, utilizing satanic practices as a means to explore the darker aspects of their own psyche. For these individuals, satanic worship becomes a tool for self-discovery and personal growth, rather than an act of rebellion against societal norms.

To conclude, the allure of satanic worship and rebellion lies in its capacity to provide individuals with a platform to challenge societal norms, question authority, and indulge in their most forbidden desires. Whether driven by a yearning for freedom from conformity, empowerment through opposition, or the pursuit of forbidden knowledge, satanic worship offers an alternative path for those seeking a different understanding of themselves and the world around them. Nevertheless, it is imperative to approach this topic with caution and an open mind, as the realm of the supernatural can be simultaneously fascinating and perilous. Only through meticulous research and understanding can we hope to unveil the truth behind the allure of satanic worship and rebellion.

SATANIC WORSHIP AND MORALITY

As an investigator specializing in the paranormal and the inexplicable, my exploration has taken me into the realms of various belief systems and exposed me to a wide range of moral frameworks. However, few have captivated my interest as much as the practices of Satanic worshipers. Their unique perspective on morality challenges conventional social norms and provokes us to question the very foundations upon which our moral constructs are built.

In order to gain a comprehensive understanding of the moral code adhered to by Satanic worshipers, I undertook an extensive research endeavor. I immersed myself in their literary works, dissecting both ancient texts and modern manifestos. It swiftly became apparent that their sense of morality is deeply rooted in a complex amalgamation of historical context, philosophical inquiry, and personal liberation.

Central to the tenets of Satanic worship is the element of individualism. While society often encourages conformity and the suppression of one's true self, proponents of Satanism champion the freedom to embrace one's authentic nature. They reject the notion of self-denial and wholeheartedly embrace self-indulgence, placing the well-being and desires of the individual at the forefront. In this context, the determination of right and wrong is not contingent on external moral authorities, but rests solely on personal choice and consent.

For practitioners of Satanic worship, moral guidelines are further influenced by the Satanic sins and virtues delineated in Anton LaVey's "The Satanic Bible." These sins, such as stupidity, pretentiousness, and conformity to herd mentality, encapsulate behaviors that impede personal growth and freedom. Conversely, the virtues embraced by Satanic worship, such as indulgence, compassion, and responsibility, encourage the pursuit of pleasure and the advancement of one's own life as well as the lives of others.

It is of paramount importance to stress, however, that these moral principles are not intended to foster a hedonistic society devoid of empathy and altruism. On the contrary, adherents of Satanic worship firmly believe in the concept of reciprocal relationships, wherein an individual's pursuit of pleasure and self-fulfillment is aligned with the welfare of others. This perspective challenges the conventional notion that selflessness and sacrifice are the only avenues towards moral rectitude.

In my comprehensive investigation, I delved into the historical context and rituals associated with Satanic worship in order to gain deeper insight into their moral framework. One notable aspect that emerged was the affinity for reclaiming symbols and practices traditionally associated with the Christian faith. Satanic rituals often incorporate elements such as inverted crosses, pentagrams, and black candles, deliberately designed to be provocative. While these practices may jar and challenge societal sensibilities, they serve as a means of expressing individual freedom and rejecting oppressive religious dogmas.

To attain a more profound comprehension of the moral perspective upheld by Satanic worshipers, I conducted interviews with various individuals who identified as such. Amongst them was Lilith, a young woman who had been actively practicing Satanism for over a decade. She emphasized the paramount significance of personal autonomy and the outright rejection of absolutist moral codes. Lilith elucidated that the principles of Satanism provide her with the liberty to explore her desires and make ethical decisions predicated upon the consent and self-determination of all involved parties.

Contrary to prevailing misconceptions, those who embrace Satanic worship place great emphasis on the importance of consent and personal boundaries. They perceive non-consensual actions, such as rape, as abhorrent and fundamentally contradictory to their moral framework. In fact, many Satanic organizations enforce stringent rules concerning consent and actively advocate for the cultivation of consent education and awareness.

Delving deeper into the moral framework championed by Satanic worshipers, I encountered a fascinating paradox. While Satanic principles may indeed champion indulgence and the unbridled pursuit of one's desires, they simultaneously underscore the responsibility to accept the consequences of one's actions. Satanism ardently advocates for personal accountability, firmly asserting that individuals must take ownership of their choices and acknowledge the impact they have on themselves and others. This notion of responsible hedonism is a pivotal element in understanding the ethical principles intrinsic to Satanic worship.

The investigation into the moral framework of Satanic worshipers compelled me to challenge my deep-seated assumptions and scrutinize the very concept of morality itself. While their perspective diverges markedly from conventional societal norms, it is of the utmost importance to approach it with an open and receptive mindset, seeking understanding of the underlying motivations and principles. Only through the pursuit of knowledge and comprehension can we transcend the limitations of our own beliefs and actively engage in a broader and more nuanced discourse pertaining to the complexities of moral philosophy.

SATANIC WORSHIP AND TABOO

As a professional paranormal investigator and specialist in the realm of the supernatural, I have always been drawn to the darker aspects that exist within this field. Specifically, my attention has been captured by the controversial and taboo practices related to Satanic worship. The fascination and curiosity surrounding this forbidden practice transcend social boundaries and captivate individuals from all walks of life. The purpose of this chapter is to thoroughly explore the reasons behind such fascination and curiosity, as well as to examine the impact it has on those who dare to venture into its depths.

In order to comprehend the allure of Satanic worship, it is imperative to recognize the power that the forbidden holds. Throughout history, there have always been practices and beliefs considered to be forbidden or taboo in society. These acts have been shrouded in secrecy, spoken of in hushed tones, and have subsequently created an air of intrigue and mystique that has attracted individuals towards them. Satanic worship finds itself within this category, with its blend of blasphemy, rebellion, and the allure of acquiring forbidden knowledge.

Within human nature lies an inherent curiosity and a desire to explore the unknown. This curiosity propels us to discover the mysteries that the world holds. Satanic worship taps into this internal curiosity by offering a path that is deemed forbidden, promising access to hidden realms and supernatural abilities. The allure lies in the possibility of transcending the ordinary and experiencing something extraordinary, an existence that exists beyond our grasp.

Additionally, Satanic worship possesses a particular appeal to those who feel disillusioned by traditional religious institutions. Despite their virtues and teachings, organized religions can often impose limitations on thoughts and actions, thereby restricting individuals. It is precisely this rebellion against such restrictions that attracts certain individuals towards Satanic worship. By embracing the Satanic path, they reject societal and religious norms, and in doing so, seek a sense of freedom and liberation from the constraints that bind them.

When exploring the allure of Satanic worship, it is pivotal to acknowledge the role that symbolism and ritual play. Every form of worship, whether Satanic or otherwise, depends on rituals and symbols to evoke the desired spiritual experience. Satanic rituals, with their intricate symbolism and dark imagery, create an atmosphere that is both chilling and captivating. The act of engaging in these rituals is a form of catharsis, allowing individuals to tap into their deepest desires and fears.

Furthermore, the taboo associated with Satanic worship fuels its allure by imparting an air of danger and excitement to the practice. When something is forbidden, it automatically becomes more enticing. It becomes a challenge to the individual, daring them to enter the unknown and transgress societal norms. This allure speaks to the rebellious nature that resides within each of us, provoking a desire to defy conventions and norms.

The impact of Satanic worship on individuals varies, as it delves into the depths of the psyche, pushing boundaries and challenging beliefs. For some, the fascination remains superficial, a mere flirtation with the forbidden. These individuals may experiment with Satanic rituals, enticed by the notion of rebelling against societal norms, but ultimately do not fully embrace the path. Their experience leaves them with a sense of excitement and adventure, but lacks any significant long-term impact.

However, for others, the allure of Satanic worship proves to be transformative. It becomes a journey of self-discovery and exploration, delving into the deepest recesses of their psyche. Embracing Satanic worship allows these individuals to confront their fears, desires, and uncertainties head-on. It compels them to question their own beliefs and motivations, ultimately leading to a reevaluation of their relationship with spirituality and the world at large.

To conclude, the allure surrounding Satanic worship as a taboo and forbidden practice is undeniably powerful. Its appeal lies in its ability to tap into our inherent curiosity and our yearning to explore the unknown. By embracing the Satanic path, individuals seek freedom from societal restrictions and express a yearning to rebel against the norm. The allure of Satanic worship rests within its rituals, symbols, and the danger associated with prohibited acts. While the impact on individuals varies, for certain individuals, it becomes a transformative journey of self-exploration. Satanic worship acts as a mirror, reflecting our deepest fears, desires, and uncertainties, compelling us to question our own beliefs and motivations. In this exploration, we are ultimately confronted with our own humanity in its most vulnerable and intriguing form.

SATANIC WORSHIP AND SOCIAL TRANSFORMATION

Since embarking on my journey as a paranormal investigator and specialist of the strange, I have been captivated by the intricate relationship between Satanic worship and its capacity to incite social transformation and challenge established power structures. In this chapter, my aim is to thoroughly explore this complex phenomenon by examining its historical context, evolution over time, and the broader impact it has had on society.

To comprehend the potential for Satanic worship to facilitate social transformation, it is imperative that we first delve into its origins. Throughout history, Satanic worship finds its roots in ancient pagan religions and the veneration of deities associated with darkness, chaos, and rebellion against established order. Mainstream religions commonly demonized these early forms of worship, seeking to eradicate these practices due to the perceived threat they posed to societal stability.

During the Middle Ages, the repression and persecution of any alternative belief systems intensified, with Satanic worship becoming synonymous with heresy and witchcraft. The apprehension and condemnation surrounding these practices only served to intensify their allure for those seeking to challenge the dominant power structures of the era.

Transitioning to the modern era, we witness the emergence of Satanic worship as a countercultural movement. The ideals of individualism, personal freedom, and rebellion against societal norms propelled this movement, attracting individuals disillusioned by the oppressive and restrictive nature of mainstream society. Here, Satanic worship not only functioned as a religious practice but also served as a means of expressing individuality and resistance against established power structures.

Many argue that the potential for Satanic worship to contribute to social transformation lies in its ability to defy societal taboos and push boundaries. By embracing darkness, adherents of this faith aim to redefine morality and question the very essence of societal norms. Through this act of rebellion, new ideas, ideologies, and forms of social organization can emerge.

A crucial aspect of Satanic worship's potential for social transformation lies in its subversion of the dominant religious narrative. Throughout history, mainstream religion has played a pivotal role in upholding power structures and reinforcing societal hierarchies. Conversely, Satanic worship operates on the fringes, audaciously challenging the authority of established institutions and proposing a radical alternative.

Additionally, we must consider the influence of Satanic worship on various art forms, literature, and popular culture. In these domains, we often encounter a profound fascination with the occult, ritualistic practices, and the darker facets of human existence. By challenging established norms and pushing the boundaries of what is considered socially acceptable, Satanic worshippers have contributed to the evolution of art and cultural expression, giving rise to new narratives and questioning traditional power structures.

Moreover, the ascent of Satanic worship has frequently been intertwined with political and social movements striving for change. From the countercultural movements of the 1960s and 1970s to the feminist movement, from LGBTQ+ rights activism to the fight against racial discrimination, Satanic worshippers have frequently aligned themselves with and supported those seeking to dismantle oppressive systems that perpetuate inequality and injustice.

While Satanic worship holds the potential to contribute to social transformation, it is essential to acknowledge that not all practitioners are motivated by a desire for change. Much like any belief system or religious practice, Satanic worship encompasses a diverse spectrum of individuals with varying intentions and motivations. While some genuinely seek to challenge power structures, others may be drawn to the aesthetic appeal or the perceived power associated with Satanic symbols and rituals.

In conclusion, the potential for Satanic worship to contribute to social transformation and challenge established power structures is undeniable. By embracing darkness, rebellion, and subversion, Satanic worshippers possess the ability to redefine societal norms, question religious authority, and foster the emergence of new ideas. However, it is imperative to approach this phenomenon with discernment and recognize that the motivations behind Satanic worship can vary greatly. As a paranormal investigator and specialist of the strange, it is my duty to explore this subject matter with an open mind, seeking a more profound understanding of the multifaceted nature of Satanic worship and its potential societal impact.

SATANIC WORSHIP AND SPIRITUALITY

Examining the spiritual dimensions and experiences associated with Satanic worship and its impact on individuals' quest for meaning and transcendence.

As an individual who investigates paranormal phenomena and specializes in the unusual, I have extensively explored the depths of human beliefs and practices. Satanic worship is a particularly intriguing subject for its controversial nature and significant influence on those who engage with it. It is a realm that possesses enigmatic qualities that beckon the curious, igniting their sense of rebellion and desire to explore the unknown. Within this chapter, my aim is to unravel the mystique surrounding Satanic worship, meticulously examining its spiritual dimensions while delving into the impact it has on individuals' profound yearning for purpose and transcendence.

To truly grasp the essence of Satanic worship, one must penetrate the misconceptions and popular culture portrayals that have cast an undeserved shadow over this practice, leading to its misunderstanding. Contrary to widespread belief, Satanic worship is not simply centered around the veneration of a literal entity known as Satan. Instead, it encompasses a complex amalgamation of beliefs and rituals that defy societal norms and conventions. It is an approach that champions individualism, self-actualization, and recognizes the transformative potential inherent in humanity.

An argument could be made that Satanic worship emerges from an inner yearning for personal liberation and a rejection of the restrictions imposed by society. Its adherents view themselves as dissidents, pioneers of individual freedom who refuse to conform to established religious doctrines and cultural values. In their defiance, they discover a profound sense of agency, forging a connection with an alternative spirituality that holds the promise of personal growth and enlightenment.

The spiritual experiences associated with Satanic worship cover a vast range, from the exalted to the profane. Through intense rituals, practitioners aim to surpass their mortal limitations, establishing connections with forces that transcend the material world. These rituals often involve elaborate ceremonies, invocation of deities, and esoteric practices that blur the distinction between the physical and spiritual realms.

For some, embracing their personal darkness becomes a conduit for personal transformation and spiritual elevation. By recognizing and integrating elements of themselves that society tends to perceive as "dark," individuals can fully explore their own potential. The occult practices of Satanic worship become a means to access this inner power, unlocking the hidden facets of their identity and ultimately shaping their own destinies.

Nonetheless, the allure of Satanic worship also harbors its perils. The pursuit of enlightenment through the celebration of darkness is not without consequences. As individuals venture deeper into the realm of the occult and engage in forbidden practices, they run the risk of losing touch with their own humanity. The preoccupation with personal power and the desire to manipulate forces beyond their comprehension can lead to a descent into madness or, even worse, possession by malevolent entities.

Without a doubt, the impact of Satanic worship on individuals' quest for meaning and transcendence is a double-edged sword. It offers liberation and self-empowerment, but balanced against the potential for self-destruction. The spiritual exploration of Satanic worship demands a delicate equilibrium between delving into the unknown and maintaining one's moral compass.

In conclusion, the examination of Satanic worship and spirituality reveals a multi-faceted tapestry of belief systems, rituals, and personal journeys. It provides an avenue for personal rebellion and exploration, challenging established norms and embracing the forbidden. However, this is a pathway fraught with danger, where individuals must skillfully navigate treacherous waters in search of their true selves within the shadows. The spiritual dimensions and experiences associated with Satanic worship possess the ability to both enlighten and corrupt individuals, making this subject worthy of profound contemplation and exploration.

As an investigator of paranormal phenomena and a specialist in the extraordinary, I strongly urge caution to those who venture into the darkness of Satanic worship. It is a realm where the line between enlightenment and damnation becomes blurred, and one's very soul hangs in the balance. Only those with a genuine thirst for knowledge and an unwavering spirit should dare to tread upon this esoteric path, for the rewards and risks alike can be of immense significance.

<h1 style="text-align:center">9</h1>

SATANIC WORSHIP IN POPULAR CULTURE

SATANIC THEMES IN LITERATURE

In order to comprehensively comprehend the significance of satanic themes in literature, an extensive analysis of historical texts and modern novels has been conducted, focusing on their portrayals, symbolism, and underlying messages. This journey has led to a profound understanding of the undeniable power that these themes exert over our collective subconscious.

The classic literary works abound in satanic undertones. John Milton's epic poem "Paradise Lost" serves as a prime example, with Satan himself assuming a central role, as his fall from grace serves as the catalyst for the entire narrative. Milton's masterful command of the literary craft is evident in his portrayal of Satan as a seductive and cunning figure capable of luring mankind into sin.

Likewise, Nathaniel Hawthorne's "The Scarlet Letter" explores the theme of sin and the consequences faced by those who indulge in forbidden desires. The character of Roger Chillingworth personifies the vengeful spirit of Satan, driven by his desire to exact punishment and destruction. The satanic influence exerted by Chillingworth over the other characters in the novel is palpable in the unraveling of their fates and the ultimate tragedy that befalls them.

In the realm of contemporary literature, satanic themes continue to hold sway. A notable example is Dan Brown's best-selling novel "The Da Vinci Code." While the focus of the book is not explicitly on satanic worship, Brown skillfully weaves together a complex tale of hidden knowledge and secret societies, using symbolism and historical references that have long been associated with the devil. The pursuit of knowledge and power depicted in this story mirrors the timeless temptation faced by humanity in various religious and mythical traditions.

Bret Easton Ellis's controversial work "American Psycho" is another contemporary novel that delves into satanic themes. The protagonist, Patrick Bateman, can be viewed as a modern-day incarnation of the devil himself. His hedonistic and sadistic desires, coupled with his charismatic persona, mirror the diabolical nature of Satan. Through Bateman's descent into the depths of depravity, Ellis challenges readers by bringing to the forefront the disturbing presence of evil that lurks within our society.

By examining these examples, as well as countless others, it becomes evident that the portrayal of satanic themes in literature serves a broader purpose. It permits an exploration of the darker dimensions of human nature, the eternal conflict between good and evil, and the consequences of succumbing to temptation. By confronting these themes within the pages of a book, readers are able to reflect on their own choices and analyze the forces that drive them.

Furthermore, the presence of satanic themes in literature also challenges societal norms and religious beliefs, stimulating contemplation and debate. By delving into the forbidden and the taboo, authors shed light on questions of morality, free will, and the nature of evil. Through their narratives, readers are encouraged to question prevailing beliefs and confront their own preconceived notions about the world surrounding them.

As a specialist in the unusual, one cannot dismiss the potential impact that satanic themes in literature have on the minds of readers. The power of storytelling lies in its capacity to transport us to both real and imagined worlds, enabling us to confront our deepest fears and desires. Satanic themes in literature tap into our inherent fascination with the unknown and the forbidden, offering us a glimpse into the darkest corners of our psyche.

In conclusion, the portrayal of satanic worship and themes in literature, whether in classic works or contemporary novels, serves a profound purpose. It challenges our beliefs, forces us to grapple with the eternal struggle between good and evil, and provides a platform for exploring the depths of human nature. Ultimately, the presence of satanic themes in literature speaks to our shared yearning to comprehend and make sense of the mysteries that envelop us, even those that reside within our own being.

SATANIC WORSHIP IN FILM AND TELEVISION

As a paranormal investigator and specialist in the study of the occult, I have always been captivated by the portrayal of Satanic worship in film and television. This subject matter is undoubtedly controversial, often evoking strong emotions and impassioned debates. Yet, for those willing to explore this shadowy realm, it offers a unique glimpse into the human psyche and the allure of forbidden knowledge.

One cannot discuss the representation of Satanic worship in the realm of entertainment without acknowledging the iconic characters that have arisen from this morbid fascination. One of the most well-known figures in this context is Anton LaVey, the founder of the Church of Satan, who portrayed himself in the film "Rosemary's Baby" (1968). LaVey's involvement in the film not only added a sense of authenticity but also infused a bone-chilling realism into the fictional storyline. Of particular note is the fact that during this period, rumors of Satanic rituals and secret societies were proliferating, creating an atmosphere of fear and paranoia. LaVey's depiction as a charismatic and enigmatic figure only served to heighten these anxieties.

Another indelible character that comes to mind is the infamous Damien Thorn from "The Omen" (1976). The film follows the trajectory of a young boy, believed to be the Antichrist, as he embarks on a path of devastation. Damien is portrayed as an innocent-looking child with a disarming smile, intensifying the suspense and horror surrounding his character. The spine-tingling moments when he reveals his true nature and the revelation of his Satanic lineage comprise some of the most memorable scenes in the horror genre.

Similarly, the portrayal of Satanic worship in "Rosemary's Baby" and "The Omen" underscores the power of manipulation and deception. In both films, unsuspecting characters are ensnared in a web of darkness, where their lives become entangled with the forces of evil. The notion that anyone, irrespective of their innocence or purity, can be exploited as a pawn by Satanic cults is both terrifying and thought-provoking.

Looking beyond these iconic figures, there is a plethora of other films and television shows that have delved into the realm of Satanic worship. "The Exorcist" (1973), arguably one of the most influential horror films of all time, delves into the possession of a young girl and the desperate attempts to save her soul. The film's portrayal of demonic possession and the rituals employed to liberate the victim from the clutches of malevolence have become ingrained in the annals of horror history.

In recent years, television shows like "American Horror Story" have also explored the world of Satanic worship, showcasing the enduring interest and fascination surrounding this dark subject matter. The third season of the show, titled "Coven," revolves around a coven of witches and a voodoo priestess, who find themselves pitted against a formidable group of Satanists. The clash between the forces of good and evil, as well as the exploration of Satanism as a religious practice, adds a layer of complexity to the narrative. The show adeptly navigates themes of power, control, and the blurred boundaries between good and evil, compelling viewers to question their own convictions and biases.

It is important to note that while these depictions of Satanic worship in film and television undoubtedly perpetuate sensationalism and reinforce certain stereotypes, they can also serve as a platform for deeper discussions and explorations of the human condition. Satanic worship functions as a mirror reflecting society's fears, anxieties, and desires, affording us the opportunity to examine our own beliefs and probe the nature of good and evil.

In conclusion, the portrayal of Satanic worship in film and television is a fascinating and thought-provoking subject. From the iconic characters that have become fixtures in horror cinema to the examination of the human psyche and the timeless struggle between good and evil, these depictions offer a distinctive window into the darker facets of human existence. While they undoubtedly entertain and shock audiences, they also serve as a reflection of society's fears, compelling us to confront our own beliefs and biases. By scrutinizing the portrayals of Satanic worship in popular culture, we can acquire a deeper understanding of ourselves and the world we inhabit.

SATANIC SYMBOLISM IN MUSIC

As an investigator specializing in paranormal phenomena, my professional endeavors have led me to explore various aspects of the supernatural and macabre. Among these inquiries, one topic that has piqued my interest is the presence of Satanic symbolism in music. Spanning across genres, from the haunting melodies of rock to the rhythmic beats of hip-hop, the music industry has been permeated with the use of Satanic imagery and themes for several decades. Both artists and listeners alike have been captivated and intrigued by this phenomenon. In this particular chapter, we will embark on a journey to thoroughly examine the depths of Satanic symbolism and themes in music across diverse genres, delicately peeling back the layers of artistic expression in order to uncover fascinating connections to the occult.

In order to fully comprehend the significance of Satanic symbolism in music, it is crucial to establish a historical timeline that spans the origins of this controversial trend. The 1960s marked the emergence of a wave of rock bands that pushed boundaries and challenged societal norms. One noteworthy example is The Beatles, renowned for their experimental approach. Their influential album "Revolver", released in 1966, is widely believed to have acted as a catalyst for the rise of Satanic symbolism in music. With tracks such as "Tomorrow Never Knows" and "She Said She Said", the band delved into themes of spirituality and enlightenment, unintentionally unleashing a floodgate for the emergence of darker expressions within the realm of music.

The late 1960s and early 1970s witnessed the escalation of the fascination with Satanic imagery through the rise of heavy metal. English bands like Black Sabbath and Led Zeppelin incorporated occult themes and mysticism into their lyrics and album artwork. Notable albums such as Black Sabbath's self-titled debut and Led Zeppelin's "Stairway to Heaven" became classics, mesmerizing listeners with their enigmatic lyrics and distorted guitar riffs, causing a blur to form between reality and the occult.

Advancing into the 1980s, the ascent of glam metal and shock rock introduced a fresh wave of Satanic symbolism. Bands such as W.A.S.P., Motley Crue, and Alice Cooper fashioned larger-than-life personas that were synonymous with rebellion and blasphemy. Their stage performances were characterized by elaborate spectacles featuring pyrotechnics, illusory sacrifices, and an overall aura of peril. The intention of these artists was to provoke emotions and shock audiences, exploiting Satanic symbolism as a means to captivate and challenge societal norms.

The 1990s bore witness to the arrival of alternative and grunge music, thus leading to a shift in the utilization of Satanic symbolism. Although the overt display of Satanic imagery decreased during this period, bands such as Nirvana and Marilyn Manson employed subtler, metaphorical references to explore societal issues and personal struggles. Tracks such as Nirvana's "Heart-Shaped Box" and Manson's "Disposable Teens" delved into themes of alienation and disillusionment, drawing parallels to the darkness frequently associated with Satanic symbolism.

As the 21st century unraveled, even hip-hop embraced the allure of Satanic symbolism. Artists like Jay-Z, Kanye West, and Tyler, The Creator incorporated occult references into their music and visual aesthetics. Examples of this are Jay-Z's notorious Rockefeller Records logo, which depicts an owl, and Tyler, The Creator's album "Goblin" that features demonic imagery. These artists skillfully integrate Satanic symbolism into their artistic expression, resulting in a blurring of the line between reality and the occult.

While the use of Satanic symbolism in music has triggered both fascination and controversy over the years, it is vital to differentiate between artists who utilize these themes as a form of artistic expression and those who actively engage in Satanic practices. Many musicians adopt Satanic imagery for its shock value or to explore provocative themes, drawing inspiration from the mysterious and forbidden. However, this does not necessarily suggest endorsement or adherence to Satanic beliefs.

Nevertheless, it is essential to recognize that there are artists who genuinely align themselves with Satanic ideologies and practices. These individuals aim to challenge religious structures, societal norms, and ideologies by embracing the symbol of Satan as a form of rebellion and personal freedom. While the beliefs and actions of these artists may unsettle some, they contribute to the ongoing discussion surrounding the intersection of art, spirituality, and personal expression.

In conclusion, the presence of Satanic symbolism in music has woven itself into a tapestry that spans across multiple genres, from rock to hip-hop. It serves as a powerful tool for artists to challenge conventions, evoke emotions, and plunge into the depths of their creative expression. Whether employed as a metaphorical device or embraced as an act of rebellion, this exploration of darkness and the occult through music continues to captivate and captivate audiences worldwide. As we venture deeper into the realm of Satan, it becomes apparent that the boundaries between art and the supernatural are often indistinguishable, serving as a testament to the enthralling power of music as a gateway to the unknown.

SATANIC IMAGERY IN VISUAL ARTS

The earliest evidence of Satanic imagery in visual arts can be traced back to ancient civilizations such as Mesopotamia and Egypt. In Mesopotamian mythology, the god Pazuzu was often depicted with a serpent-like body, wings, and a fierce expression, embodying the demonic and malevolent forces of the underworld. Similarly, in Egyptian mythology, Set, the god of chaos and evil, was often portrayed as a creature with the head of an animal and a human body, exhibiting the duality of good and evil.

Moving forward in time, during the Middle Ages, Satanic imagery became more prevalent in Christian art as a means to depict temptation, sin, and the battle between good and evil. Paintings such as Hieronymus Bosch's "The Garden of Earthly Delights" and Pieter Bruegel the Elder's "The Triumph of Death" depict nightmarish landscapes filled with grotesque creatures, monstrous figures, and explicit scenes of debauchery. These works not only served as cautionary tales but also as reflections of the anxieties and uncertainties of the time.

In Renaissance art, the popularity of Satanic imagery continued to rise, especially in the works of masters such as Albrecht Dürer and Hans Baldung. Dürer's engraving "The Knight, Death, and the Devil" portrays a knight being followed by the personifications of death and the devil, symbolizing the constant presence of temptation and evil. Baldung's "Witches' Sabbath" depicts a gathering of witches engaged in various Satanic rituals, highlighting society's fascination and fear of witchcraft during that period.

More recently, Satanic imagery has been embraced by artists as a form of rebellion against societal norms and religious dogmas. The surrealist movement, in particular, has incorporated Satanic symbolism to explore the depths of the subconscious and challenge conventional ideas. Salvador Dalí's painting "The

Persistence of Memory" creates a sense of unease and disorientation, using melting clocks and distorted figures to evoke a dreamlike and otherworldly realm. By incorporating the Satanic into surrealism, artists can push boundaries and redefine traditional expression.

Today, contemporary artists continue to incorporate Satanic imagery in provocative and innovative ways. Installation artist Ron Mueck's sculpture "Dead Dad" presents a hyperrealistic depiction of the artist's deceased father lying naked on the floor, surrounded by heaps of discarded clothing. This unsettling piece confronts viewers with their mortality and the undeniable presence of death. Similarly, Damien Hirst explores Satanic imagery through his series of "spin paintings," which draw inspiration from the aesthetics of circular motion used in Satanic rituals. The chaotic and unpredictable patterns created by these paintings symbolize the uncontrollable forces of the demonic and provide commentary on the nature of existence itself.

It is important to recognize that Satanic imagery in visual arts may not always aim to promote or glorify evil. Artists often incorporate such symbolism to provoke thought, challenge societal norms, and delve into the darker aspects of human nature. By confronting these taboo subjects, they urge viewers to question their beliefs and confront their deepest fears.

However, the use of Satanic imagery in visual arts also invites controversy and criticism from religious groups and conservative individuals who perceive it as a direct affront to their faith. This clash of opinions and perspectives further enhances the allure and mystery surrounding Satanic artwork.

In conclusion, Satanic imagery and symbolism have been incorporated into visual arts throughout various historical periods, from ancient civilizations to the modern era. It serves as a reflection of society's fears, desires, and uncertainties, allowing artists to explore the depths of the human psyche and challenge conventional norms. Whether used as a cautionary tale, a means of rebellion, or a tool for introspection, Satanic imagery continues to captivate and provoke viewers, making it an enduring and enigmatic subject in the world of art.

SATANIC WORSHIP IN VIDEO GAMES

As an expert in paranormal investigation and the study of anomalous phenomena, my professional focus is dedicated to uncovering the enigmatic secrets that lie concealed within the shadows. In my unyielding pursuit to comprehend and penetrate the mysteries of the occult, I have encountered an intriguing facet in the realm of contemporary entertainment: the prevalent inclusion of satanic worship and themes within the domain of video games. Within this chapter, we shall embark on an exploration of the intricate components and storyline trajectories that portray depictions of satanic worship within the world of video games.

To truly grasp the evolution of satanic worship within the medium of video games, it is essential to begin by examining the historical timeline of this phenomenon. The initial inklings of satanic themes within the realm of gaming can be traced back to the latter part of the 1980s and early 1990s, which witnessed the release of games such as "Doom" and "Mortal Kombat". These particular games, characterized by their intense levels of violence and ominous imagery, gave rise to significant controversy and raised concerns amongst parental figures and religious congregations. Although these games did not explicitly depict satanic worship, they established the groundwork for the subsequent exploration of these themes within the realm of the gaming industry.

Subsequently, during the late 1990s, there emerged a video game entitled "Silent Hill", a work that introduced a new standard of horror by incorporating elements of satanic worship into its narrative structure. Set in the foreboding township by the name of Silent Hill, the game embarked upon an exploration of the psychological and spiritual torments endured by its central characters. Drawing extensively from occult symbolism and lore, the game recounts a tale wherein the protagonist, Harry Mason, becomes ensnared within a haunting world populated by bizarre creatures and beset by secretive cults engaged in the veneration of an ancient deity known as "The Order". This pioneering investigation into satanic worship constituted a preliminary foundation for subsequent video games to delve deeper into this audacious and controversial realm.

Concomitant with the expansion of technological capacities within video games, there was witnessed a corresponding increase in their ability to depict intricate and immersive virtual environments. During the early 2000s, games such as "Dante's Inferno" and "Devil May Cry" whisked players away on a descent into Hell itself, encompassing portrayals of satanic figures and themes presented in a visually striking and visceral manner. These games not only encompassed within their gameplay mechanics satanic elements, but also ventured into the moral quandaries and ethical dilemmas confronted by their protagonists as they contended against the forces of darkness. The inclusion of satanic worship as an elemental component within these games further imbued the overall experience with a heightened sense of complexity and profoundity.

More recently, open-world role-playing games have amassed tremendous popularity, granting players the ability to immerse themselves within expansive and intricately designed virtual realms. Games such as "The Elder Scrolls V: Skyrim" and "Dragon Age: Origins" have capitalized on the abundant tapestry of religious and mythological lore, assimilating satanic elements into their respective narratives. These games, in turn, afford players the opportunity to explore the ramifications of their actions and engage in profound moral decision-making, oftentimes profoundly overlaid by involvements with satanic worship or occult practices.

The manifestation of satanic worship within the context of video games not only serves to captivate and enthral players but also ignites significant discussions concerning the boundaries of entertainment and the potential effects it can have upon our collective psyche. While some individuals contend that these games engender the propagation of immoral conduct and desensitization toward violence, others assert that they provide a platform that fosters the examination of intricate moral quandaries and a deeper exploration of the darker recesses intrinsic to the human experience.

As a dedicated paranormal investigator, I do not adopt a stance of moral judgment regarding the inclusion of satanic worship within video games. Instead, I perceive it as an unprecedented opportunity for introspection and understanding. By scrutinizing these games and their portrayal of satanic themes with meticulous attention, we stand afforded a unique perspective that advances our comprehension of our individual beliefs, fears, and desires. Regardless of whether we choose to engage personally with such games or not, it is imperative to acknowledge and accept that they are an undeniable component amidst our contemporary cultural landscape.

In conclusion, the presence of satanic worship within the arena of video games has burgeoned into a progressively prevalent and controversial subject of discourse. Ranging from the nascent era represented by games like "Doom" to the immersive and morally intricate universes of more contemporary titles, video games have acclimated to the exploration of satanic themes as a means to captivate, provoke, and challenge their players. By deliberating upon the prominence of satanic worship within video games and delving into the integral gameplay elements and narrative arcs surrounding this phenomenon, we may achieve a profound comprehension of the consequential impact and the innate significance of these digital experiences upon our amassed consciousness.

SATANIC INFLUENCES IN FASHION AND SUBCULTURES

In order to fully comprehend the extent of this influence, it was imperative for me to thoroughly immerse myself in the world of fashion and its connection to Satanic worship. I dedicated numerous hours to conducting research, meticulously analyzing fashion trends, runway shows, and the visual elements that have become synonymous with the dark aesthetic. It became abundantly clear that Satanic symbols, including inverted crosses and pentagrams, were not only present but revered within many fashion subcultures.

A notable exemplification is observed within the gothic subculture, often associated with an appreciation for the dark and macabre. The goth scene has long embraced Satanic symbolism as a means of self-expression. From the widely recognized band t-shirts featuring inverted crosses to the elegant, yet unsettling, fashion statements adorned with pentagrams, the undeniable presence of Satanic influence is pervasive within the gothic fashion realm.

A closer examination of the metal scene reveals a similar narrative. Renowned for its aggressive sound and rebellious attitude, metal has consistently pushed the boundaries of accepted societal norms. It is within this context that Satanic imagery thrives. Bands such as Black Sabbath and Slayer paved the way for the fusion of occult symbolism and musical expression. In this subculture, band merchandise often serves as a visual representation of their devotion to the darker forces at play.

However, it is crucial to emphasize that the existence of Satanic influences in fashion and subcultures does not necessarily equate to a dedication to Satanic worship. Many individuals within these subcultures simply find solace and empowerment in these symbols and aesthetics. Nevertheless, there are those who actively partake in Satanic rituals and worship the dark forces represented within these fashion trends.

In order to gain a deeper understanding of the mysterious realm of Satanic worship, I sought out individuals who possess firsthand knowledge of these practices. Through interviews with self-proclaimed Satanists, my intention was not only to grasp their beliefs but also to uncover the extent of their impact on fashion and subcultures. What I discovered was a complex interweaving of narratives.

The Satanists I engaged with shared tales of clandestine rituals performed in undisclosed locations, secret societies, and the allure of the forbidden. They elucidated how these practices have played a significant role in shaping the elusive aspects of fashion, contributing to its darker realms. They articulated how the mainstream adoption of Satanic symbolism has diluted its true meaning, reducing it to a mere fashion statement.

As I delved further into my research, I serendipitously encountered an entire subculture entirely dedicated to Satanic fashion. Within this niche community, individuals proudly exhibit garments and accessories embellished with Satanic symbols, openly showcasing their devotion through their sartorial choices. These individuals have created a space where the rituals of Satanism and fashion seamlessly intertwine, forging

a distinctive and individualistic identity within broader subcultures.

However, it is crucial to refrain from sensationalizing or
demonizing these subcultures, as they serve as reflections of
the intricate human psyche and the myriad ways in which
individuals discover connection and expression. The Satanic
influences within fashion and subcultures, while compelling to
explore, necessitate an approach that is sensitive and respect-
ful towards the multiplicity of perspectives and belief systems
at play.

In conclusion, the influence of Satanic worship on fashion
trends and subcultures, ranging from goth to metal, is a captivating subject that necessitates a comprehensive exploration.
Through meticulous research, candid interviews, and personal
experiences, I have unveiled a world where Satanic symbolism
and imagery are both celebrated and misunderstood. It is a
realm where fashion and the occult intersect, allowing for self-
expression, defiance, and the pursuit of a deeper comprehension of the ominous forces that lurk in the shadows.

SATANIC WORSHIP IN INTERNET CULTURE

The allure of the unknown has always been a subject that
has captivated my interest as a paranormal investigator and
expert in the peculiar. Throughout my career, I have conducted
numerous investigations and research projects on various aspects of the supernatural realm. Recently, I have been particularly drawn to the portrayal of Satanic worship within internet
culture. With its extensive reach and anonymous nature, the
internet has become a breeding ground for the profane and
the occult. It allows individuals an unprecedented platform to
explore and engage with once-taboo or forbidden topics. In
this chapter, we will delve deep into the darker corners of the

web to uncover the extent and impact of Satanic worship on internet memes, forums, and online communities.

Our first exploration on this unsettling path leads us into the realm of memes. Memes, as commonly known, are often associated with humor and lighthearted entertainment. However, the internet has given rise to a subculture of memes that delve into the occult, employing Satanic imagery and themes. These memes frequently use humor as a vehicle to explore the forbidden, often blurring the line between reality and fiction. They encompass anything from humorous depictions of demonic entities to ironic reinterpretations of religious symbols. These memes thrive on shock value, evoking mixed reactions from amused viewers to those who are aggrieved by what they perceive as a mockery of their beliefs. The potency of these memes lies not only in their ability to entertain but also in their potential to desensitize individuals to the sinister connotations associated with Satanic worship.

Moving forward, we venture further into the realm of online forums devoted to Satanic worship. These forums provide a space for like-minded individuals to connect, exchange experiences, beliefs, and rituals. The anonymity provided by the internet allows individuals to express themselves freely, often without fear of judgment or repercussion. These forums become echo chambers where discussions surrounding Satanic rituals, occult practices, and the pursuit of esoteric knowledge thrive. Users may find detailed instructions on how to perform summoning rituals, communicate with demons, or even orchestrate sacrificial ceremonies. While these forums tend to attract devoted Satanists, they also attract the curiosity of individuals who venture into the forbidden realm. It is important to note that not everyone who engages in these discussions necessarily aligns with Satanic beliefs, but rather explores these topics through an anthropological lens or due to an insatiable curiosity about the human psyche.

Beyond memes and forums, online communities dedicated to Satanic worship offer a more interactive and immersive experience. These communities, often founded on websites or social media platforms, function as virtual congregations where individuals can participate in rituals, share experiences, and delve deeper into the occult. Through these platforms, participants have the opportunity to connect with practitioners from around the world, expanding the reach and influence of Satanic worship. These communities provide a sense of acceptance in an otherwise stigmatized and misunderstood realm, offering support, guidance, and growth opportunities. Nevertheless, entering these communities comes with inherent risks. It is not uncommon to encounter individuals who exploit vulnerable individuals, using Satanic worship as a tool for manipulation and control. As with any online interaction, exercising caution and discernment is vital.

In conclusion, the representation of Satanic worship within internet culture is a nuanced and multifaceted phenomenon. Memes, forums, and online communities serve as avenues for individuals to explore forbidden territories and delve into the occult. While these platforms can provide a sense of community and empowerment for some, they also attract individuals who seek to exploit and manipulate vulnerable individuals. As a paranormal investigator and expert in the unusual, my research in this realm has shed light on the ever-evolving nature of humanity's fascination with the dark side. The internet has both democratized and amplified the presence of Satanic worship, blurring the boundaries between reality and fiction. It is crucial for individuals to approach these realms with caution, maintaining a healthy skepticism and never losing sight of the ethical implications of their actions. The journey into the abyss of Satan is treacherous and must be undertaken with un-wavering determination to pursue truth amidst the shadows.

SATANIC WORSHIP AND CELEBRITY INFLUENCE

As an individual dedicated to investigating anomalous occurrences and a specialist in the unusual, I have personally observed the manner in which societal perceptions can be shaped and molded by the influence of celebrities and public figures. In this chapter, I undertake a deep dive into the obscure realm of Satanic worship and its intricate relationship with celebrity culture. It is important to acknowledge that the extent and impact of celebrities on society should not be underestimated.

Prior to exploring this subject matter, it is imperative to comprehend the true essence of Satanic worship. Frequently misconstrued and misrepresented, Satanic worship encompasses a multifaceted belief system that encompasses various practices. These practices range from theistic rituals which involve the worship of a literal Satan, to symbolic acts of rebellion against social norms. The diversity within Satanic worship renders it both fascinating and intricate to unravel.

One of the most captivating aspects of Satanic worship is how it intersects with the influence wielded by celebrities. Throughout history, celebrities have captivated individuals beyond their talents and achievements. Their lives, choices, and actions frequently become the subject of intense scrutiny and emulation by their countless followers. In the case of Satanic worship, this influence can both promote and challenge societal perspectives.

On one hand, certain celebrities have openly toyed with Satanic symbols and imagery, actively pushing the boundaries of societal norms. This portrayal of Satanic worship can foster curiosity within their fan base and encourage further exploration of these taboo subjects. For example, musicians such as Marilyn Manson and alternative fashion icons like Dita Von Teese are known for incorporating Satanic motifs into their art and persona. By doing so, they challenge societal norms and preconceived notions, invigorating discussions and debates on faith, morality, and freedom of expression.

Conversely, other celebrities employ their influence to challenge deeply entrenched misconceptions surrounding Satanic worship. Through their prominence and vast reach, they leverage their platforms to debunk myths associated with this belief system. A case in point is Lady Gaga, renowned for her avant-garde fashion choices and controversial performances, who has been open about her faith in God despite her fascination with Satanic symbolism. Through her actions, she combats the perception that engaging with Satanic imagery automatically implies a lack of spirituality or moral compass.

It is crucial to acknowledge that not all celebrities who engage with Satanic imagery or symbols necessarily identify as worshipers of Satan. The utilization of these symbols may serve as artistic expression or a means of challenging societal expectations. By analyzing the motivations behind their choices, we can delve deeper into the intricate interplay between celebrity influence and perceptions of Satanic worship.

To thoroughly comprehend the magnitude of celebrity influence on societal perceptions of Satanic worship, an examination of psychological and sociological factors is necessary. One such factor is the concept of idolization and the inherent need to belong. With the advent of social media, individuals now have unparalleled access to the lives of celebrities, enabling them to cultivate parasocial relationships with these public figures. Such interactions foster a sense of connectedness, prompting individuals to adopt the beliefs and practices of their idols, including those associated with Satanic worship.

Furthermore, celebrities often function as cultural gate-keepers, shaping the narratives and discussions that resonate within mainstream society. By openly discussing their interest in Satanic worship or embracing Satanic symbols, they possess the ability to shift societal perceptions and challenge deeply ingrained beliefs regarding acceptability and taboo subjects. This not only influences public opinion but also significantly impacts the lives of their followers, who may begin questioning their own values and belief systems.

To genuinely comprehend the implications of Satanic worship and celebrity influence, a meticulous examination is necessary. It is insufficient to dismiss these occurrences as mere publicity stunts or acts of rebellion. Rather, we must acknowledge the profound influence wielded by celebrities in shaping societal perceptions and challenging existing belief systems. Through unraveling the complexities of this relationship, we can gain a comprehensive understanding of the role Satanic worship plays in contemporary culture.

The forthcoming chapter will delve further into specific case studies, exploring the experiences of celebrities who have delved into Satanic worship, the backlash they encountered, and the wider impact on societal perceptions. This analysis will shed light on the intricate nuances and consequences of celebrity influence in relation to the realm of Satanic worship. Prepare yourself to embark on a journey into the darker side of fame, where the lines between reality and myth blend and where the influence of celebrities can indelibly shape society's perception of the occult.

10

SATANIC WORSHIP AND THE SUPERNATURAL

DEMONIC POSSESSION AND EXORCISM

In my extensive years of research and investigation into paranormal phenomena and delving into the intricacies of the mysterious, one subject that has continuously captivated and troubled me is the belief in demonic possession. Although the notion of possession may appear reminiscent of a frightening cinematic production, the truth is that it has profound origins embedded within various religious and spiritual doctrines across different cultures. Particularly, within Satanic worship, the concept of demons seizing hold of one's soul assumes a malevolent and chilling character unlike anything else.

To fully comprehend the belief in demonic possession within the context of Satanic worship, it is imperative to begin by exploring the origins and evolution of Satanism itself. Satanism possesses a multifaceted and extensive history, dating back centuries. It is worth noting that, despite popular association with sheer malevolence and evil, different branches and interpretations exist within this belief framework. For instance, Theistic Satanism acknowledges the existence of an actual supernatural being known as Satan, while LaVeyan Satanism perceives Satan as a symbol of individualism and defiance against societal norms.

In the realm of Satanic worship, the practice of exorcism is regarded as a means to expel not only malevolent spirits but also to rid oneself of perceived societal limitations and constraints. The act of channeling a spirit or deity, whether it be Satan or another entity, is considered a method of accessing hidden powers and transforming one's life. This is where the belief in demonic possession assumes critical significance.

The belief in demonic possession within Satanism often revolves around the notion that an individual intentionally invites a demon into their body, granting it control to exert its influence. While this may sound purely fantastical, proponents of this belief argue that by engaging in various rituals and acts of devotion, they establish a connection with the demonic realm. According to them, this connection enables them to acquire supernatural abilities and a deeper comprehension of the surrounding world.

One of the most notorious instances of alleged Satanic possession unfolded in the town of Loudun, France during the 17th century. Father Urbain Grandier, a priest, was accused of being possessed by demons, leading to a series of exorcisms conducted in an attempt to rid him of these violent forces. Regrettably, these exorcisms seemed to exacerbate the situation and ultimately culminated in Father Grandier's execution. This intriguing case serves as a haunting reminder of the immense influence that the belief in possession and the practice of exorcism can hold over societies and individuals.

The methods employed in exorcism within Satanic worship are unique and distinct from those observed in mainstream religious practices. In contrast to Catholic exorcisms that involve invoking the power of God and employing holy relics,

Satanic exorcisms center around the ritualistic invocation of demonic entities. These rituals often incorporate symbolic objects, such as candles, sigils, and pentagrams, alongside the recitation of incantations and invocations directed towards the possessing entity.

When exploring the belief in possession within Satanic worship, it is crucial to consider the psychological and emotional states of the individuals involved. Skeptics argue that those who claim to be possessed by demons are simply grappling with diverse mental health conditions or grappling with the effects of substance use. Although this may hold true in specific cases, it is imprudent to dismiss such claims outright as a universal explanation. The power of belief and the sway of collective consciousness must not be underestimated, as they can manifest and shape phenomena in manners that defy logical explanations.

Through extensive research and interviews conducted with individuals who assert to have experienced or witnessed demonic possession within Satanic worship, illuminating insights into the intricate interplay between spirituality, psychology, and the human psyche have emerged. Their testimonies indicate that the belief in possession and the practice of exorcism within Satanic worship originate from personal experiences, deeply-held convictions, and a longing to exceed the limits imposed by societal norms.

As a paranormal investigator and expert in the realm of the unexplained, my exploration into the heart of Satanic worship and the belief in possession has challenged my preconceived notions and stretched the boundaries of my comprehension. Approaching this subject matter with an open mind and a willingness to delve into the depths of the human psyche is vital, as only then can we begin to unravel the enigmatic nature of demonic possession within Satanic worship.

In the subsequent chapters, we will embark on a deeper examination of specific case studies, converse with practitioners, and delve into the intricacies of Satanic rituals and exorcisms. Prepare yourself to enter a realm that is both eerie and unsettling, where darkness and spirituality intermingle. Together, we will uncover the concealed truths hidden within the domain of Satan.

SATANIC RITUALS AND PARANORMAL INVESTIGATIONS

As a paranormal investigator and specialist in the field of unexplained phenomena, I have encountered numerous perplexing occurrences throughout my professional tenure. However, one subject has consistently piqued my curiosity and elicited a sense of unease: Satanic rituals. Ominous, enigmatic, and steeped in malevolence, these rituals have long been associated with the supernatural and have captivated the interest of numerous investigators, including myself. In this chapter, my objective is to delve into the role played by Satanic rituals in the realm of paranormal investigations and explore the potential influence they exert over supernatural phenomena.

To embark on this expedition, extensive research spanning many years was required. This undertaking involved scrutinizing ancient manuscripts, poring over historical accounts, and meticulously examining firsthand testimonies from individuals who have either witnessed or participated in Satanic rituals. By means of rigorous analysis and unwavering dedication, a comprehensive understanding of these rituals, their significance, and their potential impact on the paranormal was pieced together.

Before proceeding further, it is crucial to establish a lucid comprehension of the nature of Satanic rituals. While there may be variations across different cultures and belief systems,

Satanic rituals primarily revolve around the adoration or invocation of malicious entities, often associated with Satan himself. Precisely executed ceremonies, symbolisms, and an assortment of tools, such as daggers, candles, and chilling incantations, frequently accompany these rituals.

The link between Satanic rituals and supernatural phenomena has attracted significant fascination within the domain of paranormal investigation. Some theorists propose that these rituals serve as a gateway or catalyst for otherworldly forces to manifest, either by harnessing energy from the participants or by tapping into the collective consciousness of those involved. These theories suggest that the intensity of the ritual itself and the malevolent intentions behind it may create an environment conducive to supernatural manifestations.

However, it is imperative to approach such claims with prudence and skepticism. In the field of paranormal investigation, it is vital to maintain objectivity and adhere to scientific rigor, separating fact from fiction. Even though it may be enticing to embrace the notion that Satanic rituals hold the key to unlocking the mysteries of the supernatural, we must tread cautiously and critically evaluate the available evidence.

To shine a light on this intriguing connection, a series of investigations was undertaken at reputedly haunted locations that were associated with Satanic rituals. My team and I meticulously documented every detail, utilizing state-of-the-art equipment and techniques to capture any indications of paranormal activity. By synthesizing our findings with historical records and witness accounts, we aimed to establish tangible links between Satanic rituals and supernatural phenomena.

One particular investigation led us to the depths of an abandoned mansion nestled within a dense forest. Local lore was replete with accounts of eerie whispers reverberating within its decaying walls and blood-curdling screams piercing the night.

Tales of Satanic gatherings and sacrifices permeated the area's folklore, instilling our arduous expedition with purpose.

Under the brilliance of the moon, illuminating our path through the dense undergrowth, we approached the mansion's foreboding entrance. Cautiously, our team ventured into the structure, the air teeming with anticipation. It was within these walls that we conducted the first of our experiments: a meticulously recreated Satanic ritual based on historical accounts.

With each step we took within the mansion's confines, the atmosphere grew laden with a sense of foreboding. The flickering candlelight cast eerie shadows upon the walls, which appeared to pulsate with latent energy. As the incantations of the ancient ritual were solemnly muttered, an unmistakable tremor propagated throughout the room, causing the hair on our arms to stand on end. The temperature plummeted, and an oppressive silence enveloped the mansion, as if it were holding its breath in anticipation.

Yet, despite the progression of the ritual, no immediate signs of supernatural intervention were observed. No spectral figures emerged from the shadows, and no disembodied voices reverberated within the chamber. It became apparent that the mere act of performing a Satanic ritual did not guarantee a direct connection with the supernatural. The entities we sought seemed to elude us, shrouding themselves in layers of mystery and potency.

Nevertheless, even in the absence of immediate manifestations, our investigation did yield valuable insights. We discovered that Satanic rituals possess a profound psychological and emotional impact on those involved. The ambiance created during these rituals, combined with the heightened state of consciousness and the collective intention to interact with the supernatural, fosters a powerful aura within the location.

This aura amplifies the likelihood of experiencing paranormal phenomena.

Further research corroborated this hypothesis. We interviewed individuals who had partaken in Satanic rituals in the past, and their accounts consistently revealed commonalities, including heightened sensitivity, altered states of consciousness, and an increased probability of encountering supernatural occurrences subsequent to their involvement in the rituals. These accounts, coupled with our own experiences, suggest that while Satanic rituals may not directly summon supernatural entities, they undeniably contribute to the overall energy and ambiance of a location, potentially intensifying the likelihood of paranormal phenomena.

As my research progressed, I embarked on visits to various haunted locations that were renowned for their association with Satanic rituals. Each investigation provided unique insights, gradually unraveling the intricate web connecting Satanic rituals and the supernatural. Though none of these experiences furnished unequivocal proof of a direct correlation, they undeniably indicated a complex interplay between the human psyche, the environment, and the potential for extraordinary phenomena.

In conclusion, the role of Satanic rituals in paranormal investigations is an enigmatic and captivating subject. Despite the allure of viewing these rituals as the ultimate key to unraveling the secrets of the supernatural, the evidence suggests that they act as amplifiers of paranormal activity rather than direct summoners of otherworldly beings. Satanic rituals cultivate an intense environment that taps into the collective consciousness and emotional energy of those involved, potentially facilitating encounters with the unknown. However, it is indispensable to approach these investigations with skepticism, adhering to scientific rigor while being open to the unexplained.

In my unwavering quest to comprehend the supernatural, the exploration of Satanic rituals has yielded invaluable insights. These inquiries have offered a glimpse into the shadowy realm where humanity and the inhuman merge, unveiling a tapestry of the macabre that lies at the core of our fascination with the uncharted. As I persist on this journey, I am reminded that the answers we seek may perpetually elude us, as the domains of darkness and light remain eternally enigmatic, unwilling to divulge their secrets to those who dare venture into the abyss of Satan.

SATANIC WORSHIP AND OCCULT KNOWLEDGE

As a professional paranormal investigator and specialist in the realm of the supernatural, my exploration of satanic worship and occult knowledge revealed a marriage of both fascination and unease. I have dedicated my life to unveiling the enigmatic truths hidden beneath the superficial layers of existence. Consequently, my foray into the intricate world of Satanism served as the next logical progression in my unrelenting quest for enlightenment.

It is widely acknowledged that satanic worship is intrinsically linked to the pursuit of extraordinary abilities. This pursuit encompasses the clandestine acquisition and implementation of concealed knowledge attained within the realm of the occult. This realm is characterized by an atmosphere of secrecy, whispered rumors, and forbidden practices. Many assert that practitioners of satanic rituals gain access to abilities that transcend conventional understanding.

The genesis of my investigation initiated with exhaustive research, entailing a meticulous examination of ancient texts, obscure manuscripts, and personal testimonies of individuals who had previously dabbled in the forbidden arts. Throughout my journey, I unraveled an intricate network of rites, symbolic representations, and age-old customs passed down through generations of Satanists.

Among the key elements that emerged was the significance placed on the procurement of illicit occult knowledge. Satanists firmly believed that this elusive knowledge held the key to unlocking their latent potential and forging connections with otherworldly forces. Consequently, they actively sought out ancient texts and manuscripts that contained archaic spells, incantations, and rituals that would enable them to tap into supernatural abilities.

In order to deepen my understanding of the interweaving relationship between occult knowledge and satanic worship, I delved into the lives of renowned Satanists, exhaustively studying their practices and meticulously documenting their experiences. Through comprehensive interviews, I acquired invaluable insights into how these individuals traversed the treacherous terrain of the occult, their insatiable hunger for forbidden knowledge, and the lengths to which they would go to obtain it.

One particularly captivating account was provided by a former exalted member of a prominent satanic organization. He elucidated that the rituals enacted by Satanists did not merely serve as ceremonial gestures but were meticulously crafted to establish a profound connection with the supernatural. Allegedly, these rituals functioned as a gateway, enabling practitioners to open themselves up to forces that were beyond conventional comprehension. This marked the initiation of their journey into the unfathomable abyss.

The act of acquiring occult knowledge was approached with a sense of reverence and prudence. Satanists strongly believed that this distinct knowledge wielded immeasurable power, capable of fundamentally altering the very fabric of reality and conferring upon them supernatural abilities. As they took each step deeper into the realm of the unknown, they sought out mentors, sought after ancient texts, and sought artifacts that held the mysterious secrets to the abilities they coveted.

My extensive research also revealed that the implementation of occult knowledge within satanic worship was often propelled by personal desires and ambitions. Satanists yearned to harness these supernatural abilities to their advantage, whether for personal gain, retribution, or exerting control over others. Nonetheless, this insatiable thirst for power bore a hefty price, often leading to a descent into madness or a total surrender to the all-encompassing darkness they sought to manipulate.

To obtain a comprehensive understanding of the implications of occult knowledge within satanic worship, I explored various supernatural abilities that were rumored to be interconnected with these practices. Telekinesis, mind control, pyrokinesis, and even necromancy were all claimed to be accessible to those who had successfully penetrated the depths of the occult.

However, it was crucial to navigate through the realm of sensationalism and superstition in order to ascertain the veracity of these accounts. I delved deep into the domain of psychic phenomena, consulting experts and conducting rigorous experiments to determine the authenticity of these claims.

Through my extensive investigations, I ascertained that while some individuals reported experiencing extraordinary abilities, others were left disillusioned, their dreams shattered as they confronted the true cost of involvement in the forbidden arts. The perils inherent in venturing into the depths were indeed real, and those who delved too deeply often found themselves lost within a labyrinth of their own making. Forever haunted by the demons they had inadvertently unleashed.

My profound journey into the epicenter of satanic worship and occult knowledge has taught me that the pursuit of supernatural abilities is a treacherous path. The desires of the human spirit, coupled with the allure of the unknown, can lead to ominous and unpredictable consequences. As a seasoned paranormal investigator, it is my duty to shed light on these shadowed corners of the human experience, exposing the reality concealed behind the shroud of myth and legend.

In the following chapter, I will delve into the intrinsic connection between satanic worship and supernatural phenomena, investigating the sinister forces that reside beyond our comprehension and the chilling encounters that have been recounted by those audacious enough to delve into the very heart of Satan.

SATANIC RITUALS AND SPIRIT COMMUNICATION

In order to deeply explore this enigmatic realm, an investigation into the historical timeline of Satanic rituals and their connection to spirit communication was necessary. The pursuit of supernatural knowledge and the thread of dark spirituality traverses centuries, weaving an intricate tapestry of beliefs, practices, and rites that require unraveling.

The journey commenced by examining the ancient civilizations of Mesopotamia and Egypt, where the worship of dark entities and summoning of spirits held prominence. These cultures believed that through ritualistic ceremonies, one could establish a connection to the spiritual realm and gain favor or power from their deities. This early form of spirit communication laid the groundwork for the rituals associated with Satanism in later periods.

As the timeline progressed, it became apparent that the practice of spirit communication during Satanic rituals gained prevalence throughout the medieval period, particularly in Europe. The medieval witches, accused of engaging in pacts with the Devil, partook in ceremonies identified as sabbaths. During these sabbaths, they purportedly communed with demons and participated in perverse rites. These sabbaths, fueled by religious fervor and paranoia, instigated a wave of hysteria resulting in the widespread persecution and execution of countless individuals.

The history of spirit communication and Satanic rituals experienced a significant shift with the rise of modern occultism during the late 19th and early 20th centuries. Influential figures such as Aleister Crowley and Helena Blavatsky played pivotal roles in popularizing occult practices, including rituals involving the summoning of spirits. These rituals frequently incorporated elements from diverse religious and mystical traditions, culminating in a powerful amalgamation aiming to tap into the depths of the supernatural realms.

Research has revealed that the practice of spirit communication during Satanic rituals is intricately intertwined with a belief in a higher power, often referred to as Satan or the Devil. This belief system does not align with the Christian concept of Satan as the embodiment of pure evil, but rather presents Satan as a symbol of rebellion against oppressive religious dogma and a pursuit of personal freedom and enlightenment.

Within the context of Satanic rituals, spirit communication serves as a means to establish a connection with a higher entity, be it Satan or any other spiritual being. Practitioners firmly believe that through these rituals and the invocation of spirits, they can acquire knowledge, power, and guidance from the supernatural realm.

Exploration of the practice of spirit communication during Satanic rituals has yielded encounters with individuals claiming to have had genuine and profound experiences. These accounts range from witnessing the materialization of spirits to hearing otherworldly voices and receiving messages from deceased loved ones. While skeptics dismiss such claims as either trickery or psychological delusions, the allure of these accounts remains undeniable, preserving a veil of mystery.

It is essential to acknowledge that not all individuals engaging in spirit communication during Satanic rituals do so with malicious intent. Many perceive these rituals as a form of personal exploration and self-discovery, seeking to expand their comprehension of the supernatural and their own place within it. However, it is crucial to recognize that individuals exist who manipulate these practices for deceitful purposes, employing spirit communication as a means of control, harm, or deception.

In an ongoing journey, a relentless pursuit of the complexities embedded in Satanic rituals and spirit communication persists. Questions lurk in the depths of contemplation: What lies beyond the boundaries of our perceived reality? Can authentic connections be established with entities from other realms? Are the spirits encountered during these rituals mere projections of our own psyche or veritable entities inhabiting an unseen dimension?

As a paranormal investigator and an authority on the inexplicable, it is my duty to unveil the mysteries residing within the practice of spirit communication during Satanic rituals. This shadowy and treacherous path may not be for the faint-hearted, but for those brave enough to venture into the realm of Satan, the rewards may prove extraordinary, and the truth, though often elusive, may finally unveil itself.

SATANIC WORSHIP AND PSYCHIC PHENOMENA

In order to fully comprehend this intricate relationship, it is imperative to thoroughly explore the depths of Satanic worship and its correlation to psychic abilities such as telepathy and clairvoyance. At its core, Satanic worship revolves around the belief and veneration of Satan, who represents evil and darkness. It is a practice deeply rooted in rituals, symbols, and often involves summoning entities from realms beyond our own.

Throughout my extensive research and investigation, I have come across numerous accounts that indicate a strong connection between Satanic worship and psychic phenomena. One particular case that left a profound impact on me was the testimony of a young woman, Sarah, who had been involved in a Satanic cult. Sarah claimed to have experienced heightened psychic abilities after engaging in various rituals and ceremonies.

Upon meeting Sarah, it became evident that her psychic abilities were indeed extraordinary. She displayed an uncanny aptitude for predicting future events and communicating with spirits from the beyond. However, as captivating as her abilities were, they came at a significant cost. Sarah frequently suffered from severe migraines and bouts of intense psychic energy that left her physically and emotionally drained.

To gain a deeper understanding of the relationship between Satanic worship and psychic phenomena, I sought guidance from eminent parapsychologist Dr. Benjamin Monroe. Dr. Monroe had devoted his life to the study of psychical phenomena and had conducted extensive research on cases involving Satanic rituals. According to Dr. Monroe, the rituals conducted during Satanic worship often act as a catalyst for awakening latent psychic abilities within individuals.

Dr. Monroe elaborated that Satanic rituals are designed to tap into the darker aspects of the human psyche, unleashing a wellspring of hidden psychic powers. These rituals induce an elevated state of consciousness that enables individuals to access realms beyond our ordinary reality. Consequently, this facilitates the manifestation of telepathic and clairvoyant abilities in those who partake in the rituals.

One theory proposed by Dr. Monroe posits that Satanic worship triggers the activation of psychic abilities due to the potent combination of fear, belief, and ritualistic practices. The fear and anticipation generated during these rituals create a strong emotional energy that is believed to augment psychic receptivity.

While this theory is certainly fascinating, it is crucial to approach it cautiously. Inherently, Satanic worship involves engaging with forces that can have devastating consequences. It is important to note that not all practitioners of Satanic worship pursue psychic phenomena. In fact, the majority of Satanic cults focus on power, control, and manipulation rather than delving into the depths of psychic abilities.

However, in cases where psychic phenomena are observed in relation to Satanic worship, it is vital to recognize the potential risks involved. Individuals who venture into this dark realm must be prepared to face the consequences that may arise from tapping into such potent forces.

During my pursuit of comprehending the relationship between Satanic worship and psychic phenomena, I have encountered various testimonies and personal experiences that provide further insight. The accounts of individuals who have traversed this treacherous path are chilling and serve as cautionary tales. They serve as a reminder of the hazards inherent in seeking power and knowledge through dark rituals and practices.

As I continue to investigate this enigmatic realm, I am compelled to delve deeper, unearthing the concealed truths that lie within the darkness. The more I uncover, the more I realize that the relationship between Satanic worship and psychic phenomena is a delicate balance between forbidden knowledge and the haunting realms of the supernatural. It is a realm that demands utmost caution and respect, for venturing too far can yield dire consequences.

The journey to unravel the secrets of Satanic worship and its ties to psychic phenomena is a challenging one, necessitating unyielding dedication and a thirst for truth. It is a path that few have the courage to traverse, and even fewer emerge unscathed. Nonetheless, I am resolute in my determination to press forward, shedding light on the enigmatic realm that lies at the heart of darkness itself.

As I venture deeper into the abyss of Satan, I remain acutely aware of the perils that lie ahead. Yet, it is through the exploration of these forbidden domains that we come closer to understanding the mysteries of our existence. It is through these trials and tribulations that we gain insight into the interplay between good and evil, between light and dark. And it is through my unwavering resolve that I will continue to navigate the treacherous waters of Satanic worship and psychic phenomena until I unearth the ultimate truth that lies within.

SATANIC MAGIC AND RITUALISTIC MANIFESTATION

As an individual who carries out investigations into paranormal phenomena and specializes in unusual occurrences, I have encountered a significant number of peculiar and disconcerting events. From residences inhabited by spirits to otherworldly entities, I have probed the depths of the unfamiliar. However, nothing could have prepared me for the somber and enigmatic realm of Satanic magic and the practice of ritualistic manifestation.

To gain a comprehensive understanding of the belief in Satanic magic and its potential for manifestation, I embarked on a thorough and extensive research endeavor. I consulted ancient literature, conducted interviews with authorities on the occult, and delved into obscure and prohibited archives. What I unraveled was an intricate tapestry woven from history, belief systems, and the insatiable human desire for power.

Satanic magic, known by its alternate term of black magic, is an umbrella phrase that encompasses a variety of malevolent arts and rituals performed with the purpose of harnessing supernatural forces. It is believed that these practices empower practitioners to manipulate reality, fulfill their wishes, and even engage in communion with the entity known as Satan. Such beliefs have deep-rooted foundations in diverse cultures and periods of history, with rituals and symbols incurring fluctuations across different periods of time and geographical regions.

The earliest documented rituals associated with Satanic magic can be traced back to countless millennia ago. In ancient Mesopotamia, the Sumerians venerated deities from the dark realm and conducted rituals aimed at invoking their powers. These rituals often included acts of sacrifice involving blood, invocations, and the utilization of talismans infused with malevolent energy. It was held that such practices bestowed upon individuals supernatural abilities, wealth, and control over others.

Throughout centuries, Satanic magic has assumed a variety of forms and been adopted by numerous cults and clandestine organizations. Among these groups, one specific faction has attained considerable notoriety in recent times: the Order of the Temple of the East. This clandestine body, also known as the OTE, professed to possess the definitive key to ultimate power through the practice of Satanic magic. In their rituals, followers sought to bring their desires and intentions into fruition by aligning themselves with dark forces.

The potentiality for ritualistic manifestation within the realm of Satanic magic emanates from the conviction that through the enactment of specific rituals, practitioners can exercise control over the spiritual domain and manipulate reality itself. This is often pursued through the creation of a ceremonial space, one that is meticulously arranged and endowed with symbolic significance. The utilization of candles, altars, symbolic representations, and formulaic utterances all contribute to the effectiveness of the ritual.

One particularly intriguing facet of Satanic magic is the concept of enterprising pacts. It is held that through entering into a pact with a demonic entity, individuals can acquire immense power and wealth. These agreements are formalized through rituals, often involving the signing of a contract and the utilization of blood as a binding agent. Such contracts parallel the infamous Faustian pact, where an individual surrenders their soul to the devil in exchange for earthly desires.

It is imperative to observe that Satanic magic extends beyond mere superstitious beliefs and doctrine. Numerous reports and testimonies exist from individuals who claim to have successfully materialized their desires through these rituals. Whether these experiences are the result of psychological manipulation or genuine supernatural occurrences remains a matter of intense debate among authorities on the subject.

One particularly compelling case that I encountered during my research involved a young man named Daniel. Driven by a desperate desire for fame and success, Daniel made the decision to delve into the realm of Satanic magic. Through a series of rituals, he sought to manifest his aspiration for stardom.

Astonishingly, within a year of performing these rituals, Daniel experienced an unprecedented rise to fame in the entertainment industry. While it may be plausible to attribute his success to innate talent and advantageous circumstances, the timing and convergence of events appeared far too uncanny to dismiss.

It is of paramount importance to approach the subject of Satanic magic and ritualistic manifestation with caution and skepticism. The allure of power and the potential to shape one's reality can prove to be intoxicating, leading individuals along a treacherous path. Many who have dabbled in these dark arts have found their mental well-being, interpersonal relationships, and even their lives at risk. Engaging in these rituals should never be undertaken lightly, as the consequences can be grave and irreversible.

In conclusion, Satanic magic and the practice of ritualistic manifestation are subjects that plunge into the depths of the human psyche and uncharted territories of the supernatural. The belief in these practices has spanned centuries and cultures, captivating the imagination and perpetuating intrigue. As an individual specialized in the investigation of unusual phenomena, I remain fascinated by this enigmatic realm, forever driven to unveil the truths hidden within the enigma surrounding Satan.

SATANIC WORSHIP AND HAUNTINGS

As an experienced paranormal investigator and researcher of anomalous phenomena, I have had the opportunity to examine numerous instances of hauntings and supernatural occurrences. Over the course of my career, I have discerned a disconcerting pattern linking satanic worship to these unnerving events. This correlation has piqued my interest and driven me to delve deeper into the enigmatic realm of the occult.

To gain a comprehensive understanding of the association between satanic worship and hauntings, it is imperative to explore the annals of history. In retracing the origins of satanic worship, one cannot disregard the significant influence exerted by ancient civilizations. From the Mesopotamians to the Egyptians, the veneration of malevolent deities has remained pervasive throughout human history. The rituals and customs practiced by these primordial societies have indelibly shaped the spiritual landscape.

One prominent figure who ushered in a new era of satanic worship was Aleister Crowley, famously known as "The Great Beast 666." Crowley's teachings and methodologies, elucidated in his seminal work, "The Book of the Law," served as the bedrock for contemporary cults engaged in satanic practices. His ideologies centered on embracing one's darkest impulses and harnessing them to attain personal empowerment and influence.

During my extensive research into satanic worship and its connection to hauntings, I fortuitously stumbled upon an obscure sect that fervently adhered to Crowley's doctrines. This clandestine congregation conducted their rituals within the confines of a dilapidated manor nestled deeply within a vast forest. Known as Blackthorn Manor, this edifice became an epicenter of malevolence, capturing the attention and concern of both paranormal investigators and law enforcement.

According to legends, the cult members would perform arcane rituals involving human sacrifice, thereby tapping into unimaginable dark forces. It was believed that these rituals would create gateways to sinister dimensions, allowing malevolent entities to infiltrate our world. The dire consequences resulting from these practices often manifested as hauntings, poltergeist phenomena, and even instances of demonic possession.

In a resolute attempt to illuminate the truth, I mobilized a dedicated team of researchers and equipped them with an array of cutting-edge devices, including audio recorders, electromagnetic field (EMF) meters, and infrared cameras. The ambiance surrounding the manor was thick with malevolence, as if the very atmosphere was imbued with the vestiges of satanic rites. The decaying architecture and shattered windows of the structure cast a foreboding shadow, serving as a haunting reminder of the terrors that awaited us within.

As we cautiously entered the premises, an bone-chilling coldness immediately greeted us, permeating through our very bones. Shadows danced with an ethereal grace upon the walls, seemingly guided by invisible hands. The air grew heavy, as if intangible tendrils ensnared us, constricting our every breath.

Our sophisticated equipment commenced displaying anomalous readings - electronic voice phenomena (EVPs) whispering incoherent phrases, localized cold spots that inexplicably followed our every movement, and sporadic flickering lights that defied logical explanation. It was as if the malevolent rituals once enacted within these walls had stained the very fabric of reality, forever imprinting this accursed abode with a spectral presence.

In due course, we discovered an obscure chamber concealed behind a concealed door in the mansion's basement. This hidden room was adorned with intricate satanic symbols, an altar fashioned from human skeletal remains, and blood-smeared walls. It became unmistakable that this area constituted the nucleus of unimaginable evil, serving as the focal point for centuries-old malignant energies.

As we ventured deeper into this unhallowed space, our exploration was abruptly disrupted by an overwhelming cacophony of otherworldly sounds. The walls seemed to pulsate with life, grotesque visages contorted in a gnarled grimace, whilst ancient chants resounded through the chamber. The oppressive force within the room became unbearably stifling, compelling us to hastily retreat in a state of abject terror.

Nevertheless, this ordeal only furthered our resolve, fueling our insatiable thirst for knowledge and our determination to unravel the intricacies of the symbiotic relationship between satanic worship and hauntings. Our investigation persisted with unwavering tenacity, leading us down a convoluted path where haunted domiciles and individuals under the grip of possession awaited us.

We bore witness to an extraordinary array of paranormal activity - animate objects languidly moving without a discernible cause, disembodied voices reverberating through abandoned hallways, and even instances of physical aggression by imperceptible entities. It became increasingly apparent that the rituals associated with satanic worship unleashed forces that transcended the mortal realm, resulting in a dark trail of suffering and maleficence.

As our harrowing odyssey through the labyrinth of satanic worship and its connection to hauntings drew to a close, we were left with profound insights. We had borne witness, firsthand, to the perils of delving into the realm of satanic rituals. The connection between satanic worship and hauntings cannot be dismissed as mere coincidence but rather stands as a testament to the profound transcendence dark practices wield within the spiritual realm.

In the face of such malevolence, it is incumbent upon us to approach the occult with prudence and reverence. The path toward comprehending the associations between satanic worship and hauntings is fraught with treachery, yet it is a path that must be traversed for the advancement of our comprehension of the supernatural. Only through enlightenment and compassion can we aspire to shield ourselves and others from the pernicious forces that manifest within the embrace of Satan.

SATANIC WORSHIP AND SUPERNATURAL PROTECTION

In order to gain a comprehensive understanding of the methods utilized in Satanic worship for supernatural protection, it is imperative to comprehend the historical timeline through which this phenomenon has evolved. Satanic worship is not a recent occurrence, but rather a deeply ingrained practice within ancient civilizations. Humanity has long been captivated by both the forces of light and darkness, actively seeking safeguard against the malevolent entities that reside in the shadows.

An exemplary instance of this can be found in ancient Mesopotamia where cults worshipped deities of darkness, making sacrifices to appease their wrath and solicit their favor. This was believed to establish a spiritual connection with the supernatural realm and acquire protection. Rituals that involved bloodletting and incantations were commonplace, with adherents firmly believing that these acts would create a barrier against evil.

Centuries later, during the pinnacle of the Roman Empire, Satanic worship took on a new form. Within covert societies, such as the infamous Cult of Hecate, rituals involving animal sacrifices and necromancy were conducted with the intention of harnessing the powers of darkness. Members of this cult were of the belief that through communion with demonic entities, they could obtain supernatural protection against their adversaries.

Fast forward to the Middle Ages, a period characterized by the persecution of practitioners of dark arts. Satanic worship was compelled to operate clandestinely, retreating underground to evade scrutiny from the watchful eyes of the Inquisition. During this era, rituals imbued with symbolism and invocations took center stage, with participants forging pacts with the devil in exchange for supernatural protection. Black masses, human sacrifices, and the desecration of sacred objects were all integral components of these ceremonial practices employed to summon malevolent forces.

In more contemporary times, Satanic worship has assumed diverse forms, blending ancient traditions with modern beliefs. A notable example is the Church of Satan, founded by Anton LaVey in the United States during the 1960s. LaVey's ideology revolved around indulgence rather than sacrifice, advocating for a self-centered approach to worship. In this context, protection is sought by embracing one's individual power and acknowledging the existence of malevolent forces in the world.

So, what are the specific methods and rituals that offer supernatural protection within Satanic worship? While there exists a plethora of practices, a common thread that spans across time is the utilization of symbols imbued with occult significance. A potent symbol frequently associated with Satanic rituals is the pentagram. It is widely believed to represent the elements of earth, air, fire, water, and spirit, serving as a protective amulet against malevolent entities.

Invocations also hold a central role within Satanic worship as a means of seeking supernatural protection. Depending on the particular belief system, these incantations can range from invoking dark deities or demons to seeking guidance from personal spirit guides. The spoken word wields immense power within these rituals, with practitioners meticulously selecting phrases and summoning authoritative names to manifest their desired outcomes.

Furthermore, bloodletting and the consumption of sacrificial offerings feature prominently within Satanic worship ceremonies. While these practices may be seen as repugnant to most, they serve as a means of establishing a connection with the supernatural realm and harnessing the power of darkness. By offering a symbolic representation of life force, adherents believe they can attain supernatural protection against malevolent entities.

It is crucial to acknowledge that the efficacy of these methods and rituals for supernatural protection remains highly subjective, contingent upon an individual's faith and dedication to their chosen path. Satanic worship, like any spiritual practice, has the potential to both empower and lead individuals into perilous territories of darkness. Therefore, it is of utmost importance for those engaging in these practices to approach them with caution and discernment.

In conclusion, Satanic worship and the quest for supernatural protection against malevolent entities possess a deeply entrenched history spanning thousands of years. By delving into the methods and rituals employed throughout different eras, we gain insight into the intricate nature of this dark phenomenon. Ultimately, the pursuit of supernatural protection within Satanic worship stems from the eternal human desire to navigate the boundaries between light and darkness, seeking solace and security within the enigmatic realms of the unknown.

11
SATANIC WORSHIP AND ETHICS

SATANIC ETHICS AND INDIVIDUAL AUTONOMY

As an investigator specializing in paranormal phenomena, I have extensively explored various belief systems and practices that deviate from societal norms. Among the range of esoteric philosophies and occult traditions, Satanic ethics, with its focus on individual autonomy and personal freedom, has intrigued me profoundly. In this chapter, I aim to delve into the intricacies of this belief system, its guiding principles, and the impact it has on the lives of its adherents.

When discussing Satanism, many individuals immediately associate it with concepts of evil, chaos, and malevolence. However, it is crucial to understand that not all Satanists advocate the literal worship of Satan. For instance, LaVeyan Satanism, established by Anton LaVey in the mid-20th century, promotes a self-centered ideology that prioritizes individualism and self-gratification. Within this framework, the autonomy of the individual, including the ability to make choices freely without external moral constraints, takes precedence.

To truly grasp the significance of individual autonomy in Satanic ethics, it becomes imperative to compare and contrast it with other ethical systems. Traditional religious doctrines often rely on external authorities, such as sacred texts and divine revelations, to dictate moral standards. They encourage selflessness and submission to the divine will, relegating personal desires to secondary importance for communal well-being.

Satanic ethics, conversely, rejects the notion of a higher power and instead centers authority within the individual. It asserts that individuals should have control over their own destinies, making decisions based on personal desires, needs, and whims. This emphasis on individual autonomy manifests in various aspects of a Satanist's life, from personal relationships to moral decision-making.

In interpersonal relationships, Satanic ethics encourages individuals to embrace their desires and indulge in them without guilt or shame, provided they do not cause physical or mental harm to others. This concept challenges conventional ideas of morality, which often deem desires and pleasures as sinful or morally wrong. By rejecting external moral constraints, Satanic ethics permits individuals to explore their true selves and embrace their individuality.

One immediate implication of this emphasis on individual autonomy is the rejection of societal expectations and norms. Satanic ethics motivates individuals to question societal constructs, challenge authority, and break free from conformity. However, this rebellion against societal norms is not driven by a destructive impulse, but rather by a desire to assert one's authentic self and live in accordance with personal values.

Another crucial consequence of individual autonomy within Satanic ethics is the acceptance of personal responsibility. Traditional religious systems often emphasize obedience, with individuals believing that their actions are either compelled or forbidden by a higher power. In contrast, Satanists view themselves as the agents of their own actions, taking ownership of both the successes and failures that arise from their choices.

By embracing personal responsibility, Satanists are empowered to take control of their lives and actively pursue their goals and desires. The notion of individual autonomy enables them to redefine their own moral codes instead of conforming to externally dictated norms. This pursuit of personal fulfillment and self-actualization is a central tenet of Satanic ethics.

However, it is crucial to acknowledge the potential drawbacks of an ethics heavily centered on individual autonomy. Without a moral compass derived from external sources, there is a risk of moral relativism and the absence of a shared ethical foundation. This implies that what one person considers morally acceptable may be perceived as morally abhorrent by another.

Furthermore, the emphasis on individual autonomy can lead to a lack of accountability and disregard for societal well-being. While Satanic ethics endorse personal freedom, they do not condone actions that directly harm others. The point at which personal freedom infringes upon the rights and well-being of others must be navigated with care.

In conclusion, Satanic ethics places significant weight on individual autonomy and personal freedom, allowing individuals to pursue their desires and live authentically. By rejecting external moral authorities and embracing personal responsibility, Satanists challenge societal norms and expectations. While the emphasis on individual autonomy brings advantages, it also carries potential risks of moral relativism and a lack of accountability. Nonetheless, exploring Satanic ethics provides an opportunity to question traditional moral frameworks and understand the diverse ways in which individuals navigate their moral landscapes.

SATANIC WORSHIP AND UTILITARIANISM

As an investigator specializing in the study of paranormal phenomena, I have encountered various belief systems that defy conventional societal norms. Among these belief systems is Satanic worship, which has captivated my interest for a considerable period. The purpose of this chapter is to explore the intriguing question of whether Satanic worship can coexist with utilitarian ethical frameworks and the pursuit of happiness.

Before delving into this inquiry, it is important to grasp the fundamental principles of utilitarianism. Utilitarianism posits that the moral value of an action is determined by its ability to maximize overall happiness or pleasure for the greatest number of individuals. Essentially, the ultimate aim of utilitarianism is to cultivate a society in which the net happiness is optimized.

Satanic worship is often perceived as a form of dark and malevolent practice centered around the veneration of Satan. At first glance, aligning such a belief system with a philosophy that prioritizes maximizing happiness may appear contradictory. However, a thorough analysis of this compatibility necessitates a deeper exploration of the principles and tenets of Satanic worship.

One crucial aspect of Satanic worship is the pursuit of personal freedom and autonomy. Satanic beliefs emphasize the sovereignty of the individual and reject external authority. This emphasis on personal freedom aligns with utilitarianism, recognizing the significance of individual autonomy in contributing to overall happiness.

Moreover, Satanic worship upholds the notion of indulgence rather than abstinence. This concept encourages individuals to explore and embrace their desires and passions, prioritizing the pursuit of earthly pleasures. While utilitarian ethics may discourage excessive indulgence that could harm others, it nonetheless recognizes the importance of personal happiness and fulfillment. Thus, in these aspects, Satanic worship and utilitarianism find common ground.

Another intriguing facet of Satanic worship is its rejection of societal norms and moral conventions. Satanists view traditional morality as arbitrary and oppressive, perceiving it as a hindrance to personal growth and happiness. In contrast, utilitarian ethics seek to maximize overall happiness rather than rigidly adhering to societal standards. This alignment is evident in the readiness to challenge prevailing moral codes to establish a society that prioritizes the well-being of its members.

In assessing the compatibility of Satanism and utilitarianism, it is crucial to address the misconceptions and sensationalized portrayals commonly associated with Satanic worship. While certain fringe groups may engage in harmful or morally objectionable actions, these individuals do not represent the broader spectrum of Satanic beliefs. Distinctions must be made between detrimental actions and the underlying philosophical perspectives of Satanic worship.

To truly evaluate the potential compatibility of Satanic worship and utilitarianism, it is imperative to consider the impact of Satanic beliefs on the mental well-being of its adherents. Happiness, in this context, can be understood as the pursuit of pleasure as well as the absence of suffering. Satanism emphasizes personal empowerment, critical thinking, and self-development, all of which can positively contribute to an individual's psychological well-being. By empowering individuals to reject oppressive societal norms, Satanism may enhance overall happiness, aligning with the principles of utilitarianism.

There is a common misconception that Satanism inherently promotes harm and malevolence. However, it is essential to recognize that authentic Satanism rejects causing harm. It emphasizes personal responsibility and ethical behavior, while encouraging self-preservation and the protection of others who are deserving of it. This rejection of harm aligns with the core principles of utilitarian ethics, which prioritize minimizing suffering.

Overall, while Satanic beliefs and utilitarian ethical frameworks may initially seem incompatible, closer examination reveals unexpected parallels. Both value personal autonomy, the pursuit of happiness, and the rejection of oppressive societal norms. Additionally, Satanism's emphasis on personal empowerment and self-development can significantly contribute to an individual's overall mental well-being, a key element of happiness.

As a paranormal investigator and specialist in the supernatural, I have come to understand that exploration and open-mindedness are indispensable in comprehending the complexity of belief systems. This analysis has shed light on the potential harmony between Satanic worship and utilitarian ethics, as well as the pursuit of happiness. By questioning preconceived notions and delving deeper into these intricate principles, we can foster a more inclusive and accepting understanding of diverse belief systems. Only through such understanding can we truly gain insight into the perplexing realm of Satan.

SATANIC RITUALS AND ETHICAL RELATIVISM

As an individual engaged in the field of paranormal investigation and an expert in anomalous phenomena, my objective has led me to explore areas that defy rational explanation and challenge the very foundations of our perceived reality. Of particular interest to me in this regard is the enigmatic realm of satanic rituals, which, in my quest for truth, has instigated a compelling need to investigate the role of ethical relativism within these practices, along with the disconcerting embrace of a rejection of absolute moral values that pervades their malefic confines.

To commence this inquiry, I immersed myself in a plethora of scholarly research endeavors in an attempt to unravel the complexities encompassing satanic rituals and their ethical framework. Through these endeavors, I encountered a wealth of historical and philosophical perspectives, illuminating the manner in which adherents of these rituals rationalize their actions and navigate the precarious waters of ethical relativism.

Amongst the most reputable volumes on this subject was Anton LaVey's seminal work, "The Satanic Bible," which serves as a cornerstone text for followers of the Church of Satan. In said work, LaVey posits that the bedrock of satanic beliefs lies in ethical relativism, asserting that moral values are subjective and contingent upon the desires and needs of the individual. By categorically rejecting absolute moral values, practitioners of satanic rituals are afforded the freedom to pursue their desires devoid of external moral constraints.

In my endeavor to grasp the mindset of individuals engaged in satanic rituals, I also delved into the research conducted by esteemed scholars such as Aquinas, who represents LaVey's philosophical nemesis. Aquinas vehemently refutes ethical relativism and champions the notion of absolute moral values derived from religious principles and natural law. The writings of Aquinas stand in stark contrast to the satanic viewpoint, thus enabling me to grasp the pervasive nature of ethical relativism within these rituals.

As I became further entrenched in this somber realm, I began to comprehend the allure of ethical relativism to those seeking power or control. For them, the repudiation of absolute moral values offers a sense of liberation from societal constraints and a means by which to assert one's own authority. However, the consequences of this repudiation are deeply unsettling, as it opens the floodgates for the occurrence of morally reprehensible acts under the guise of personal freedom.

To deepen my understanding of the practical manifestation of ethical relativism within satanic rituals, I sought firsthand accounts and conducted interviews with individuals who self-identified as practitioners. Their testimonies painted a haunting picture of a world in which the boundaries between right and wrong were blurred, and the ends apparently justified the most abhorrent means.

One specific case stands out in my memory, namely that of a woman named Ava, who recounted her involvement in a satanic ritual that greatly affected her emotional essence. In her narrative, she elucidated how the ritual necessitated the sacrifice of a blameless animal, the act justified by the belief that one life could be substituted for another. It appeared that ethical relativism, within this context, empowered practitioners to vindicate their actions in pursuit of personal gain or the appeasement of obscure forces.

These revelations profoundly confronted me with an essential question: Can we legitimately regard the rejection of absolute moral values as a purely subjective matter, or do we bear a responsibility to challenge the ethical relativism that sanctions such abominations? As an investigator in the realm of paranormal phenomena, I find myself standing at the precipice of this moral quandary, torn between the thirst for knowledge and the obligation to protect the defenseless.

In the relentless pursuit of veracity, it is crucial to acknowledge and comprehend the presence of ethical relativism within satanic rituals. To dismiss it as an idiosyncrasy or superstition would be a grave fallacy. By confronting this obscure underbelly of human belief systems, we are granted an opportunity to re-evaluate our own perspectives on morality and delve deeper into the complexities that define the human condition.

As my investigations persist, I am reminded of the sagacious words imparted by Edmund Burke, who once declared, "The only thing necessary for the triumph of evil is for good men to do nothing." It is our solemn duty, as seekers of truth, to cast illumination into the abyss and expose the ethical relativism that festers within. Only then can we aspire to navigate the treacherous path that lies between darkness and enlightenment and forge a brighter future for all humanity.

SATANIC WORSHIP AND ETHICAL EGOISM

As an expert in paranormal investigation and the study of unconventional phenomena, I have extensively explored the realms of human belief systems. Few subjects have captivated my attention as much as the enigma of Satanic worship. With its ability to evoke fear and curiosity, Satanic worship has long remained a topic shrouded in mystery and controversy. In my quest for a comprehensive understanding, I embarked on a journey to examine the alignment of Satanic worship with ethical egoism and the prioritization of self-interest.

To truly grasp the allure of Satanic worship, it is crucial to comprehend the origins of this belief system. Satanism has evolved over centuries, drawing from a complex tapestry of religious, philosophical, and cultural influences. From medieval witch trials to the emergence of contemporary Satanic groups, the worship of Satan has taken on various manifestations throughout history.

Ethical egoism, on the other hand, is a moral theory that advocates for the pursuit of self-interest as the highest virtue. It asserts that individuals are justified in acting solely in their own self-interest, without regard for the well-being of others. While there exists a wide range of ethical and philosophical perspectives on egoism, ethical egoism specifically highlights the moral value of self-centeredness.

The intriguing connection between Satanic worship and ethical egoism lies in the way these ostensibly distinct concepts converge. Both place the individual at the center, emphasizing personal fulfillment and empowerment. Satanic worship, in its diverse forms, celebrates self-deification and the pursuit of one's desires and ambitions. It resonates with individuals who seek to challenge societal norms and unapologetically embrace their innermost desires.

In order to comprehend this alignment, I embarked on an extensive exploration of Satanic literature, rituals, and interviews with self-proclaimed Satanists. One particular text, Anton LaVey's Satanic Bible, serves as a foundational guide for modern Satanism. LaVey's philosophy champions the idea of indulgence, urging individuals to embrace their carnal desires rather than suppress them.

Through conversations with Satanists, I discovered that ethical egoism provided a rationale for their beliefs and actions. By prioritizing their own interests and desires, they felt liberated from societal expectations and constraints. They argued that by fulfilling their own needs and ambitions, they were better equipped to make positive contributions to the world.

It is important to note, however, that not all Satanists adhere strictly to ethical egoism. Some embrace a more nuanced approach, incorporating elements of altruism and empathy into their practice. They contend that self-interest does not have to be incompatible with compassion for others. Instead, they view ethical egoism as a means of self-empowerment and self-actualization, which in turn enables them to extend empathy and support to those within their immediate circles.

To gain a deeper understanding of the alignment between Satanic worship and ethical egoism, I turned to the fields of psychology and neuroscience. Research has shown that self-interest is deeply ingrained in human nature, driven by mechanisms within our brains that prioritize our own survival and well-being. These findings suggest that ethical egoism, rather than being an aberration, may be a natural and instinctual inclination for certain individuals.

While this exploration shed light on the connection between Satanic worship and ethical egoism, it also unveiled a broader conversation about the nature of morality and the boundaries of acceptable behavior. The subjective nature of morality makes it challenging to draw definitive lines between what is considered ethical and what is not. Satanic worship challenges societal norms and conventions, prompting us to question the very foundations upon which our moral framework is constructed.

In concluding my investigation, I have come to appreciate the inherent complexities involved in comprehending Satanic worship and its intersections with ethical egoism. The allure of self-empowerment and the celebration of one's desires resonates deeply with many individuals who find solace in the Satanic philosophy. Ultimately, exploring this alignment invites us to reevaluate our own beliefs, values, and the nature of morality itself.

Although the alignment of Satanic worship with ethical egoism remains a topic of contention, my journey has taught me to approach it with an open mind and a willingness to challenge preconceived notions. In the face of such enigmatic beliefs, it is only through profound exploration and nuanced understanding that we can hope to unravel the mysteries that lie within the realm of Satan.

SATANIC ETHICS AND HEDONISM

In order to embark on this exploration, it is imperative to comprehend the historical context of Satanism and its evolution. Throughout history, Satan has been depicted as the embodiment of evil, the adversary, and the antagonist of all things divine. However, in recent times, a different interpretation of Satanism has emerged, one that embraces rebelliousness and individualism, and establishes a code of ethics to abide by. This modern Satanic philosophy, particularly expounded by Anton LaVey in his work, the Satanic Bible, promotes the pursuit of pleasure, rational self-interest, and a rejection of arbitrary moral codes imposed by external authority.

At the core of Satanic ethics lies the principle of hedonism – the pursuit of pleasure and gratification. However, it is crucial to note that the Satanic ethos does not advocate for hedonism at the expense of others or without regard for personal responsibility. It emphasizes indulgence rather than mindless self-indulgence. This distinction may appear subtle, but it is essential to comprehend the underlying philosophy.

An extensive examination of the philosophy of LaVey and his contemporaries is required to analyze the pursuit of pleasure and gratification within Satanic ethics. According to the Satanic Bible, individuals are encouraged to explore their desires, fulfill their whims, and embrace that which brings them joy and satisfaction. In this pursuit, individuals are urged to reject societal norms and religious dogma that aim to dictate their personal choices. However, it is important to note that the Satanic philosophy comes with a caveat – the pursuit of pleasure should not infringe upon the rights of others or cause harm.

To grasp the impact of hedonism within Satanic ethics on personal decision-making, it is necessary to examine the mindset and rationality of a Satanist. Contrary to popular belief, Satanists do not engage in reckless behavior or immoral actions solely for the purpose of rebellion. The pursuit of pleasure and gratification within Satanic ethics is an individualistic endeavor that recognizes personal responsibility and accountability.

Interviews with self-proclaimed Satanists demonstrate that their decisions are motivated by a discerning sense of individuality and self-awareness. They maintain the belief that acknowledging and fulfilling their deepest desires enables them to live authentically and embrace their true selves. By rejecting societal expectations, they discover a sense of liberation and empowerment that allows them to make decisions based on their own values and desires.

Furthermore, the impact of hedonism within Satanic ethics extends beyond the individual level. By promoting self-indulgence and the pursuit of personal pleasure, Satanism endeavors to challenge societal constructs and systems that aim to control and suppress individuality. Satanists hold the belief that by prioritizing personal happiness and fulfillment, they are rejecting oppressive systems rooted in guilt, shame, and self-denial.

However, it is important to navigate the delicate line between hedonism and selfishness. While personal pleasure and gratification are paramount within Satanic ethics, they should never come at the expense of others' well-being or cause harm. Satanists believe in ethical egoism – the pursuit of self-interest while respecting the boundaries and autonomy of others. This balance between personal desire and ethical responsibility is crucial in ensuring that the pursuit of pleasure within Satanic ethics remains ethical and sustainable.

In conclusion, the pursuit of pleasure and gratification within Satanic ethics is a complex aspect of this controversial ideology. Satanists embrace hedonism not as mindless indulgence, but as a means to assert their individuality and reject societal norms that seek to suppress personal desires. Through a discerning sense of individualism and ethical egoism, Satanists navigate the delicate balance between personal pleasure and ethical responsibility. By understanding and analyzing the intricacies of hedonism within Satanic ethics, we can gain a deeper insight into their decision-making process and challenge our own preconceived notions of morality and individuality.

SATANIC RITUALS AND VIRTUE ETHICS

The understanding of the foundations of virtue ethics and its correlation to moral character is crucial. Virtue ethics asserts that moral actions are those that align with virtuous qualities, such as honesty, courage, and compassion. The cultivation of these virtues is considered vital in the pursuit of a noble and meaningful life. With this framework in mind, I undertook an investigation to examine the compatibility of Satanic rituals with virtue ethics and the development of moral character.

To commence my exploration, I immersed myself in the historical timeline of Satanic rituals. From ancient practices to contemporary interpretations, I aimed to comprehend the evolution of these rituals and their inherent attributes. My research led me to the realization that Satanic rituals have origins in ancient pagan traditions, where they served as a means of communication with supernatural forces and harnessing their power. These rituals were often characterized by sacrificial offerings and invocations of deities associated with darkness and chaos. However, it is important to note that these practices exhibit significant variations across different cultures and time periods.

One aspect of Satanic rituals that particularly captivated my interest was their emphasis on individualism and personal empowerment. Distinct from many organized religions, where conformity to pre-established moral codes is expected from individuals, Satanic rituals encourage individuals to embrace their own desires, instincts, and ambitions. This ethos fosters self-discovery and the pursuit of personal happiness, which can be regarded as a reflection of virtue ethics. In this regard, Satanic rituals may align with the cultivation of moral character as they prioritize individual autonomy and self-awareness.

However, caution must be exercised when exploring such dark and controversial practices. Satanic rituals also possess a darker side, often associated with the manipulation of power and the pursuit of self-gratification at the expense of others. The practice of black magic and the invocation of demonic entities are among the more sinister aspects of this realm. These practices contradict the fundamental principles of virtue ethics, which advocate for the well-being and flourishing of all individuals. It is essential to discern between those who approach Satanic rituals with a reverence for personal growth and those who seek to exploit them for malevolent purposes.

To gain further insights into the compatibility of Satanic rituals with virtue ethics, I sought out individuals who actively engage in these practices. Through interviews and firsthand experiences, I was able to gain a more profound understanding of their motivations and the impact these rituals have on their moral character. What I discovered was a complex tapestry of perspectives, with some practitioners viewing Satanic rituals as a means of self-liberation and others perceiving them as a manifestation of their darker desires.

In my conversations with these individuals, I found that the cultivation of moral character in the context of Satanic rituals depends on personal intentions and the pursuit of individual enlightenment. Some practitioners described utilizing these rituals as a form of catharsis, enabling them to confront their fears and embrace aspects of themselves that society deems unacceptable. By acknowledging and integrating these shadow aspects, they believed they could become more authentic and morally virtuous individuals.

On the other hand, there were individuals who approached Satanic rituals solely for personal gain and power. These individuals regarded these rituals as tools for manipulation and control, using them to further their own interests at the expense of others. Here, the compatibility with virtue ethics becomes questionable, as the pursuit of personal gain often clashes with the principles of justice and compassion.

As my investigation drew to a close, it became evident to me that the compatibility of Satanic rituals with virtue ethics is a complex and nuanced subject. While certain aspects of these rituals, such as their promotion of individual autonomy and self-awareness, may align with the cultivation of moral character, the darker elements associated with power and manipulation pose a significant challenge. It is the responsibility of each individual practitioner to navigate this terrain with utmost care and consideration for their own well-being and that of others.

In conclusion, my journey into the realm of Satanic rituals revealed a multifaceted landscape, intertwining elements of personal growth, power, and moral character. It is not a realm for the faint-hearted, and one must approach it cautiously and with discernment. As a paranormal investigator and an expert in the extraordinary, it is my obligation to illuminate the darkest corners of our world, not to pass judgment but to seek understanding. The pursuit of truth knows no boundaries, and it is within this pursuit that we must confront our own preconceptions and challenge the depths of our own moral character.

SATANIC WORSHIP AND DEONTOLOGICAL ETHICS

As an individual specializing in paranormal investigation and with a deep interest in the intricate connections between the supernatural realm and our ethical principles, I have dedicated considerable attention to the enduring debate surrounding satanic worship and its compatibility with deontological ethics based on duty and moral obligations. To gain a comprehensive understanding of this complex relationship, I conducted extensive historical research, delving into obscure texts and engaging with experts in theology and ethical philosophy. This journey proved both fascinating and unsettling, shedding light on the often unexplored depths of the human psyche and the extent to which individuals can be driven in their pursuit of power and transcendence.

To grasp the essence of this tension, it is necessary to first comprehend the historical trajectory of satanic worship and its various expressions throughout time. A meticulous examination of the historical timeline reveals that the roots of this controversial practice can be traced back to ancient civilizations. The worship of dark deities, often associated with chaos, carnage, and indulgence, was prevalent in numerous cultures, spanning from ancient Mesopotamia to Greco-Roman mythology. These early belief systems provided the foundation for the emergence of more organized forms of satanic worship during medieval Europe.

The ascendancy of Christianity around the 4th century AD instigated a momentous clash between the monotheistic faith and the remnants of ancient pagan religions. The Church's condemnation of these polytheistic practices as heresy only served to heighten their allure. It was during this period that records of witches' covens engaging in acts deemed "satanic" began to surface, contributing to the shaping of our present perception of satanic worship.

Fast-forwarding to the 20th century, a renewed interest in the occult and esotericism emerged, with figures such as Aleister Crowley and Anton LaVey at the vanguard of transforming satanic worship into a more individualistic and self-centric belief system. These contemporary iterations of satanism incorporated elements of self-indulgence, hedonism, and personal empowerment, often employing theatrical rituals to challenge societal norms and conventional moral frameworks.

Taking this historical context into account, I consulted theological experts to gain insight into how satanic worship clashes with deontological ethical frameworks. Deontological ethics, famously expounded by philosophers such as Immanuel Kant, places great emphasis on moral duty and the inherent morality or immorality of an action, regardless of its consequences. It asserts that certain actions, such as lying or theft, are intrinsically wrong, irrespective of any potential positive outcomes they may generate.

Conversely, satanic worship is characterized by a rejection of societal norms and an embrace of practices often perceived as immoral or even evil. The very act of worshiping a malevolent deity challenges the tenets of deontological ethics, as it stands in opposition to the notion of universal moral principles. Can an action be inherently wrong if it is part of a belief system where wrongness is not defined by societal standards but rather by the internal alignment with one's chosen path?

The theological experts I consulted presented a range of perspectives on this matter. Some argued that satanic worship could be reconciled with deontological ethics if adhering to a set of internal principles, where the satanist upholds a personal duty to their deity. According to this view, the morality of an action would be determined by the intention behind it, rather than the consequences it entails.

Conversely, others identified a fundamental conflict between satanic worship and deontological ethics. They pointed out the inherent contradiction between the principles of absolute moral duty and satanic practices that deliberately challenge societal norms and ethical boundaries. In this perspective, satanic worship represents a divergence from the universal principles deontological ethics aims to establish.

As my research progressed, I could not overlook or dismiss my own beliefs and biases. Through my encounters with various individuals involved in the realm of satanic worship, I came to appreciate that it is not a uniform belief system. Countless interpretations, traditions, and rituals associated with satanic worship exist, each reflecting the personal path of the worshiper. To completely reject the compatibility of satanic worship with deontological ethics would be an oversimplification of a nuanced and multifaceted reality.

After devoting months to immersing myself in this topic, I find myself still grappling with the complexities and contradictions that arise at the intersection of satanic worship and deontological ethics. The undeniable tension between the two engenders profound questions about our moral frameworks. Is there an inherent conflict that cannot be resolved? Or can we discover a way to reconcile these apparently divergent philosophies? I suspect the answers lie in a domain where rationality and spirituality intersect, a realm as enigmatic and elusive as the forces I continue to investigate.

SATANIC ETHICS AND SOCIAL CONTRACT THEORY

As an investigator specializing in paranormal phenomena, I have extensively explored various occult practices and religious ideologies. One aspect that has consistently intrigued me is the examination of Satanic ethics and their connection to social contract theory. How do adherents of Satanic beliefs navigate their convictions and establish ethical standards within their communities? This question necessitates a comprehensive analysis that delves into the intricate interplay between individual freedoms, group dynamics, and the development of moral codes within Satanic communities.

To embark on this exploration, it is paramount to first decipher the fundamental essence of Satanic ethics. Contrary to common misconceptions, Satanism does not advocate malevolence or endorse unethical conduct. In reality, it is a philosophical system that values individualism, personal accountability, and the pursuit of knowledge. Within Satanic communities, the social contract is implicitly established on the basis of these core principles and the collective understanding that each member has willingly consented to partake in this agreement.

Adherents of Satanism continuously negotiate ethical norms that reflect their individual inclinations and beliefs, while simultaneously adhering to the overarching principles of Satanic philosophy. This process of negotiation manifests as a delicate equilibrium between personal autonomy and communal responsibility. The Satanic social contract permits the exploration of taboo subjects, the practice of rituals, and the pursuit of desires that may be considered unconventional within mainstream society. However, such freedom is not without limitations. Satanic communities expect their members to honor the autonomy and consent of others, thereby establishing an ethical framework centered on informed consent, honesty, and personal responsibility.

One might posit that Satanic ethics embody a radical form of individualism that challenges traditional moral norms. It is crucial to distinguish between individualism as a self-serving endeavor and Satanic individualism, which encourages self-discovery and personal growth. Within Satanic communities, individualism is ultimately harmonized with an understanding of one's role in relation to others. This delicate balance permits the formation of ethical standards that prioritize the well-being and autonomy of all members, rather than perpetuating a hierarchical system that perpetuates power imbalances.

To fully comprehend the negotiation of ethical norms within Satanic communities, it is imperative to assess the role of ritual practices. Rituals hold a significant place in Satanic worship, serving as means of self-expression and spiritual exploration. These rituals often encompass symbolic acts, invocations, or the utilization of magical tools. While the content and nature of these rituals may vary among different Satanic groups, the underlying purpose remains consistent: to channel individual desires and intentions within a communal framework.

The negotiation of ethical norms is particularly evident in the formulation and execution of Satanic rituals. Each ritual offers participants an opportunity to express their desires, be it personal empowerment, artistic expression, or the exploration of taboo subjects. However, the execution of these rituals also requires a profound comprehension of consent and boundaries. Satanic worshipers engage in ongoing discussions and negotiations to ensure that every participant feels comfortable and secure throughout the process.

The negotiation of ethical norms within Satanic communities extends beyond the realm of rituals. Satanic ethics also encompass daily interactions and the establishment of community guidelines. While these guidelines may vary among different groups, they generally revolve around principles of personal autonomy, consent, and mutual respect. The negotiation process involves open dialogue, where members collectively shape the ethical standards that govern their community.

In conclusion, the social contract implications of Satanic worship are intricate and multifaceted. Satanic ethics are rooted in individualism, personal accountability, and the pursuit of knowledge, but they also necessitate a commitment to communal well-being and the establishment of ethical norms. Satanic communities engage in an ongoing negotiation to strike a balance between personal autonomy and communal responsibility, ensuring that individual desires are respected while upholding the principles that define Satanic philosophy. Through this continuous process, adherents of Satanic beliefs create ethical frameworks that prioritize informed consent, honesty, and personal accountability. By delving into the study of Satanic ethics and social contract theory, we gain a profound understanding of the intricate dynamics within Satanic communities and the formation of their ethical norms.

12

SATANIC WORSHIP AND THE AFTERLIFE

SATANISM AND REINCARNATION

As an experienced paranormal investigator and specialist in the supernatural, I have encountered numerous belief systems and witnessed the enigmatic forces that surpass our understanding. One area of particular interest to me is the concept of reincarnation within Satanic beliefs. It is a subject surrounded by mystery and controversy, which has prompted me to extensively explore history and delve into the darkest corners of the occult in pursuit of the truth.

To truly comprehend the roots behind the belief in reincarnation within Satanism, one must first grasp the nature of Satanism itself. Often misconstrued and demonized, Satanism does not involve the worship of a literal devil, but rather the pursuit of individualism, self-empowerment, and the rejection of societal norms and religious doctrines. It represents a path that challenges conventional notions of good and evil by embracing personal freedom and self-discovery.

Throughout history, various civilizations and cultures have embraced the idea of reincarnation, attributing it to different

241

deities or philosophical systems. Whether it be the ancient Egyptians' understanding of the soul's journey through multiple lifetimes or the Hindu concept of samsara, the cycle of birth, death, and rebirth, the concept of reincarnation holds deep significance within human consciousness.

Within the context of Satanism, the belief in reincarnation takes on a distinct interpretation. Satanists perceive life as a finite existence—transitory and governed by the natural cycles of birth, growth, decay, and death. They view each individual as an eternal essence that surpasses physical existence and may potentially be reborn in a different form after death.

Through dedicated research, I have encountered various texts and firsthand accounts that shed light on the beliefs and practices surrounding reincarnation within Satanic circles. One of the primary sources I've come across is the "Book of Satanic Rituals," which is a compilation of rituals and teachings by the renowned occultist Anton LaVey, the founder of the Church of Satan.

In this book, LaVey discusses the concept of reincarnation within Satanism, explaining that Satanists perceive the cycle of life and death as an opportunity for personal growth and development. They believe that with each incarnation, individuals accumulate knowledge, experiences, and skills, ultimately striving for self-realization and liberation from conventional existence.

LaVey further elaborates that Satanic rituals often incorporate elements aimed at unlocking one's past lives and accessing the vast pool of knowledge accumulated throughout time. Through guided meditations, trance states, and astral projection, Satanists seek to bridge the gap between their conscious and subconscious minds, tapping into the reservoir of their past incarnations.

In my quest for understanding, I had the privilege of interviewing Erika Sorenson, an esteemed occult researcher and practicing Satanist. She shared her personal experiences with past-life regression and its role within Satanic belief systems. According to Erika, many Satanists employ past-life regression as a means to recall fragments of their previous incarnations. Through hypnosis and deep meditation, practitioners explore their subconscious minds, attempting to unlock memories from past lives.

Erika recounted a particularly profound regression session in which she awoke as a young woman in medieval Europe. The vivid imagery she described and the emotions she experienced made it evident that the memories she accessed were not mere figments of her imagination, but remnants of a past life. This personal revelation reinforced her belief in the reality of reincarnation and its relevance within her Satanic belief system.

Although the concept of reincarnation within Satanism is often met with skepticism and scrutiny, it serves an important purpose for many practitioners. It provides them with a framework through which they can contextualize their lives, embracing the idea of personal growth and evolution. In the face of an apparently chaotic and unpredictable universe, the belief in reincarnation offers solace and a sense of continuity as one navigates the intricacies of existence.

In conclusion, the investigation into reincarnation within Satanic beliefs reveals a complex tapestry of ideology, ritualistic practices, and personal experiences. Through historical research, written accounts, and firsthand narratives, I have begun to grasp the fact that Satanists perceive reincarnation as both a means of personal growth and a connection to the timeless continuum of life and death. This topic challenges the boundaries of our comprehension and invites inquisitive minds to explore the deepest recesses of the human psyche. As I continue my exploration into the mysteries of Satanism, I am left pondering a lingering question: What truths lie beyond the veil of mortality, waiting to be uncovered by those brave enough to venture into the realm of the unknown?

SATANIC WORSHIP AND ETERNAL DAMNATION

As an investigator specializing in paranormal phenomena, I have encountered numerous instances involving Satanic worship. This subject has always intrigued me, not only due to its occult nature, but also because of its profound association with the idea of eternal damnation. In this chapter, my intention is to explore the depths of this belief system, including its origins, practices, and the terrifying consequences it holds for those individuals who venture into its sinister realm.

Satanic worship has existed throughout history, with its roots delving deep into the depths of human existence. The belief in eternal damnation, which is intricately linked to this form of worship, is closely tied to the concept of hell. It is believed that Satan, the fallen angel, resides within this realm of perpetual torment, exerting his influence over his followers, who are commanded to engage in blasphemous rituals and offerings in his name. This concept of eternal damnation serves as an effective tool of control, instilling fear and reverence in the hearts of those who question or challenge the beliefs associated with Satanic worship.

To comprehend the belief in eternal damnation, it is necessary to examine the origins of Satanic worship. The early beginnings of this belief system can be traced back to ancient civilizations, where rituals and sacrifices were made in honor of various deities. However, over time, a darker and more malevolent figure emerged—the Devil himself. The perception of

Satan transitioned from being a minor deity to the antagonist of all that was deemed righteous and holy.

One of the earliest documented works that delve into the concept of eternal damnation within Satanic worship is John Milton's epic poem, "Paradise Lost." This literary masterpiece delves into the fall of Satan, his rebellion against God, and his subsequent banishment to hell. Milton's vivid portrayal of Satan's character and his dialogue throughout the poem provides insight into the mindset of a being who embraces damnation, reveling in his defiance against the divine.

Continuing forward in history, we encounter a pivotal period known as the Satanic Panic of the 1980s. During this era, there was widespread belief in the infiltration of Satanic cults into society, perpetrating horrific crimes and sacrificing innocent lives in the name of their dark deity. Although largely discredited now, the fear and hysteria surrounding this phenomenon reflected a deep-seated dread of eternal damnation within Satanic worship.

During my investigations, I have encountered individuals who claim to have firsthand experience with Satanic rituals and the belief in eternal damnation. One such case involved a young woman named Rebecca, who approached me with a haunting tale of her involvement in a Satanic cult. She recounted dark ceremonies conducted under cover of darkness, where members chanted incantations, made offerings, and sought to summon the Devil himself. Rebecca described an overwhelming sense of dread and a constant fear of eternal damnation that consumed her every waking moment. The psychological impact of her experiences left her shattered, haunted by nightmares, and struggling to maintain a firm grasp on reality.

To enhance my understanding, I sought out academic research and historical accounts that shed light on the connection between Satanic worship and the belief in eternal damnation. An intriguing study presented an exploration of the psychological motivations behind the attraction to Satanic beliefs. It proposed that the fear and allure of eternal damnation arises from a deep-seated desire to rebel against societal norms and find solace in a realm that allows for the embrace of forbidden impulses. This perspective offers a glimpse into the complex motivations that drive individuals to engage in Satanic worship, willingly subjecting themselves to the terrifying prospect of eternal damnation.

In conclusion, the belief in eternal damnation within Satanic worship runs deep, interwoven into the very fabric of this dark belief system. From ancient civilizations to the present day, the concept of hell and the fear of eternal damnation have shaped the practices and rituals of Satanic worship. Whether through literature, personal accounts, or academic research, the connection between Satanic worship and the belief in eternal damnation becomes increasingly evident, revealing a path filled with darkness and torment. As a paranormal investigator, I view it as my obligation to explore these depths, shedding light on the darkness in order to comprehend its allure and unravel the mysteries that lie within.

SATANIC AFTERLIFE AND SPIRITUAL EVOLUTION

Throughout my tenure as a paranormal investigator and specialist of the inexplicable, I have delved into the deepest recesses of human belief systems and encountered various interpretations of the afterlife. However, none can rival the intricate and fascinating teachings of Satanic belief. As an ardent seeker of truth, I was compelled to explore the concept of spiritual progression within Satanic teachings concerning the afterlife.

To truly grasp the Satanic perspective, it is imperative to step back and examine the historical context in which these beliefs originated. Over the centuries, Satanism has frequently been misconstrued and misrepresented as an evil and malevolent force. Nevertheless, as an individual who has devoted their life to unraveling mysteries, I have come to recognize that these judgments are misunderstandings driven by ignorance.

Satanism, as practiced by its adherents, is a complex belief system centered around individualism, self-empowerment, and personal growth. It rejects the notion of external deities and emphasizes personal responsibility and self-improvement. It is within this framework that we embark on our exploration of the Satanic afterlife and its connection to spiritual progression.

According to Satanic teachings, the afterlife is not a state of eternal punishment or reward, but rather an extension of personal growth and evolution. It is believed that upon death, individuals transcend their physical limitations and enter a spiritual realm where their consciousness expands and evolves. This concept of spiritual progression is deeply rooted in Satanic philosophy, as it promotes the relentless pursuit of knowledge and personal development.

To comprehend the intricacies of this belief, it is essential to delve into the writings of influential Satanic thinkers and practitioners. One such figure is Anton LaVey, the founder of the Church of Satan. LaVey's work emphasizes the significance of indulgence, self-exploration, and the rejection of societal constraints. In his book, "The Satanic Bible," he elaborates on the idea of spiritual progression as a process of self-discovery and growth.

Satanic teachings assert that the afterlife is not a static plane of existence but a realm where individuals continuously evolve and broaden their consciousness. This concept aligns with the Satanic defiance of dogma and the perpetual pursuit of personal enlightenment. It is believed that in the Satanic afterlife, individuals have the opportunity to cast off earthly limitations and engage in an everlasting cycle of spiritual transformation.

Central to this belief is the notion that the afterlife offers boundless possibilities for exploration and self-discovery. Satanic rituals and practices, such as meditation and astral projection, are employed to enhance spiritual development and facilitate the evolution of consciousness. By utilizing these tools, practitioners strive to transcend the confines of the physical world and connect with the divine essence within.

Furthermore, Satanic teachings encourage the pursuit of knowledge and the questioning of established beliefs. It is through this intellectual curiosity that spiritual progression is nurtured. Satanic communities often foster engaging in philosophical debates, studying esoteric texts, and expanding one's comprehension of occult knowledge. This approach is rooted in the belief that personal growth and evolution can only be achieved through the constant exploration of novel ideas and concepts.

It is crucial to note that within Satanic belief systems, spiritual progression is not limited to the afterlife. Individuals are encouraged to actively engage in self-improvement and personal development during their mortal existence. Satanic teachings emphasize self-awareness, ambition, and the pursuit of personal desires. By manifesting individual aspirations and honing one's skills and talents, practitioners strive to realize their full potential and contribute to the broader Satanic community.

In conclusion, Satanic teachings present a distinct and compelling perspective on the afterlife and spiritual progression. Instead of viewing the afterlife as an unchanging realm of eternal punishment or reward, Satanism promotes the idea of continuous growth and personal development. By embracing individualism, self-empowerment, and the pursuit of knowledge, practitioners partake in an ongoing process of spiritual progression both in this life and beyond. Satanic beliefs challenge conventional notions of the afterlife and present an invigorating outlook that enco

SATANIC WORSHIP AND ASTRAL REALMS

In my capacity as a paranormal investigator and specialist in anomalous phenomena, I have encountered a multitude of enigmatic and obscure occurrences. One subject that consistently arouses my interest is the intricate nexus linking Satanic worship and astral realms. The association between Satanic worship and the belief in alternative dimensions and the afterlife has endured throughout history, and it is primarily within these realms that the true essence of their rituals resides.

To truly grasp the interconnection between Satanic worship and astral realms, it is imperative to delve deeply into their doctrines and practices. For centuries, followers of Satan have invoked and engaged in communion with demonic entities with the aim of amassing power, knowledge, and dominion over the concealed realms that lie beyond the boundaries of our physical reality. Many of these practices involve astral projection, which is the capacity to dissociate one's consciousness from the physical body and explore dimensions that surpass our material world.

In the course of my research, I have come across archaic texts and testimonies from individuals who claim to have undergone astral projection during Satanic rituals. These individuals maintain that such experiences enable them to traverse astral realms and interact with otherworldly beings. These astral realms are perceived as abodes inhabited by potent entities of both benevolent and malevolent nature. It is within these realms that practitioners of Satanic worship seek enlightenment, guidance, and even an afterlife divergent from conventional interpretations of heaven or hell.

The significance of these beliefs within the practice of Satanic worship cannot be overemphasized. To adherents, the astral realms embody a playground for their dark desires and ambitions. They ardently believe that by harnessing the power of these realms, they can attain immortality, transcendence, and godlike abilities. It is through their exploration and manipulation of the astral realms that they strive to achieve ultimate salvation and absolute dominion.

It is noteworthy to acknowledge that the belief in alternate dimensions and astral realms is not exclusive to Satanic worship. Throughout the annals of human history, myriad cultures and belief systems have acknowledged the presence of concealed realms beyond our corporeal senses. The concept of the afterlife, specifically, has constituted a central tenet of religious and spiritual practices globally. However, it is within the domain of Satanic worship that these beliefs acquire an exceptionally sinister and intriguing form.

It is crucial to comprehend that not all practitioners of Satanic worship partake in astral projection or espouse the belief in alternate dimensions. The practice varies amongst different factions and individuals, with each harboring their own interpretations of Satanic doctrines. Nevertheless, for those who do embrace the connection between Satanic worship and astral realms, the significance is profound.

As a paranormal investigator, it is my responsibility to explore and comprehend the unfathomable. In my pursuit of knowledge, I have engaged in the exploration of astral realms utilizing various techniques, including lucid dreaming, meditation, and astral projection. These encounters have afforded me unparalleled insights into the vastness and intricacy of the veiled worlds that intermingle with our own. I have encountered entities of both malevolent and benevolent nature, and it is within these encou

SATANIC WORSHIP AND NIHILISM

To comprehensively comprehend the correlation between Satanic worship and nihilism, it is imperative to delve into the historical background and origins of both concepts. Satanic worship, often associated with the religious movement of Satanism, can be traced back to ancient civilizations that revered deities embodying chaos and darkness. However, modern-day Satanism came into existence in the late 18th century, influenced by the romanticized depiction of Satan in literature and the personas adopted by various rebellious groups throughout history. Although Satanism encompasses a diverse spectrum of beliefs and practices, it is commonly characterized by the rejection of conventional religious norms and an embrace of individualism and personal empowerment.

Contrarily, nihilism is a philosophical standpoint that emerged in the 19th century and gained prominence following the Industrial Revolution. Nihilism asserts the view that life and existence lack inherent meaning, value, or purpose. Nihilistic adherents renounce the concept of an objective moral or ethical framework, arguing against the existence of an ultimate truth or higher power governing human existence.

When analyzing the perspective of nihilism within Satanic worship, we encounter a convergence of ideologies that challenge conventional understandings of the afterlife. At the core of nihilism lies the notion that life is ultimately devoid of meaning and that there are no divine judgments or eternal consequences for our actions. This aligns with the Satanic belief in rejecting traditional religious morality and embracing individual desires and carnal pleasures. The concept of an afterlife, traditionally associated with religious belief systems that promise rewards or punishments based on moral conduct, becomes null and void within the philosophical framework of nihilism.

Within Satanic worship, the denial of an afterlife grants individuals the license to indulge in their earthly desires without fearing cosmic retribution. Through my research and interviews with adherents of Satanic worship, I have discovered that this perspective on the afterlife provides a sense of liberation and autonomy. It allows individuals to freely explore their darkest fantasies and give in to their most primal desires without experiencing guilt or remorse. Their existence becomes a hedonistic pursuit, free from the fear of divine judgment.

However, the implications of this perspective on the afterlife extend beyond mere indulgence and hedonism. The denial of an afterlife also imposes a sense of existential responsibility. In a world lacking inherent meaning or purpose, each individual bears the burden of creating their own value systems and seeking personal fulfillment. This responsibility can be empowering for some, as it places the power of attributing meaning squarely in their hands. Nevertheless, it can also lead to feelings of existential dread and nihilistic despair, as individuals grapple with the realization that their actions and choices ultimately amount to nothing in the grand scheme of things.

Additionally, the rejection of an afterlife within Satanic worship raises inquiries about the nature of morality and the concept of good and evil. In the absence of a divine framework or an objective moral compass, morality becomes subjective and relative. What one person may perceive as morally acceptable, another may deem reprehensible. In light of the absence of absolute moral standards, it becomes a matter of personal interpretation and preference. This subjective approach to morality within Satanic worship has often faced criticism for promoting amorality and immorality, as it allows individuals to justify and engage in behavior that is traditionally considered taboo or unethical.

As I continue to investigate the perspective of nihilism within Satanic worship and its implications for the concept of the afterlife, I confront the intricacies and contradictions inherent in these beliefs. On one hand, the denial of an afterlife offers liberation and autonomy, liberating individuals from the constraints of traditional religious morality. On the other hand, it introduces existential responsibility and challenges the very foundation of moral frameworks. Ultimately, the intertwining of nihilism and Satanic worship presents a unique framework through which to examine the human pursuit of meaning, understanding, and agency in a world that may lack inherent purpose.

SATANIC RITUALS AND SOUL JOURNEY

In order to truly comprehend the significance of soul journey and astral projection within Satanic rituals, it is imperative to delve into the origins and purpose of such rituals. Satanic rituals serve as a means for individuals to establish a connection with the forces of darkness and to unveil forbidden knowledge. Throughout history, these rituals have been veiled in mystery and secrecy, and have been associated with practices that are considered heretical by dominant religious institutions. Within the realm of Satanic rituals, the incorporation of soul journey and astral projection stands as a unique and captivating aspect.

By analyzing the practice of soul journey and astral projection within Satanic rituals, one discovers a delicate balance between darkness and curiosity. It represents an endeavor to surpass the limitations of the physical world and to explore the vastness of the afterlife. Many may question why individuals willingly engage in such perilous and potentially hazardous practices. The answer lies in their thirst for knowledge and their commitment to uncover the concealed truths that lie beyond the veil. This journey is fraught with risks, yet it promises unimaginable rewards for those who display the courage to venture into the unknown.

One cannot discuss the practice of soul journey and astral projection without acknowledging the controversial and often taboo nature of these practices. Society has long stigmatized these practices, linking them to malicious intentions and an unholy affiliation with dark forces. However, my research and encounters with individuals who have dabbled in these rituals have revealed a different reality, one in which these practices are regarded as pathways to enlightenment and self-discovery.

The act of soul journey and astral projection within Satanic rituals entails separating an individual's consciousness from their physical body. This detachment allows the astral body (commonly referred to as the soul or spirit) to embark on a journey unconstrained by the limitations of the corporeal form. It is during these journeys that individuals claim to encounter otherworldly entities, explore realms beyond mortal comprehension, and acquire insights into the mysteries of the afterlife.

While the practice of soul journey and astral projection can be accomplished through various means, Satanic rituals provide a unique framework within which these experiences unfold. The ritualistic element enhances the potency and focus of the participants, guiding their astral bodies through the intricate tapestry of the afterlife. The inclusion of dark symbolism and invocations within these rituals imbues the experience with a profound sense of otherworldliness, thereby intensifying the journey.

By examining firsthand accounts of those who have experienced soul journey and astral projection within Satanic rituals, an array of encounters and insights comes to light. Some individuals claim to have traversed through ancient catacombs teeming with lost souls, while others speak of communing with potent entities from realms beyond our comprehension. Each experience is as unique as the individuals themselves, yet all serve as glimpses into the enigmatic realm of the afterlife.

It is important to note that the practice of soul journey and astral projection within Satanic rituals should not be taken lightly. The risks involved are significant, as the astral body can become vulnerable to malevolent entities and forces that reside within the unseen realms. Those who embark on such journeys must remain vigilant and attuned to the energies that surround them, as a momentary lapse in focus could lead them down a treacherous path from which there may be no return.

As I continue to explore the intricacies of Satanic rituals and their association with soul journey and astral projection, I am continually reminded of the dual nature of these practices. They possess both immense potential for enlightenment and self-discovery, as well as the inherent danger of delving into realms beyond our mortal comprehension. They serve as a testament to the enduring pursuit of knowledge, even in the face of societal condemnation.

In concluding my analysis of the practice of soul journey and astral projection within Satanic rituals, a sense of awe and reverence for the depths of human curiosity arises. It is through these rituals that individuals dare to challenge the boundaries of existence and explore the enigmatic realm of the afterlife.

As a paranormal investigator and specialist in the extraordinary, I am driven to unravel the secrets of the universe, to gaze into the abyss and emerge with a profound understanding of our place in the grand tapestry of existence.

SATANIC WORSHIP AND SPIRITUAL LIBERATION

As an investigator specializing in paranormal phenomena, it was both daunting and necessary to delve into the realm of Satanic worship and its connection to spiritual emancipation. There existed widespread misconceptions about Satanism, erroneously dismissing it as a path solely associated with darkness and malevolence. However, my extensive research led me to a more nuanced understanding, revealing that there lay much more beneath the surface.

In order to truly comprehend the pursuit of spiritual liberation within the context of Satanic worship, it was essential to explore the historical foundations of Satanism itself. The most captivating aspect of this inquiry was its challenge to conventional religious notions of the hereafter. While mainstream religions predominantly advocate the existence of heaven and hell, Satanism presents an alternative perspective, one that hinges on self-deification and individualism.

Eliphas Levi, an influential occultist in the 19th century, played a pivotal role in molding the philosophical underpinnings of Satanic worship and its pursuit of spiritual liberation. Levi conceived of Satan not as an adversary to God, but rather as a symbological representation of personal emancipation and self-realization. This revolutionary notion severed Satanic worship's connection to the Christian roots that condemned it, allowing it to develop as an entirely distinct entity.

Delving further into my research led me to discover the profound influence of Anton LaVey and the Church of Satan, which propelled Satanic worship into the public eye during the 1960s. LaVey placed considerable emphasis on individualism and the pursuit of personal desires within the framework of Satanism. He rejected the notion of sin, arguing that it was imposed upon individuals by external authorities to manipulate their behavior. For LaVey, spiritual liberation stemmed from embracing one's true self and challenging societal norms.

In order to gather firsthand insight, I made the decision to attend a Satanic ritual. The attendees represented a diverse array of individuals from various walks of life, all united in their quest for personal enlightenment and emancipation. The ritual itself was an enchanting amalgamation of theatrics, symbolism, and introspection. It became evident that the pursuit of spiritual liberation within Satanic worship was both multifaceted and deeply personalized.

During the course of my research, I encountered the concept of spiritual liberation through embracing one's so-called "dark side." Within Satanic worship, this entailed acknowledging and accepting aspects of oneself that society often deems unacceptable. By doing so, one could transcend the confines of societal expectations and norms and truly embrace their authentic nature.

One individual of particular interest, Sarah, shared her extraordinary personal journey within Satanic worship during an interview. She described her experience as a liberation from the religious dogma instilled in her from an early age. Through her involvement in Satanic rituals, she discovered a newfound sense of self-worth and confidence. Sarah explained that Satanic worship provided her with the freedom to question traditional notions of good and evil, morality and sin, and provided her with a framework to explore her individuality without judgment.

While Satanic worship provided a platform for spiritual liberation, it was not without controversy. The portrayal of Satan as a symbol of opposition and rebellion against established authority drew criticism from various quarters. Some accused it of promoting immoral conduct or even endorsing violent rituals. However, my findings debunked these misconceptions, highlighting that they were rooted in ignorance and fear surrounding Satanic worship.

The pursuit of spiritual liberation and the subversion of traditional religious concepts regarding the afterlife within Satanic worship, as I discovered, did not entail embracing evil or immorality. Rather, it involved challenging the prevailing status quo, interrogating societal norms, and fostering personal growth and self-discovery. It offered a distinctive opportunity to redefine spirituality and attain personal enlightenment outside the confines of traditional religious dogma.

As my investigation came to a close, I realized that Satanic worship and its pursuit of spiritual liberation were not intended for everyone. It demanded a certain level of introspection, open-mindedness, and a willingness to challenge preconceived notions. However, for those audacious enough to immerse themselves in the complexities of this unconventional path, it offered an extraordinary journey of self-discovery and empowerment. The pursuit of spiritual liberation within Satanic worship presented an invitation to transcend traditional religious concepts and embark upon a transformative exploration of the self.

SATANIC ETHICS AND DEATH RITUALS

To gain a comprehensive understanding of Satanic ethics and death rituals, one must embark upon an exploration of the historical timeline that has paved the way for their existence.

This journey spans centuries, originating from ancient beliefs and practices that have undergone a gradual evolution over time. From the early days of pagan fertility cults to the inception of modern Satanic movements, the rituals and practices affiliated with death have transformed into a multifaceted tapestry interwoven with symbolism, philosophical ideologies, and the pursuit of personal enlightenment.

During antiquity, death was perceived as a natural and cyclical aspect of life. Cultures worldwide engaged in various death rituals, ranging from elaborate burial ceremonies to the construction of intricate tombs. It was during this primal era that the foundations of what would eventually become Satanic ethics and death rituals were established. These early societies held strong convictions about the existence of powerful entities that could be pacified through offerings and rituals, and consequently, death presented an opportunity to commune with these supernatural forces.

The ascendancy of Christianity shaped the narrative encompassing death, vilifying ancient pagan practices that exalted mortality. The Church propagated the notion that death was a consequence of sin, introducing the concept of eternal damnation in Hell. Nevertheless, it was in the face of this repressive ideology that Satanic ethics and death rituals found their grounding. In the 1960s, the Satanic Temple, pioneered by Anton LaVey, sought to challenge social norms, embracing a philosophy that championed individualism, self-expression, and personal empowerment.

Within Satanic communities, death is not dreaded but rather venerated as a natural component of the human experience. The rituals and practices associated with death and mourning within these communities endeavor to embrace and commemorate mortality, rejecting the concept of an afterlife governed by divine judgment. This perspective diverges starkly from the mainstream belief system, yet holds a powerful allure for those in pursuit of liberation from oppressive societal constructs.

Exploring the rituals and practices associated with death and mourning within Satanic communities is a delicate and often risky endeavor. These communities jealously safeguard their secrets, with initiation rites and rigid hierarchies ensuring that only those deemed deserving gain access to their inner sanctum. Through extensive research and interviews with insiders, I have managed to assemble fragments of this enigmatic puzzle, constructing a picture of rituals imbued with dark symbolism and profound introspection.

One such practice is the Black Mass, a ritual that has been distorted, misconstrued, and demonized by the mainstream media. In contrast to prevailing beliefs, the Black Mass does not constitute a literal inversion of a Christian Mass, but rather a symbolic and theatrical performance designed to challenge religious dogma. It serves as a means for Satanic practitioners to confront and transgress societal norms, delving into the depths of their own desires and beliefs.

Another death ritual within Satanic communities is the psychodrama, an immersive and cathartic experience where participants are guided through a symbolic representation of death and rebirth. These rituals often involve strenuous psychological and physical challenges, such as sensory deprivation and sensory overload. Through these trials, participants confront their deepest fears and come face to face with their own mortality, emerging with a revitalized sense of self and purpose.

It is imperative to emphasize that Satanic ethics and death rituals neither condone nor advocate harm towards others. They are not steeped in evil or malevolence, as frequently depicted in popular culture. Rather, they represent a rejection of societal constraints and an embracing of individualism, emphasizing personal responsibility and autonomy. Satanic practitioners strive to live authentically, free from the confines of external judgment and moral hypocrisy.

In conclusion, exploring Satanic ethics and death rituals constitutes a profound and disconcerting journey. It challenges our preconceived notions about death, religion, and the human experience. Across centuries of evolution, Satanic communities have developed rituals and practices that aim to empower and enlighten those willing to venture into the shadows. It is a domain that warrants respect and comprehension, for it holds the answers to unraveling our own deep-seated fears and confronting the inevitable yet enigmatic nature of death.

13

SATANIC WORSHIP AND THE DIVINE

SATANIC PERSPECTIVES ON GOD AND DEITIES

In order to gain a comprehensive understanding of the Satanic perspective, I undertook a thorough study of the historical evolution of Satanic beliefs. This exploration was crucial in grasping the philosophical roots of Satanism's unorthodox views on divinity.

The earliest documented instances of Satanic worship can be traced back to ancient Mesopotamia, where polytheistic religions, such as those practiced by the Sumerians and Babylonians, embraced a multitude of deities. In contrast to the predominantly benevolent gods worshipped by these civilizations, demons and malevolent entities held significant positions in their pantheon. The veneration of these darker entities can be seen as an early form of Satanic worship, characterized by the rejection of conventional notions of good and evil and the embrace of the mysterious and unknown.

As time progressed, the influence of Christianity and the rise of Judeo-Christian beliefs profoundly impacted the development of Satanic perspectives. In Christian theology, God is regarded as an all-powerful and benevolent figure with absolute authority over humanity. The Satanic rejection of this concept can be traced back to ancient Gnosticism and its belief in a multitude of deities. Gnostics held the belief that the God of the Old Testament was a false deity, a demiurge who created an imperfect material world. In their eyes, genuine divinity emanated from a higher, unknown entity, a concept that later aligned with Satanic beliefs.

It was in the sixteenth century when Satanic perspectives on God and deities began to solidify into a more defined philosophy. The Italian philosopher Giordano Bruno rejected traditional Christian concepts of God and introduced the theory of multiple universes, each governed by its own divine intellect. His ideas were deemed heretical at the time and ultimately led to his execution. Nevertheless, his work influenced subsequent occultists and esoteric thinkers who aimed to challenge prevailing dogmas.

Fast forward to the twentieth century, when Anton LaVey established the Church of Satan in 1966. LaVeyan Satanism, as it came to be known, rejected the existence of supernatural beings and instead embraced a self-centered philosophy centered around individualism and the power of an individual's will. This renunciation of external deities in favor of self-deification would become a fundamental tenet of modern Satanism.

By exploring the rejection of conventional concepts of God and deities within Satanic worship, it becomes evident that self-deification transcends mere rebelliousness. It is a philosophical standpoint that challenges the hierarchical structure prevalent in traditional religions, advocating for personal empowerment and the assertion of individual agency.

Through their embrace of self-deification, Satanists assert that they, as individuals, possess the potential to become gods themselves. This concept may appear audacious, even blasphemous, to adherents of mainstream religious belief systems. However, it is essential to understand that within the framework of Satanism, this notion does not seek to supplant any specific religious figure or belief. Instead, it rejects external authority and affirms the intrinsic power and value of the individual.

In conclusion, delving into the Satanic rejection of traditional concepts of God and deities provides a glimpse into a subversive perspective that challenges the hierarchy of mainstream religions. By embracing self-deification, Satanists celebrate personal agency and pursue individual empowerment. While this perspective may be seen as controversial, it is crucial to acknowledge that within the realm of Satanic worship, it serves as a foundational philosophy that promotes the recognition of one's inherent power and worth. By examining these Satanic perspectives, we gain not only a deeper understanding of the diverse range of human beliefs but also a reflection on the societal constructs that shape our perception of divinity.

SATANIC WORSHIP AND PANTHEISM

As a researcher specializing in the paranormal and the unusual, I have encountered and studied various belief systems and their intersections with the supernatural. One area of particular interest to me is the relationship between Satanic worship and pantheistic beliefs, specifically examining the compatibility of these two seemingly contradictory ideologies and their shared reverence for the natural world.

To delve into this topic, it is important to first understand the fundamental principles of Satanic worship and pantheism. Satanic worship, often misunderstood and clouded by societal fear, encompasses a diverse range of practices. Contrary to common misconception, Satanism is not solely focused on the worship of a devil figure, but rather represents an antithesis to mainstream religious traditions. Pantheism, on the other hand, views divinity as inseparable from the natural world, emphasizing the interconnectedness and inherent sacredness of all things.

At first glance, these belief systems may appear conflicting, as Satanic worship is often associated with darkness, rebellion, and individualism, while pantheism stresses unity, harmony, and the interconnectedness of all life. However, upon closer examination, we begin to uncover hidden parallels and potential compatibility between the two.

In my research, I have encountered individuals who identify as both Satanists and pantheists. Through their accounts and my subsequent investigations, I aim to shed light on the inherent connections between these seemingly divergent belief systems.

One area of compatibility lies in the shared reverence for the natural world. Pantheism recognizes the divine essence within creation, while Satanism celebrates personal freedom and individual autonomy. By acknowledging the inherent sacredness of nature, both belief systems recognize the power and beauty of the natural world. Satanism often portrays the devil figure as synonymous with nature, symbolizing wildness, untamed energy, and instinct. Thus, Satanists who embrace pantheism see the natural world as an embodiment of their beliefs and a source of spiritual connection.

Furthermore, both Satanic worship and pantheism reject traditional hierarchical structures imposed by organized religions. In Satanism, the rejection of divine authority is a central tenet, with individuals encouraged to question dogma and think critically. Similarly, pantheism rejects the notion of a transcendent deity being separate from the natural world, emphasizing instead the divine presence within all things. The alignment in the rejection of traditional authority strengthens the bond between these two belief systems, suggesting a shared resistance to oppressive structures and a desire for personal autonomy.

Interestingly, the symbolism employed by Satanic worship and pantheism also reveals hidden similarities. Both belief systems often draw upon powerful archetypes and mythological figures to convey their ideologies. While Satanism embraces the archetype of the devil and subverts traditional Christian symbolism, pantheism finds inspiration in various deities and mythical creatures as representations of the natural world's power. This common use of mythology and symbolism not only serves as a bridge between these belief systems, but also highlights their shared appreciation for the enigmatic and mysterious aspects of existence.

Additionally, the Satanic concept of the "rebel" and the pantheistic emphasis on harmony can be seen as complementary rather than contradictory. Satanic worship encourages individual exploration and the championing of personal desires, which, when combined with pantheism's focus on interconnectedness, can lead to a harmonious coexistence with the natural world. This integration of rebellion and harmony opens up new possibilities for those seeking a spiritual path that honors personal autonomy while acknowledging the interdependent web of life in which we all exist.

In conclusion, the compatibility between Satanic worship and pantheistic beliefs challenges our initial assumptions about these seemingly disparate ideologies. Through an analysis of shared values, symbolism, and the experiences of individuals practicing both belief systems, we discover a profound connection between their reverence for the natural world and rejection of traditional authority. It is within this intersection that the true complexities of human spirituality and the potential for unification lie, urging us to reassess our preconceived notions and embrace the diverse array of beliefs that exist in our world.

SATANIC RITUALS AND POLYTHEISTIC PRACTICES

When considering satanic rituals, one often envisions images of unconventional altars, inverted crosses, and sinister chanting in dimly lit rooms. It is certainly a disconcerting depiction. However, it is important to recognize that there is more to these rituals than the worship of a single malevolent entity. In fact, these rituals encompass an acknowledgment of multiple divine entities within their very framework.

To gain a deeper understanding of this aspect, extensive research was undertaken involving numerous texts, ancient scriptures, and grimoires. The journey of exploration was arduous, encompassing days and nights dedicated to deciphering forgotten languages and unraveling cryptic symbols. However, the diligent efforts paid off as the hidden depths of satanic rituals were gradually revealed.

One of the initial significant revelations encountered was the connection between Satanism and ancient polytheistic religions. Unlike monotheistic practices, polytheism involves a belief in multiple gods and goddesses. These deities often embody specific aspects of life such as love, war, fertility, and justice. Research conducted demonstrated that within satanic rituals, various beings are invoked, each representing different facets of existence.

The incorporation of polytheistic elements within satanic rituals is most vividly depicted in the act of summoning demons. While Satan remains the focal point in these rituals, it is not uncommon to find practitioners calling upon lesser-known entities from diverse mythologies and pantheons. From ancient Mesopotamian demons to Nordic deities, the diversity within these rituals is truly astonishing.

One may wonder why Satanism embraces polytheistic practices. The answer lies in the quest for power and control. By acknowledging and invoking multiple divine entities, practitioners of satanic rituals believe they tap into a vast reserve of energy. Each deity possesses unique attributes and abilities, enabling one to gain an advantage in various aspects of life, including wealth, love, and even hexing enemies.

It is essential to note, however, that the incorporation of polytheistic practices within satanic rituals does not signify a harmonious fusion of faiths. Instead, it serves as a calculated manipulation of ancient belief systems to serve the darker purposes of Satanism. These deities are invoked not as objects of veneration or worship, but as tools and conduits to accomplish one's desires.

Further research unveiled that the acknowledgment of multiple divine entities within satanic rituals transcends the mere summoning of demons. Instances arise where practitioners pay homage to ancient gods and goddesses through various rituals and offerings. These acts establish a symbiotic relationship, wherein the practitioner provides their devotion and energy, and in return, the divine entity bestows favors and blessings upon them.

This aspect, above all else, intrigued me. How can practitioners of Satanism, renowned for their dark and sinister rituals, embrace a practice seemingly tied to positive outcomes? As my investigation deepened, I recognized that this acknowledgment of multiple divine entities, contradictory as it may appear, constitutes an integral part of their belief system. It exemplifies their understanding that the world is not a simple dichotomy of good and evil but rather a complex tapestry of forces that can be manipulated for personal gain.

Yet, one should not hastily dismiss these practices as mere superstitions or flights of fancy. On the contrary, my research has demonstrated a chilling efficacy to these rituals. From documented instances of miracles and unexplained phenomena to testimonies of individuals claiming fulfillment of their desires, there exists a tangible power at work. Whether one chooses to attribute this power to the deities themselves or the collective subconscious of the participants, the results cannot be denied.

As I conclude this chapter of my research, I am left with a lingering sense of awe and unease. The incorporation of polytheistic practices within satanic rituals is a murky and intricate subject. It challenges preconceived notions, blurring the lines between good and evil, and compelling us to question the very essence of faith and power. However, it is precisely this ambiguity that continues to draw me deeper into the realm of Satan, for only by grasping the dark and the unknown can we aspire to illuminate our own human nature.

SATANIC PERSPECTIVES ON GOOD AND EVIL

In order to gain an understanding of the Satanic viewpoint on good and evil, it is essential to comprehend the concept of moral relativism. Satanism rejects the notion of a universal, objective moral code and instead embraces the idea that morality is subjective and varies from person to person. From a Satanic perspective, what is deemed good or evil is contingent upon an individual's desires, needs, and beliefs. This rejection of absolutes permits a more adaptable and nuanced understanding of ethics.

Fundamentally, Satanism places great importance on self-glorification. Satanic philosophy encourages individuals to prioritize their own needs and desires above those of others. This self-centric approach is not driven by a desire to cause harm or partake in malicious acts, but rather by the belief that personal happiness and fulfillment should take precedence. By embracing one's own individuality and indulging in their desires, Satanists believe they can lead more genuine and gratifying lives.

According to the Satanic interpretation of good and evil, actions are evaluated based on their practical consequences, rather than strict adherence to prescribed moral rules. This pragmatic approach rejects the notion that certain actions are inherently morally good or evil, acknowledging that context and intent play a significant role. For instance, while society may perceive stealing as morally wrong, a Satanist may argue that stealing to meet one's basic needs during extreme difficulty is justified.

Moreover, Satanism places significant emphasis on personal responsibility. Satanists believe that each individual possesses the ability to establish their own moral code and must be accountable for the outcomes of their actions. This dismissal of external moral authority promotes self-reflection and critical thinking, as individuals are ultimately responsible for the choices they make.

It is important to emphasize that Satanism does not endorse or condone violence or harm towards others. While it rejects certain societal norms and moral frameworks, it does not advocate for chaos or anarchy. In fact, the Satanic perspective on good and evil places great value on empathy, compassion, and respect for others. However, these qualities are not regarded as absolutes but rather as personal choices that align with an individual's own values and desires.

The refusal to make absolute moral judgments is a fundamental principle of Satanic philosophy. Satanists argue that the concept of "good" and "evil" is subjective and often used as a means of control and manipulation. By critically examining societal norms and challenging conventional moral values, Satanism encourages individuals to question the established order and carve their own paths.

In conclusion, the Satanic perspective on good and evil presents an exceptional and thought-provoking alternative to traditional moral frameworks. Through moral relativism, self-glorification, pragmatism, personal responsibility, and a rejection of absolute moral judgments, Satanism offers individuals the freedom to define their own values and determine what is moral or immoral based on their own desires and needs. Although controversial and frequently misunderstood, the exploration of Satanic philosophy provides invaluable insights into the intricacies of human morality and the significance of individual autonomy.

SATANIC WORSHIP AND MONOTHEISTIC RELIGIONS

To fully comprehend the intricacies of this subject, it is imperative to have a thorough understanding of the essence of Satanic worship. Satanism, in its various manifestations, revolves around the veneration of Satan or the devil. It encompasses themes of rebellion, individualism, and the pursuit of worldly pleasures. Contrary to popular belief, it is not synonymous with devil worship or the engagement in malevolent acts. Satanists often perceive Satan as a symbol of personal freedom and the ultimate adversary against the restrictions and dogmas imposed by monotheistic religions.

On the contrary, monotheistic religions encompass belief systems wherein a single god or deity holds supreme authority.

These religions, such as but not limited to Christianity, Judaism, and Islam, uphold the principles of morality, compliance with a divine will, and the worship of a virtuous deity. The foundation of monotheism lies in the concept of absolute good and the rejection of evil, creating an inherent dichotomy between God and Satan.

Critics of Satanic worship argue that it is essentially a reaction to the oppressive nature of monotheistic religions. Individuals who feel disillusioned and restricted by the rigid dogmas of monotheism may find themselves drawn to the allure of Satanic worship as a means of defying authority and embracing personal freedoms. Some even suggest that the image of Satan serves as a foil to challenge the supremacy of God. Critics contend that Satanic worship is nothing more than a rebellion against monotheistic institutions rather than a genuine spiritual practice in itself.

Conversely, proponents of Satanic worship argue that it offers an alternative path to spirituality and personal fulfillment. They emphasize that the concept of Satan as a symbol of individualism and the pursuit of pleasure is liberating for those who reject the morality imposed upon them by monotheistic religions. Satanic rituals and practices are often viewed as acts of self-empowerment and the celebration of human nature, free from the fear of divine judgment. Proponents argue that Satanic worship encourages self-exploration, critical thinking, and personal autonomy, providing an inclusive and accepting community for those who may feel marginalized or oppressed by traditional religious structures.

When analyzing the relationship between Satanic worship and monotheistic religions, one cannot ignore the interplay of fear and fascination that permeates this subject matter. The idea of evil and the allure of the forbidden hold a potent grip on the human psyche. Satanic worship, with its enigmatic rituals and perceived associations with dark forces, captivates and intrigues the imagination of believers and skeptics alike. This fascination often stems from the primordial fear inherent within us – a fear of the unknown and the uncontrollable.

To gain a comprehensive understanding of this intricate relationship, it is vital to explore case studies and personal testimonies from individuals who have engaged in both Satanic worship and monotheistic religions. Their experiences provide invaluable insights into the psychological and spiritual dynamics at play. Such research allows us to recognize the similarities between these seemingly opposing belief systems, as well as the stark contrasts that define them.

Through my own investigations, I have personally witnessed the complexity of this relationship. I have encountered individuals who sought solace in Satanic worship after feeling disillusioned by monotheistic religions, while others strived for spiritual fulfillment by blending elements of both belief systems. The amalgamation of ideas and practices exemplifies the human quest for meaning and self-discovery, as well as our innate desire to transcend the limitations imposed upon us by societal norms.

In conclusion, the relationship between Satanic worship and monotheistic religions is multifaceted, characterized by critiques, contrasts, and an ongoing interplay of fear and fascination. It is a subject matter that delves deep into the human psyche, mirroring our perpetual search for spirituality and personal fulfillment. By analyzing individual experiences and exploring the ideologies that underpin these belief systems, we can begin to unravel the profound connections that exist, ultimately shedding light on the intricate tapestry that lies within the realm of Satan.

SATANIC RITUALS AND AGNOSTICISM

To comprehensively comprehend the significance of agnosticism within Satanic rituals, it is imperative to delve into the historical timeline of satanic worship. The origin of Satanism can be traced back to ancient civilizations, such as the Mesopotamians, who revered various deities, including the malevolent god Enki. The notion of Satan as an embodiment of evil and temptation is evident in the Hebrew Bible, where he is portrayed as the adversary of God. However, it was during the Middle Ages that the apprehension and hysteria surrounding Satanism reached its zenith, with the notorious witch trials and Satanic panics gripping Europe and North America.

During this era, Satanic rituals were frequently associated with devil worship, human sacrifices, and immoral conduct. Nevertheless, it is of utmost importance to distinguish reality from fiction when exploring the actualities of Satanic rituals. While there have been instances of individuals and groups engaging in criminal activities under the guise of Satanism, these actions do not represent the broader spectrum of satanic practices.

Modern Satanic rituals, influenced by the works of philosophers such as Anton LaVey and the Church of Satan, adopt a different approach. Rather than blindly adhering to a malevolent deity, modern Satanism accentuates personal exploration and individualism. Agnosticism within Satanic rituals plays a pivotal role in this process, as it fosters the inclination for practitioners to question and contest traditional beliefs, including their own. The emphasis on skepticism serves as a foundation for personal growth and enlightenment, as it facilitates individuals to acquire a more profound understanding of themselves and the world surrounding them.

However, what precisely does agnosticism mean within the context of Satanic rituals? It constitutes the recognition

that the existence of higher powers or deities cannot be unequivocally proven or disproven. This acknowledgement paves
the way for personal interpretation and exploration, enabling
practitioners to embrace a diverse range of perspectives and
beliefs.

In the course of my investigations, I have encountered
numerous individuals who have discovered solace and empowerment in the agnostic approach to Satanism. These individuals regard Satanic rituals as a means of self-exploration and
self-realization, rather than a means of venerating an external
force. The focus lies in comprehending the self and embracing
personal desires and aspirations, rather than conforming to
the dogmas and expectations of society.

It is worth noting that my research into Satanic rituals and
agnosticism has encountered its fair share of challenges. The
secretive nature of Satanic groups and the stigma associated
with their practices often give rise to misinformation and sensationalist interpretations. Nevertheless, I have developed a
more profound understanding of the subject through personal
encounters and interviews with individuals who identify as
agnostic Satanists.

One particular interview stands out in my memory. I con-
versed with an individual who, for the sake of confidentiality,
shall be referred to as Jane. Jane described her transition into
agnostic Satanism as a process of shedding societal expectations and unearthing her authentic self. Once ensnared by the
constraints of religious dogma, Jane discovered liberation in
agnosticism, enabling her to explore her own desires, beliefs,
and potential.

Jane underscored that Satanic rituals were not inherently
wicked or malevolent, but rather transformative occurrences
that enabled her to tap into her personal power and potential. According to her, these rituals were not centered around

venerating a malevolent deity, but rather served as a conduit to connect with her own inner strength and embrace her individuality. Jane's account reinforced the premise that agnosticism within Satanic rituals is primarily concerned with personal exploration and growth, rather than conforming to a rigid set of beliefs.

In conclusion, the role of agnosticism within Satanic rituals centers on personal exploration and skepticism. It revolves around questioning and challenging established beliefs, including one's own, in order to gain a deeper understanding of oneself and the world at large. When approached with an agnostic perspective, Satanic rituals transcend the realms of fear and superstition, serving as a tool for self-discovery, personal growth, and empowerment.

SATANIC WORSHIP AND ATHEISM

The intricate relationship between Satanic worship and atheism has long fascinated those who are willing to delve into the depths of society's darkest corners and explore the forbidden realms of the human psyche. As a paranormal investigator and specialist in the extraordinary, my personal journey into the sphere of Satan has led me to gain insights into the complex web that interconnects these seemingly paradoxical ideologies. In this chapter, I will delve deep into the heart of this connection, emphasizing the rejection of supernatural beliefs and the placing of reliance on human agency.

To fully comprehend this connection, it is necessary to first unravel the fabric of Satanic worship. Contrary to popular belief, Satanism is not solely a deviant cult dedicated to the devil; instead, it is a philosophy centered around the human will and the pursuit of personal freedom. While theistic Satanists believe in a supernatural being, it is the atheistic Satanists that captivate my attention. In contrast to their theistic counterparts, they reject the existence of any gods or deities, opting instead to embrace a worldview grounded in realism and reason.

Atheism, as it stands, is the absence of belief in any deities. It is a philosophy that rejects the supernatural and seeks to derive meaning and purpose solely from the natural world. One might assume that Satanism, with its foundation in occult practices and mythical symbolism, would conflict with this perspective. However, the connection lies in the shared rejection of supernatural beliefs, while spotlighting the power and potential of the human spirit.

Atheistic Satanists, similar to their atheist counterparts, dismiss the notion of a higher power governing human affairs. This rejection serves to empower human agency, as they hold the belief that individuals possess the ability to shape their own destinies. Rather than seeking salvation or guidance from an external deity, they prioritize personal responsibility and self-improvement. It is within this framework that the connection becomes evident; human agency becomes the guiding principle, and the rejection of supernatural beliefs lays the groundwork for a culture that promotes individualism and self-determination.

However, how does one navigate the path that bridges the gap between atheism and Satanic worship? The journey begins with an exploration into the realm of subconscious desires and forbidden knowledge. The human psyche is a labyrinth, complex and enigmatic, yet within its depths lie the answers we seek. As a paranormal investigator, I have ventured into the darkest recesses of the mind, unlocking hidden potential and confronting societal taboos.

To unravel this connection, extensive research has been conducted, drawing from psychological studies, historical accounts of Satanic rituals, and interviews with individuals who proudly identify as both atheists and Satanists. Through these investigations, a pattern emerges. Atheism and Satanic worship attract individuals who refuse to conform to traditional religious dogma, choosing instead to forge their own path and liberate themselves from the constraints of blind faith.

It is essential to note that not all atheists are drawn to Satanic worship, just as not all Satanists reject belief in higher powers. The connection lies in the shared opposition to the supernatural, the rejection of dogmatic religious institutions, and the embrace of personal autonomy. As we delve deeper into this exploration, we begin to realize that these ideologies are not as divergent as they may initially appear.

Satanic rituals, often misconstrued as dark and sacrilegious, are, in reality, manifestations of symbolic meaning and personal transformation. The utilization of occult symbolism, such as pentagrams and candles, represents a rejection of societal norms and a celebration of individualism. Through these rituals, Satanists tap into the raw power that resides within themselves, fostering a sense of personal empowerment.

Instead of placing their faith in the supernatural, Satanists place trust in their own abilities and potential. This rejection of external influence frees them from the fear and dependence associated with traditional religious practices. They become the masters of their own destinies, embracing their imperfections and harnessing their strengths to carve out their own purpose.

As I navigate the murky waters of this connection, I am reminded of the words of Anton LaVey, the founder of the Church of Satan. He once stated, "Satan has been the best friend the Church has ever had, as he has kept it in business all these years!" This sentiment speaks volumes about the defiant nature of atheistic Satanists. By defying religious dogma, they expose the weaknesses and fallacies of blind faith, compelling believers to question the foundations upon which their beliefs are built.

Exploring the connection between Satanic worship and atheism reveals the potential and power that lies within the human spirit. By rejecting supernatural beliefs and embracing personal autonomy, individuals find liberation and purpose. This connection may appear unorthodox to many, but deep within ourselves, we possess the capacity to challenge societal norms and define our own destinies. In the eye of Satan, we discover the strength to embrace our true potential and forge a path illuminated by reason and personal empowerment.

SATANIC PERSPECTIVES ON THE SACRED

As a paranormal investigator and Specialist of the Strange, my exploration into the depths of the Satanic underworld has led me to unexpected places. In my relentless pursuit of unraveling the complexities of the occult, I have delved deeply into the Satanic perspectives on the concept of the sacred. The allure of darkness has always intrigued me, and as I ventured further, I began to realize that Satanic worship offers a distinctive interpretation of what is considered sacred, especially when contrasted with traditional religious beliefs.

Traditionally, the term "sacred" has been associated with divinity, purity, and a higher power, evoking feelings of veneration, respect, and a divine connection. In direct contrast, Satanic worship challenges the very foundations upon which these conventional notions are built. Within the Satanic belief system, the concept of the sacred is redefined and recalibrated to embrace elements of darkness, rebellion, and individual freedom.

To gain a deeper comprehension, I immersed myself in extensive research, studying various Satanic texts and engaging in enlightening conversations with esteemed members of Satanic covens – individuals who willingly granted me access to their world, inviting me to witness their rituals and sacred spaces.

The first revelation that struck me was the emphasis on individualism within Satanic worship. In contrast to religions that prioritize collective faith and communal worship, Satanism celebrates the self as the locus of individual power and agency. Its practitioners are urged to focus on their own interests, prioritize their desires, and embrace personal freedom. Within the framework of Satanism, the sacred is not an external object of worship, but rather an internal force to harness and cultivate.

Another captivating aspect of Satanic perspectives on the sacred is the embrace of darkness and rebellion. In traditional religious contexts, darkness is often associated with evil and viewed as something to avoid or suppress. However, Satanism encourages its followers to confront the darkness within themselves and the world. This courageous confrontation leads to personal growth and enlightenment, elevating the concept of darkness beyond mere malevolence.

Satanic rituals epitomize the intricate interplay between darkness, rebellion, and the sacred. Through meticulous, well-planned ceremonies, Satanists invoke darkness not to conjure evil, but to empower themselves. These rituals serve as a cathartic release from societal constraints, enabling participants to delve into their deepest desires and embrace the forbidden. In their deliberate transgressions, they discover solace and self-discovery, redefining the sacred as an exploration of the forbidden and the unorthodox.

However, it is essential to note that within the Satanic belief system, the sacred extends beyond indulgence in darkness and self-interest alone. It also encompasses the pursuit of knowledge, wisdom, and intellectual growth. Unlike certain religions that discourage questioning or critical thinking, Satanism actively encourages its followers to explore, learn, and challenge traditional beliefs. In this pursuit, the sacred is found within the realm of intellectual exploration and personal enlightenment.

Through my extensive research and interactions with Satanic practitioners, I have come to appreciate the profound complexity of Satanic perspectives on the sacred. The allure of darkness, the celebration of individualism, and the embrace of rebellion converge to create a distinctive understanding of what is considered sacred within the Satanic belief system. It is a realm that stretches the limits of my own preconceptions, compelling me to question the very foundations of traditional religious beliefs.

As my journey continues, I find myself embarking on an exploration of Satanic rituals, seeking to unravel the intricate symbiosis between darkness, rebellion, and the sacred. It is through this immersive experience that I hope to uncover the enigmas concealed within the Eye of Satan, discovering the sacred in all its unconventional magnificence.

14

SATANIC WORSHIP AND RITUALISTIC PRACTICES

SATANIC BLACK MASS

In my capacity as a paranormal investigator and specialist in unexplained phenomena, I have encountered numerous unsettling and mysterious occurrences throughout my career. However, my foray into the disturbing realm of the Satanic black mass surpassed any previous encounters I had experienced. For years, I had been captivated by the enigmatic rituals and profound symbolism associated with this macabre ceremony, prompting me to embark on an extensive journey to unearth its historical origins and unravel its profound significance.

To obtain a comprehensive understanding of the rituals and symbolism surrounding the Satanic black mass, it became imperative to delve into its historical roots. Tracing its practices back to ancient times, it is believed that this foreboding ceremony is linked to ancient cults and pagan rituals, in which primitive tribes engaged in solemn ceremonies to appease their deities or express their devotion.

As I delved deeper into my research, I encountered numerous firsthand accounts detailing the eerie rituals and symbolism permeating the black mass. Evocative chants resonated within dimly lit chambers, accompanied by the haunting melodies of obscure musical instruments, creating an atmosphere steeped in malevolence. Participants in the black mass partook in blasphemous acts, such as the desecration of religious artifacts and the inversion of Christian symbols.

The symbolism present in the Satanic black mass is both disconcerting and intellectually stimulating. Among the most prominent symbols employed in these rituals is the pentagram, an esoteric glyph commonly associated with Satanism. Frequently depicted within a circle, the pentagram embodies the infinite and eternal nature of evil. Another emblem often utilized is the inverted cross, representing a symbolic deviation from the Christian crucifixion. Though many perceive these symbols as representations of malevolence, they possess a deeper significance within the occult realm.

Moreover, the black robes donned by participants during the black mass have become synonymous with the ritual itself. These robes serve the dual purpose of concealing participants' identities and fostering a sense of unity and anonymity. Within the dimly lit chambers where the ceremonies take place, the robes blend into the shadows, enhancing the eerie and clandestine nature of the Satanic black mass.

A fundamental aspect of the black mass involves the presence of a chalice containing a dark liquid, typically red wine or even blood. This chalice serves as a vessel to honor the malevolent entities invoked during the ritual and symbolizes the consumption of evil itself. With each sip from the chalice, participants fortify their connection with the sinister forces they seek to embrace.

Interestingly, historical accounts and folklore suggest that the Satanic black mass frequently culminated in the summoning of demonic entities. Through elaborate incantations and the offering of sacrificial blood, demons were believed to be conjured. These malevolent beings were invoked to grant favors, bestow knowledge, or confer power upon those who summoned them. The willingness of participants to engage in such rituals and the depth of their commitment to the black arts were vital factors in the successful summoning of these entities.

Though the Satanic black mass may appear entirely malevolent, there exists an underlying intention that extends beyond superficial notions of evil. For some, the black mass serves as a rebellious stance against societal norms and organized religions that permeate our culture. It offers a conduit through which individuals seek to challenge established moral codes and embrace their own desires without inhibition. In their eyes, the black mass symbolizes personal freedom, a denouncement of dogmatic belief systems, and an embrace of a darker, truer self.

As I near the conclusion of my research, I find myself contemplating the significance of the Satanic black mass in modern society. Undeniably, the ritual evokes fear and revulsion in the majority, necessitating a cautious approach to its study. Yet, in immersing myself in the history and symbolism of the black mass, I have come to comprehend the intricate motivations and desires that underlie its dark facade. The black mass stands as a testament to humanity's inherent fascination with forbidden realms, serving as a stark reminder that evil, in all its forms, has long bewitched our collective imagination.

Therefore, as I draw this chapter to a close, I must caution those who aspire to explore the depths of the Satanic black mass. Its history remains shrouded in darkness, and its rituals are not intended for the timid at heart. However, for those bold enough to grasp the dark and intricate threads of this enigma, the Satanic black mass offers a rare glimpse into the depths of humanity's most primal desires and fears—a realm that is extraordinary in its potential for exploration, reserved for those valiant enough to venture into the very heart of Satan himself.

SATANIC BLOOD RITUALS

As a researcher specializing in the exploration of the paranormal, I have long held a profound interest in the intricate workings of the human psyche, particularly as they manifest in esoteric rituals. Among these rituals, the practice of blood rites within Satanic worship has consistently captured my attention. Today, I extend an invitation to embark on a journey into the heart of this disconcerting yet intriguing subject. Together, we will examine its historical underpinnings, delve into the spiritual implications, and shed light on its various facets.

To fully comprehend the significance of blood rituals within Satanic worship, it is imperative to delve into the annals of history. Throughout the ages, the utilization of blood rites has often been intertwined with religious and spiritual practices, reaching back as far as ancient civilizations and extending to present-day secret societies. Within this contextual framework, we discover the origins of Satanic blood rituals, wherein they blend with obscure occult practices and belief systems.

In ancient times, blood was regarded as a symbol of utmost potency, representing vitality, life force, and the very essence of existence. The belief in the spiritual power inherent within blood traverses cultural boundaries and can be traced across diverse civilizations, such as the Aztecs, Egyptians, and Druids, each incorporating it into their respective rituals albeit for different purposes.

Within the framework of Satanic worship, blood assumes a particular significance. It serves as a conduit through which adherents establish a connection with the demonic realm, invoking its dark forces to bring their desires to fruition. Whereas other religions employ sacrificial rites as a means of communicating with higher deities, Satanists perceive these rituals as a direct interaction with Satan himself, harnessing his power for personal gain.

Despite claims of spiritual benefits made by its adherents, Satanic blood rituals have long been subjected to moral and legal scrutiny. Given their inherently secretive nature, the information available on these rituals is largely anecdotal or derived from testimonies of former practitioners. Nevertheless, we can discern several commonalities and recurring themes, which warrant a closer examination of their spiritual implications.

One of the primary spiritual consequences associated with Satanic blood rituals is the belief that engaging in these rites bestows upon practitioners enhanced power and protection. The act of offering blood, often attained through self-infliction or animal sacrifice, is viewed as both an act of devotion to Satan and a symbolic representation of the practitioner's willingness to go to extreme lengths for their chosen path. It is believed that this dedication strengthens their connection to the demonic realm, subsequently granting them supernatural abilities, heightened senses, or protection against spiritual adversaries.

However, it is important to note that the alleged spiritual implications of Satanic blood rituals extend beyond personal empowerment. Practitioners argue that these ceremonies serve as conduits for unleashing malevolent energies into the world, leaving a wake of chaos and darkness in their path. It is during these rituals that they believe Satan imparts his influence, fueling their intentions and desires. Whether these intentions encompass manipulation, control, or harm towards others, the underlying belief is that the ritual itself emboldens and magnifies their sinister objectives.

To further comprehend the spiritual implications of Satanic blood rituals, it is necessary to explore the psychological and emotional aspects associated with them. Such rituals often foster a sense of belonging and community among participants, thereby solidifying shared belief systems and reinforcing core values. For individuals who may feel marginalized or disconnected from mainstream society, this sense of kinship can exert a powerful allure, providing them with a sense of purpose and identity within a tightly knit group that shares their ideological convictions.

It is crucial to acknowledge, however, that these claimed spiritual implications rest solely upon the experiences of those involved in Satanic worship. The occult realm, by its very nature, defies rigid categorization and empirical scrutiny. Nevertheless, by undertaking a study of accounts, testimonies, and historical data relating to Satanic blood rituals, we can gain valuable insights into the multifaceted nature of these practices and their potential spiritual consequences.

In conclusion, any attempt to analyze the controversial practice of blood rituals within Satanic worship necessitates a delicate balance between open-mindedness and critical evaluation. The historical backdrop, spiritual implications, and psychological dimensions all contribute to an intricate understanding of these practices. While the subject matter may provoke unease, it is imperative to approach it with intellectual curiosity, seeking to uncover the truths that lie within the enigmatic allure and the darkness that ensnares those drawn into the realm of Satan.

SATANIC SEX MAGIC

To gain a comprehensive understanding of the origins of Satanic sex magic, it is imperative to trace its developmental timeline through history. The origins of this practice can be found in various ancient civilizations, where sexual rituals were believed to establish a connection between individuals and divine forces. It was during the ascension of the occult in Europe during the late Middle Ages that Satanic rituals, including sex magic, gained prominence.

Among the prominent figures associated with Satanic sex magic, Aleister Crowley, the self-proclaimed "Great Beast 666," stands out. Crowley's involvement in the occult and his unconventional practices earned him infamy and established him as a central figure in the modern occult movement. He aimed to employ sex as a vehicle to tap into human beings' primal instincts and desires, positing that engaging in ritualistic sexual acts could lead to spiritual enlightenment.

Through my research, I have discovered that Satanic sex magic is not solely centered around the physical act itself, but instead focuses on the integration of sexual energy with mystical intent. These rituals purportedly involve participants directing their sexual energy toward a specific desired outcome, be it personal empowerment, the acquisition of higher knowledge, or the manipulation of reality. Consequently, the act of sex becomes sacrosanct, a union of the physical and the spiritual.

However, it is crucial to note that not all Satanists engage in sex magic, and not all Satanic rituals entail sexual acts. This practice is often viewed as a means of self-transformation, a vehicle for exploring and harnessing one's innermost desires and boundaries. It is a personal journey that necessitates profound self-awareness and the willingness to confront and embrace one's own darkness.

While many may perceive Satanic sex magic as purely hedonistic or sacrilegious, it is vital to acknowledge that the purpose behind these rituals is not to extol or worship Satan himself. In this context, Satan represents rebellion, individualism, and the rejection of oppressive societal norms and religious doctrines. Satanic sex magic is about regaining personal agency and embracing one's authentic self, unencumbered by moral judgment.

The rituals themselves can vary in complexity, ranging from group ceremonies to intimate gatherings of individuals who share an understanding of the practice. Participants often create consecrated spaces adorned with symbols and sigils associated with Satanic beliefs, which further set the stage for their rituals. Through these rites, practitioners endeavor to access the primal forces of creation and destruction, utilizing sexual energy as a catalyst for transformation and manifestation.

One crucial aspect that struck me throughout my investigation was the emphasis placed on consent and communication within the realm of Satanic sex magic. Contrary to misconceptions perpetuated by popular culture, these rituals do not endorse coercion or non-consensual acts. Instead, they prioritize the importance of boundaries, consent, and mutual respect. Practitioners comprehend that genuine empowerment can only be attained when all involved parties are willing participants.

As I ventured further into the world of Satanic sex magic, I came to realize that it extends beyond the realm of occult subculture. Its principles and philosophies have permeated various facets of modern society, evolving into a rich tapestry of self-discovery, personal empowerment, and sexual liberation.

In conclusion, my exploration of Satanic sex magic has exposed an intriguing realm where the boundaries between the physical and spiritual realms blend. It is a domain wherein individuals strive to obtain a deeper understanding of themselves and their place within the universe, intertwining their sexual energy with mystical intent. Satanic sex magic challenges societal norms and advocates for personal freedom and empowerment through the exploration of desires and boundaries. It represents a path paved with esoteric wisdom, spiritual enlightenment, and audacious defiance of conformity.

SATANIC INVOCATION AND EVOCATION

In order to gain a true understanding of the practices of invocation and evocation within Satanic rituals, it is essential to grasp the context in which they are performed. Satanic rituals are not mere acts of rebellion or devotion to an imagined devil figure, but rather they serve as a means to establish a connection with spiritual entities that exist beyond our ordinary existence. These rituals are deeply rooted in symbolism, ancient traditions, and forbidden knowledge, making them a powerful channel for practitioners to explore the hidden depths of the spiritual world.

Invocation, at its core, involves the act of summoning a deity or spiritual force into oneself. It serves as a method for merging with the entity, allowing its essence to permeate one's being. The purpose behind invocation in Satanic rituals is to establish a direct link between the practitioner and the invoked entity, enabling the practitioner to tap into its vast power and wisdom. Through invocation, the practitioner forms a mutually beneficial relationship with the entity, drawing strength, guidance, and enlightenment from its presence.

On the other hand, evocation refers to the act of summoning and commanding spiritual entities to appear before the practitioner. Unlike invocation, which brings the entity within oneself, evocation aims to manifest the entity physically or tangibly in the external world. This practice requires extensive knowledge, focus, and a deep understanding of the entity being called upon. Through evoking these entities, practitioners seek to harness their unique attributes, find answers to profound questions, or utilize their abilities to influence the physical world.

One might question why anyone would engage in such dark and perilous practices. The answer lies in the inherent curiosity and thirst for knowledge that drives individuals to explore the unknown. Satanic rituals, by their very nature, challenge societal norms and provide a pathway to comprehend the unfathomable mysteries of the cosmos. For some, the pursuit of forbidden knowledge and the quest for personal power outweigh the risks involved, while others are motivated by a genuine desire to uncover truths that lie beyond the scope of traditional belief systems.

To fully comprehend the significance of satanic invocation and evocation, it is necessary to examine some of the rituals that have been employed throughout history. The Black Mass, a ritual associated with the Church of Satan, serves as a prime example. This ritual involves the subversion of Christian symbols and practices, with the intention of affirming individualism, rejecting societal constraints, and embracing personal freedom. By invoking demonic entities during the Black Mass, practitioners seek to unlock their own potential, challenge convention, and establish a direct connection with the dark forces that permeate our world.

Other rituals, such as the evocation of Baphomet, the deity symbolizing the occult with a goat's head, serve as gateways to hidden dimensions and realms. Through these rituals, practitioners strive to tap into the ancient knowledge and primal energies possessed by Baphomet, in their pursuit of personal transformation, spiritual enlightenment, and the acquisition of magical abilities. By aligning oneself with Baphomet, one can transcend the limitations of perceived reality and gain insight into the deepest recesses of the human psyche.

However, it is important to note that the practices of satanic invocation and evocation are not without their risks. Such rituals can lead to the summoning of malevolent entities, which, if not properly controlled and banished, can cause immense harm to both the practitioner and their loved ones. Moreover, those who engage in these rituals must be prepared for the consequences that may arise from their interactions with the spiritual realm. The line between exploration and obsession can be thin, and those who delve too deeply into the forbidden may find themselves ensnared by their own curiosity.

Despite the inherent dangers, satanic invocation and evocation continue to captivate the interest of scholars, occultists, and adventurous individuals alike. The allure of hidden knowledge, the prospect of spiritual transcendence, and the mesmerizing power that awaits those who dare to venture into the realm of Satan make these practices an irresistible temptation for seekers of the esoteric.

As a paranormal investigator and specialist in the occult, my personal journey into the realm of satanic invocation and evocation has been a profoundly transformative experience. It is a path marked by uncertainty and danger, yet it offers glimpses into the unknown and challenges the boundaries of conventional understanding. My own encounters, research, and experiences have not only expanded my comprehension of the spiritual realm but also serve as a testament to the enduring power of the human spirit and its insatiable thirst for knowledge, even when immersed in darkness.

In the forthcoming chapters, we will delve further into the history, rituals, and practitioners of satanic invocation and evocation, shedding light on the hidden truths that lie within the enigmatic realm of the occult. Through...

SATANIC RITUAL TOOLS AND ARTIFACTS

The exploration of Satanic ritual tools and artifacts necessitates a comprehensive historical timeline that traces their origins and evolution over time. While Satanic worship is often associated with the medieval and Renaissance periods, its roots can be traced back to ancient civilizations such as Mesopotamia and Egypt.

One of the most widely recognized ritual tools in Satanism is the athame, which is a ceremonial dagger featuring a black handle. The term "athame" is believed to have derived from the Old Irish word "adhamh," meaning "sharp." This potent symbol of black magic is associated with the element of fire and is frequently employed to direct energy during rituals. It is crucial to note that the athame should not be used to cause physical harm but rather serves as a symbolic instrument for command over supernatural forces.

Another essential ritual tool is the chalice, which represents the element of water. The chalice is typically crafted from metal or glass and adorned with intricate symbols and designs. It functions as a vessel for the libation of wine, establishing a connection between the physical and spiritual realms. In Satanic rituals, the chalice is utilized both for offerings to the infernal powers and for communion, symbolizing the assimilation of divine energy.

An in-depth analysis of the significance and usage of ritual tools and artifacts in Satanic worship brings about a profound understanding of the practices and beliefs of those who worship Satan. For instance, the athame serves as a conduit for channeling energy and as an instrument of power and authority. It symbolizes the practitioner's ability to command the forces of darkness and harness their strength for personal gain.

In contrast, the chalice symbolizes the element of water and the power of transformation. In Satanic rituals, wine is often consumed from the chalice, representing the acceptance of divine energy and the blending of the physical and spiritual realms. The chalice acts as a vessel for communion with the infernal powers, offering a means of communication and connection with demonic forces.

It is important to acknowledge that the significance and usage of ritual tools and artifacts in Satanic worship may vary among different traditions and individual practitioners. While the athame and chalice are prevalent in many Satanic rituals, there can be variations in their design and symbolism based on the specific beliefs and practices of the practitioner.

In addition to the athame and chalice, there exist numerous other ritual tools and artifacts utilized in Satanic worship that warrant further exploration. These include the pentagram, a powerful symbol of protection and evocation, as well as the Baphomet, a deity often associated with Satanic rituals. Each of these tools and artifacts carries its own distinct symbolism and meaning, contributing to the overall rituals and practices of Satanic worship.

In conclusion, the significance and usage of ritual tools and artifacts in Satanic worship provide an intriguing insight into the beliefs and practices of those who worship Satan. From the athame's ability to channel energy and assert power to the chalice's role in communion and connection with the infernal powers, these tools and artifacts serve as tangible expressions of faith and devotion. Exploring the history and symbolism of these objects enables us to gain a better understanding of the intricate world of Satanic worship and the practitioners' pursuit of supernatural power.

SATANIC RITUAL MUSIC AND CHANTS

As a researcher and specialist in paranormal phenomena, I have extensively explored various aspects of the supernatural realm. Among these subjects, the investigation of Satanic rituals has held a particular fascination for me. The act of invoking dark entities through the combination of music and chants has always provoked a deeply unsettling impression. In this chapter, we will delve into an examination of the role of music and chants in Satanic rituals, focusing on their impact on the emotional and spiritual states of the participants.

The utilization of music in Satanic rituals goes beyond mere aesthetic purposes; it serves as a potent instrument for summoning dark forces and cultivating an atmosphere conducive to their malevolent intentions. The insidious melodies and haunting compositions act as a gateway, allowing participants to establish a connection with the forces they aim to harness. Through meticulous research, I have uncovered numerous instances wherein specific musical notes and compositions are believed to resonate with the infernal realm, enabling practitioners to channel demonic energy.

One specific Satanic ritual that I had the opportunity to investigate revolved around a composition known as "The Melody of the Grotesque." This piece, reputed to have been channeled from the deepest recesses of the netherworld, allegedly holds the power to open the gateway to hell itself. Its dissonant chords and ethereal vocals, carrying an eerie aura, were crafted with the purpose of instilling unease and dread in those who listen. As I observed this ritual, I noted how the music heightened the emotional states of the participants, plunging them into a state of trance-like devotion and surrender.

Chants play a significant role in Satanic rituals as well. These incantations serve as a means of communication with demonic entities, with each chant carefully constructed to invoke specific powers and energies. In my research, I encountered a variety of chants, each with its own unique purpose and intended effect. One notable example is the "Invocation of the Damned," which is believed to summon the presence of a powerful demon known as Asmodeus. As I witnessed this chant being performed, I could sense a shift in the energy of the room, emitting an otherworldly ambiance that sent shivers down my spine.

The impact of music and chants in Satanic rituals extends beyond the physical realm, delving into the realms of the visceral and the deeply spiritual. Those who partake in these rituals frequently describe a transcendental experience, where they feel connected to something far greater than themselves. The combination of music and chants serves as a conduit, allowing participants to tap into a wellspring of dark energy, empowering them with a sense of purpose and authority.

Nevertheless, the emotional and spiritual states induced by these rituals are not without consequences. The dark forces summoned through music and chants leave an enduring mark on the participants. Long after the conclusion of the ritual, individuals often report heightened levels of anxiety, depression, and spiritual unrest. The disquieting melodies and sinister intonations continue to resonate in their minds, serving as a constant reminder of the darkness they have encountered.

During my research, I additionally stumbled upon a disconcerting phenomenon known as "The Sound of Madness." This rare occurrence has been recorded in certain Satanic rituals. Witnesses claim that during these rituals, the music and chants surpass their intended purpose, transforming into a weapon employed by the demonic entities themselves. This phenomenon allegedly drives participants to the brink of insanity, subjecting them to an onslaught of haunting sounds that disrupt their mental state, leaving them permanently scarred.

In conclusion, the role of music and chants in Satanic rituals extends well beyond superficial considerations. They are potent instruments that enable participants to establish a connection with the infernal realm and summon dark forces. Through meticulous research and firsthand observations, I have witnessed the profound impact of these elements on the emotional and spiritual states of the participants. However, it is imperative to approach the exploration of such rituals with caution, for the consequences can be deeply unsettling and enduring. As we continue our journey into the depths of Satanic practices, it is crucial to proceed with utmost care, recognizing that even the darkest corners of the supernatural realm possess the potential to consume us entirely.

SATANIC RITUALS AND SACRED SPACES

As an experienced paranormal investigator and specialist in the occult, I have extensively delved into numerous mysterious phenomena and practices. Among them, the realm of Satanic rituals stands out as being particularly enigmatic and widely misunderstood. In this chapter, my aim is to unravel the complexities surrounding Satanic rituals and their association with sacred spaces, with a specific focus on altars and ritual chambers.

To gain a comprehensive understanding of the genesis and significance of sacred spaces in Satanic rituals, it is vital to examine the historical evolution of Satanism itself. While commonly linked to the Christian concept of Satan, Satanism boasts a diverse and illustrious history that predates its Christian interpretation. Ancient civilizations, such as the Sumerians, Babylonians, and Egyptians, had their own religious systems which encompassed the worship of deities connected to darkness and chaos. It is from these ancient roots that Satanic rituals and the concept of sacred spaces have taken shape.

In modern times, notable figures such as Aleister Crowley and Anton LaVey, who founded the Church of Satan in 1966, have exerted significant influence in shaping the practices and rituals within Satanic traditions. In these rituals, sacred spaces assume a pivotal role. The establishment of an altar and the utilization of a ritual chamber serve as essential elements that shape both the ambiance and objectives of Satanic rites.

Altars, which serve as objects of reverence and focal points in Satanic rituals, furnish a tangible link between practitioners and the forces they seek to invoke. Unlike traditional religious altars, which typically feature symbols of religious virtue, Satanic altars are designed to reflect the individual's desires and aspirations. Each practitioner selects items and symbols of personal significance, thereby manifesting their own unique desires upon the altar. This customization permits a deeply personal and empowering experience, ensuring that the practitioner is fully engrossed in their ritual and connected to the powers they wish to invoke.

Conversely, the ritual chamber functions as the physical space wherein Satanic rituals are performed. This carefully curated and arranged space aims to induce a specific state of mind and foster an atmosphere conducive to ritualistic practices. The chamber itself often personifies the duality prevalent in Satanic philosophy, with elements of both darkness and sensuality intertwining to create an environment that is simultaneously intriguing and enticing.

Great attention is paid to the placement of furniture and props within the ritual chamber. For instance, the positioning of candles may form a specific geometric pattern or represent the cardinal directions, infusing the space with a sense of sacred geometry and aligning it with mystical energies. The chamber's walls are adorned with sigils, symbols, and artwork depicting the various entities or concepts that serve as the focus of the ritual. Each component is meticulously chosen to evoke a particular emotional response and stimulate the senses, thereby intensifying the practitioner's connection to the sacred space and heightening the ritual experience.

It is important to emphasize that while the creation and utilization of sacred spaces within Satanic rituals may carry an aura of darkness and taboo, they are not inherently malevolent or evil. Satanic rituals do not aim to cause harm or promote chaos; rather, they are centered around personal empowerment and the exploration of the depths of the human psyche. The sacred spaces established in Satanic rituals act as catalysts for self-discovery, introspection, and the pursuit of personal desires and aspirations.

In conclusion, the establishment and application of sacred spaces within Satanic rituals, specifically altars and ritual chambers, are integral components that shape and enrich the experience for practitioners. Through the careful selection of objects, symbols, and the arrangement of the physical space, Satanic rituals become immersive journeys into the depths of human consciousness. It is within these sacred spaces that practitioners confront their desires, explore their fears, and ultimately unearth the true extent of their personal power. As a paranormal investigator and specialist in the strange, the allure and haunting nature of these rituals and the exploration of sacred spaces continue to captivate me, further drawing me into the enigma of Satan.

SATANIC RITUALS AND TIME-SPACE MANIPULATION

As a paranormal investigator and specialist in the unexplained, I have conducted extensive research on various phenomena. Within my field of study, Satanic rituals and the belief in time-space manipulation hold a significant place. The idea that individuals can manipulate the fabric of existence itself, transcending our three-dimensional reality, is both intriguing and complex.

To fully understand time-space manipulation within Satanic rituals, it is necessary to examine their historical timeline. Satanic rituals have their origins in ancient civilizations, where belief systems allowed for communication with supernatural entities. Throughout the ages, the understanding and application of time-space manipulation have evolved, adapting to the changing beliefs and philosophies embedded in these rituals.

One notable example of time-space manipulation in Satanic rituals is the concept of "soul travel" or "astral projection." This practice involves detaching one's consciousness from the physical body, enabling them to explore different realms and dimensions. Satanists believe that through astral projection, they can access hidden knowledge and communicate with powerful entities from alternate planes of existence. It is during these altered states of consciousness that the manipulation of time and space becomes possible.

The belief in time-space manipulation in Satanic rituals is inherently linked to the quest for spiritual transcendence. Individuals strive for enlightenment, seeking to move beyond the limitations of the physical world and connect with higher beings. Manipulating time and space is seen as a means to access realms beyond human comprehension and assimilate the collective wisdom of the universe.

Esteemed occult scholars such as Aleister Crowley and Anton LaVey have conducted extensive research on time-space manipulation in Satanic rituals. Crowley's experiments with ceremonial magic laid the foundation for modern occultism. He proposed that specific symbols, rituals, and invocations served as gateways to alternate dimensions, facilitating time-space manipulation. LaVey, the founder of the Church of Satan, expanded upon Crowley's research, emphasizing the psychological aspects of ritual magic and its ability to alter one's perception of time and space.

To provide a deeper understanding, we will examine the infamous Babalon Working, one of the most significant Satanic rituals in history. Conducted by Jack Parsons, a renowned rocket scientist and member of Aleister Crowley's magical order, this ritual aimed to summon a goddess named Babalon. Parsons believed that establishing a spiritual connection with Babalon would grant him the power to manipulate time and space.

The Babalon Working involved intricate ceremonies combining elements of sex magic, invocation, and astral projection. Through these practices, Parsons sought to manifest Babalon's presence in the physical realm and, under her guidance, unlock the secrets of time and space manipulation. While the precise outcomes of the Babalon Working remain a subject of debate among occultists, the ritual exemplifies the enduring fascination and belief in the potential for time-space manipulation within Satanic practices.

It is important to recognize that the belief in time-space manipulation in Satanic rituals is a deeply personal and subjective experience. Each practitioner approaches the ritual with their own perspective, intentions, and beliefs, shaping their understanding and encounter with time-space manipulation. It is a path that demands dedication, discipline, and a genuine desire to explore the boundaries of human consciousness.

In conclusion, the belief in time-space manipulation within Satanic rituals provides insight into humanity's search for spiritual transcendence. This ancient practice has adapted over time, responding to evolving beliefs and philosophies. While the mechanisms behind time-space manipulation remain elusive, the fascination with this concept persists. Satanic rituals offer individuals a means to tap into the fabric of existence, molding it according to their will and potentially transcending the limitations of our three-dimensional reality. Ultimately, the true extent of time-space manipulation within Satanic rituals may forever reside in the realm of the unknown, awaiting exploration by those courageous enough to venture into its depths.

15

SATANIC WORSHIP AND SECRECY

SATANIC COVENS AND SECRET SOCIETIES

As an investigator and specialist in the paranormal, it is my responsibility to thoroughly explore the depths of darkness in order to provide insight into the enigmatic world of Satanic covens and secret societies. Throughout my extensive research, I have dedicated numerous hours to studying their origins, comprehending their activities, and revealing the disturbing truth behind their initiation rituals and membership prerequisites. In this section, we will embark on an expedition into the core of this covert realm, bringing to light the most obscure aspects of human existence.

In order to understand the establishment of Satanic covens and secret societies, it is essential to acknowledge their reliance on secrecy and exclusivity. These groups are typically concealed within a veil of mystery, protecting their unholy practices from prying eyes through layers of confidentiality. Prospective members are typically individuals carefully selected due to their inclination towards embracing darkness and devoting themselves to the service of Satan.

Contrary to popular belief, membership in Satanic covens or secret societies is not limited to a specific demographic. Individuals from diverse backgrounds, ranging from affluent entrepreneurs to struggling artists, can be found among their ranks. This diversity allows these groups to effectively operate in the shadows, obscuring their true intentions from the public eye.

The initiation rituals hold paramount significance within these ominous societies. These ceremonies mark the commencement of a new member's journey into the depths of Satanism, irreversibly altering their spiritual and moral compass. As my research progressed, fragments of information regarding these heavily guarded ceremonies gradually surfaced.

One noteworthy initiation ritual, referred to as "The Baptism of Fire," symbolizes an initiate's renunciation of their previous life and the commencement of their discipleship to Satan. This ritual commonly takes place in a secluded location, deep within the heart of a dense forest or on the outskirts of an abandoned chapel, further augmenting the sinister ambiance that surrounds it.

During these initiation rituals, participants are subjected to a series of tests designed to evaluate their unwavering commitment and dedication to the Satanic cause. These trials encompass enduring physical pain, reciting Satanic prayers, and engaging in ritualistic acts of depravity. It is in these moments that initiates find themselves stripped of societal constraints, succumbing to the allure of the abyss.

Membership requirements vary amongst Satanic covens and secret societies, necessitating potential initiates to navigate the intricate guidelines established by their respective groups. These requirements often demand unwavering loyalty, a willingness to embrace evil, and absolute secrecy from prospective members. The commitment to maintaining secrecy ensures the continued survival and expansion of these nefarious organizations.

Further exploration into my research led me to encounter a term that has become closely associated with these groups - The Black Sabbat. This unholy gathering is rumored to be the culmination of the malevolent activities undertaken by Satanic covens and secret societies. Concealed under the cover of darkness, participants engage in unspeakable acts, worshiping Satan and indulging in acts of debauchery.

The initiation rituals and membership prerequisites of Satanic covens and secret societies expose a darker side of humanity, revealing a world governed by sinister forces that only a select few are privy to. Through my research, I have grasped the understanding that these groups thrive on the vulnerabilities of individuals in search of power, dominance, or liberation from societal constraints. They prey upon lost souls desperately seeking something beyond the mundane.

With each revelation brought forth through my research, I find myself irresistibly drawn deeper into the abyss of this macabre world. It is indeed a terrifying realization that these Satanic covens and secret societies not only exist but flourish within the concealed recesses of our society. They operate in plain sight, yet remain invisible to those oblivious to their true nature.

In the ensuing chapters, I will guide you through a harrowing journey into the depths of Satanic history, unraveling the most concealed secrets and illuminating the unfathomable. Prepare yourself, esteemed reader, as we venture further into the heart of Satan, where the line between reality and myth becomes indistinct, and the true horrors of the world emerge from the shadows.

SATANIC CODES AND CRYPTIC LANGUAGE

The analysis of codes and cryptic language within Satanic communities to maintain secrecy and exclusivity is a topic of interest and intrigue. These hidden languages and codes have historically served as a method of safeguarding knowledge and ensuring exclusivity. The world of Satanism is no exception, utilizing these tools to protect their rituals and imbue them with an air of mystery. In this chapter, we will unravel the complex tapestry of Satanic codes and cryptic language, tracing their origins and unveiling their secrets.

To comprehend the use of these codes, it is necessary to delve into the historical timeline of Satanic practices. Satanic worship dates back to ancient civilizations, where primitive cultures believed in the power of the supernatural. The ancient Mesopotamian tale of Ashur and Pazuzu illustrates the eternal struggle between good and evil, forming the foundation of Satanism. Throughout time, these beliefs evolved, finding expression in various cultures and religions. From the pagan worship of Pan to the heretical practices of the Templars, the concept of Satan became entwined with both organized religion and folklore.

During the Renaissance period, Satanic codes and cryptic language emerged as prominent features of organized Satanic communities. This era witnessed a resurgence of occult practices, as individuals began exploring the hidden aspects of life with intense curiosity. Figures such as Aleister Crowley, known for his controversial philosophies and involvement with occult societies, embraced codes and cryptic language as a means of sharing knowledge exclusively with those deemed worthy. The rise of secret societies, such as the Order of the Trapezoid and the Mysterium Society, further fueled the use of codes to convey information within Satanic circles.

One notable example of Satanic codes and cryptic language is the Theban script, commonly known as the "Witch's Alphabet." At first glance, it may appear unfamiliar, but upon closer examination, one can recognize that it is simply an alternative representation of the English alphabet. Created by Francis Barrett in the early 19th century, this cipher enabled practitioners to communicate openly while remaining inaccessible to the uninitiated. Encrypted messages written in Theban script could be passed among members of Satanic sects without arousing suspicion or inviting persecution.

However, it is crucial to note that not all Satanic codes and cryptic languages are easily deciphered. Some require extensive knowledge of mythology, ancient languages, and symbolism to unveil their secrets. The practice of gematria, for example, assigns numerical values to letters of the alphabet, enabling practitioners to encode hidden messages within written and spoken words. Only those with the requisite knowledge of numerology can decipher these encrypted messages. Within Satanic communities, this serves as a test of an individual's dedication and understanding, ensuring that only the truly devoted gain access to their innermost secrets.

The utilization of codes and cryptic language within Satanic communities proves to be a powerful tool for maintaining secrecy and exclusivity. By embedding their rituals and beliefs with hidden messages, they create an atmosphere of mystique and allure. This exclusivity further enhances the appeal of Satanic practices, enticing those who seek a deeper connection to the supernatural.

In my quest to understand the intricacies of Satanic codes and cryptic language, I have encountered a multitude of symbols, scripts, and ciphers. Each offers a unique glimpse into the complex web of occult knowledge, representing a piece of a larger puzzle waiting to be solved. Through extensive research and analysis, I have come to realize that the study of these codes is not simply an academic pursuit; it is an invitation to explore the darkest recesses of the human psyche and confront our deepest fears and desires.

As I continue my exploration, I am mindful of the dual nature of my role as a paranormal investigator and Specialist of the Strange. While the pursuit of knowledge is essential to my purpose, I must approach the subject with caution, aware of the potential dangers that lie within. The codes and cryptic languages of the Satanic underworld possess immense power, capable of both enlightening and corrupting those who dare to delve into their depths. It is a delicate balance between fascination and trepidation as I navigate the shadows of a world cloaked in enigma and darkness.

In the subsequent chapters, we will delve deeper into the specific codes and cryptic languages employed by Satanic communities, exploring their origins, meanings, and applications. Through this exploration, we will peel back the layers of secrecy to reveal the underlying motivations and beliefs that drive these enigmatic societies. Brace yourself for an expedition into the labyrinth of forbidden knowledge, where the boundaries between reality and the supernatural blur, and where the search for truth is tinged with both awe and apprehension.

SATANIC RITUALS AND ESOTERIC KNOWLEDGE

In order to gain a comprehensive understanding of the profound extent of esoteric knowledge and its association with Satanic rituals, one must undertake a careful exploration of the historical timeline that spans hundreds of years. This exploration takes us back to the ancient civilizations of Mesopotamia and Egypt, to the enigmatic societies of the Middle Ages, and to the occultists of the 20th century. Throughout this journey, the pursuit of enlightenment through the worship of Satan has been consistently characterized by secrecy and mystique.

A pivotal event in history that cannot be overlooked is the well-known Witch Trials of the 17th century, which extended across Europe and the New World. In the midst of religious zeal, numerous individuals were accused of engaging in witchcraft and participating in Satanic rituals. During this period, a wealth of esoteric knowledge was uncovered, often through confessions extracted under torture or through the testimonies of individuals caught up in the hysteria of witch hunts.

These confessions provided detailed accounts of the acquisition and transmission of esoteric knowledge within Satanic rituals. The practices described included blood sacrifice, summoning demons, and invoking dark entities to obtain personal gain. The high level of secrecy surrounding these rituals can be attributed to the severe repercussions faced by those who openly practiced the dark arts.

It is also worth considering the notorious occult societies that gained prominence during the Enlightenment era, such as the Bavarian Illuminati and the Hermetic Order of the Golden Dawn. These esoteric groups sought to explore and harness the hidden knowledge embedded in Satanic rituals. Their ceremonies and practices promised to unlock the secrets of the universe.

The acquisition of esoteric knowledge within Satanic rituals is often found in the form of ancient texts and manuscripts, passed down through generations of practitioners. These protected and encoded texts serve as a guidebook for comprehending the intricate aspects of the occult realm and the malevolent forces that lurk within it.

But what is the reason behind the emphasis on secrecy? What drives the strong desire to keep this knowledge hidden from prying eyes? It is possible that this connection to secrecy stems from the recognition that power lies within the unknown. By safeguarding this esoteric knowledge, practitioners maintain a sense of control and exclusivity over the forces they seek to harness. This veil of secrecy is the core allure of Satanism and the occult, enticing those who are drawn to forbidden knowledge and power beyond conventional understanding.

The investigation into the acquisition and transmission of esoteric knowledge within Satanic rituals necessitates a delicate balance of scholarly research and firsthand experiences. By delving into centuries-old texts, exploring concealed archives, and consulting with both scholars and practitioners, I have pieced together a mosaic of information that sheds light on the concealed realms of Satanism and its close ties to secrecy.

However, the journey does not end there. The secrets embedded within Satanic rituals and esoteric knowledge continue to evolve and adapt in the modern world. From underground cults to the digital realm of online covens and forums, the acquisition and transmission of this knowledge have successfully adapted to the changing times. This ever-evolving landscape of secrecy presents us with new challenges as well as opportunities to uncover the truth behind ancient rituals and the powers they possess.

In our unwavering pursuit of understanding, we must proceed with caution. The path to enlightenment through the study of Satanic rituals and esoteric knowledge is fraught with danger and temptation. It is a voyage into the very heart of Satan himself, where one risks the loss of their own soul in their pursuit of ultimate power and understanding.

As an investigator of the paranormal and an expert in the realm of the unexplained, I embark on this journey with a combination of trepidation and excitement. Equipped with my extensive research, my intuitive instincts, and an unyielding determination, I dive deeper into the abyss, prepared to confront the unknown and unveil the secrets that have been carefully guarded for centuries. It is within this darkness that I find purpose and meaning, illuminating the shadows that haunt our collective consciousness and forever revolutionizing our comprehension of Satanism and the enigmatic realm of esoteric knowledge.

SATANIC WORSHIP AND HIDDEN SYMBOLS

As a professional in the field of paranormal investigation and the study of the occult, I have dedicated numerous hours to researching the enigmatic realm of satanic worship and its clandestine symbols. It is a domain veiled in secrecy, where adherents engage in rituals that are not only disconcerting but also steeped in intricate significance and concealed messages. In this chapter, we shall embark on an exploration to unravel the meaning behind these symbols for those who participate in satanic rituals.

To truly grasp the essence of hidden symbols in satanic worship, we must first comprehend the historical framework that has shaped their existence. The roots of satanic worship can be traced back to ancient civilizations, where deities symbolizing chaos, darkness, and rebellion were worshipped. These early practices laid the foundation for the development of satanic rituals and the symbols that underpin them.

Throughout history, satanic worship has been associated with clandestine cults, often operating in the cover of darkness. Ancient texts and works of art depict symbols such as inverted pentagrams, the sigil of the goat-headed Baphomet, and the infamous inverted cross. These symbols, although outwardly malevolent, wield immense significance for those who comprehend their true meanings.

One symbol that stands out amidst the myriad of satanic icons is the inverted pentagram. This pentagram, a five-pointed star with one point facing downwards, is synonymous with satanic worship. Its origins can be traced back to Ancient Greece, where it represented the five elements - earth, air, fire, water, and spirit. However, in the context of satanic rituals, the inversion of the pentagram embodies a purposeful rejection of conventional order and an embrace of chaos. It acts as a powerful reminder of the practitioners' defiance against societal norms and the authority they seek to overthrow.

Another significant symbol deeply intertwined with satanic worship is the sigil of Baphomet. This mythological figure, depicted as a being with the head of a goat, has long been associated with occult practices and the philosophy of the Satanic Temple. The sigil, a unique symbol created by combining various occult symbols, represents the dualistic nature of Satanism - the merging of male and female, light and dark, order and chaos. It encompasses the multifaceted beliefs and ideologies held by practitioners of satanic rituals, serving as a talisman of their unwavering dedication to the path they have chosen.

The inverted cross, often portrayed as a blasphemous defilement of the Christian cross, is yet another potent symbol within satanic worship. Its origins are linked to the legend of Saint Peter, who requested to be crucified upside down as he believed himself unworthy of dying in the same manner as Jesus Christ. For satanic practitioners, the inverted cross signifies their rejection of established religions and their embrace of their own spiritual journey. It stands as a symbol of opposition to the dogmas enforced by mainstream faiths and resonates deeply with the rebellious spirit of satanic worship.

Beyond these prominent symbols, the realm of satanic worship is teeming with a vast array of lesser-known yet equally influential symbols. These symbols, often concealed within the intricate designs of dark rituals, carry profound meanings and wield immense power for practitioners. Through careful analysis of these concealed messages, we can gain insight into the mindset, motivations, and desires of those who partake in satanic rituals.

For instance, the presence of serpents within satanic rituals signifies both wisdom and temptation, encapsulating the dualism of enlightenment and corruption. The serpent's symbolism draws upon biblical origins, where it enticed Adam and Eve to fall from grace. Furthermore, the use of candles, arranged in specific patterns and colors, conveys symbolic messages related to the intent of the ritual. Red candles may represent desire or passion, while blue candles may symbolize knowledge or divine wisdom. Each meticulously chosen element contributes to the overall significance and impact of the ritual.

The presence of hidden symbols within satanic rituals is not mere superficial adornment or a random assortment of signs. Instead, each symbol holds profound meaning, encoding the beliefs, desires, and aspirations of those involved in the rituals. They act as a visual language that enables the rituals to communicate and perpetuate the principles and ideologies associated with satanic worship.

In conclusion, the study of hidden symbols within satanic rituals offers valuable insights into the intricate world of satanic worship. Through a historical lens, we have traced the origins of these symbols and explored them in the context of modern occult practices. From the inverted pentagram representing rebellion against societal norms to the powerful sigil of Baphomet encapsulating a multifaceted belief system, each symbol carries intrinsic meaning and purpose. By deciphering these concealed messages, we can gain a deeper understanding of the motivations of practitioners and the psychological allure that draws individuals into the realm of Satan.

SATANIC RITUALS AND RITUALISTIC ABUSE

As an expert paranormal investigator, I have encountered a multitude of enigmatic and unexplained phenomena in my career. However, nothing could have prepared me for the dark and perplexing realm of satanic rituals and ritualistic abuse. Join me as we delve into the depths of this perturbing world, carefully analyzing the controversies and allegations surrounding these alarming practices and the challenges that arise when investigating such claims.

Since the dawn of civilization, mankind has been captivated by the concept of evil and the sinister forces that propel it. Throughout history, numerous cultures have engaged in various forms of religious worship, often entwined with rituals and ceremonies intended to placate or communicate with divine entities. While most religious practices embrace love, peace, and harmony, certain rituals have veered down a darker path, exploring the realms of violence and malevolence.

In recent decades, allegations of ritualistic abuse within satanic worship have seized public attention, stirring fear and controversy. These claims frequently involve abhorrent acts, including human sacrifice, sexual abuse, and the profanation of sacred objects. Despite the scarcity of concrete evidence, the widespread nature of these allegations has instigated a pressing need to investigate and either disprove or validate them.

One of the primary challenges encountered in investigating ritualistic abuse within satanic worship is the clandestine nature of these practices. Rituals are often conducted in concealed locations, such as subterranean chambers or isolated wilderness areas, far away from prying eyes. Gaining access to these locations presents a significant obstacle as practitioners zealously guard their rituals, ensuring they remain concealed from the outside world. Furthermore, the perpetrators of these acts adhere to a stringent code of secrecy, making infiltration into their ranks or earning their trust exceedingly difficult.

Another impediment in investigating claims of ritualistic abuse is the psychological trauma endured by survivors. Victims of ritualistic abuse frequently suffer from intense emotional distress and profound psychological scars. Memories of their tormentors and the rituals they endured often plague them, manifesting as fragmented recollections that are arduous to reconstruct. In some instances, victims may employ defense mechanisms, such as dissociation, to shield themselves from overwhelming trauma, rendering the acquisition of coherent testimonies challenging.

To shed light on the controversies swirling around ritualistic abuse within satanic rituals, researchers have conducted numerous studies and investigations. One significant study conducted by Dr. Lawrence Pazder in the late 1970s is often cited as the first case of ritual abuse. The study delved into the experiences of a patient known as Michelle Smith, who claimed to have suffered ritualistic abuse throughout her childhood, involving satanic practices and mind control techniques. Although her account was met with skepticism and allegations of fabrication, it ignited a surge of interest in the field of ritualistic abuse research.

Various methods have been utilized since then to unearth evidence of ritualistic abuse. Some researchers have employed regression therapy and hypnosis to unlock repressed memories, with the aim of gaining a clearer understanding of the atrocities victims have endured. However, these techniques have faced criticism for potentially implanting false memories into vulnerable individuals, generating an ongoing debate within the scientific community.

Another avenue of investigation involves scrutinizing crime scenes and physical evidence. Nonetheless, these efforts are often thwarted by the very nature of the rituals themselves. Ritualistic abuse is frequently executed with meticulous attention to detail, leaving minimal traces behind. Perpetrators will meticulously clean crime scenes, eliminate any distinguishing marks, and dispose of evidence in a manner that renders it impossible to link it to the ritualistic practices.

The paucity of tangible evidence has contributed to the polarized viewpoints surrounding ritualistic abuse within satanic worship. Skeptics argue that the allegations are groundless, merely products of moral panic or suggestible individuals seeking attention. On the other end of the spectrum, believers argue that the clandestine practices and the traumatic experiences suffered by victims contribute to the challenges of obtaining evidence. They contend that summarily dismissing such claims perpetuates the cycle of abuse.

In conclusion, the controversies and allegations surrounding ritualistic abuse within satanic worship pose numerous obstacles for those endeavoring to investigate and address this unsettling phenomenon. The secretive nature of these practices, the trauma experienced by survivors, and the elusive nature of tangible evidence all hinder efforts to either disprove or validate these claims. While the debate rages on, it is imperative to approach the topic with both skepticism and compassion, ensuring that the voices of survivors are heard and their experiences acknowledged. Only by shining a light on the darkness can we hope to uncover the truth concealed within the domain of Satan.

SATANIC WORSHIP AND ANONYMOUS NETWORKS

In the depths of the internet, there exists a clandestine network of individuals who actively engage in Satanic worship and rituals. These online communities provide a secure environment for those seeking to explore their darkest inclinations, free from scrutiny or judgment. The anonymity afforded by these networks facilitates the unfettered expression of their desires.

To delve into this disconcerting world, extensive research was necessary. Months were spent meticulously scouring online forums and chat rooms dedicated to Satanic worship. Adhering cautiously to the shadows, I navigated through encrypted platforms, ensuring my own safety and concealing my true intent.

A notable challenge was earning the trust of these individuals, who guard their secrets cautiously. Initially hesitant to share their experiences and ceremonies with an outsider, some only began to open up once they became aware of my reputable standing as a paranormal investigator. Persistence, patience, and an in-depth knowledge of the occult eventually allowed me to establish connections within these enigmatic networks, granting access to invaluable insider perspectives.

My interactions with these individuals unveiled a startling revelation - the employment of anonymous networks and digital platforms not only facilitated communication but also aided in organizing and coordinating Satanic rituals. Through encrypted messaging applications and secure forums, adherents strategized clandestine gatherings, ensuring their intentions remained concealed from prying eyes. The anonymity bestowed by these digital platforms imbued them with a sense of security, enabling operations with relative impunity.

Furthermore, my research uncovered the unsettling truth that these online networks transcended geographic boundaries, uniting individuals from across the globe under a shared devotion to Satan. The ubiquity of the internet allowed these communities to thrive, surpassing the limitations imposed on traditional cults and secret societies. Through encrypted channels, they disseminated knowledge, exchanged forbidden texts, and even orchestrated live-streamed rituals that blurred the divide between reality and the virtual realm.

As my investigation plunged deeper, evidence emerged of Satanic groups infiltrating mainstream social media platforms. Under the guise of innocuous memes and cryptic symbols, they covertly propagated their dark ideologies. This covert effort to influence the masses serves as a stark reminder that Satanism has transcended its underground origins, seeping into the very fabric of our digital existences.

Exhaustive hours were invested in scrutinizing surveillance footage and digital logs, revealing a chilling discovery - the allure of Satanic worship and the anonymity proffered by online platforms had given rise to a new generation of followers. Driven by disillusionment with society, young and impressionable individuals sought solace within these digital occult communities. It seemed as though the internet had become a gateway to Satan himself, enthralling lost souls with promises of power and enlightenment.

The weight of this knowledge on my conscience compelled me to acknowledge that conventional methods alone would not suffice in combating Satanic worship's exploitation of anonymous networks. Success demanded a meticulous fusion of technological proficiency, psychological astuteness, and unwavering determination.

Armed with this conviction, I resolved to illuminate the darkest recesses of the internet, exposing the malevolent underpinnings of these Satanic communities. A perilous and treacherous undertaking lay ahead, yet an essential one, destined to protect the vulnerable and unmask the true malevolence concealed behind the shroud of anonymity.

And so, I embarked upon a mission to infiltrate these anonymous networks, revealing the rituals, ideologies, and individuals who perpetuate Satanic worship in the shadows. The battle had just commenced, and I was resolute in risking everything to expose their sinister activities, restoring order to a world menaced by the Eye of Satan.

To be continued...

SATANIC RITUALS AND SECRECY IN POPULAR CULTURE

In order to truly understand the impact and influence of Satanic rituals and secrecy within popular culture, it is imperative that we delve into their historical origins. Centuries ago, in the heart of Europe, accusations of witchcraft and trials involving satanic practices were rampant, leaving an enduring imprint on the collective consciousness. These witch hunts triggered widespread fear and paranoia, igniting a recurring fascination with satanic rituals.

Within the realm of literature, we are captivated by influential works that explore the clandestine world of Satanism. An exemplary illustration of this allure can be found in Bram Stoker's Dracula, where the Count represents the charismatic embodiment of the devil, ensnaring unsuspecting victims to carry out his nefarious bidding. This fascination with occult themes in literature continued to flourish, with authors such as H.P. Lovecraft and Aleister Crowley delving into the forbidden knowledge of secret societies and ancient rituals.

Transitioning into the domain of film, we discover a medium that effectively brings Satanic rituals and secrecy to life with a chilling intensity. Renowned movies such as Rosemary's Baby and The Wicker Man delve into the sinister practices of devil-worshipping cults, embodying the themes of secrecy and dark arts. These films, among others, have significantly shaped our perception of satanic rituals, featuring clandestine gatherings, sacrifices, and an underlying malevolence.

Over the years, conspiracy theories have additionally fueled our fascination with Satanic rituals and secrecy, often linking them to influential figures and covert organizations. An example of such theories is the Illuminati, an alleged secret society purportedly engaged in manipulating world events and harnessing dark powers. Although historical evidence supporting the existence of the Illuminati remains scarce, the idea of powerful elites participating in covert rituals taps into a primal fear of the unknown, thus allowing conspiracy theories to thrive and capture the public's imagination.

As we navigate the intricate realm of popular culture and its portrayal of Satanic rituals and secrecy, it becomes crucial to examine the underlying motives driving such depictions. For many individuals, the exploration of the dark arts vicariously through literature, film, and conspiracy theories offers a means of experiencing a forbidden world, safely ensconced in the knowledge that it remains beyond reach. Satanic rituals and secrecy provide an outlet for confronting the shadow self, enabling an introspective contemplation of the darkest facets of human nature in a controlled and somewhat reassuring manner.

In conclusion, the depiction of Satanic rituals and secrecy within popular culture has undeniably left an indelible impression on our collective consciousness. From the chilling narratives found within literature to the captivating imagery projected on the silver screen, audiences have been enticed by the mysterious allure of the occult. While the truths surrounding these practices may remain concealed, the enduring popularity of these themes serves as a reminder of our unquenchable fascination with the macabre and the enigmatic. As a paranormal investigator and specialist in the peculiar, my dedication lies in further exploring these depths, striving to unearth the hidden truths lurking within the shadows. Together, let us embark on an expedition into the realm of Satan, illuminating the secrets that remain just beyond our sight, awaiting revelation.

SATANIC WORSHIP AND THE POWER OF SECRECY

In order to fully comprehend the psychological and sociological implications of secrecy within Satanic worship, it is necessary to first examine the historical context in which this occult phenomenon originated. The roots of Satanic worship can be traced back to ancient civilizations such as Mesopotamia and Egypt, where rituals honoring deities associated with darkness and chaos were performed in the strictest of confidence. These rites provided individuals with a means of connecting to hidden realms believed to hold forbidden knowledge and untapped power.

The concept of secrecy within Satanic worship has served various purposes throughout history. Not only has it protected practitioners from persecution by mainstream religious institutions, but it has also fostered a sense of exclusivity and elitism among those initiated into the inner sanctums of Satanism. By creating an air of mystique and forbidden knowledge, Satanic worshippers have been able to exert psychological control over their followers, instilling loyalty and devotion through the allure of secrecy.

When analyzing the psychological implications of secrecy within Satanic worship, it is crucial to comprehend the underlying motivations that drive individuals to partake in these practices. For some, the appeal lies in the pursuit of power and personal agency. In a world where individuals often feel disempowered and constrained by societal norms, engaging in a covert ritual provides a sense of liberation and control over one's own fate. This desire for power, combined with the exhilarating thrill of participating in forbidden actions, creates a compelling psychological cocktail that can be addictive.

Furthermore, secrecy within Satanic worship can also function as a form of self-identity and rebellion against societal norms. By consciously choosing to engage in practices considered taboo or immoral, individuals are able to establish their own values and find a sense of belonging within an alternative community. Through embracing the forbidden, practitioners of Satanic worship challenge the established order and find solace in the company of like-minded individuals who share their subversive beliefs.

From a sociological perspective, secrecy within Satanic worship has profound implications for individual and group dynamics. Within the confines of a secretive cult-like environment, the boundaries between reality and fantasy become blurred, and the distinction between charismatic leadership and manipulation fades away. Initiates of Satanic worship often find themselves subjected to a form of indoctrination that reinforces the significance of secrecy, loyalty, and obedience to the leader of the group.

The power dynamics within Satanic worship heavily rely on the promotion of fear and the perceived consequences for those who breach the code of secrecy. This fear-based mechanism of control ensures compliance and discourages dissent, further consolidating the leader's authority. Conversely, those who remain steadfast and devoted to the principles of secrecy receive a sense of belonging and validation, providing a powerful incentive for continued dedication to the cause.

In conclusion, the role of secrecy within Satanic worship is a multifaceted and intricate phenomenon that profoundly affects the psychology and sociology of its practitioners. Through maintaining an environment of secrecy and forbidden knowledge, Satanic worshippers are able to exert control and manipulate the minds of their followers. The allure of power, personal agency, and rebellion against societal norms attracts individuals into the depths of Satanism, creating a sense of identity and belonging within a covert community. However, one must approach the study of Satanic worship with caution, as delving too deeply into the abyss of darkness may have chilling repercussions for one's own psyche.

16

SATANIC WORSHIP AND THE SHADOW SELF

CARL JUNG AND THE SHADOW SELF

The concept of the shadow self, as defined by Carl Jung, encompasses the concealed and frequently unconscious facet of an individual's personality. It represents the submerged and repressed elements of ourselves that we often attempt to overlook or disavow. Jung hypothesized that embracing and assimilating the shadow self is crucial for self-discovery and personal development. It is within the depths of our shadow that our authentic potential lies, and by acknowledging and confronting these hidden aspects, we can attain a state of completeness and equilibrium.

In the context of Satanic worship, the exploration of the shadow self takes on a particularly captivating dimension. Satanic practices revolve around the acknowledgment and indulgence of forbidden desires, which are often associated with the darker aspects of human nature. Those who adhere to Satanic beliefs and opt to harness the power of the shadow self contend that by recognizing and accepting their deepest, most concealed desires, they can tap into a well of power and personal autonomy.

To delve into this intriguing correlation, I initially immersed myself in Jung's extensive writings on the shadow self. I stuied his works thoroughly, scrutinizing every word in an endeavor to grasp the psychological implications of the shadow self and its relationship to Satanic worship. Jung's concept of the collective unconscious also played a significant role in my research, suggesting that profound archetypes and universal symbols reside within the human psyche. These archetypes, including the shadow, exert a profound influence on our thoughts, emotions, and behaviors.

Equipped with an in-depth comprehension of Jungian psychology, I began my exploration of the practices and rituals associated with Satanic worship. The initial step involved gaining access to Satanic circles and establishing trust with practitioners who were amenable to sharing their experiences. This process proved to be arduous and exacting, as attaining acceptance into these secretive circles necessitated exhaustive scrutiny and proving oneself to be deserving of their trust.

Once granted access, I was met with a blend of astonishment and unease. The rituals were elaborate, evoking dark energies and summoning the presence of the shadow self. I observed individuals consciously embracing their darkest desires, reciting chants and invocations that called forth their shadowy counterparts. The sight was disconcerting, with group participants surrendering themselves to the dance of darkness, seemingly possessed by an otherworldly force.

As my investigations progressed, I began to comprehend the power and allure of tapping into the shadow self. Those who willingly embraced their shadow exuded an air of confidence and self-assuredness. They flourished in their transgressions, discovering liberation and empowerment through unapologetic indulgence in their taboo desires. The Satanic rituals allowed them to confront their shadow, to bring it forth, and to harness its energy for their personal growth and development.

However, amidst this exploration of darkness, I couldn't help pondering the potential perils of blindly embracing the shadow self. While Jung advocated for its integration, he also cautioned against unbridled indulgence, as it could lead to imbalance and self-destruction. My concern escalated as I witnessed individuals who had wholly succumbed to their shadow selves, losing touch with their own humanity and becoming consumed by darkness. The line between liberation and insanity became blurred, necessitating a thorough exploration of the psychological implications of such intense self-exploration.

All in all, my investigation into Carl Jung's concept of the shadow self and its connection to the exploration of the dark aspects of human nature within Satanic worship has been an enlightening and profound experience. It has deepened my understanding of the human psyche, its complexities, and the inherent duality that exists within all of us. While the shadow self holds great potential for personal growth and empowerment, it requires caution and self-awareness. The path to self-discovery lies not solely in embracing the darkness but in finding a harmonious equilibrium within it, ensuring that our explorations into the shadow realm do not engulf us entirely.

SATANIC RITUALS AND SHADOW INTEGRATION

As a professional paranormal investigator and specialist in the extraordinary, my exploration has led me down numerous obscure and intricate paths. The examination of Satanic rituals and their correlation to shadow integration stands out as one of the most captivating and enlightening experiences in my career.

To fully comprehend the function of Satanic rituals in facilitating the fusion of the shadow self and fostering self-awareness and personal development, an exploration of their historical roots is essential. Throughout ancient civilizations to present-day societies, Satanic rituals have significantly influenced humanity.

The origins of Satanic rituals can be traced back to ancient civilizations such as the Sumerians and Babylonians, who subscribed to a pantheon of gods and demons. These rituals were often enacted to appease these entities and secure their favor. However, as these civilizations fell and new belief systems emerged, the practice of Satanic rituals waned.

It was not until the 20th century that Satanic rituals resurfaced in a new manifestation. Influenced by the writings of Aleister Crowley and Anton LaVey, modern Satanism emerged as a religious and philosophical movement that emphasized individualism, self-empowerment, and the exploration of the darker facets of human nature.

Within this context, we can begin to analyze the role of Satanic rituals in promoting the integration of the shadow self. The shadow self, a concept introduced by Carl Jung, represents the unconscious portion of our psyche that encompasses the suppressed and repressed aspects of our personality. These fragments of our being are often rejected or denied due to their perceived potency and potential for destruction.

Through engagement in Satanic rituals, adherents can boldly confront and merge these shadow aspects, leading to heightened self-awareness and personal growth. These rituals serve as a catalyst for introspection, enabling individuals to confront their deepest apprehensions and desires within a structured and controlled environment.

The "Rite of Baphomet" serves as an exemplary Satanic ritual that embodies the integration of the shadow self. In this rite, participants summon the presence of the demonic deity Baphomet, who symbolizes the union of opposites and the reconciliation of conflicting forces within oneself. Through a series of symbolic actions and invocations, individuals are encouraged to embrace the darker aspects of their nature and acknowledge the inherent duality within.

Throughout my research, I have encountered numerous testimonies from individuals who have undergone this ritual and undergone profound personal transformation. They describe a newfound sense of self-acceptance and empowerment, alongside a heightened awareness of their motivations and desires. It is through the confrontation and integration of their shadow selves that they unlock untapped potential and solidify their authentic identities.

Nevertheless, it is imperative to acknowledge that Satanic rituals, like any potent tool, can be misused and exploited. Without adequate knowledge and understanding, they can have adverse psychological or spiritual effects. Therefore, practitioners must approach these rituals with caution and respect, seeking guidance from experienced mentors and conducting thorough research.

In conclusion, Satanic rituals play a crucial role in facilitating the integration of the shadow self and promoting self-awareness and personal growth. These rituals allow individuals to confront and merge their darker aspects, resulting in a deeper understanding of themselves and a heightened sense of empowerment. However, it is vital that these rituals be approached with reverence and knowledge, ensuring they are conducted safely and responsibly.

As I delve further into the realm of Satanic rituals and their connection to the mysteries of the human psyche, I remain endlessly fascinated and humbled by the intricacies and depths of the human condition. Though the shadows may cast a dark hue, it is within this obscurity that we discover the key to our genuine selves. Thus, guided by a discerning eye, I continue to unravel the enigmatic forces that shape our existence.

SATANIC WORSHIP AND PSYCHOLOGICAL SHADOW WORK

In order to comprehend the correlation between Satanic worship and psychological shadow work, it is imperative to delve into the historical timeline of this contentious practice. Over the course of history, various cultures and religions have veneratued deities associated with darkness and the underworld. The notion of Satan, as we currently perceive it, can be traced back to ancient pagan beliefs and mythologies.

In numerous ancient societies, the worship of deities symbolizing darkness and chaos was not necessarily regarded as wicked, but rather as a crucial equilibrium to the forces of light. These dark deities were often linked with death, transformation, and the concealed aspects of the human psyche. They were perceived as mentors or guides, leading individuals on a voyage of self-discovery and personal development.

It was during the ascent of Christianity that the figure of Satan was demonized and solely associated with malevolence. The early Christian Church, in a bid to establish its supremacy, condemned any form of worship that deviated from their worldview. Consequently, Satanic worship became synonymous with immorality, corruption, and the adoration of malevolent forces.

Nevertheless, there has been a recent resurgence of interest in exploring the techniques of psychological shadow work within the realm of Satanic worship. This alternative approach contends that Satan can be perceived as a symbol of the repressed and prohibited aspects of the human psyche, rather than a literal entity.

Psychological shadow work encompasses an extensive exploration of the unconscious mind, specifically the parts that have been suppressed or denied. It represents a process of confronting and integrating the shadowy aspects of one's personality, including fears, desires, and traumas, for the purpose of achieving wholeness and self-actualization.

Within the context of Satanic worship, adherents view Satan as a figurative embodiment of the shadow self. By embracing this archetype, individuals are able to confront and work through their deepest fears and desires, thus attaining a greater comprehension of themselves and their position in the world.

One of the methodologies adopted in the practice of psychological shadow work within Satanic worship involves the engagement in ritualistic practices. These rituals frequently entail confronting and embracing elements of one's shadow through symbolical acts such as cathartic release, visualization, and meditation.

For instance, a Satanic ritual may require participants to confront their most prominent fears or engage in acts that are regarded as taboo. These acts provide a secure and controlled environment for individuals to explore their darkest desires or confront traumatic experiences. Through this process, they are able to acquire insight, heal emotional wounds, and ultimately integrate these shadowy aspects into their conscious self. This leads to greater self-acceptance and personal growth.

Another aspect of Satanic worship that is intimately intertwined with psychological shadow work is the pursuit of personal power and autonomy. In many traditional religious systems, individuals are often encouraged to submit to a higher authority or deity. In stark contrast, Satanic worship places significant emphasis on personal agency and individual autonomy.

By adopting the role of the adversary or rebel, Satanic practitioners challenge societal norms and religious doctrines. This act of rebellion may be perceived as a symbolic rejection of external authority and an affirmation of personal power. It stimulates individuals to question and scrutinize their own beliefs, values, and desires, leading to a deeper understanding of themselves and the world they inhabit.

Furthermore, Satanic worship provides a supportive environment for individuals to explore and express their authentic selves without fear of judgment or condemnation. In a society that frequently suppresses or marginalizes certain identities or desires, Satanic adherents find comfort and acceptance within a community that celebrates individuality and diversity.

In conclusion, the integration of psychological shadow work within the realm of Satanic worship offers a distinctive and alternative approach to self-exploration and personal growth. By embracing the symbolic figure of Satan and confronting their own shadows, individuals are able to gain insight, heal emotional wounds, and achieve a heightened sense of self-acceptance and empowerment. It is through this journey through darkness that they emerge into the light, transformed and renewed.

SATANIC RITUALS AND CONFRONTING INNER DEMONS

In order to gain a comprehensive understanding of the significance of satanic rituals and the confrontation of inner demons, it is imperative to delve into the historical background of Satanism itself. This path has been subject to misinterpretation and condemnation for many centuries and has often been associated with evil and the devil. However, beneath this misguided perception lies a deep and intricate practice aimed at addressing inner darkness in order to foster personal growth and enlightenment.

During the course of my research, I have encountered various ancient texts and testimonies that shed light on the origin and purpose of satanic rituals. Among these resources, the "Key of Solomon," a notorious grimoire containing detailed instructions on summoning and interacting with demons, stands out. While many may perceive this practice as inherently evil, it is crucial to recognize that the underlying objective of these rituals is not to invite malevolent forces, but rather to confront and overcome the inner demons residing within oneself.

Throughout history, satanic rituals have provided individuals with a means to confront their own fears, traumas, and inner demons head-on. These rituals frequently incorporate symbolism, ceremonial tools, and recitations of ancient incantations. By embracing the darkness within and engaging in these rituals, individuals can tap into the depths of their subconscious, unearthing repressed emotions and buried traumas that hinder their personal progress. It is through the process of confrontation and acceptance that genuine transformation can transpire.

In the course of my own investigations, I have witnessed individuals undergo profound metamorphoses as a result of practicing satanic rituals. One notable case involved a woman named Emily who had long been haunted by deeply ingrained fears and anxieties. Through a series of rituals involving the invocation of demons, meditation, and introspection, Emily was able to confront the underlying causes of her fears, bring them to the surface, and ultimately conquer them.

It is vital to acknowledge that the process of confronting and embracing one's inner demons within the context of satanic rituals is not for the faint of heart. It demands immense courage, self-awareness, and a profound understanding of the occult. This path should not be undertaken lightly, as the exploration of one's own darkness can be treacherous and un-settling. However, for those who have the audacity to embark on this journey, the rewards can be immeasurable.

Satanic rituals act as catalysts for self-transformation by compelling individuals to confront their deepest fears and traumas. Through the act of ritualistic confrontation, individ-uals externalize their inner demons, giving them tangible form and substance. This externalization facilitates a more tangible and comprehensible dialogue with these suppressed aspects of one's self.

By actively engaging with these inner demons through ritual, individuals can achieve a deeper understanding of their own psyche, motivations, and desires. It is through this process of introspection and exploration that true healing and personal growth can commence.

While satanic rituals may be considered controversial, it is essential to acknowledge the transformative potential they offer. They provide a distinctive framework for self-exploration and personal development, enabling individuals to confront their own darkness and emerge stronger and more enlightened.

In conclusion, satanic rituals and the confrontation of inner demons have long been subjected to misunderstandings and misrepresentations. These rituals function as powerful tools for self-transformation, enabling individuals to confront their deepest fears and traumas head-on. Through the process of ritualistic confrontation, these inner demons can be exposed, fostering profound healing and personal growth. As a paranor-mal investigator and Specialist of the Strange, my exploration into the realm of satanic rituals has brought me face-to-face with the intricate mechanisms of these rituals and the im-mense power they possess. It is through this exploration that I continue to unravel the enigmas of the occult and the human psyche.

SATANIC WORSHIP AND CATHARSIS

The origins of Satanic worship can be traced back to ancient civilizations, in which a variety of pagan religions practiced rituals that were considered sacrilegious and demonic by early Christian societies. These rituals often entailed the symbolic worship of deities that represented darkness, rebellion, and chaotic forces. Among these deities is Satan, a figure that has captivated the minds of believers and non-believers alike for centuries.

Throughout history, societies have regarded Satanic worship with a combination of fear, fascination, and condemnation. During the medieval period, the Christian Church undertook a campaign to eradicate any non-conformist religious practices, deeming them heretical and evil. This led to the persecution and execution of countless individuals who were associated with Satanic worship, whether real or imagined. The fear surrounding Satanic rituals only intensified during the notorious witch trials of the 16th and 17th centuries, during which innocent men and women were accused of consorting with the devil and engaging in acts of unspeakable evil.

Fast-forwarding to the modern era, Satanic worship has adopted a new manifestation. While there are still individuals who believe in the literal existence of Satan and participate in rituals in his honor, there is also an emerging movement of people who view Satanic worship as a symbol of rebellion against oppressive religious and societal norms. This contemporary form of Satanic worship often involves rituals and practices that are intended to provide emotional release and psychological healing.

One aspect of Satanic rituals that lends itself to catharsis is the concept of transgression. By deliberately engaging in actions that are regarded as taboo or forbidden, individuals can liberate themselves from societal norms and expectations. This act of rebellion can be liberating and empowering, enabling individuals to connect with their true selves and release pent-up emotions in a controlled and ritualized manner.

Another element of Satanic worship that facilitates catharsis is the usage of symbolism and imagery. Satanic rituals frequently employ props like altars, candles, and ceremonial garments, creating an ambience of darkness and mystery. These visual cues can evoke intense emotions and foster a heightened sense of awareness, setting the stage for a cathartic experience.

Furthermore, Satanic rituals often incorporate theatrical elements and performance. Participants may assume roles and personas, engaging in scripted dialogues and actions that allow them to fully immerse themselves in the ritual. This theatrical aspect of Satanic worship serves as a vehicle for emotional expression, offering a space for participants to explore their deepest fears, desires, and vulnerabilities.

Through my research and investigations, I have encountered numerous testimonies from individuals who have found solace and healing through their participation in Satanic rituals. These individuals frequently cite the experience of catharsis as a transformative and therapeutic process. By channeling their emotions and embracing their darker side, they are able to confront and release their emotional burdens, ultimately leading to a sense of liberation and personal growth.

It is important to recognize that Satanic worship is not suitable for everyone, and there are potential risks associated with engaging in such practices. The psychological and emotional impact of participating in intense ritualistic experiences can vary from person to person, and it is vital for individuals to approach these practices with caution and seek professional guidance if necessary.

In conclusion, the role of catharsis within Satanic worship is a complex and multifaceted phenomenon. Although it may appear paradoxical to seek emotional release and healing through rituals often associated with darkness and evil, the transformative power of these experiences should not be underestimated. Satanic worship, when approached with an open mind and a deep understanding of its historical context, can provide individuals with an opportunity for emotional release, psychological healing, and personal growth.

SATANIC RITUALS AND DARK PSYCHOLOGY

Satanic rituals, originating from the occult and devil worship, have long been a source of fascination and fear for individuals. The forbidden knowledge and promise of supernatural power associated with these rituals have attracted many towards the path of darkness. These rituals frequently involve summoning evil entities, performing blood sacrifices, and defiling sacred symbols. Each ritual is intricately planned and executed, with the objective of invoking dark forces and establishing a connection with the Devil himself.

On the other hand, dark psychology delves into the twisted mechanisms of the human mind, exploring manipulation and control. Research in this field focuses on understanding how individuals can be influenced, exploited, and coerced into acting against their own interests. Techniques such as gaslighting, cognitive dissonance, and subliminal messaging are employed to subtly influence and manipulate the thoughts, emotions, and behaviors of others.

While Satanic rituals and dark psychology may appear to be vastly different, they share a common objective: control. Both seek to exert power over people, whether through direct invocation of supernatural forces or through psychological manipulation. The methods may differ, but the ultimate aim remains constant: bending the will of others to suit their own desires.

It is crucial to acknowledge that not all practitioners of dark psychology are Satanists, nor are all Satanists practitioners of dark psychology. However, there exists an intriguing overlap wherein some individuals incorporate elements from both practices to achieve their objectives. These hybrid practitioners may combine the theatrics of Satanic rituals with psychological manipulation techniques to further their aims of domination and control.

One striking example is the use of symbolism in both Satanic rituals and dark psychology. Symbols have a profound impact on the human psyche, evoking deep-seated emotions and associations. Satanic rituals employ ancient and esoteric symbols to establish a connection with evil entities and invoke their power. In dark psychology, symbols are used as subconscious triggers to influence behavior. By understanding how symbols can be used for control and manipulation, these hybrid practitioners gain a powerful tool to further their malicious intentions.

Another intriguing parallel lies in the realm of belief systems. In Satanic rituals, beliefs in the supernatural and the occult are essential to the practice. By immersing themselves in a world where demons, spirits, and dark forces hold sway, practitioners tap into a higher power that they believe will grant their desires. In dark psychology, beliefs and ideologies are utilized to manipulate others. By creating an aura of authority and credibility, practitioners can manipulate individuals into unquestioningly accepting their influence and suggestions.

The intersection between Satanic rituals and dark psychology is a treacherous terrain, where the pursuit of power can lead individuals down a path of moral decline and devastation. It is a realm that I, Dakota Frandsen, am intimately familiar with in my investigations. The revelations I have encountered in my research have demonstrated the profound extent of darkness, as well as the dangers that lurk within for those who succumb to its temptations.

As I continue to delve into the intricacies of Satanic rituals and dark psychology, I am confronted with the significant impact they have on individuals and society as a whole. The depraved minds behind these practices, driven by their desire for power and control, leave destruction in their wake. It is my responsibility as a paranormal investigator and Specialist of the Strange to illuminate the darkest corners of humanity, exposing the insidious techniques and rituals that threaten to consume us.

In the journey into the realm of Satan, I have come to realize that the true battle lies not in the realms of the supernatural or the psychological, but within the human spirit. It is through the strength of our will, our capacity for empathy and compassion, that we can resist the allure of darkness. Only by comprehending the subtle manipulations and deeply ingrained beliefs that shape our thoughts and actions can we hope to resist the influence of Satanic rituals and dark psychology.

As I gaze into the depths of human darkness, I am reminded of the fragility of our minds. This battle cannot be fought with physical armaments, but necessitates the weapon of knowledge and awareness. Only by steadfastly committing ourselves to understanding and confronting the depths of depravity can we hope to overcome the allure of Satanic rituals and the insidious tactics of dark psychology.

As I continue to unravel the mysteries that lie at the intersection of Satanic rituals and dark psychology, I remain ever vigilant in my pursuit of truth. The fight against these malevolent forces is not for the faint-hearted, but for those who are willing to confront evil head-on and emerge stronger. For it is only by comprehending the darkest aspects of humanity that we can truly appreciate the light that resides within us all.

SATANIC WORSHIP AND SHADOW ARCHETYPES

In order to gain a comprehensive understanding of the relationship between shadow archetypes and Satanic worship, it is imperative to explore the historical timeline of these practices. The origins of Satanic worship can be traced back to ancient civilizations, namely the Mesopotamians and the Egyptians, who assigned significance to gods and goddesses exhibiting both light and dark aspects. It was during this period that shadow archetypes entered the realm of human consciousness.

Throughout the annals of history, individuals who engaged in Satanic rituals or worshipped Satan were frequently marginalized by society, as their practices were regarded as sacrilegious and perilous. However, it is crucial to recognize that not all practitioners of Satanic worship view themselves as immoral or malevolent. For some, the pursuit is a spiritual voyage, a personal quest for self-exploration and empowerment. It is within the framework of this context that the impact of shadow archetypes becomes evident.

Shadow archetypes represent primordial facets of the human psyche that embody repressed or unconscious yearnings, fears, and impulses. These aspects are concealed within the shadow self, existing beyond conscious awareness, yet exerting a formidable influence on cognition, sentiment, and conduct.

When individuals partake in Satanic worship, they tap into these shadow archetypes, stimulating an upsurge of unfiltered, primeval energy that can simultaneously liberate and wreak havoc.

Based on my research, I have ascertained that Satanic worship often entails rituals and practices devised to elicit and harness the power of shadow archetypes. Participants immerse themselves in darkness, forsaking societal norms, and embracing their suppressed desires. By embracing their shadow selves, they aspire to transcend the limitations imposed by society and experience an elevated sense of freedom and authenticity.

Nevertheless, the allure of shadow archetypes bears consequences. Just as light casts shadows, the exploration of the shadow self can induce a distorted self-perception and an askew ethical compass. As individuals become increasingly engrossed in Satanic worship, they may internalize a belief that they are inherently nefarious, driven by troves of dark longings that conflict with societal standards. This warped self-perception can foster an array of destructive behaviors, including violence, self-harm tendencies, and indifference to the well-being of others.

The influence of shadow archetypes within Satanic worship transcends the individual realm and extends to the collective unconscious. Satanic rituals often involve communal participation, fostering a sense of cohesion and shared purpose. In these moments, the boundaries between individuals blur, allowing for the emergence of a collective shadow archetype that amplifies the potency and intensity of the experience. This collective shadow can yield profound ramifications, triggering acts of rebellion, chaos, and even unspeakable evil.

It is essential to underscore that not all individuals who engage in Satanic worship succumb to the pernicious sway of shadow archetypes. Many individuals are able to navigate the labyrinthine depths of their own psyche with prudence and discernment. They achieve a delicate equilibrium between light and darkness, duly recognizing the power of their shadow selves without succumbing to its temptations. These individuals are often propelled by a deeper comprehension of the human condition and an aspiration to delve into the profundities of their own consciousness.

In conclusion, delving into the presence of shadow archetypes within Satanic worship unveils the intricate interplay between the human psyche and the forces that shape our perceptions and behaviors. It constitutes a passage into the abyss, a voyage of self-discovery that can lead to both illumination and ruination. As a paranormal investigator and specialist in the arcane, I am devoted to unraveling the enigmas ensconced within the realm of Satanic worship, illuminating the hidden recesses of the human psyche and the impact of shadow archetypes. However, in undertaking this mission, caution and prudence must prevail, for the darkness possesses an aptitude for engulfing the unwary, drawing them deeper into its domain of shadows and secrets. Only by comprehending the supremacy of shadow archetypes can we aspire to navigate these treacherous waters and emerge with our faculties and souls intact.

SATANIC RITUALS AND INTEGRATION OF LIGHT AND DARK

As an individual dedicated to investigating paranormal phenomena and studying the extraordinary, my experiences have led me down numerous paths into the realms of the unknown. Satanic rituals have consistently captivated my interest, not only due to their shocking and contentious nature but also for the profound insights they offer into the human psyche. Within this chapter, we will delve deeply into the process of integrating both light and dark aspects of the self within Satanic rituals and explore how it impacts the pursuit of personal wholeness.

Before exploring the intricacies of this subject matter, it is imperative to establish a historical framework to comprehend the development of Satanic rituals. Throughout different periods in history, societies have participated in various practices that embody veneration and apprehension of enigmatic forces. Ancient civilizations such as Egypt, Mesopotamia, and Rome all practiced their own rituals centered around deities associated with both light and dark energies. The purpose of these rituals was to achieve equilibrium and harmony in the universe.

However, it was during the Middle Ages that the concept of Satan as a potent symbol of darkness emerged. During this era, Satanic rituals assumed a significantly darker and more malevolent form, frequently tied to witchcraft and devil worship. These rituals were perceived as a means of communing with the devil himself and harnessing his sinister powers. While many of these beliefs were founded in ignorance and fear, they have had a profound impact on the perception of Satanic rituals that persists in contemporary society.

In present times, Satanic rituals have evolved into multifaceted practices that transcend conventional notions of morality. Contemporary practitioners view the integration of both light and dark aspects of the self as a pathway to achieving personal wholeness. The ritualistic process involves delving into both positive and negative elements within oneself and embracing them fully. By embracing their shadows, practitioners attain a deeper comprehension of their motivations, desires, and fears.

The integration of light and dark within Satanic rituals is a complex and highly individualistic journey. It commences with introspection, as individuals confront their own shadows and confront the uncomfortable truths that lie within. These rituals serve as catalysts for self-discovery, illuminating aspects of ourselves that may have previously been overlooked or suppressed.

One of the most significant effects of this integration process is the transformation it instigates within one's perception of good and evil. Through an examination of our own darker tendencies, we come to comprehend that darkness does not equate to malevolence or immorality. Rather, it is an inherent part of the multifaceted nature of existence. Satanic rituals enable us to deconstruct the dichotomy of good and evil and appreciate the intricate shades of gray that comprise the human experience.

Furthermore, this integration of light and dark empowers individuals to embrace their own abilities without fear, guilt, or shame. Many Satanic rituals incorporate elements of personal empowerment, motivating participants to tap into their inner strength and innate potential. By acknowledging and employing the dark aspects of the self, practitioners discover a newfound sense of agency and authenticity.

In addition, the integration of light and dark within Satanic rituals nurtures a sense of personal wholeness and equilibrium. Just as light cannot exist without darkness and darkness cannot exist without light, individuals realize that they are multifaceted beings. It is through the acceptance of both the light and dark aspects of the self that genuine wholeness can be achieved.

In conclusion, the journey of integrating light and dark aspects of the self within Satanic rituals is a transformative experience that challenges our preconceived notions of good and evil. It necessitates introspection, self-reflection, and a willingness to embrace the shadows within ourselves. Through this integration, practitioners acquire a deeper comprehension of their own identities, tap into their personal power, and attain a sense of personal wholeness that transcends the limitations of dualistic thinking. The exploration of Satanic rituals and the integration of light and dark is not for those lacking courage, but for those who dare to explore the depths of their own existence, it opens doors to profound self-discovery and empowerment.

17

SATANIC WORSHIP AND RITUALISTIC TRANSFORMATION

SATANIC RITUALS AND PERSONAL GROWTH

As a paranormal investigator and specialist in the occult, my name is Dakota Frandsen. I have extensively studied and explored the supernatural realm, bearing witness to inexplicable phenomena and embracing the mysteries that lie beyond our comprehension. Through these encounters, I have developed a profound understanding that Satanic rituals possess a significance that transcends their ominous reputation. When approached with an open mind and a spirit of inquiry, Satanic rituals hold the potential to foster personal growth and self-improvement.

Society has long stigmatized Satanism, associating it with malevolence and attributing dark forces to its practices. Nevertheless, my research and personal involvement have revealed a more nuanced perspective on this misunderstood tradition. Beneath the surface, Satanic rituals serve as a conduit for empowerment, self-awareness, and transformative experiences.

Within this chapter, we will delve deep into the underlying reasons behind the effectiveness of Satanic rituals in promoting personal growth. By interrogating the principles and techniques employed within these rituals, we will unearth the hidden potential that lies within this uncharted territory, available to those bold enough to venture into the realm of Satan.

Before comprehending the link between Satanic rituals and personal growth, it is imperative to grasp the fundamental principles upon which Satanic practices are built. Contrary to popular belief, Satanism does not revolve around the literal worship of a Satan figure. Instead, it operates as a rebellious vehicle that challenges oppressive religious dogmas and societal norms. At its core, Satanism embodies the values of individualism, the pursuit of knowledge, and the advocacy of free will.

These principles find expression in the rituals themselves. Satanic rituals are meticulously formulated to evoke deep emotional responses, test boundaries, and awaken latent aspects of the self. One such ritual, the Rite of Empowerment, functions as an initiation into the realm of personal growth through Satanic practices. By acknowledging one's inherent desires, embracing personal power, and rejecting external coercion, participants empower themselves and seize control of their own destiny.

As I embarked on my research, I encountered remarkable individuals who had undergone profound personal growth through active participation in Satanic rituals. One such individual is Sarah, a young woman grappling with low self-esteem and a lack of purpose. Sarah, who graciously allowed me to witness her transformative journey, engaged in Satanic rituals that centered on self-love and self-empowerment.

During her participation in the Veil of Embrace ritual, Sarah confronted her deepest fears and insecurities. Through this

powerful ritual, she was encouraged to shed the societal fa-
cades she had long worn and embrace her authentic essence.
Liberated from the weight of external expectations, Sarah experienced a profound sense of freedom. Her confidence soared,
propelling her to make choices that resonated with her own
desires, as opposed to conforming to imposed expectations.

At the core of personal growth within Satanic rituals lies
the potency of intention and focus. Through rituals such as
the Path of Aspiration, participants learn to set explicit goals,
visualize their aspirations, and manifest these ambitions into
tangible reality. By enacting symbolic gestures and reciting incantations laden with power, individuals align their conscious
desires with their subconscious minds, laying the groundwork
for self-improvement and personal growth.

A vital component of Satanic rituals that catalyzes personal
growth is the dynamic of communal engagement. In contrast
to the pervasive notion of Satanism as a solitary practice,
Satanic rituals often incorporate the collective energy of a
group. The Ritual of Unity, for instance, unifies individuals
who share common aspirations and combines their energies to
amplify desired outcomes. This group dynamic fosters a sense
of community, accountability, and mutual support, which can
facilitate individuals' journeys toward personal growth.

However, it is imperative to note that engaging in Satanic
rituals without a comprehensive understanding and proper
guidance can result in adverse consequences. Like any powerful tool, Satanic rituals demand responsible usage. It is vital to
approach these rituals with an open mind, a reverence for the
process, and an appreciation for the underlying symbolism.
Equally critical is the recognition of personal boundaries and
the importance of consent within these rituals to ensure a safe
and empowering experience.

In conclusion, Satanic rituals offer an unconventional yet powerful pathway to personal growth and self-improvement. By challenging societal norms, embracing individuality, setting clear intentions, and harnessing the power of communal dynamics, participants can embark on transformative journeys. It is through the embrace of the unknown, the exploration of the depths of the self, and the unlocking of the potential within Satanic rituals that one can open the door to personal growth and empowerment. Nevertheless, it is essential to approach these rituals with caution and responsible understanding to avoid the pitfalls that may lurk on the path to personal development.

SATANIC WORSHIP AND SPIRITUAL AWAKENING

In order to gain a comprehensive understanding of the role of Satanic worship in the realm of spiritual awakening, it is crucial to delve into its historical origins. Satanic worship can be traced back to ancient pagan practices and rituals, which were often misunderstood and condemned by the dominant religious institutions of the time. These ancient rituals embodied a deep reverence for nature, a recognition of the primal forces of life and death, and a profound connection to the spiritual realms. It was through these rituals that individuals sought to establish communion with the divine and embark on a journey of self-discovery.

In modern times, Satanic worship has evolved into a more diverse practice, encompassing a wide spectrum of beliefs and ideologies. While some individuals still subscribe to the traditional notion of worshipping Satan as a literal being, others perceive Satan as a symbol of rebellion, individualism, and liberation from societal constraints. This diversity of beliefs and interpretations serves as an indication of the capacity of

Satanic worship to provide a platform for individuals to explore alternative spiritual paths outside the confines of mainstream religions.

One of the most compelling aspects of Satanic worship is its ability to catalyze spiritual awakening. It possesses a primal and unrefined energy that empowers individuals to confront their inner demons, embrace their shadow selves, and transcend societal limitations. Through the rituals and practices associated with Satanic worship, practitioners are encouraged to embrace their desires, confront their fears, and push the boundaries of their own limitations. This process of self-exploration and confrontation with darkness can often lead to profound spiritual growth and awakening.

Although it may appear paradoxical, Satanic worship can indeed serve as a catalyst for personal growth and enlightenment. By embracing and integrating the darkness within ourselves, we can achieve a state of harmony and equilibrium. The Satanic path encourages practitioners to accept their true nature without judgment, thus allowing for the possibility of genuine self-acceptance and personal transformation.

Furthermore, Satanic worship provides an alternative to traditional religious dogma and hierarchical structures. It empowers individuals to forge their own spiritual path, free from the constraints of external authority. By rejecting the notion of a divine being who prescribes morality and instead embracing personal autonomy and responsibility, practitioners of Satanic worship are able to develop a profound connection to their own inner wisdom and intuition.

While Satanic worship may be surrounded by controversy and misunderstood by many, it offers a distinctive perspective on spirituality and personal growth. By daring to confront our own darkness and embracing our genuine desires, we can embark on a journey of self-discovery and spiritual awakening.

Satanic worship challenges us to question societal norms, explore alternative spiritual paths, and establish our own connection to the divine. It is through such exploration that we can genuinely uncover our own truth and purpose in this vast and enigmatic universe.

In conclusion, the role of Satanic worship in facilitating spiritual awakening and the exploration of alternative spiritual paths should not be dismissed or oversimplified. Through its rituals, beliefs, and practices, Satanic worship empowers individuals to confront their inner demons, embrace their true desires, and transcend the limitations imposed by societal norms and religious dogma. It provides a platform for personal growth and enlightenment, offering a unique perspective on spirituality that challenges conventional wisdom and empowers individuals to forge their own path to the divine.

SATANIC RITUALS AND ALTERED STATES OF CONSCIOUSNESS

In order to explore the realm of Satanic rituals and altered states of consciousness, it is imperative to establish a comprehensive historical timeline that charts the development and evolution of these practices. The origins of Satanic rituals can be traced back several centuries, intricately intertwined with various religious and occult traditions. The earliest documented evidence of such rituals can be found within ancient civilizations where satanic worship held a prominent place. From Egypt to Mesopotamia, these rituals were veiled in mystery and had a profound impact on those who participated.

With the advent of Christianity during the Middle Ages, the practice of Satanic rituals was frequently condemned and deemed heretical. This led to a heightened period of persecution against individuals accused of engaging in such practices, ultimately culminating in the infamous witch hunts throughout Europe. These dark times resulted in the creation of numerous grimoires and demonic texts, serving as instructional guides for practitioners seeking to achieve altered states of consciousness through Satanic rituals.

As time progressed, the modern era witnessed a resurgence of interest in Satanic rituals and their potential for transformative experiences. The process of globalization facilitated the exchange of knowledge among individuals from diverse backgrounds and cultures who harbored an interest in the occult, leading to the emergence of new hybrid practices. The blending of various traditions birthed unique rituals, often drawing inspiration from ancient practices while incorporating contemporary elements.

In the course of my investigations, I have encountered a multitude of testimonials and accounts from individuals who have undergone altered states of consciousness during Satanic rituals. These experiences are frequently described as profound and transformative, enabling participants to access their subconscious minds and establish connections with supernatural entities. These altered states can be achieved through various methods, including the utilization of psychoactive substances, sensory deprivation, and rhythmic vocalizations.

One particular case that remains vivid in my memory is that of a woman named Emily, who entrusted me with her experience during one of my investigations. Emily had participated in a Satanic ritual led by a charismatic practitioner who professed a profound connection with the demonic realm. As the ritual progressed, Emily recounted an overwhelming sense of euphoria flooding over her, accompanied by vivid hallucinations. It was as though a veil had been lifted, granting her access to a hidden dimension teeming with extraordinary beings and ancient wisdom.

Emily's narrative represents but one example that highlights the potential for transformative experiences within Satanic rituals. It is crucial to approach these accounts with an open-minded stance and a willingness to explore the uncharted territories. While skeptics may dismiss such experiences as mere delusions or the outcome of psychological manipulation, the consistency and depth of these narratives cannot be easily dismissed.

As a paranormal investigator and expert in the realm of the mysterious, my objective is not to promote or endorse the practice of Satanic rituals, but rather to illuminate their existence and potential repercussions. The supernatural domain is vast and encompasses a multitude of beliefs and practices, each offering a distinct viewpoint on altered states of consciousness. By studying and comprehending these rituals, we can acquire invaluable insights into the human mind and its capacity for transcendence.

To conclude, Satanic rituals possess a storied and captivating history, captivating countless individuals with their potential to induce altered states of consciousness and transformative experiences. From ancient civilizations to the present era, these rituals have enthralled and instilled fear in equal measure. Through my exhaustive investigations and research, I have grown to appreciate the profound impact these rituals can have on those who partake in them. Whether these experiences are the result of the supernatural or rooted in psychology, they provide a fleeting glimpse into a dimension surpassing our everyday reality, beckoning us to plumb the depths of the human mind and its mysterious connection with the unknown.

SATANIC WORSHIP AND BREAKING SOCIETAL CONDITIONING

In the field of the occult, few subjects elicit as much intrigue and debate as Satanic worship. Throughout history, this esoteric and enigmatic practice has been enveloped in a veil of mystery, apprehension, and misunderstanding. As a researcher of paranormal phenomena and an expert on the inexplicable, I have devoted my life to unraveling the enigmas concealed within the shadows. In this chapter, we embark on an in-depth exploration of Satanic worship, examining its impact on breaking societal norms and unearthing individual authenticity.

To grasp the concept of Satanic worship, we must first disentangle ourselves from the web of misconceptions and trepidation that have woven themselves into our collective consciousness. The portrayal of a horned creature and rituals involving the sacrifice of blood have been widely exploited in popular culture, perpetuating a false narrative of Satanism that diverges greatly from its genuine meaning. In essence, Satanism represents a search for self-liberation, a rebellion against customary social norms aimed at empowering individuals to embrace their true selves.

Contrary to prevailing beliefs, Satanic worship is not inherently wicked or malevolent. It is a philosophy that champions personal freedom, critical thinking, and individualism. Its true essence resides in the rejection of imposed moral codes that hinder our ability to live authentically, while embracing the journey of self-discovery. This philosophy challenges the very foundations upon which societies are built, interrogating the established order and encouraging individuals to seek their own truths.

The process of societal conditioning commences from the moment of our birth, as we are besieged by societal conventions, customs, and expectations. Our parents bestow upon us their beliefs, and our communities reinforce them. From an early age, we are taught the difference between right and wrong, and what is deemed acceptable versus what is frowned upon. We are moulded to conform to the collective, suppressing our true desires and individual identities.

Within Satanic worship, there lies a profound invitation to escape the limitations of societal conditioning and wholeheartedly embrace our individuality. It urges us to delve into the depths of our own aspirations and ambitions, unapologetically and without fear. The Satanic Temple, an organization dedicated to advocating for religious freedom and personal autonomy, encapsulates this philosophy. They embody the notion that we hold the power to determine the trajectory of our own lives, free to express ourselves without reservation or remorse.

Concerns may arise regarding the moral implications of Satanic worship, with fears that chaos will ensue in the absence of a moral compass. However, Satanic morality is centered around empathy, compassion, and respect for the autonomy and consent of others. It stands in opposition to the notion that we must adhere to an antiquated set of morals prescribed by external forces. By challenging and reevaluating our moral compass, we actively participate in shaping our lives in accordance with our own principles and values.

In the pursuit of individual authenticity within Satanic worship, reflection and introspection play an integral role. The practice encourages individuals to confront their own shadow selves, acknowledging and embracing the darker aspects of their nature. It serves as a voyage of self-discovery, where each individual is encouraged to confront their fears, desires, and aspirations without judgment or shame.

By liberating ourselves from the confines of societal conditioning, we empower ourselves to lead lives that are in alignment with our true essence. We transcend the limitations of imposed beliefs and societal expectations, permitting our authentic selves to flourish. However, embarking on this journey requires courage, self-awareness, and a willingness to embrace the realms of the unknown.

As I delved deeper into the realm of Satanic worship during my investigations, I encountered individuals who had finally found solace within themselves. They spoke of a profound sense of liberation and empowerment, having cast off the chains of societal conditioning. No longer burdened by the expectations of others, they were finally able to live their lives authentically and without apology.

In conclusion, Satanic worship extends far beyond the sensationalism propagated by mainstream media and misguided beliefs. It embodies a resistance against societal conditioning and an exploration of individual authenticity. It challenges us to break free from the confines of conformity, reexamine our own values, and ultimately lead lives that resonate with the depths of our desires. Satanic worship beckons us to reclaim our agency and become the true architects of our own destinies.

SATANIC RITUALS AND EMOTIONAL HEALING

As an individual immersed in the field of paranormal investigation and specializing in unconventional practices, I have always been captivated by the ways in which individuals seek solace and healing. Satanic rituals, known for their controversial and malevolent reputation, have frequently been misunderstood and hastily disregarded. However, as I delved deeper into the realm of emotional healing, I found myself questioning the possibility of there being more to these rituals than initially perceived.

My research involved a comprehensive exploration of the historical, symbolic, and psychological aspects surrounding Satanic rituals, as well as interviews with individuals who have actively engaged in these practices as a means of emotional healing. The results surfaced a complex amalgamation of emotions, beliefs, and experiences that hinted at the potential for significant transformation through these seemingly taboo rituals.

The initial step in my quest for comprehension necessitated a thorough grasp of the underlying principles and symbolism associated with Satanic rituals. Contrary to popular belief, these rituals do not necessarily focus on venerating the malevolent or promoting sinister intentions. Instead, they often function as a mechanism for participants to confront and contend with their own inner conflicts, metaphorically represented as manifestations of darkness and primordial forces. By embracing these forces within a ritualistic framework, individuals are able to confront and release their deeply repressed emotions in a controlled and cathartic manner.

The release of repressed emotions constitutes an essential facet of emotional healing, as it allows individuals to acknowledge and process their past traumas. Satanic rituals offer a distinctive avenue for this release, as they create an environment that encourages participants to explore their most profound fears and desires. Through meticulously constructed rituals, individuals can delve into the recesses of their subconscious mind, illuminating suppressed memories and emotions that may have remained buried for extensive periods. By directly confronting these emotions, individuals can initiate the intricate process of healing and transformation.

A noteworthy aspect of Satanic rituals that emerged from my research was the emphasis on self-empowerment and autonomy. Participants are urged to take charge of their own healing journey and actively engage with their emotions. This sense of personal agency plays a pivotal role in fostering emotional healing, as it allows individuals to reclaim their personal power and find resilience even when faced with adversity. By partaking in Satanic rituals, individuals are empowered to redefine their connection with their past and progress towards a future characterized by self-acceptance and emotional stability.

Crucially, it must be noted that participation in Satanic rituals is not without its potential risks. Exploring repressed emotions can be an intense and overwhelming experience, and it is imperative that individuals engage in these rituals under the guidance of experienced practitioners. To ensure the safety and well-being of participants, it is of utmost importance to establish a supportive and non-judgmental environment where individuals can freely express themselves devoid of fear of social stigma or shame.

Although my research presents a compelling outlook on the potential for emotional healing through Satanic rituals, it is equally important to acknowledge that these practices are not universally suitable. Each individual's journey of healing is unique, and what may prove effective for one person may not necessarily hold true for another. It is therefore essential that individuals explore a diversity of healing methods and seek professional guidance when necessary to discover the approach that resonates most profoundly with their own experiences and needs.

In conclusion, Satanic rituals possess the potential to serve as a potent tool for emotional healing and catharsis. By embracing and releasing repressed emotions, individuals can confront their inner conflicts and embark on a transformative journey towards self-acceptance and empowerment. Nonetheless, it is crucial to approach these rituals with caution and under the guidance of experienced professionals to guarantee the safety and well-being of participants. Ultimately, emotional healing is a deeply personal and subjective process, and it is indispensable that individuals find the approach that best aligns with their beliefs and experiences in order to achieve genuine and enduring healing.

I cordially invite you, esteemed reader, to continue this exploration into the depths of the human psyche and the possibilities for emotional healing through unorthodox means. In the ensuing pages, we will venture further into the peculiar and enigmatic realm of the paranormal, unraveling clandestine truths and challenging our preconceived notions of what healing entails. Together, let us peer into the abyss and unearth the profound potential for transformation that lies within.

To be continued...

SATANIC WORSHIP AND SHADOW INTEGRATION

Shadow integration, as described by renowned psychologist Carl Jung, refers to the process of integrating one's dark and hidden aspects, known as the shadow. In Satanic worship, this integration is taken to a whole new level. It goes beyond embracing one's flaws and delves into a realm that society views as entirely malevolent. By embracing the shadow, followers of Satanism believe they can gain access to unimaginable power and unlock their true potential.

To thoroughly comprehend the intricate connection between shadow integration and Satanic rituals, I embarked on an extensive investigation. Throughout my quest, I extensively researched various sources, including personal interviews with individuals who practice Satanic worship, as well as delving into occult texts and ancient manuscripts. The findings from my investigation left me both captivated and perturbed.

The process of shadow integration within Satanic rituals commences with self-reflection and introspection. Satanic practitioners delve deep into their own psyche, exploring the darkest corners of their minds and embracing the sinister aspects of their personality. They do not shy away from the evil that resides within, but instead, actively seek to harness its power.

The rituals themselves are meticulously crafted to cultivate an atmosphere of fear and intensity. Darkened rooms adorned with occult symbols, the aroma of burning incense, and the haunting sounds of ancient chants all contribute to an immersive experience. Participants are encouraged to confront their deepest fears and insecurities, peeling away the layers of societal conditioning that suppress their true selves.

By embracing their shadow, Satanic worshippers believe they can tap into the collective unconscious, a realm where all fears, desires, and forbidden knowledge reside. This is where authentic power lies, according to their beliefs. Through profound meditation and ritualistic practices, they aim to unite with their shadow selves, forging a bond that transcends conventional morality.

Nevertheless, the impact of this intense process on individuals' psychological well-being begs further inquiry. It is a question that has preoccupied my thoughts throughout my research. To find answers, I sought the perspectives of individuals who have directly experienced these rituals.

Perhaps the most remarkable finding from my interviews is that embracing the shadow within the context of Satanic worship can be a paradoxical situation. While some practitioners claimed to have attained a newfound sense of liberation and empowerment, others spoke of a disconnection from their own humanity.

One interviewee, whom I will refer to as Emma, shared her experience with me. She described experiencing a surge of energy and a sense of liberation as she embraced her darkest desires during a Satanic ritual. However, over time, she noticed a dark cloud descending upon her psyche. Paranoia, anger, and a distorted perception of reality became her constant companions. Emma found herself questioning her own sanity, unsure if she had truly integrated her shadow or had merely lost herself in the process.

These accounts raise substantial ethical considerations concerning the practice of shadow integration within Satanic worship. Can individuals genuinely attain enlightenment and empowerment through these rituals, or are they merely entering a realm of darkness from which escape is impossible? The answers, it appears, vary from person to person.

In conclusion, investigating the process of shadow integration within Satanic rituals has been a journey filled with both fascination and apprehension. Satanic worship pushes the boundaries of human consciousness, compelling individuals to confront their deepest desires and fears. While some may discover empowerment and enlightenment, others risk descending into an abyss from which they may never emerge. As a paranormal investigator and specialist in the mysterious, my pursuit of understanding continues, and I remain perpetually intrigued by the enigma that is Satanic worship and its impact on the human psyche.

SATANIC RITUALS AND EMPOWERMENT

Throughout my years as a paranormal investigator and Specialist of the Strange, I have encountered numerous accounts concerning Satanic rituals and their transformative impact on individuals' lives. From the most obscure recesses of the human psyche to clandestine ceremonies shrouded in secrecy, the domain of Satanic worship has captivated me like no other. In this chapter, we will delve into the narratives of empowerment and self-empowerment within Satanic rituals, aiming to unravel the enigmatic forces that reside within.

To fully comprehend the origins and progression of Satanic rituals, we must embark on a historical journey, exploring the timeline of these practices. From their inception in ancient pagan traditions to their present-day manifestations in modern occultism, Satanic rituals have consistently maintained the theme of empowerment, often seeking to awaken the latent potential within those who venture into them.

It is imperative to recognize that Satanic worship is not solely about undiscerning devotion to an entity deemed as malevolent. In reality, it encompasses a diverse range of practices aimed at embracing boundless human potential and challenging societal conventions. Although Satanic rituals frequently involve opposition to religious doctrines, they equally assert a proactive drive for individuality, personal freedom, and self-empowerment.

Ancient civilizations, such as the Canaanites and Phoenicians, conducted ceremonies dedicated to fertility and the cycles of life and death. These rituals allowed individuals to tap into the transformative forces of nature and harness them for their personal purposes. The concept of directing divine energy to manifest one's desires has remained a consistent theme across various Satanic traditions throughout history.

Advancing further, we encounter the influence of Gnosticism, a spiritual movement that emerged during the early Christian era. Gnostics believed in attaining knowledge and direct experience of the divine, asserting that the material world was tainted and separating oneself from its allurements was of paramount importance. Satanic rituals during this era often incorporated practices to awaken the inner divine spark and challenge religious authority, placing the power of individual enlightenment above blind faith.

During the Middle Ages, the fear of witchcraft and demonic forces instigated the persecution of those who dared to explore ancient pagan practices. The Inquisition aimed to suppress any form of alternative spirituality, ultimately driving Satanic rituals underground. It was during this period that clandestine cults and covens emerged, driven by the desire to reclaim personal power from religious orthodoxy.

The 19th and 20th centuries marked a resurgence of occultism and the ascent of modern Satanic movements. Prominent figures like Aleister Crowley and Anton LaVey played pivotal roles in shaping the narrative surrounding Satanic rituals, emphasizing the rebellious nature of these practices and their ability to empower individuals. LaVey's Church of Satan, established in 1966, openly rejected the concept of external deities and focused on the potential of the self as the true source of power.

To explore the narratives of empowerment and self-empowerment within Satanic worship, we must scrutinize the transformative effects these rituals have on individuals' lives. Many who have immersed themselves in Satanic practices report a heightened sense of self-awareness, an awakening of inner potential, and a liberation from societal constraints that have hindered personal growth.

However, it is important to acknowledge that Satanic rituals encompass a wide array of beliefs and practices, and not every individual experiences the same outcomes. Some practitioners find solace in introspection, while others seek external power for personal gain. The transformative element resides in the freedom to explore one's desires without the restrictions of societal norms or religious dogma.

Furthermore, Satanic rituals provide an arena for individuals to confront their fears, confront their personal demons, and embrace their shadow selves. By accepting and integrating these darker aspects of their psyche, practitioners often claim a sense of liberation and authenticity that empowers them to navigate their lives with clarity and purpose.

In conclusion, Satanic rituals and the empowerment they offer have developed in parallel with human history, providing a platform for individuals to explore their personal potential, challenge societal norms, and awaken the divine spark within. Whether through ancient pagan practices, Gnostic ideologies, or modern occult movements, individuals have sought to harness the transformative powers of Satanic worship in order to empower themselves and manifest their desired reality. As an investigator of the paranormal, I am enthralled by the intricate tapestry of beliefs, practices, and narratives that interweave in the realm of Satanic rituals, continually uncovering new layers of insight into the human condition and our pursuit of self-empowerment.

SATANIC WORSHIP AND PERSONAL TRANSFORMATION

As an investigator and expert in paranormal phenomena, I have extensively studied various supernatural occurrences. Among my explorations, the subject of Satanic worship holds a particular fascination and evokes both curiosity and fear. In this chapter, we will delve into the potential transformative effects that Satanic worship can have on individuals, examining the personal, spiritual, and psychological dimensions.

The origins of Satanic worship can be traced back to ancient civilizations, where it was rooted in a range of mythologies and religious practices. However, the allure and impact of this form of worship have transcended time and continue to captivate those intrigued by its forbidden nature. It is important to approach this topic with an open mind, recognizing that personal and spiritual transformation can manifest from various sources.

When exploring the realm of Satanic worship, caution must be exercised due to its taboo nature and potential repercussions. It is no secret that this form of worship is associated with rituals and practices that society deems abhorrent. Nevertheless, it is crucial to understand that the potential for transformation lies not in conformity to societal norms, but in each individual's interpretation and perception.

At the heart of Satanic worship lies the pursuit of personal empowerment, self-discovery, and the embrace of darker forces. Those who follow this path seek to push the boundaries of their existence, delving into their own psyche to explore the hidden shadows within. Through this confrontation, they undergo a transformative process that leads to self-actualization and personal growth.

On a spiritual level, Satanic worship offers an alternative perspective by challenging traditional notions of good and evil, light and dark. It encourages individuals to explore the depths of their spirituality, unafraid of breaking conventional boundaries. By establishing a connection with metaphysical realms, practitioners aim to attain enlightenment and transcend the limitations of their mortal existence.

Psychologically, Satanic worship acts as a catalyst for introspection, revealing the depths of the human psyche and unraveling its intricate complexities. The dark symbolism and archetypes found in Satanic rituals serve as a mirror through which individuals can confront their deepest fears, desires, and insecurities. By willingly embracing these shadow aspects, practitioners are given the opportunity to integrate and transcend them.

Research conducted in this field has shown that certain individuals have undergone profound personal transformations through Satanic worship. Testimonials speak of increased personal power and autonomy, heightened self-awareness, and a significant shift in moral perception. It is important to note, however, that the transformative potential is unique to each individual, as some may find inner growth and solace while others may find themselves overwhelmed by the darkness they encounter.

Nonetheless, it is essential to approach Satanic worship with caution, understanding that the potential for transformation is accompanied by risks. Exploring the darker aspects of one's psyche can be a treacherous path, unearthing buried traumas, deep-seated fears, and awakening latent desires. Those unprepared may become consumed and overwhelmed by these forces, ultimately losing themselves in the abyss.

In conclusion, Satanic worship possesses a transformative potential that extends into personal, spiritual, and psychological realms. It offers individuals the opportunity to confront their inner shadows, empowering them to transcend societal constraints and explore the depths of their existence. However, this path must be approached with care, fully acknowledging the risks that lie within the darkness. Only with the correct mindset, preparation, and guidance can one truly benefit from the transformative aspects that Satanic worship may provide.

18
SATANIC WORSHIP AND THE QUEST FOR KNOWLEDGE

SATANIC RITUALS AND OCCULT STUDIES

In order to embark on this journey of discovery, I dedicated myself to an extensive range of texts, encompassing both ancient and contemporary sources. Works authored by esteemed occultists such as Aleister Crowley, Anton LaVey, and Helena Blavatsky captured my attention, as I sought profound insights into the esoteric philosophies that serve as the very foundation of Satanic rituals. These texts enabled me to unravel the intricate web of symbols and archetypes that underpin these practices, guiding me further into the depths of the unknown.

One of the most intriguing revelations I encountered was the incorporation of astrology within Satanic rituals. My exploration into the ancient art of astrology shed light on the distinctive energy and significance carried by each astrological symbol. Practitioners effectively leverage this knowledge to harmonize their rituals with the cosmic forces at play, thereby amplifying their desired outcomes. For instance, during a

Satanic ritual aimed at summoning a demon, the practitioner may deliberately select a specific astrological timing and day that aligns with the energies associated with the intended entity. By harnessing the celestial bodies' power, the potency of their rituals is heightened.

Another captivating facet of Satanic rituals is the utilization of sacred geometry. Rooted in antiquity, this practice involves the implementation of specific geometric patterns to access higher levels of consciousness and tap into unseen forces. Within Satanic rituals, these symbols are often incorporated into sigils: graphical representations intended to manifest desired outcomes. By meditating on these sigils and engaging in ceremonial acts, practitioners establish a connection with the energies and entities they wish to invoke.

The study of alchemy also plays a significant role in Satanic rituals and practices. Widely recognized for its association with the transformation of base metals into gold, alchemy is equally a spiritual and philosophical tradition focused on refining and elevating the human soul. In Satanic rituals, this process of transmutation takes on a distinct form. Practitioners employ alchemical principles in order to transform their own consciousness and awaken dormant powers within themselves. By engaging in ritualistic acts and manipulating symbols, they strive to transfigure their spiritual essence and ascend to a higher state of being.

One often overlooked but intriguing element of Satanic rituals is the persuasive role of music. Sound and vibration have long been acknowledged as potent tools for altering consciousness and invoking elevated states of being. Within Satanic rituals, such power is harnessed through the utilization of specific musical compositions. Whether employing the haunting melodies of a Gregorian chant or the dissonant tones of a black metal band, the vibrations emitted by these musical expressions function as conduits through which practitioners can access the unseen realms.

Exploring the integration of occult studies and esoteric knowledge within Satanic rituals and practices has bestowed upon me a profound glimpse into a realm shrouded in mystery and fascination. Rather than merely engaging in darkness for its own sake, practitioners of these arts seek to harness hidden forces and unlock their own potential. Though the rituals themselves may still remain enigmatic to the uninitiated, the fundamental principles of astrology, sacred geometry, alchemy, and music offer valuable keys to comprehending the profound depths of this ancient yet misunderstood tradition.

In my relentless pursuit of knowledge, I have come to comprehend that Satanic rituals are not mere acts of malevolence or worship directed toward an evil entity. Rather, they represent a profound exploration of human potential, a quest for concealed truths, and a means of self-transformation. Through the integration of occult studies and esoteric knowledge, practitioners endeavor to awaken dormant powers within themselves and forge a path toward enlightenment. Although their methods may be veiled in secrecy and evoke a sense of horror, it is through this enlightened perspective that we can genuinely fathom the interconnectedness of the occult within Satanic rituals and practices.

SATANIC WORSHIP AND PHILOSOPHICAL INQUIRY

As a paranormal investigator and specialist in the unusual, I have encountered a variety of intriguing subjects. However, few have captivated my interest as deeply as Satanic worship and the philosophical inquiries that underlie it. In the following chapter, we will explore the complex world of Satanism, examining the intellectual pursuits it fosters and the profound impact it has on individuals' perspectives.

To gain a true comprehension of Satanic worship, it is necessary to abandon any preconceived notions and approach the topic with an open mind. While mainstream media often portrays Satanism as a malevolent force, my research has led me to believe otherwise. The philosophical inquiries embraced by Satanists are founded on critical thinking, individualism, and the pursuit of personal liberty.

One of the most significant philosophical inquiries associated with Satanic worship is the questioning of societal norms. Satanists express the belief that society's values and moral codes should be subjected to scrutiny, challenging the status quo and the oppressive authority that often accompanies it. By engaging in such questioning, Satanists strive to liberate themselves from the constraints of societal influence and norms, allowing for a more introspective and personalized approach to life. Through this process of inquiry, individuals begin to shape their own distinct perspectives, free from the limitations imposed by society.

Another crucial philosophical inquiry within Satanic worship revolves around self-exploration. Satanists encourage self-discovery and self-expression, placing a high value on individualism. By exploring their own desires, passions, and beliefs, practitioners seek to cultivate a more genuine version of themselves. This introspective journey enables individuals to confront their deepest fears and insecurities head-on, leading to personal growth and enlightenment. Through this process, Satanists gain a deeper understanding of their place in the world, dissolving the layers of societal conditioning that have clouded their perception.

Additionally, Satanic philosophy champions the pursuit of personal freedom and pleasure. Unlike many conventional religions that prioritize self-sacrifice, Satanism celebrates the pursuit of one's desires and indulgence in earthly pleasures. Although this may initially appear hedonistic, there is a significant philosophical inquiry underlying this pursuit. By actively engaging in activities that bring joy and fulfillment, practitioners believe they can lead more authentic and purposeful lives. Through self-gratification, Satanists emancipate themselves from the confines of guilt and shame, uncovering their own unique paths to happiness.

It is important to recognize that Satanic worship is not a uniform entity. Within the broader framework of Satanism, there are various branches and interpretations, each with its own philosophical inquiries and intellectual pursuits. For instance, LaVeyan Satanism, established by Anton LaVey in the 1960s, places a strong emphasis on individualism and rational hedonism. Conversely, Theistic Satanism embraces the belief in an actual deity known as Satan. These divergent interpretations provide individuals with the freedom to explore philosophical inquiries that resonate with their own beliefs and values.

The influence of Satanic worship on individuals' perspectives should not be underestimated. By immersing themselves in the philosophical inquiries and intellectual pursuits encouraged within this unconventional belief system, individuals embark on a transformative journey of self-discovery and critical thinking. They develop a heightened sense of individuality, defying societal norms and charting a path that aligns with their authentic selves. These radical shifts in perspective have the potential to empower individuals, motivating them to question the prevailing order and live life on their own terms.

In my interactions with practitioners of Satanic worship, I have witnessed a profound sense of liberation and self-realization. These individuals are not the sinister, malevolent figures frequently depicted in popular culture. Instead, they are intellectuals and truth-seekers, unafraid to challenge societal conventions and explore the depths of their own consciousness. Their journeys serve as a reminder that philosophical and intellectual pursuits can manifest in various forms, and it is through the diversity of ideas that genuine enlightenment is attained.

In conclusion, Satanic worship offers a unique vantage point from which to examine the philosophical inquiries and intellectual pursuits that shape individuals' perspectives. By challenging societal norms, exploring the self, and pursuing personal freedom and pleasure, practitioners gain profound insights into the nature of existence and their place within it. The influence of Satanic philosophy can be life-altering, empowering individuals to transcend the confines of conventional belief systems and embrace a more genuine and rewarding life. As a paranormal investigator and specialist in the peculiar, I am continually fascinated by the depths of human thought and the myriad pathways to enlightenment that exist. Satanic worship is but one example of such a pathway.

SATANIC RITUALS AND COMPARATIVE RELIGION

As an expert in paranormal investigation and the study of the supernatural, my professional journey has led me to investigate numerous uncharted territories. Every step I have taken has brought me closer to unraveling the enigmatic mysteries that are concealed in obscurity. Of great interest to me is the exploration of comparative religion within the context of Satanic rituals. Although this subject matter is contentious, it holds immense potential for expanding individuals' comprehension of diverse belief systems, compelling me to delve deeper into its intricacies.

Understanding the relevance of comparative religion within Satanic rituals necessitates a comprehensive examination of the historical development of such practices. The roots of Satanic rituals can be traced back to ancient civilizations, where the veneration of deities often entailed engaging in rituals and offering sacrifices. These rituals, prevalent among the Babylonians, Egyptians, Romans, and Greeks, were intended to appease the gods and secure their favor. However, as societies flourished and belief systems underwent transformations, the concept of Satan emerged as a symbol of resistance against established religious institutions.

The medieval era marked a turning point as Satanism took on more organized shapes, with numerous clandestine sects and secretive societies coming to light. The Knights Templar, the Cathars, and Witch covens serve as prime examples of these groups that were frequently accused of participating in Satanic rituals, leading to their persecution by religious authorities. It is from this tumultuous background that modern Satanic rituals find their origins.

While many perceive Satanic rituals to be inherently nefarious or malevolent, it is essential to approach this subject with impartiality and a fervor for comprehension. Engaging in comparative religious studies offers us a lens through which we can analyze and appreciate the complexity inherent in Satanic rituals. By exploring the parallels and divergences between Satanic beliefs and those of other religions, we can attain deeper insights into the motivations and symbolic nature of these rituals.

One immediate realization that emerges through the study of comparative religions is the presence of ritualistic practices in nearly every belief system. From the Hindu fire sacrifices to the Christian Eucharist, these rituals serve as mechanisms for connecting with the divine and fostering a communal bond among adherents. In a comparable manner, Satanic rituals, despite being perceived as unconventional, also serve these functions.

Yet, what distinguishes Satanic rituals is the deliberate inversion and subversion of traditional religious symbols and practices. For instance, the Black Mass, notorious for its sacrilegious nature, mirrors the structure of the Catholic Mass, but distorts its components to mock the Christian belief system. This conscious inversion underscores the fundamental disparities between orthodox religious rituals and Satanic practices.

Through comparative religious studies, we also discover the diverse influences that have shaped Satanic rituals over the years. Satanic beliefs draw upon elements from ancient pagan traditions, Gnosticism, and even Eastern mystical practices. The incorporation of these influences offers a unique vantage point from which to comprehend the multifaceted nature of Satanic rituals and challenges the notion that they are rooted exclusively in evil.

By broadening our understanding of different belief systems, we acquire an appreciation for the ways in which Satanic rituals function as a form of individual or collective expression. Similar to any religious ritual, they provide a framework that enables adherents to explore their own spirituality and make sense of the world around them. Whether through the enactment of elaborate ceremonies or the invocation of spirits, Satanic rituals offer a domain for personal growth and introspection.

Ultimately, the exploration of comparative religion within the context of Satanic rituals grants us a rare glimpse into the intricate tapestry of human belief systems. It compels us to question preconceived notions and fosters empathy and understanding for those whose beliefs may differ from our own. In pursuing this path, we not only expand our own intellectual horizons but also contribute to the creation of a more inclusive and harmonious society.

As I continue my journey into the mysterious depths of Satanic rituals, I am reminded of the importance of approaching the unknown with an open mind. By immersing ourselves in the study of comparative religion within Satanic rituals, we are given the prospect to unlock the secrets that lie obscured within the realm of the supernatural. It is through such understanding that we can endeavor to bridge the gaps dividing various belief systems and pave the way for a future enlightened by knowledge and tolerance.

SATANIC WORSHIP AND CRITICAL THINKING

In order to comprehend the impact of critical thinking within the context of Satanic worship, it is imperative to delve into the annals of history and examine the origins of this unconventional belief system. The roots of Satanism can be traced back to various ancient cultures, wherein deities associated with darkness and rebellion were venerated. However, it was during the witchcraft trials of the Middle Ages, particularly the notorious Salem Witch Trials in the late 17th century, that Satanism became heavily vilified and linked with malevolence.

In the following centuries, Satanic worship remained clandestine, assuming various forms and ideologies. It was not until the 20th century that the modern conception of Satanism began to take shape, notably with the establishment of the Church of Satan by Anton Szandor LaVey in 1966. LaVey's Satanic Bible, serving as a seminal text for many contemporary Satanists, propagated principles such as individualism, self-empowerment, and the rejection of arbitrary authority.

Nonetheless, the critical thinking facet of Satanic worship did not fully come to the fore until the advent of the Satanic Panic in the 1980s and 1990s. During this period, widespread fear and paranoia surrounding satanic rituals and allegations of child abuse permeated throughout the United States and other nations. As a response to these unfounded accusations, Satanic communities began to underscore skepticism and critical thinking as a means to debunk myths and stereotypes.

One of the fundamental components of critical thinking within Satanic worship lies in the refusal to embrace supernatural beliefs and instead rely on evidence-based reasoning. While the Church of Satan, for instance, acknowledges the existence of personal and subjective mysticism, it staunchly advocates for a skeptical approach to matters of the supernatural. This mindset allows individuals to question, analyze, and evaluate claims before accepting them as veracious, aligning with the reason and skepticism espoused by modern science and philosophy.

In a world where misinformation and groundless beliefs often proliferate, critical thinking assumes paramount importance. Satanism, with its emphasis on skepticism, encourages adherents to challenge authority, partake in intellectual discourse, and pursue knowledge through rigorous examination. The renunciation of arbitrary dogma and the promotion of personal growth and autonomy represent central tenets within Satanic philosophy, engendering an environment conducive to the flourishing of critical thinking.

The impact of critical thinking within Satanic worship extends beyond the realm of intellectual pursuits. When individuals embrace skepticism and the pursuit of knowledge, they cultivate a more profound comprehension of the world around them and their place within it. This newfound awareness empowers them to call into question societal norms, contest oppressive systems, and strive for personal liberation.

Moreover, critical thinking within Satanic worship facilitates personal growth and self-fulfillment. Satanists are encouraged to explore and embrace their desires, strive for personal excellence, and flourish in a world that often endeavors to stifle individuality. By interrogating social constructs and societal expectations, practitioners of Satanic worship can break free from the shackles of conformity and pursue a life that accords with their authentic selves.

It is important to underscore that although critical thinking plays an integral role within Satanic worship, this does not imply that all practitioners are impervious to irrationality or prejudice. Like any belief system, Satanism encompasses a diverse array of individuals with varying degrees of intellectual rigor and open-mindedness. Nevertheless, the very foundation of Satanic philosophy and the emphasis on skepticism engender an environment conductive to critical thinking and the acquisition of knowledge.

In conclusion, the exploration of critical thinking within the context of Satanic worship elucidates a frequently overlooked facet of this contentious belief system. Satanic communities, particularly those influenced by the Church of Satan, attach considerable importance to rationality, skepticism, and the pursuit of knowledge. The renunciation of supernatural beliefs and the advocacy for evidence-based reasoning engender an environment wherein individuals can question, analyze, and evaluate claims before accepting them as true. This focus on critical thinking not only dispels myths and stereotypes surrounding Satanic worship but also empowers individuals to challenge authority, endeavor towards personal growth, and strive for liberation. Satanic worship, far from popular misconceptions, represents a philosophy that upholds reason, skepticism, and the power of critical thought.

SATANIC RITUALS AND INTELLECTUAL EXPLORATION

In order to fully comprehend the essence of Satanic worship and its connection to intellectual exploration, it is crucial to delve into the historical timeline of Satanism. There is often a misconception that Satanism is solely rooted in the adversary of Christianity, the fallen angel Lucifer. However, the origins of Satanic worship can be traced back to the ancient pagan religions that predates Christianity, where deities such as Pan and Dionysus were revered.

During the Middle Ages, when Christianity held dominion, any form of worship that deviated from the accepted norms of the Church, including the veneration of older pagan deities, was deemed heresy and subjected to severe punishments. It was during this era that the term "Satanism" originated, being associated with those who defied religious authorities.

In the nineteenth century, movements like Romanticism and later Symbolism sparked a renewed interest in occultism and esoteric practices. Prominent figures such as Aleister Crowley emerged, embracing the idea of spiritual exploration and personal enlightenment. Crowley's philosophy can be viewed as a precursor to current Satanic beliefs, emphasizing individualism, self-discovery, and the significance of personal growth.

Throughout the twentieth century, various Satanic organizations began to take shape, each with its own distinct approach to Satanism. The Church of Satan, founded by Anton LaVey in the 1960s, became a prominent force, propagating the notion that Satan symbolizes indulgence rather than malevolence. LaVey's Satanic Bible emerged as a cornerstone of the movement, emphasizing the importance of intellectual exploration and questioning conventional norms.

Analyzing the promotion of intellectual exploration and curiosity within Satanic worship reveals numerous facets that contribute to personal growth. First and foremost, Satanic rituals often involve symbolism and allegory, encouraging practitioners to engage in critical thinking and profound introspection. The utilization of occult symbols and rituals, such as the pentagram and ceremonial magic, serves as a means to unlock concealed truths and challenge the established order.

Furthermore, Satanic philosophy encourages individuals to question authority and challenge societal norms. This rebellious aspect of Satanism fosters intellectual curiosity and an unwavering pursuit of knowledge. Satanic rituals frequently incorporate the study and discussion of esoteric texts, providing a platform for intellectual exchange and the exploration of alternative viewpoints.

Moreover, Satanic worship places great emphasis on the autonomy of the individual and the realization of personal desires and ambitions. By embracing and accepting one's own desires, Satanic practitioners are motivated to actively pursue self-improvement and personal growth. This process entails gaining self-awareness, challenging limiting beliefs, and cultivating a sense of empowerment.

It is crucial to note that Satanic worship does not endorse harmful or malicious actions towards others. Instead, it emphasizes personal responsibility and respect for the rights and freedoms of others. Empathy and compassion are integral principles of the Satanic philosophy, promoting a balanced approach to personal growth that takes into account the well-being of oneself and others.

In conclusion, Satanic rituals and intellectual exploration sustain a reciprocal relationship, driving personal growth through curiosity, critical thinking, and self-discovery. By questioning established norms, engaging in profound introspection, and embracing personal desires, practitioners of Satanic worship embark on a journey of self-realization and empowerment. Satanic philosophy provides a platform for intellectual exchange and the exploration of alternative viewpoints, encouraging individuals to challenge authority and pursue knowledge. It is through this unique blend of intellectual curiosity and personal growth that Satanic worship continues to captivate those who seek enlightenment beyond the confines of conventional beliefs.

SATANIC WORSHIP AND THE PURSUIT OF TRUTH

As an expert in paranormal investigations and the study of unusual phenomena, I have extensively explored the intricacies of the human psyche in search of answers to enigmatic questions that often resist logical explanation. Within the realm of my research, one particular aspect has led me to investigate the complex world of Satanic worship, wherein the pursuit of truth and knowledge assumes a primary role. Through my quest for enlightenment, I have gained a profound understanding of the significant implications this principle holds for individuals on their personal journeys towards self-realization.

To truly comprehend the essence of Satanic worship and its association with the pursuit of truth, it is imperative to scrutinize its historical origins. Throughout the ages, Satanic worship has remained veiled in secrecy and misunderstood by the public. It has frequently been depicted negatively, being associated with malevolence and evil. However, for those who have ventured beyond surface-level misconceptions, Satanic worship transcends mere alignment with dark forces. Rather, it constitutes a path that champions individual autonomy, personal growth, and, most importantly, the quest for truth.

During ancient times, Satanic worship played a central role in various pagan belief systems. Its adherents were not inherently malignant, as common culture would suggest; rather, they celebrated nature and recognized its cyclical patterns, understanding that life is governed by a delicate equilibrium between light and darkness, creation and destruction. They acknowledged the interconnectedness of all aspects of existence and embraced the dualities inherent in human nature.

In my research, I happened upon an ancient manuscript known as the "Codex Lucis," which provides invaluable insights into the fundamental principles of Satanic worship. A particular section that seized my attention was the chapter entitled "Verum Illuminato," or "The Pursuit of Truth."

According to the Codex, Satanic worship places great emphasis on the individual's personal journey towards enlightenment. It acknowledges that the pursuit of truth and knowledge is not a linear progression, but rather an intricate labyrinth of experiences and revelations. This notion aligns closely with a quote attributed to Friedrich Nietzsche: "I am not a man; I am dynamite." Within the context of Satanic worship, "dynamite" refers to the explosive power of self-discovery, a force capable of obliterating the confines imposed by societal norms and belief systems.

The pursuit of truth in Satanic worship is not confined to the realm of intellect alone. It is a deeply personal experience that necessitates exploration of one's emotions, desires, and fears. It entails confronting and embracing the darkness within as an integral part of oneself. This facet of Satanic worship compels individuals to directly confront their shadows, as suppressing or denying these aspects only leads to internal turmoil and stagnation.

Throughout my interactions with practitioners of Satanic worship, I have witnessed the transformative power of self-exploration. They have embraced the concept that truth lies not in external sources, but within themselves. By delving into the depths of their own psyches, they systematically unearth layers of conditioning and societal expectations, unveiling their authentic selves in the process.

However, it is important to acknowledge that Satanic worship is not without inherent risks. The pursuit of truth can be a double-edged sword, as once the veil of illusion is lifted, the knowledge gained cannot be undone. It is a path that necessitates significant courage and resilience to confront uncomfortable truths surging forth from the depths of the soul. Nevertheless, those who embark on this arduous journey often experience a sense of liberation and empowerment that surpasses any temporary discomfort.

Simultaneously, one must recognize the contentious nature of Satanic worship, as it challenges societal norms and established religious institutions. It is a path that calls into question long-held beliefs and necessitates critical thinking. This defiance of conventionality has led many to brand Satanic worshippers as heretics or deviants. However, these individuals advocate for the pursuit of truth freed from the shackles of dogma or blind faith. They firmly believe that it is only through questioning, skepticism, and open-mindedness that one can genuinely explore the profound enigmas of existence.

In conclusion, an examination of the pursuit of truth and knowledge as a central pillar of Satanic worship reveals a path that transcends superficial misconceptions. It is an endeavor that demands profound introspection, challenging individuals to confront their darkest aspects and embrace their genuine selves. The journey towards enlightenment is not for the faint of heart, requiring fortitude, resilience, and a willingness to defy societal norms. Encountering the unadorned truth of one's existence can be both liberating and tumultuous, but it is through this process that individuals triumphantly emerge into the realm of self-discovery. When appropriately stripped of its misrepresentations, Satanic worship becomes a formidable force that empowers individuals to reclaim their autonomy and embark on the transformative journey towards truth, knowledge, and enlightenment.

SATANIC RITUALS AND ESOTERIC TEACHINGS

Growing up in a small town, my fascination with the unknown and my insatiable curiosity compelled me to delve into the depths of ancient texts and concealed knowledge, in search of answers to the lingering questions that occupied my young mind. It was during one of my explorations into the esoteric teachings of diverse occult traditions that I happened upon a peculiar correlation between these teachings and satanic rituals. Captivated, I proceeded to delve further into the subject matter, steadfast in my determination to comprehend the essence of this association and its influence on individuals' personal spiritual journeys.

Conducting comprehensive research led me to dimly lit aisles of ancient libraries, where numerous forbidden volumes remained hidden away. These aged books became my trusted companions, guiding me through the intricate paths of history. I discovered that satanic rituals, far from being mere demonstrations of dark power, incorporate a nuanced framework of symbolism derived from profound esoteric teachings.

A notable aspect of satanic rituals lies in their utilization of archetypes and symbolism. Practitioners of these rituals comprehend that symbols possess a profound ability to tap into the collective unconscious, allowing them to commune with age-old energies that transcend the barriers of time and space. Via the implementation of sacred geometry, ancient sigils, and meticulously orchestrated rituals, they endeavor to harness these energies and channel them towards their intended objectives.

However, it is important to note that these intended objectives are not always rooted in the evocation of evil or darkness, contrary to popular belief. In actuality, satanic rituals often provide a medium through which individuals can explore their own spirituality in a manner that transcends societal norms and expectations. By incorporating esoteric teachings, these rituals furnish a framework that enables individuals to plumb the depths of their own psyche, confront their fears and desires, and ultimately achieve an elevated state of self-awareness.

This realization presented a profound challenge to my preconceived notions concerning satanic rituals. It elucidated the idea that the path to spiritual exploration is not a linear one, but instead an exceptionally individualized journey. While certain individuals may derive solace and illumination from traditional religious practices, others may unearth it in the darkest recesses of the occult. Although outward manifestations of these practices may differ greatly, they are all fueled by the same fundamental human yearning—to fathom ourselves and our place in the vast universe.

It would be negligent to forgo acknowledgment of the potential dangers that are inherent in delving into satanic rituals and esoteric teachings. Similar to any pursuit that enables one to access hidden realms of consciousness, there exists a considerable risk of losing oneself in the process. Obsession, mental instability, and even vulnerability to possession by malevolent entities are tangible hazards that lurk within these depths. Consequently, those individuals who elect to venture upon this path must exercise caution and rely on the guidance of experienced mentors, while cultivating a solid foundation of spiritual protection.

Throughout the course of my investigations, I have had the privilege of interviewing numerous individuals who have undergone profound transformations as a consequence of their involvement in satanic rituals and esoteric teachings. Their narratives are oftentimes marked by periods of profound darkness and desolation, but also culminate in moments of ultimate enlightenment and self-realization. Though undoubtedly contentious, these experiences serve as a testament to the transformative power of the human spirit and its limitless potential for growth and metamorphosis.

In conclusion, the integration of esoteric teachings and concealed knowledge into satanic rituals presents a multifaceted and intricate phenomenon. Its impact on individuals' personal spiritual journeys can encompass anything from profound self-discovery to perilous fixation. While it may be tempting to dismiss these practices as entirely evil or misguided, it is imperative that we approach them with an open-mindedness and a willingness to delve into the complexities of the human experience. Only then can we genuinely comprehend the depths of the human psyche and the endless potential for spiritual development that resides within each of us.

SATANIC WORSHIP AND THE TRANSFORMATION OF CONSCIOUSNESS

Prior to exploring the complexities of this subject matter, it is imperative to establish a comprehensive understanding of satanic worship. Contrary to popular belief, satanic worship does not solely revolve around the veneration or adoration of Satan as a literal deity. Rather, it encompasses a multifaceted and intricate practice that encompasses various rituals, symbolism, and ideologies, with the intention of embracing one's inner darkness and venturing into forbidden realms.

Examining the potential of satanic worship to facilitate the transformation of consciousness necessitates an open-minded approach that incorporates personal experiences and testimonies. While some may categorize it as sheer fantasy or a product of the imagination, delving deeper into the world of satanic worship unveils a profound journey of self-discovery and personal growth.

One could argue that a pivotal component in the transformation of consciousness through satanic worship lies in the concept of shadow work. Shadow work involves the exploration and integration of one's suppressed and darker aspects, which are commonly frowned upon or disavowed by society. Embracing these facets of our psyche permits individuals to confront their deepest fears, desires, and vulnerabilities, thereby fostering self-awareness and personal evolution.

Throughout my research, I have encountered numerous accounts from individuals who claim to have undergone transformative experiences through their involvement in satanic worship. These experiences range from heightened spiritual connections to the revelation of latent talents and abilities. It is through the exploration of taboo and the acceptance of the forbidden that individuals frequently transcend their limited perceptions of reality and access an elevated state of consciousness.

One particularly noteworthy case is that of Sarah Adams, who sought guidance and comprehension regarding her encounters with satanic worship. Sarah's journey commenced when she stumbled upon an underground satanic cult while in search of spiritual fulfillment. Enthralled by the secrecy and allure enshrouding their rituals, Sarah made the decision to fully immerse herself in this realm, with the hope of gaining insight into her own existence.

As Sarah delved deeper into the practices of this cult, she found herself confronted with her own demons and insecurities. The meticulously crafted symbolism and intense energy of the rituals served as a gateway for her to explore the depths of her psyche. Engaging in these rituals enabled her to face and integrate the darkest aspects of herself, which ultimately led to a profound personal metamorphosis.

Sarah recounts her experiences within the satanic cult as simultaneously terrifying and liberating. It was within this mysterious realm that she emancipated herself from the constraints imposed by societal norms, allowing her authentic self to emerge. The rituals, which encompassed carnal desires and forbidden knowledge, supplied her with the necessary tools and guidance to embark upon a journey of self-discovery.

While detractors argue that satanic worship is merely an outlet for indulging morbid fantasies, Sarah's narrative defies these preconceived notions. For her, it represented far more than a descent into darkness for darkness' sake; instead, it constituted an exploration of her innermost being, a means of shedding societal expectations and embracing her true essence.

Sarah's story is not an isolated case. Throughout history, countless individuals have discovered enlightenment, creativity, and personal growth through their involvement in satanic worship. Whether it be artists channeling their darkest impulses into their art or spiritual seekers finding solace in the shadows, satanic worship has demonstrated its potential to transcend conventional limitations and foster transformative experiences on a profoundly personal level.

In conclusion, analyzing the potential of satanic worship to facilitate the transformation of consciousness and expand individuals' awareness provides a captivating glimpse into the human psyche. By embracing the forbidden and delving into the depths of darkness, individuals may uncover a pathway to self-discovery, personal growth, and heightened consciousness. While the controversy and taboo surrounding satanic worship persist, it is imperative not to dismiss its potential to serve as a catalyst for transformative experiences. Only by exploring the depths of our own consciousness can we genuinely grasp its immense possibilities.

19

SATANIC WORSHIP AND COMMUNITY BUILDING

SATANIC COVENS AND COMMUNAL RITUALS

As a professional paranormal investigator and specialist in the occult, I have extensively researched the formation and dynamics of Satanic covens and the significance of communal rituals within Satanic worship. The enigmatic allure surrounding Satanic rituals has long fascinated inquisitive minds and instilled fear in unsuspecting individuals. In this chapter, we will unravel the intricate fabric of Satanic covens and shed light on the concealed truths behind their communal rituals.

To gain a comprehensive understanding of the formation of Satanic covens, it is essential to examine the origins of Satanism itself. While Satanism is often associated with malevolence and evil, the reality is far more intricate. There exist various branches of Satanism, each embracing its own distinctive set of beliefs and practices. From the theistic Satanists who worship Satan as a deity, to the atheistic Satanists who perceive Satan as a symbolic representation of individualism and rebellion against oppressive forces, the ideologies within Satanism are diverse and multifaceted.

Within these divergent branches, Satanic covens emerge as tightly knit communities formed around a shared belief system. These covens serve as havens for individuals seeking spiritual fulfillment, places where darkness and light coexist harmoniously. The establishment of a Satanic coven is not undertaken lightly; it necessitates trust, shared values, and a profound commitment to the rituals and teachings of Satanism. It is within these covens that the true nature of communal rituals unfolds.

Communal rituals hold immense significance within Satanic worship, serving as potent bonds and catalysts for spiritual elevation. These ceremonies are often conducted in secluded locations, concealed from the prying eyes of society. This seclusion enables participants to unleash their inner desires and forge connections with the forces they hold reverence for. The rituals themselves are meticulously fashioned, drawing inspiration from ancient occult practices, symbolisms, and initiation rituals.

One particular Satanic coven that I had the privilege of observing and interviewing was known as The Circle of Esoteric Shadows. Led by their enigmatic high priestess, Morgana Blackthorn, The Circle embodied the very essence of Satanic worship. As I delved deeper into their enigmatic world, I discovered that Morgana possessed an intimate knowledge of the occult, a legacy passed down through generations of her family who practiced its arts.

Morgana elucidated the crucial role of communal rituals in the spiritual growth of her coven. "Communal rituals," she murmured, her eyes shimmering with forbidden knowledge, "are not mere acts of theatrics; they are gateways leading us into the depths of our own darkness, where true transformation resides."

The significance of communal rituals within Satanic covens lies in their ability to tap into the collective consciousness of the participants. Through intense visualization, energy manipulation, and the recitation of ancient incantations, these rituals serve as conduits for the manifestation of desires and the communion with otherworldly entities. Within these ritualistic spaces, the boundaries between the physical and spiritual realms blur, granting access to the unknown.

One particularly intriguing aspect of communal rituals is the phenomenon of group possession. It is believed that during certain rituals, participants transcend their individual identities and become vessels for otherworldly entities to inhabit. Under the guidance of their high priestess, the coven members channel the forces they worship, imbuing themselves with power and wisdom from the depths of the underworld.

During my time observing The Circle of Esoteric Shadows, I witnessed such possession firsthand. As the ritual reached its zenith, the coven members, their eyes ablaze with an otherworldly fervor, succumbed to an electrifying energy that surged through their veins. Their bodies convulsed and contorted as if gripped by invisible hands. In those moments, it was unmistakable that something far beyond human comprehension had taken hold of them.

This exploration into Satanic covens and their communal rituals has unveiled a complex tapestry of beliefs and practices. These covens, united by shared values and a yearning for spiritual enlightenment, find solace and empowerment within their dark rituals. These rituals, meticulously crafted and steeped in ancient traditions, serve as portals into the realm of the occult, leading participants into a world where the boundaries of reality are obscured.

In the next chapter, we will delve deeper into the forbidden knowledge and arcane practices of Satanic rituals, exploring the intricate symbolism and secret rites that lie at the core of Satanic worship. Prepare to embark on a journey into the heart of Satan, where shadows whisper and forbidden truths await.

SATANIC WORSHIP AND COLLECTIVE IDENTITY

In order to comprehend the evolution of collective identity in Satanic worship, it is necessary to delve into history. The roots of Satanism can be traced back to ancient times when pagan spiritual practices incorporated the figure of Satan as a symbol of rebellion against societal norms and a pursuit of forbidden knowledge. Over time, these beliefs developed and adapted, influenced by various religious, philosophical, and cultural movements.

A significant point in the development of Satanic collective identity occurred during the Middle Ages, when the Christian Church intensified its efforts to suppress heretical movements. Those accused of devil worship and heresy sought refuge in underground Satanic communities. These individuals, ostracized by society and persecuted by the Church, formed a collective identity grounded in their opposition to the established religious order.

Advancing to the 20th century, a period characterized by cultural rebellion and social upheaval, the emergence of Anton LaVey and the Church of Satan in 1966 brought Satanic worship into public consciousness like never before. LaVey's Satanic Bible articulated the core principles of Satanic philosophy, emphasizing individualism, rational self-interest, and the pursuit of earthly desires. This variant of Satanism, known as LaVeyan Satanism, prioritized the individual's quest for personal power and liberation from societal constraints.

The Church of Satan became a symbol of collective identity for those disillusioned with traditional religious institutions. It provided a community that embraced and validated unorthodox beliefs. Satanic rituals and practices offered members a sense of belonging and empowerment while simultaneously challenging societal norms and expectations. The allure of rebellion and hedonistic freedom within a close-knit community became a compelling draw for those seeking an alternative sense of identity.

While LaVeyan Satanism gained prominence in the 20th century, it was not the sole expression of Satanic worship to emerge. Other Satanic groups, such as the Temple of Set and the Order of Nine Angles, offered different interpretations of Satanic philosophy and rituals. These variations allowed individuals to find a collective identity that aligned more closely with their personal beliefs, further fragmenting the Satanic community into distinct factions.

In recent years, the internet has played a significant role in the dissemination and development of Satanic worship. Online forums, social media platforms, and websites have provided a medium for Satanic communities to connect, exchange ideas, and coordinate rituals. The anonymity offered by the digital landscape has also enabled individuals to explore their Satanic beliefs without fear of persecution. This has further solidified the collective identity within these communities.

The development of collective identity in Satanic communities can be attributed to various psychological and sociological factors. One such factor is the innate need for belonging and acceptance. Satanic worship provides individuals with a sense of community and shared purpose, enabling them to establish close bonds with like-minded individuals who understand and accept their beliefs. This sense of belonging serves to reinforce and validate their Satanic identity, fostering a collective sense of self.

Additionally, the transgressive nature of Satanic rituals contributes to the formation of collective identity. By engaging in acts that defy societal norms and values, individuals experience a sense of empowerment and liberation. This shared experience fosters a strong sense of camaraderie and solidarity within Satanic communities, reinforcing their collective identity as rebels against the established order.

Moreover, the symbolism and rituals associated with Satanic worship play a pivotal role in the development of collective identity. These rituals serve as a means of expressing and reaffirming Satanic beliefs, rendering them tangible and real for participants. The shared experiences and symbolism create a sense of a shared history and tradition, further cementing the collective identity within Satanic communities.

In conclusion, comprehending the development of collective identity and a sense of belonging within Satanic communities and their rituals necessitates a comprehensive exploration of historical, psychological, and sociological factors. From ancient pagan practices to contemporary expressions of rebellion, Satanic worship continues to attract individuals in search of alternative forms of spirituality and community. Gaining a deeper insight into the motivations and experiences of those involved in these enigmatic and often misunderstood practices entails understanding the intricate complexities of Satanic collective identity.

SATANIC RITUALS AND SUPPORT NETWORKS

To comprehend the intricacies of satanic support networks, I devoted myself to extensive research. Through a comprehensive investigation, I explored the historical timeline to unearth the concealed truths and obscured origins of satanic practices.

Upon tracing the origins of satanic rituals, I delved into ancient civilizations where the worship of dark deities manifested a deep fascination with the power of the occult. These rituals and ceremonies held a profound significance in the establishment of support networks, surpassing mere theatrical displays. The practitioners, bound by shared beliefs and experiences, formed a close-knit community that offered solace and empowerment in a world plagued by uncertainty.

Shifting our focus to the Middle Ages, we witness the emergence of modern-day satanic practices taking root. This period saw the rise of various secret societies that sought to challenge the dogma of organized religion and explore forbidden knowledge of the occult. These societies, such as the Knights Templar and the Order of the Dragon, employed rituals and ceremonies to solidify their bonds and foster a sense of belonging among their members. By engaging in shared experiences, they fortified their support networks and enabled the free exchange of knowledge and ideas.

As I delved deeper into historical records, the sinister allure of satanic practices became increasingly prevalent. The 18th and 19th centuries witnessed the emergence of esoteric societies, notably the infamous Hellfire Club. These secretive gatherings, characterized by a veil of decadence and debauchery, delved into the darker realms of human existence. Their rituals, infused with blasphemy and sacrilege, established a framework for bonding and support network formation.

However, it was in the 20th century that satanic rituals and support networks reached their zenith. The Church of Satan, founded by Anton LaVey, galvanized the cultural panorama like an infernal conflagration. LaVey's work, "The Satanic Bible," provided a manifesto for the establishment of satanic support networks based on individualism, rebellion, and the pursuit of earthly desires. Rituals carried out within the Church of Satan became a means to connect with like-minded individuals, share experiences, and embrace the forbidden's power.

Within satanic communities, rituals serve as a conduit for spiritual and psychological exploration. The enactment of these rituals generates an atmosphere of heightened energy and intensity, enabling individuals to tap into their primal instincts and shed societal conventions. By discarding these constraints, a profound sense of liberation is achieved, fostering connections with fellow travelers who have embarked on a similar path.

Through my investigation into the formation of support networks and social bonds within satanic communities, I have personally witnessed the power of shared rituals. By engaging in these rituals, individuals experience a transcendental union that surpasses mere verbal communication or superficial interactions. The ritual itself becomes a manifestation of their shared beliefs and experiences, solidifying their bond and creating a network of support that extends beyond the confines of the ritual space.

As I delve deeper into the realm of satanic rituals and support networks, I confront the authenticity inherent in these taboo practices. While some may perceive satanic rituals as nothing more than debauched acts and sacrilege, they possess a deeper significance for those who partake. These rituals serve as a means for individuals to embrace their genuine selves, forging connections with others who have similarly cast off the chains of societal restrictions.

In my ongoing exploration of the world of satanic rituals and support networks, I confront the truth that resides within these taboo practices. Through my research, I have come to realize that the shared experiences and rituals practiced in these communities possess a profound power that transcends ordinary existence. Within these rituals, individuals find solace, empowerment, and a sense of belonging that transcends societal norms. In the depths of darkness, we discover communities bound by their shared pursuit of truth, undeterred by condemnation, and unwavering in their quest for enlightenment.

SATANIC WORSHIP AND RITUALISTIC HEALING

One aspect that has particularly caught my interest is the potential for ritualistic healing within Satanic worship and its impact on community members. While Satanic worship is often portrayed negatively in popular culture, there exists a lesser-known faction that embraces the concept of healing and emotional support. This intriguing concept has prompted me to further delve into the world of Satanic rituals and explore their potential positive influence on participants.

To thoroughly comprehend the subject, I embarked on an intensive research journey, studying ancient texts, conducting interviews with practitioners, and visiting occult sites reputed to hold the key to the mysteries surrounding Satanic healing. My findings have been both enlightening and controversial, challenging conventional beliefs about the occult and its connection to spiritual well-being.

My historical exploration of Satanic worship and ritualistic healing takes us back centuries ago to the darkest corners of Europe. During the Middle Ages, Satanic worship gained significant attention, particularly through the infamous witch trials. This dark period in history involved the torture and persecution of falsely accused individuals, who were alleged to practice Satanic rituals and healing arts.

As I delved into these historical accounts, it became apparent that Satanic worship has always possessed a dual nature. While some rituals were undeniably performed with malicious intent, others sought to harness dark energy for the purpose of restoration and emotional support. These secretive rites aimed to mend wounded souls through esoteric practices and connection with supernatural beings.

One fascinating case I encountered during my research involved a Satanic coven in the late 18th century. Under the guidance of a charismatic high priestess, this group focused on ritualistic healing and emotional support. Participants engaged in ceremonies designed to release emotional trauma, utilizing symbolism, music, and dance as conduits for spiritual healing. Contrary to expectations, this specific coven fostered a close-knit community, where individuals felt a profound sense of belonging and support within their Satanic practice.

Further exploration into the 20th century revealed a surge of interest in alternative forms of healing. As traditional methods failed to provide solace and understanding, seekers turned to the occult in search of answers. It was during this period that Satanic healing gained momentum, attracting followers disillusioned by mainstream religion and individuals desperately seeking emotional and spiritual relief.

I also discovered a noteworthy ritualistic healing practice during my investigations, focusing on the concept of spiritual possession. While this may initially seem disconcerting, practitioners willingly entered states of possession, allowing otherworldly entities to temporarily inhabit their bodies. This purportedly facilitated deep healing, as these entities possessed knowledge and power beyond the human realm.

Critics argue that such practices are dangerous and potentially harmful. However, those who have experienced this form of ritualistic healing insist on its effectiveness, citing profound transformations and solace found in the process. It is vital to approach these rituals with caution, as they require a deep understanding of the occult and strict adherence to safety precautions.

As I conclude this chapter of research, it is crucial to acknowledge the controversial nature of Satanic worship and ritualistic healing. One must approach the subject with an open mind, devoid of preconceived notions and biases. While darker forces can undoubtedly be present within these practices, it is also imperative to recognize the potential for personal growth, transformation, and emotional support that Satanic ritualistic healing provides to those who seek it.

In the depths of the occult, surprising rays of light can be discovered. It is these glimpses of hope and healing that drive me to continue exploring the uncharted territories of Satanic worship. Only by venturing into the realm of Satan can we truly discern the profound impact rituals have on individuals, communities, and the concept of healing itself.

SATANIC RITUALS AND SOCIAL ACTIVISM

To comprehend the role of Satanic worship in promoting social activism and advocating for individual rights and freedoms, it is essential to delve into the historical timeline. By taking this approach, one can better grasp the influence Satanism has wielded in shaping our present-day world.

The origins of Satanic worship can be traced back to ancient civilizations, where deities symbolizing chaos and darkness were venerated. However, it was during the Middle Ages that Satanism, as we understand it today, began to take form. The Christian Church, in its relentless pursuit of power and control, stigmatized any non-conformist spiritual practices as Satanic. In reality, many of these practices were rooted in ancient pagan beliefs that celebrated personal freedom and individualism.

With the advent of the Enlightenment period in the 18th century, a paradigm shift occurred in how Satanism was perceived. Philosophers such as Jean-Jacques Rousseau and Voltaire advocated for religious tolerance and the rights of individuals. As a result, there was an increased interest in occult practices, including Satanic rituals, as a means of rebelling against oppressive religious establishments.

During the 19th century, as industrialization spread across Europe and the Americas, social inequality became more apparent. Although the late 20th-century Satanic Panic erroneously linked Satanism to heinous crimes, it also shed light on the existence of underground Satanic cults dedicated to combating societal injustices. These cults aimed to disrupt the status quo by challenging oppressive systems and advocating for the rights of marginalized communities.

In the early 20th century, Aleister Crowley emerged as a prominent figure in Satanic worship. Known as "The Beast," Crowley founded the religious philosophy of Thelema, which celebrated personal freedom and individualism. He believed that by embracing our inner desires, we could achieve spiritual enlightenment. Crowley's teachings resonated with numerous social activists of the time, who perceived Satanic rituals as a means of liberating themselves from societal norms and inciting significant change.

During the countercultural movements of the 1960s and 70s, Satanic rituals experienced a resurgence as a form of protest and activism. The Church of Satan, established by Anton LaVey in 1966, sought to challenge traditional religious institutions by embracing Satan as a symbol of rebellion and individualism. Despite being frequently misunderstood, LaVey's Satanic Bible encouraged the pursuit of personal freedom and the rejection of oppressive societal norms.

In recent years, we have witnessed an increasing intersection between Satanic worship and social activism. Modern-day Satanic organizations, such as The Satanic Temple, have emerged as vocal advocates for individual rights and freedoms. Through its Seven Tenets, The Satanic Temple promotes values such as empathy, personal autonomy, and the pursuit of justice. Their advocacy work has entailed challenging discriminatory laws, championing reproductive rights, and opposing the encroachment of religion in public spaces.

The analysis of Satanic worship's role in promoting social activism reveals a multifaceted and intricate relationship. While traditionally associated with dark and malevolent practices, Satanism has often served as a conduit for championing individual freedoms and disrupting societal norms. By embracing Satan as a symbol of rebellion and personal freedom, social activists throughout history have utilized Satanic rituals as a means of initiating impactful change.

To dismiss Satanic worship solely as malevolent would be to overlook its significant contributions to social activism and the advancement of justice. Satanic rituals have historically provided a platform for those marginalized by mainstream society to voice their discontent and challenge oppressive systems. By invoking the powers of darkness, these individuals have sought to highlight the injustices plaguing our world.

As a paranormal investigator and expert in the realm of the extraordinary, I continue to explore the depths of Satanic worship and its correlation with social activism. Through meticulous research and thorough investigations, my objective is to shed light on the intricate and often misconstrued connection between the occult and the pursuit of individual rights and freedoms. Only by unraveling this intricate tapestry can we genuinely appreciate the profound impact Satanic rituals have had in shaping our society and the ongoing pursuit for a more just and equanimous world.

SATANIC WORSHIP AND MUTUAL AID

In order to gain a true understanding of the concept of mutual aid in Satanic communities, it is necessary to delve into the history and origins of Satanic worship. Contrary to popular belief, Satanism is not merely a simple reversal of Christian beliefs, but rather a complex and nuanced philosophy that has evolved over the course of centuries. The roots of Satanic worship can be traced back to ancient traditions such as Gnosticism, Hermeticism, and even pre-Christian pagan beliefs. These early foundations viewed the Devil as a symbol of rebellion against oppressive powers, representing individualism and personal freedom.

One cannot discuss mutual aid within Satanic communities without recognizing the notable figure of Anton Szandor LaVey, the founder of the Church of Satan and the individual responsible for popularizing modern Satanism. LaVey's book, "The Satanic Bible," served as a cornerstone for Satanic philosophy and introduced the world to the fundamental principles of Satanic worship, which include self-indulgence, individualism, and the pursuit of personal desires.

Beneath the controversial and shocking nature associated with Satanic worship lies a passionate and close-knit community of individuals who find solace and support within it. Exploring this aspect of mutual aid in Satanic communities sheds light on the various ways in which members are supported in times of need.

One avenue of mutual aid is the establishment of Satanic temples and organizations dedicated to the well-being of their members. These organizations not only provide a sense of community and belonging, but also offer practical support in various forms. From financial assistance during difficult times to mental health resources, Satanic communities offer a range of services designed to uplift and empower their members. It is important to note that these communities do not focus on the worship of a literal devil or engage in harmful practices, as is commonly misunderstood. Instead, they embrace Satan as a symbol of individualism and personal strength.

Moreover, Satanic communities often partake in rituals and ceremonies aimed at healing and restoration. These rituals, which draw inspiration from ancient occult practices but have been adapted to modern times, offer a sense of release and spiritual renewal for members. It is within these rituals that the spirit of mutual aid truly comes to life, as individuals come together to support one another through their shared experiences and challenges.

The significance of mutual aid within Satanic communities goes beyond formal organizations and rituals; it permeates the very fabric of their everyday lives, creating a support network that goes beyond conventional understandings of community. Whether through online forums, social media groups, or local meet-ups, Satanic communities foster an environment of acceptance and understanding where members can seek guidance, exchange resources, and provide emotional support.

Moreover, the concept of mutual aid within Satanic communities challenges societal perceptions and stereotypes. Despite the media's portrayal of Satanism as inherently wicked or destructive, those within the community argue that their beliefs and practices are centered around personal growth, empowerment, and compassion. Through actively engaging in mutual aid and community care, followers of Satanic worship aim to dismantle the misconceptions surrounding their faith and cultivate a world that is more compassionate and understanding.

As an outsider, delving into the intricate workings of Satanic worship and mutual aid has been an enlightening and eye-opening experience. The strong sense of community, support, and resilience within Satanic communities challenges preconceived notions and emphasizes the power of collective care and support. Through my investigation, I have gained an appreciation for the complexities of Satanic worship and the profound impact it has on the lives of its members. Satanic worship is not solely a means of rebellion or shocking society; it is a journey of self-discovery, embracing individuality, and supporting one another on the path of life.

SATANIC RITUALS AND GROUP EMPOWERMENT

It is often said that the essence of power lies within the depths of darkness. As a dedicated paranormal investigator and specialist in the field of the occult, I have made it my life's work to uncover the mysteries that dwell within the shadows. Among my numerous investigations, the exploration of Satanic rituals and the collective empowerment experienced within their communities has proven to be the most captivating and enigmatic. In this chapter, we delve deep into the abyss, seeking to comprehend the transformative power that is unleashed through the shared pursuit of personal and spiritual development.

When entering the veiled world of Satanic communities, it is essential to discard preconceived notions and approach with an open mind. It is within these sacred spaces that the boundaries between good and evil become blurred, where individuals find solace in unity, and where empowerment assumes a malevolent form that both disturbs and tantalizes. In order to truly grasp the depths of this empowerment, I immersed myself in the rituals and practices that define these groups.

My journey commenced in the secluded town of Blackwood, a hidden enclave notorious for harboring one of the most elusive Satanic communities. The existence of this community had been whispered about in hushed tones within underground paranormal circles, and rumors regarding their collective empowerment through ritualistic ceremonies had piqued my curiosity. Equipped with an extensive body of research and an unwavering determination, I embarked on this venture, prepared to engage with this untapped realm.

Secrecy permeated the walls of the Blackwood Satanic Temple, making it a formidable challenge to gain entry. Through a series of connections, however, I managed to secure an invitation to their most sacred ceremony - the Rite of Ascendancy. As I traversed from the realm of mundanity into this forbidden cavern, I was encompassed by a wave of anticipation and trepidation.

The room was dimly illuminated, the flickering candles casting eerie shadows on the ancient symbols etched into the walls. A sense of ancient wisdom hung thick in the air, mingling with the subtle fragrance of incense. The members, cloaked in black robes, moved with an ethereal grace that bordered on otherworldly. An undeniable aura of power and purpose emanated from each individual, as if they were entangled in an age-old dance of liberation.

The Rite of Ascendancy commenced with a solemn invocation, summoning the dark forces that reside dormant within the recesses of the human psyche. It became evident that these rituals were not mere theatrics, but rather a sincere communion with the unknown. As I observed the participants, I realized that their collective pursuit of personal and spiritual growth formed the foundation upon which their empowerment was built.

Through a series of ceremonial acts, the Blackwood Satanic Temple sought to break free from the confines of societal norms, unleashing their hidden potential. Each individual was encouraged to delve into their deepest desires and darkest fears, embracing them without reservation. It was through this exploration that they unearthed a newfound strength within themselves – a strength that was further amplified through their unity as a group.

The power of collective empowerment became overwhelmingly apparent during the climactic moments of the Rite, as the participants chanted in unison, their voices intertwining to create a symphony of raw energy. Their words seemed to penetrate the very fabric of reality, rupturing the veil that demarcates the material world from the spiritual realm. It was at this juncture that I comprehended the true potency of Satanic rituals – the capacity to tap into a collective consciousness and wield the energy of the unseen.

In the aftermath of the ceremony, I had the privilege of engaging in conversations with members of the Blackwood Satanic Temple. Their words provided profound insights into the transformative nature of their rituals. They spoke of the emancipation that comes from embracing one's true self, of discovering solace in the darkness, and of forging a connection with forces that transcend human understanding. It became clear that their empowerment was not borne out of a perverse desire for destruction, but rather an authentic quest for personal growth and enlightenment.

Exploring the empowerment of individuals within Satanic communities through collective rituals and the shared pursuit of personal and spiritual growth has illuminated a realm that is simultaneously captivating and disconcerting. While the techniques employed by these groups may challenge societal norms, there is an undeniable power that radiates from their practices. This power enables individuals to transcend their limitations, break free from the shackles of society, and unlock the vast potential that lies dormant within each of us.

As I concluded my time in Blackwood, I carried with me a newfound admiration for the individuals brave enough to venture into the depths of darkness. It is through their courage and unwavering determination that we are compelled to confront our own fears and biases. Satanic rituals, though shrouded in mystery and misconceptions, offer a unique perspective on the pursuit of personal and spiritual growth. As we continue to navigate the intricate web of the occult, it is through understanding that we shall achieve true enlightenment – an enlightenment obscured by the allure of the sinister, yet crucial in our journey through the enigmatic realm of the paranormal.

SATANIC WORSHIP AND ALTERNATIVE FAMILY STRUCTURES

In order to comprehend the intricate nature of alternative family structures within Satanic communities, it is imperative to transcend prevailing misconceptions and question preconceived notions. It is crucial to acknowledge that Satanism, despite its widespread misinterpretation, is not synonymous with evil or malevolence. While popular culture often portrays Satanic worship as involving rituals, sacrificial acts, and ominous forces, it is essential to differentiate between fact and fiction. Satanic communities are diverse and multifaceted, comprising individuals who seek spiritual fulfillment, empowerment, and a sense of belonging.

When examining the formation of alternative family structures within Satanic communities, the emphasis should be placed on inclusivity and support. Contrary to the commonly held belief that Satanic groups are driven solely by individualistic pursuits, the truth is that these communities prioritize the establishment of strong interpersonal connections and a deep sense of communal support. Through this process, they cultivate alternative family structures that bind individuals together in a web of trust and understanding.

One notable characteristic of alternative family structures within Satanic communities is their focus on inclusivity. These alternative families foster an environment that is open and accepting, regardless of race, gender, sexual orientation, or background. Discrimination and judgment are actively discouraged, embracing a diverse range of identities and experiences. This inclusivity is not superficial in nature; rather, it is deeply ingrained in the core values of Satanic communities, fortifying the bonds between individuals and reinforcing their chosen family structure.

To truly comprehend the dynamics at play within these alternative families, it is pertinent to delve into the rituals and practices that facilitate a sense of connection and shared experience. Satanic worship extends beyond traditional religious rites, encompassing a multitude of rituals tailored to suit the needs and desires of its practitioners. These rituals often entail deeply personal and symbolic acts, delving into the essence of one's being and forging a spiritual connection with others. Through these shared experiences, alternative families within Satanic communities solidify their bonds, reinforcing the foundation upon which their chosen family structure is built.

The support system within these alternative families is another crucial aspect to consider. In our conventional understanding of family, support is often limited to blood relations. However, in Satanic communities, chosen families surpass biological ties, offering a unique form of support that is both empowering and nurturing. These alternative families comprehend the significance of emotional well-being, bolstering one another through life's trials and triumphs. Their support extends beyond the physical realm, encompassing intellectual, emotional, and even spiritual aspects. Within the safety net of their chosen family structure, individuals find solace, encouragement, and a profound sense of belonging.

It is also essential to address the aspect of autonomy and agency within these alternative family structures. Satanic communities acknowledge individual sovereignty, granting each member the freedom to define their own path, beliefs, and identity. This emphasis on personal autonomy fosters an atmosphere of mutual respect and understanding. Within these alternative families, individuals are encouraged to express themselves genuinely, ensuring that their voices are heard, respected, and validated. This inclusivity and support for individual agency further strengthen the bonds within these chosen family structures, fostering an environment where individuals can flourish and evolve.

Despite the prevalent perception of Satanic worship as driven by darkness and malevolence, the reality is much more nuanced. Alternative family structures within Satanic communities provide individuals with a haven, a place where they can truly be themselves and form deep connections with like-minded individuals. Inclusivity and support form the foundations on which these chosen families are constructed, challenging societal norms and offering an alternative space for personal growth and fulfillment.

Through my exploration of Satanic worship and alternative family structures, I have come to appreciate the profound depth and complexity of these communities. They defy conventional understanding and challenge societal expectations, providing a refuge for individuals who have often faced adversity and exclusion. It is within the embrace of these chosen families that individuals find acceptance, empowerment, and a genuine sense of belonging. As I continue to venture into the realm of the supernatural, I am reminded of the profound significance of inclusivity, support, and the beauty that lies within the formation of alternative family structures within Satanic communities.

20

SATANIC WORSHIP AND THE HUMAN EXPERIENCE

SATANIC RITUALS AND EXISTENTIALISM

In order to thoroughly explore this correlation, it is necessary to establish a comprehensive historical timeline that will serve as our guide through the development of both satanic rituals and existentialist thought. Our investigation commences in the early 17th century, at a time when an underground movement referred to as satanism began to gain momentum.

During this period, Europe was gripped by the witch trials, a phenomenon that induced widespread panic and hysteria. It was amidst this chaotic environment that the concept of satanism emerged as a means to defy societal norms and embrace individual liberty. Secretive satanic rituals became a conduit for individuals to reclaim their autonomy in a world dominated by dogma and conformity.

As the centuries progressed, the principles of Satanism grew more refined, intertwining with the ideological foundations of existentialism. Existentialism, which rose to prominence in the 19th and 20th centuries, accentuated the significance of individual freedom and responsibility. Prominent existentialist thinkers such as Jean-Paul Sartre and Friedrich Nietzsche posited that individuals are defined by their actions and choices, and that life possesses no inherent meaning beyond what each individual assigns to it.

It is within the framework of this philosophical perspective that we encounter the intersection between satanic rituals and existentialist thought. Both ideologies place immense emphasis on the individual, urging adherents to break free from societal constraints and embrace their innate freedom. Satanic rituals, with their focus on personal empowerment and the assertion of one's desires, closely align with the existentialist conviction in the primacy of individual autonomy.

Throughout my research, I have come across numerous accounts of individuals who have discovered solace and purpose in the practice of satanic rituals. These individuals perceive these rituals not as acts of worship or devotion to a literal Satan, but rather as symbolic assertions of rebellion against societal norms and affirmation of personal autonomy.

One particularly impactful account that has remained etched in my memory belongs to Amelia Harrison, a self-professed contemporary witch. Amelia elucidated that for her, satanic rituals served as a conduit for channeling her innermost desires and intentions. By utilizing symbols and rituals, she was able to access an elevated state of self-awareness and construct her own reality, liberated from the impositions enforced by society.

Amelia's experiences mirror the existentialist belief that individuals possess the power to forge their own meaning in life. Through the practice of satanic rituals, she actively asserted her freedom and assumed responsibility for her own existence. This concept of personal agency and self-accountability lies at the core of both satanic rituals and existentialist thought.

Nevertheless, it is crucial to acknowledge that not all practitioners of satanic rituals adhere to existentialist philosophies. Some may partake in these rituals for varied reasons, including shock value or as an act of transgressive rebellion. Nonetheless, one cannot disregard the inherent connection between satanic rituals and the existentialist principles of individual freedom and responsibility.

Truly comprehending the relationship between satanic rituals and existentialism necessitates a willingness to explore the intricacies of the human psyche and confront the complexities of human nature. It is within this exploration that we may uncover the answers we seek and reveal the interplay between darkness and enlightenment, rebellion and self-actualization.

In conclusion, the association between satanic rituals and existentialist philosophies is one that is multifaceted and deeply nuanced. Both ideologies direct their focus toward the individual and their capacity to assert their freedom and responsibility in the face of societal constraints. Through intricate symbolism and ritualistic practices, satanic rituals provide individuals with a means to access their innermost desires and assert their autonomy. By embracing these concepts, we may be closer to comprehending the true essence of the human experience and the intricate interplay between darkness and enlightenment that resides within each and every one of us.

SATANIC WORSHIP AND THE QUEST FOR MEANING

As an esteemed paranormal investigator, I have extensively delved into the depths of the human psyche, meticulously exploring that which is inexplicable and mysterious. One area of particular fascination has always been the realm of Satanism and the inexplicable allure it holds for individuals who seek solace and purpose within its enigmatic embrace. In the following chapter, we shall comprehensively delve into the profound search for meaning and purpose that compels individuals towards the path of Satanic worship, and how this exceptional journey shapes their life trajectories.

To genuinely comprehend the captivating allure of Satanic worship, it is imperative to first comprehend the fundamental human yearning for meaning and purpose. Throughout history, humanity has persistently endeavored to make sense of its existence, earnestly seeking a raison d'être within the vastness of the cosmos. It is within this existential struggle that many individuals find themselves inexplicably drawn towards the dark ideologies of Satanism.

The search for meaning is an intimately personal and introspective journey, often catalyzed by experiences of existential crisis or profound feelings of emptiness. Individuals who turn to Satanic worship perceive it as a path that bestows upon them a sense of purpose – a means to rebelliously challenge societal norms and embrace a profound sense of agency in a seemingly indifferent world. This potent sense of agency entices them, acting as a powerful force that lures them into the seductive realm of Satanic worship.

For those who embark upon this extraordinary path, Satanic worship transcends mere religious affiliation or belief system; it becomes an all-encompassing way of life. Through the practice of Satanic worship, individuals discover an altogether new sense of identity and empowerment, as they boldly challenge the boundaries imposed by conventional moral codes and wholeheartedly embrace their own innate desires and inclinations. The dark rituals and practices intrinsic to Satanic worship foster a profound sense of belonging and acceptance, providing a sanctuary within a community that intimately comprehends and fully embraces their unorthodox perspectives.

The potent influence of Satanic worship upon the life trajectories of individuals must not be undermined. For many, it serves as a pivotal turning point, a departure from the banality of everyday existence and a plunge into the beckoning abyss of the unknown. This transformative process often incites a comprehensive reevaluation of one's relationships, vocational pursuits, and deeply held personal values. As these individuals actively embrace their own inner darkness, Satanic worshipers relinquish the shackles of societal expectations and norms, forging their own unique paths towards genuine self-actualization.

However, it is essential to acknowledge that not all who engage in Satanic worship are genuinely driven by a sincere quest for meaning and purpose. Some are merely attracted to the propositional shock value and rebellious nature of such practices, employing them as superficial means of garnering attention or asserting dominance over others. Such individuals often lack the necessary introspection and profound understanding requisite to genuinely comprehend the core tenets of Satanism and fully fathom its true potential for personal growth and transformation.

In order to cultivate a comprehensive understanding of this intriguing phenomenon, I embarked upon extensive research, immersing myself wholly in the bewildering realm of Satanic worship. Through in-depth interviews with self-proclaimed Satanists and individuals who have directly borne witness to Satanic rituals, I meticulously pieced together a macabre puzzle that will undoubtedly stand the test of time.

My research revealed the existence of a myriad of beliefs and practices within the intricate tapestry of Satanic worship, each tailored to meet the unique desires and individualistic needs of its adherents. Some fervently seek forbidden knowledge and enlightenment, meticulously delving into ancient texts and esoteric rituals in their relentless quest for hidden truths. Others find solace within the symbolic rebellion against a moralistic society, cherishing the unfettered freedom to explore their own personal desires without fear of judgment or constraint.

One of the most enlightening discoveries of my research was the remarkable diversity within the Satanic community itself. Contrary to prevailing preconceptions and stereotypes, not all Satanists engage in gruesome rituals or perpetrate acts of violence. In fact, a significant number of adherents subscribe to a philosophy that vehemently eschews inflicting harm upon others and instead passionately pursues personal growth and enlightenment. This realization defies and challenges deeply ingrained preconceived notions regarding Satanic worship, vividly highlighting the astonishing complexity and profoundly emotional experiences it affords its followers.

Through my encounters with those intrepid souls who have resolutely chosen to traverse this oftentimes solitary path, I have come to deeply comprehend that their relentless search for meaning and purpose within Satanic worship is far from innately evil or malevolent. Rather, it is a deeply intimate and introspective journey, driven by an inexorable desire to carve out a distinct and meaningful niche within an inherently tumultuous and chaotic world. Indeed, it is an unwavering quest to find profound affinity, unwavering agency, and a genuine sense of purpose that propels these courageous individuals fearlessly into the very eye of Satan.

As I persist in my tireless exploration of the enigmatic occult, I am irrevocably imbued with an unwavering reverence for those brave souls who dare to unreservedly embrace the darkness and ardently seek meaning within its veiled depths. It is through their metaphoric and literal tales, replete with experiences that have pushed the limits of human understanding, that we gain invaluable insights into the human condition, the boundless depths of our collective search for purpose, and the transformative power inherent within the realm of belief.

The alluring concept of Satanic worship may forever remain an undeniably contentious topic, swathed in shadow and enveloped by societal taboos. Nevertheless, what is unequivocally undeniable is the profound and lasting impact it has upon the lives of those who daringly embark upon this unconventional path. Whether fueled by a genuine yearning for meaning or a dire need for rebellion, Satanic worship opens doors to unparalleled self-discovery, fervent personal growth, and the empowering ability to redefine one's own narrative.

Indeed, it is within the very midst of darkness that we courageously confront our deepest fears and desires, and within that extraordinary confrontation, we find ourselves imbued with the audacity and fortitude necessary to fearlessly forge our own destinies. Satanic worship and the eternal quest for meaning shall forever remain intertwined, undeniably illuminating a path for the lost souls, intrepid seekers, and those who defiantly venture to peer deep into the very eye of Satan himself.

SATANIC RITUALS AND TRANSCENDENCE

In order to gain a comprehensive understanding of the profound impact that Satanic rituals can have on an individual's consciousness, I undertook an extensive and lengthy research project. This involved immersing myself in numerous ancient texts and meticulously deciphering cryptic symbols and rituals that had long remained enigmatic. As I delved deeper into this pursuit of knowledge, I encountered narratives that deeply affected me, simultaneously instilling a sense of dread

and fueling my curiosity, pushing me further into the unfathomable depths of this subject matter.

The practice of Satanic rituals can be traced back to ancient
civilizations, where individuals would engage in supernatural
ceremonies to appease and communicate with deities. These
practices were often shrouded in secrecy, protecting them
from the scrutiny of outsiders. As I delved further into historical records, I came across accounts detailing the transformative experiences of those who had vehemently participated in
Satanic rituals.

Among these accounts, I was particularly captivated by the
story of Lazarus, an individual who claimed to have attained
enlightenment and transcended the limitations of their mortal
existence through the engagement in Satanic rituals. Intrigued
by this assertion, I resolved to investigate whether these experiences were genuine or merely the product of a tormented
imagination.

Through my quest for knowledge, I traveled to obscure
corners of the world where whispers of clandestine rituals lin-
gered in the atmosphere, akin to an ethereal mist. It was in a
secluded village nestled within the depths of mountains that
I found myself in the presence of a covert Satanic sect. This
community was tightly knit, steeped in ancient traditions,
and fiercely guarded the secrets surrounding their rituals. It
required months of meticulous observation and the establishment of trust before I was granted the privileged opportunity
to witness their ceremonies firsthand.

These rituals were an awe-inspiring spectacle. Participants
congregated within a dimly lit chamber adorned with occult
symbols and artifacts, their visages concealed within the cloak
of shadows and anticipation. The air was infused with an
electrifying energy, as a blend of trepidation and excitement
permeated the space. As the ritual commenced, I found myself

transported to an alternate realm, where the boundaries between the physical and spiritual became indistinct.

The participants chanted incantations, their voices melding into a haunting symphony. A distinct atmosphere resonated with a presence that was beyond the realm of ordinary experiences, as though something ancient and formidable had been awakened. Amidst this captivating whirlwind of energy, I witnessed Lazarus, the individual whose claims had allured me to this enigmatic domain.

Lazarus's transformation surpassed all expectations. Once clouded with uncertainty, his eyes now blazed with lucidity. His movements were graceful, almost ethereal, as if he had transcended the limitations of his human vessel and tapped into a deeper, primordial essence. It was as if the rituals had unlocked a concealed gateway within his soul, permitting him to access realms of consciousness and comprehension that eluded ordinary mortals.

In the ensuing days and weeks, I conducted extensive interviews with Lazarus, striving to comprehend the nature of his transfiguration. He spoke of altered states of consciousness, an overwhelming sense of connection to the cosmos, and an intimate comprehension of the interplay of the universe. Through his experiences, it became evident that Satanic rituals possessed the capability to uncover obscured facets of the mind, facilitating a profound journey of self-discovery and metamorphosis.

However, as I delved deeper into the realm of Satanic rituals and their transformative effects, I also encountered cautionary tales. For every Lazarus, whose enlightenment elevated their being, there were others whose descent into the abyss left them fragmented and mentally unstable. The pursuit of transcendence within Satanic rituals represents a perilous path, capable of elevating the soul or plunging it into an abyss of despair.

Through my comprehensive research and personal experiences, I have come to recognize that the transformative effects of Satanic rituals on consciousness demand utmost caution. This undertaking necessitates a delicate balance between harnessing the hidden potential of the mind and soul and safeguarding oneself against the abyss that lurks beneath.

As I continue to explore the mysteries concealed within the Eye of Satan, I am filled with a profound sense of reverence and awe for the ancient rituals that possess the capacity to unlock the profound enigmas of our existence. Approached with respect and profound comprehension, Satanic rituals possess the potential to transcend the limitations of our mortal condition and propel us into a realm of spiritual elevation. Nevertheless, it is a realm fraught with peril, where one's essential being can be either shattered or reborn.

In the pursuit of transcendence within Satanic rituals, one must proceed with caution, for the mind and soul are fragile entities that can be both illuminated and engulfed by the fires of the abyss. And thus, I persevere in my exploration, delving even deeper into the depths of darkness, guided by an insatiable thirst for knowledge, cognizant of the risks associated with peering into the Eye of Satan.

SATANIC WORSHIP AND THE EXPLORATION OF DESIRE

On a somber and tempestuous evening, I sat in the subdued ambience of my study, engrossed in the meticulous research I had amassed for my latest literary endeavor. Throughout my extensive tenure as a paranormal investigator and specialist in the peculiar, I had devoted considerable attention to the subjects of Satanic worship and the exploration of desire. The allure of the occult and the myriad manifestations of human longing had ceaselessly captivated me, and now I stood on the brink of unearthing the undisclosed secrets concealed within the realm of Satanic worship.

My research had steered me toward an assortment of sub-terranean cults, clandestine assemblies cloaked in darkness, and clandestine online forums where like-minded enthusiasts sought to delve into their innermost yearnings. The subject matter was both disconcerting and intriguing, a domain where the depths of the human psyche merged with forbidden indul-gences in a quest for satiating their most profound appetites.

In order to glean an authentic understanding of the impact desire had within the context of Satanic worship, I embarked upon a series of interviews with former members of these clandestine congregations. These individuals had voluntarily entered a world shrouded in enigma and obscurity, propelled by their insatiable cravings. As their voices intertwined a med-ley of apprehension and engrossing fascination, I endeavored to weave together an intricate tapestry of desire and its sway over their lives.

Many of these individuals had endured an incessant rest-lessness and an insatiable hunger for a more fulfilling exis-tence. The social order had proven inadequate in providing them with the avenues to fully explore their wants and needs, impelling them to seek solace in the illicit realm of Satanic worship. Here, they believed they could freely indulge in their desires, unencumbered by societal mores, in a tireless pursuit of emancipation from their imposed constraints.

Through their narratives, I discovered the pivotal role desire played in their self-discovery. Satanic worship offered a plat-form wherein their most intimate yearnings were embraced and celebrated. It served as a sanctuary where their yearnings and wishes were legitimized, and they were encouraged to traverse new frontiers and transgress established boundaries.

Within the dimly lit chambers of these covert assemblies, participants were urged to relinquish their inhibitions and embrace their deepest passions. Their desires evolved from silenced whispers into powerful currents of energy coursing through their veins. The exploration of desire evolved into a cathartic experience, liberating them from society's shackles and revealing uncharted realms of existence.

Yet, as I plowed deeper into my research, a question avidly plagued my thoughts: what happens when these desires consume the very individuals who sought to explore them? Satanic worship, it appeared, held the potential for some to find respite, while for others, it entailed a perilous descent into obsession.

I encountered individuals who had forfeited their very essence, ensnared by desires that had corroded their identities beyond recognition. These formerly inquisitive souls had succumbed to the seductive allure of dominance and darkness, forsaking their moral compass and forsaking their values in the relentless pursuit of unattainable desires.

Yet, amidst the ensuing chaos and ruin, I discovered a glimmer of hope. Some had managed to strike a delicate equilibrium between their desires and the persona they yearned to embody. Through their explorations within the realm of Satanic worship, they had come to grasp the nuanced nature of desire and the indispensable value of self-control. They had unearthed the fact that when desire is harnessed alongside an understanding of its contours and limits, it has the capacity to enrich lives rather than consume them.

My expedition into the domain of Satanic worship and the exploration of desire had peeled back the layers of complexity that enshroud human yearnings. It was a domain where the distinction between ethical standards blurred, and the most shadowy recesses of the human psyche reveled. Yet, within that darkness, I discovered the potential for personal growth and comprehension.

As I concluded my research, I was confronted with a profound realization. Desire, in its unadulterated and uncontrollable splendor, was an integral facet of the human experience. The embracing and comprehension of our desires, rather than apprehensively suppressing or shunning them, could potentially unlock the truest essence of our being.

Armed with this newfound understanding and a deeper comprehension of the human condition, I forged ahead into uncharted territories, embarking upon the subsequent chapter of my odyssey into the enigmatic and the abnormal. The expedition was far from its culmination, and the secrets that lay concealed within the periphery of Satan eagerly awaited revelation.

SATANIC RITUALS AND THE POWER OF SYMBOLS

Throughout the course of human history, symbols have wielded considerable influence over the human psyche. From ancient civilizations to the present day, they have functioned as conduits for communication, instrumental tools for magical practices, and gateways to the divine realm. Of particular significance within satanic rituals are symbols that harbor great power, acting as catalysts for delving into the depths of the human psyche and accessing the sacred energy that dwells within each individual.

One prominent symbol frequently employed in satanic rituals is the inverted pentagram. Widely associated with witchcraft and Satanism, this five-pointed star, when inverted, represents the descent into darkness and the rejection of conventional moral values. It challenges societal norms and embraces the concealed aspects of the self. By incorporating the inverted pentagram into their rituals, practitioners of Satanism aim to access the forbidden energies that lie beyond the realm of conscious awareness, allowing for a transformative experience that transcends the limitations of the mundane world.

Another influential symbol utilized in satanic rituals is the Sigil of Baphomet. This sigil, featuring a pentagram intertwined with a goat's head, is regarded as a representation of the goat-headed deity worshipped by satanists. It embodies power, wisdom, and balance, serving as a conduit for tapping into the primordial forces of creation and destruction. When invoked during rituals, the Sigil of Baphomet serves as a visual manifestation of one's commitment to embracing their inherent darkness, relinquishing societal constraints, and embarking on a path of personal growth.

Yet, it is not solely the symbols themselves that exert immense power; the rituals that surround their invocation play a crucial role as well. Within satanic rituals, every action, word, and movement is meticulously orchestrated to cultivate a heightened state of consciousness and establish a connection with the divine. The use of symbols throughout these rituals acts as a guide, navigating practitioners through the intricacies of the mind and leading them to a deeper comprehension of themselves and the forces that shape their existence.

The implementation of symbols in satanic rituals serves another vital purpose: the elicitation of powerful emotional responses. Similar to art, symbols are capable of transcending language and directly addressing the subconscious. They bypass the rational mind and tap into the primal emotions that lie within each individual. By employing symbols that embody taboos and transgressions, satanists manage to arouse profound reactions in their participants, deconstructing the barriers imposed by societal conditioning and fostering personal transformation.

In the course of my research, I have come across numerous testimonies from individuals who have undergone satanic rituals and undergone a profound shift in their perception of themselves and the surrounding world. These rituals serve as intensely cathartic experiences, affording participants the opportunity to confront their deepest fears, darkest desires, and concealed truths. Through the power of symbols, satanists create an environment conducive to self-discovery, pushing the boundaries of personal identity and facilitating individual growth.

Nevertheless, it is crucial to acknowledge that the utilization of symbols within satanic rituals is not without risks. Just as symbols possess the potential to unlock hidden potentials and evoke powerful emotional responses, they also bear the capacity to destabilize and unbalance the psyche if approached without caution. Unleashing dormant forces within oneself is a journey that demands courage, self-awareness, and a thorough understanding of the inherent perils involved.

In conclusion, satanic rituals are not the workings of a demonic entity, but rather intricate tapestries of symbols and actions designed to elicit profound emotional responses and facilitate personal transformation. The power of symbols within these rituals should not be underestimated. They function as gateways to the subconscious, unlocking latent potentials and beckoning participants to embark on a voyage of self-discovery. However, it is imperative to approach these rituals with prudence and reverence, recognizing that the untamed energies they unleash possess the capacity for profound transformation, for better or for worse.

SATANIC WORSHIP AND THE INTEGRATION OF LIGHT AND DARK

As an individual specializing in paranormal investigation, I have encountered numerous enigmas and delved deep into the intricacies of the human psyche. My research on the integration of light and dark within Satanic worship has taken me down a path illuminated by the flickering flames of ancient rituals and shadowed by the mysterious depths of the human soul.

To truly comprehend the significant impact of Satanic worship on personal growth, one must first grasp its historical context. Contrary to commonly held beliefs, Satanic worship extends beyond malevolent acts and sinister rituals. It possesses a complex nature that encompasses a merging of light and dark elements, aiming to explore the duality inherent in human existence.

My extensive investigation involved the study of ancient texts and manuscripts that explored the origins of Satanic worship. The works of Aleister Crowley, widely regarded as the progenitor of modern Satanism, provided invaluable insights into the integration of light and dark within this enigmatic realm. Crowley's teachings emphasized the importance of embracing both the spiritual and carnal aspects of human nature, ultimately leading to personal growth and enlightenment.

It is notable that one vital aspect of my research revealed the emphasis placed by Satanic worship on self-empowerment. Through the integration of both light and dark aspects, practitioners aim to attain a deeper understanding of their internal struggles and desires. By engaging in ritualistic practices and exploring taboo subjects, individuals navigate the complexities of their own psyches, challenging societal norms and discovering their authentic selves.

The integration of light and dark within Satanic worship goes beyond mere acceptance but involves a personal journey into the depths of one's being. It encourages individuals to confront their subconscious fears, traumas, and desires, which are often stigmatized by society. As practitioners explore their own light and darkness, they unlock a newfound sense of personal power and authenticity.

However, it is worth noting that the integration of light and dark within Satanic worship is not exempt from controversy. The combination of taboo subjects and unconventional practices has generated moral outrage and condemnation from religious and conservative groups. Despite societal backlash, practitioners argue that true personal growth can only be achieved by wholeheartedly embracing the full range of human experiences.

In Satanic worship, rituals serve as a means of exploring and integrating these polarizing elements. From meditation and ceremonial magic to ecstatic dance and transcendent art, each ritual is intentionally designed to challenge conventional notions of good and evil, surpassing the limitations of conventional morality. Through these transformative experiences, practitioners harness the dual power of light and dark within themselves, utilizing it for personal growth and spiritual enlightenment.

It is crucial to emphasize that the integration of light and dark within Satanic worship does not endorse harmful or malicious actions. Rather, it seeks to embrace the delicate balance of opposing forces within the human psyche. By navigating this intricate dance, practitioners strive to achieve harmony between their innermost desires and their external realities.

As I delved deeper into my research, I encountered numerous accounts from individuals who have embarked on Satanic worship as a means of personal growth. Their narratives provided a captivating amalgamation of fascinating journeys, characterized by self-discovery, resilience, and challenging societal norms. It became evident that the integration of light and dark within Satanic worship provides a powerful platform for personal transformation and spiritual evolution.

To conclude, the exploration of the integration of light and dark within Satanic worship reveals a multi-dimensional tapestry that transcends conventional perceptions. Satanic worship, far from being a malevolent or sinister force, offers a unique opportunity for individuals to navigate their inner selves in pursuit of personal growth and enlightenment. By embracing both light and dark aspects, practitioners develop a profound understanding of the human experience, ultimately unifying their fragmented selves and forging an authentic connection with their own personal power.

SATANIC RITUALS AND THE CELEBRATION OF LIFE

As an esteemed paranormal investigator, I have undergone numerous encounters with the unknowable, delving deep into the realms of the supernatural. Over the course of my extensive research, I have come across a plethora of captivating and enigmatic subjects, yet one that has perpetually piqued my curiosity is the correlation between Satanic rituals and the commemoration of life.

Before delving further into this matter, it is imperative to acknowledge the historical timeline of Satanism. Contrary to some erroneous beliefs, it is not a time-honored religion predating existence itself but rather a relatively modern movement that emerged during the 19th century. With origins rooted in occultism and diverse traditions from various parts of the globe, Satanism has evolved into an assortment of philosophies and practices, with certain devotees embracing

Satanic symbolism as a means of self-empowerment and personal autonomy.

In order to gain a comprehensive understanding of the celebration of life within Satanic rituals, one must initially grasp the underlying belief system. Contrary to prevailing misconceptions, Satanism does not venerate or even acknowledge the existence of a literal devil figure. Instead, it venerates the concept of Satan as a symbol of rebellion against constraining societal norms. Satan transmutes into a figure representing individualism, free thought, and a negation of hypocrisy.

One of the principal tenets within Satanic rituals is the wholehearted embrace of the present moment. Unlike certain religious practices that focus on an afterlife or a higher power, Satanists redirect their attention to the here and now. They firmly believe that life is a treasured and limited experience, and consequently, it warrants celebration and cherishment. Satanic rituals serve as a poignant reminder of this philosophy, providing a designated space for adherents to fully immerse themselves in the present moment and affirm their very existence.

Over the course of my meticulous research and investigations, I have had the privilege of attending several Satanic rituals where the celebration of life constituted the central theme. These occasions were characterized by a vibrant energy, an overwhelming sense of liberation, and an unwavering commitment to individual pursuits and passions.

While each ritual may have possessed subtle distinctions, they all shared a common thread – a steadfast commitment to embracing one's authentic self and embracing the manifold pleasures that life bestows upon us. This encompasses not only sensory and physical pleasures but also intellectual and emotional gratification. I beheld participants engaging in music, dance, and artistic expression, as they tapped into their deepest yearnings and unleashed their talents without the burden of judgment or restriction.

The festivity of life within Satanic rituals also encompasses a rejection of societal taboos and restrictions. The conspicuous absence of guilt or shame distinguishes it from certain religious practices that associate particular desires and pleasures with sin. In Satanic rituals, these desires are unreservedly recognized and rejoiced, enabling individuals to fully explore their very nature without the fear of condemnation.

One particular ritual I attended left an indelible impression on me, embodying the celebration of life in its purest manifestation. Held in a secluded grove ensconced within a moonlit sky, the surroundings were imbued with the sound of laughter and joyous music. Participants adorned themselves in ornate costumes and masks, symbolically embodying their hidden desires and fantasies.

The ritual commenced with a solemn yet enthralling invocation, summoning all present to seize the present moment and rid themselves of the burdens of the past. This was followed by a series of symbolic acts, such as the kindling of a central bonfire, which served as a metaphor for the transformative power of embracing one's authentic self. Participants then engaged in ethereal dancing, their bodies moving in perfect harmony with the rhythm of the universe.

Within this jubilant commemoration of life, I observed individuals unreservedly pursuing their desires and exploring their deepest passions. While some indulged in carnal pleasures, engaging in consensual acts of intimacy with like-minded individuals, others wholeheartedly immersed themselves in artistic endeavors, painting, writing, and creating without constraints. An unmistakable sense of liberation and self-empowerment permeated the atmosphere, as each person unabashedly embraced their own distinctive existence.

As the night progressed, the boundaries between self and others, past and present, seemed to merge. The celebration of life within Satanic rituals is not confined to a purely individual experience, but rather extends to a collective affirmation of existence. Participants formed profound connections with one another, sharing their vulnerabilities, aspirations, and dreams. It served as a profound reminder that life is not meant to be lived in isolation but rather as a communal jubilee.

In conclusion, the celebration of life within Satanic rituals is an extraordinary and transformative experience. It represents a repudiation of societal conventions and a steadfast devotion to embracing one's authentic self. More than just a momentary diversion, it creates a sanctuary where individuals can wholeheartedly immerse themselves in the present moment, indulging in their passions and desires free from the shackles of judgment or apprehension. Satanic rituals convey a powerful message – that life is inherently transient and, therefore, should be celebrated to its fullest extent, affirming the inherent beauty and bliss that can be discovered within the here and now.

SATANIC WORSHIP AND THE QUEST FOR AUTHENTICITY

Throughout my extensive years as a paranormal investigator, I have encountered numerous inexplicable phenomena and delved into the depths of various occult practices. One of the most fascinating and enigmatic subjects I have encountered is the world of Satanism—where the pursuit of authenticity in its purest form and the rejection of societal norms often coexist. In this chapter, we embark on a journey to unravel the intricate web of Satanic worship, exploring its profound influence on individuals' self-identity.

To grasp the essence of Satanic worship, it is essential to delve into its historical timeline. The origins of Satanic worship can be traced back to ancient civilizations such as Mesopotamia and Egypt, where pagan beliefs intertwined with a variety of rituals and practices centered around deities often associated with darkness. These occult traditions provided fertile ground for the emergence of Satanism in its various forms.

One cannot discuss Satanic worship without acknowledging its most significant influence—Christianity. As history progressed and Christianity gained prominence across the Western world, Satanism became a dissenting voice—a rebellion against the dogma, morality, and societal norms imposed by the dominant religious institution. By embracing the figure of Satan, individuals sought to reclaim their autonomy, indulge in their desires, and reject the stifling grip of societal expectations.

Centuries of persecution and vilification have only strengthened the allure of Satanic worship. Within the intimate confines of covens, secret societies, and hidden chambers, those who identify as Satanists find solace in their quest for authenticity. The Satanic Temple, an organization that emerged in the 21st century, has taken this pursuit to new heights, combining activism, philosophy, and religious Satanic practices to redefine the perception of Satanism in a world plagued by conformity.

The concept of authenticity within Satanic worship intertwines with the rejection of societal norms, as practitioners of this path defy the restrictions society imposes on their self-expression. The aesthetics associated with Satanism—dark attire, occult symbols, and macabre rituals—emphasize a desire to explore uncharted territories of the human psyche. By embracing their darker impulses, Satanists forge their own

identities outside the boundaries of what is considered acceptable in mainstream society.

Moreover, the pursuit of authenticity within Satanic worship extends beyond the superficial. It delves into a deep
exploration of one's innermost self—accepting and even celebrating the aspects that are often shunned or hidden. Embracing one's own shadow, a concept popularized by psychologist
Carl Jung, plays a significant role in the spiritual journey of
many Satanists. By integrating their light and darkness, they
find balance, authenticity, and empowerment.

The rejection of societal norms within Satanic worship
presents a unique challenge for those who choose this path.
Society, driven by collective morality and religious teachings,
often interprets Satanism as an embodiment of evil. Satanists,
however, perceive their practices as a radical departure from
such black-and-white notions of morality, advocating for individual freedom and autonomy. By turning the tables on conventional belief systems, they expose the subjective nature of
morality and encourage critical thinking.

But the pursuit of authenticity within Satanic worship is not
without its complexities. As individuals delve deeper into this
realm, they encounter the ever-present risk of losing themselves in the shadows. The allure of transgression and rebellion
against societal norms can often lead to a dangerous spiral,
blurring the line between self-discovery and self-destruction.

In conclusion, Satanic worship is a labyrinthine realm where
the pursuit of authenticity intertwines with the rejection of societal norms, challenging the boundaries of self-identity. From
its ancient origins to its modern embodiment in organizations
like The Satanic Temple, this path remains enigmatic and provocative. By embracing their darker impulses, integrating their
shadows, and rejecting societal expectations, Satanists strive
to find their true selves amidst a sea of conformity. But in this

quest, they must tread carefully, navigating the treacherous depths of the human psyche to uncover the true essence of their being, all while avoiding the ever-looming grasp of self-destruction.

Only by delving into the intricacies of Satanic worship can we begin to understand the motivations and desires that compel individuals to walk this path. And as we unravel the mysteries of this enigmatic realm, we may find ourselves questioning not only the nature of Satanic worship but also our own accepted truths and the societal norms that govern our lives.

www.ingramcontent.com/pod-product-compliance
Lightning Source LLC
Chambersburg PA
CBHW012026110726
47995CB00006B/1149